Mobility, Labour Migration and Border Controls in Asia

Other books by the editors:

WAGE LABOUR IN SOUTHEAST ASIA SINCE 1840 (*A. Kaur*)

WOMEN WORKERS IN INDUSTRIALISING ASIA (*A. Kaur*) (*Ed*)

THE SHAPING OF MALAYSIA (*A. Kaur and Ian Metcalfe*)

Mobility, Labour Migration and Border Controls in Asia

Edited by

Amarjit Kaur and Ian Metcalfe

First published in 2006 by
PALGRAVE MACMILLAN
Houndmills, Basingstoke, Hampshire RG21 6XS and
175 Fifth Avenue, New York, N.Y. 10010
Companies and representatives throughout the world.

PALGRAVE MACMILLAN is the global academic imprint of the Palgrave
Macmillan division of St. Martin's Press, LLC and of Palgrave Macmillan Ltd.
Macmillan® is a registered trademark in the United States, United Kingdom
and other countries. Palgrave is a registered trademark in the European
Union and other countries.

ISBN-13: 978–1–4039–8745–7 hardback
ISBN-10: 1–4039–8745–9   hardback

This book is printed on paper suitable for recycling and made from fully
managed and sustained forest sources.

A catalogue record for this book is available from the British Library.

Library of Congress Cataloging-in-Publication Data

Mobility, labour migration and border controls in Asia / edited by Amarjit
Kaur and Ian Metcalfe.
       p. cm.
    ISBN 1–4039–8745–9 (cloth)
      1. Migrant labor – Asia. 2. Asia – Emigration and immigration – Government
policy. 3. Globalization. I. Kaur, Amarjit. II. Metcalfe, Ian, 1949–

HD5856.A78M63 2006
331.5′44095—dc22   2005055348

10 9 8 7 6 5 4 3 2 1
15 14 13 12 11 10 09 08 07 06

Printed and bound in Great Britain by
Antony Rowe Ltd, Chippenham and Eastbourne

Contents

List of Tables	vii
List of Figures	xi
List of Maps	xii
List of Abbreviations	xiii
Acknowledgements	xv
Preliminary Note	xvi
Notes on Contributors	xvii

Part I   Divided We Move: Migration Challenges in Asia

1   Introduction
Amarjit Kaur and Ian Metcalfe 3

2   Changing Border Control Regimes and their Impact on
Migration in Asia
Tessa Morris-Suzuki 8

3   Order (and Disorder) at the Border: Mobility,
International Labour Migration and Border Controls
in Southeast Asia
Amarjit Kaur 23

4   Coping With Cross-Border Labour Flows Within Southeast Asia 52
Chris Manning and Pradip Bhatnagar

5   Women, Work and International Migration in Southeast Asia:
Trends, Patterns and Policy 73
Graeme Hugo

Part II   Crossing Borders: The State, Migration Strategies and Temporary Migrant Worker Schemes

6   Trading Labour: Socio-economic
and Political Impacts and Dynamics of Labour Export from the
Philippines, 1973–2004 115
Rochelle Ball

7 Indonesian Labour Migration after the 1997–98 Asian
Economic and Financial Crisis 139
Carunia Mulya Firdausy

8 The Feminisation of Migration: Gender, the State and Migrant
Strategies in Bangladesh 155
Ishrat Shamim

9 'White-Collar Filipinos': Australian Professionals
in Singapore 172
Melissa Butcher

10 Indian Professional Workers in Singapore 193
Seema Gaur

**Part III Managing the Border: Governance of
Recruitment, Facilitation of Remittances and
Migrant Workers' Rights**

11 The Recruitment of Foreign Labour in Malaysia: From
Migration System to Guest Worker Regime 213
Diana Wong

12 After Nunukan: The Regulation of Indonesian
Migration to Malaysia 228
Michele Ford

13 The State and Labour Migration Policies in Thailand 248
Patcharawalai Wongboonsin

14 The State and Facilitation of Financial Flows (Remittances)
by Temporary Workers: The Case of Bangladesh 274
Kenneth Jackson

15 Regional Perspectives on the 1990 UN Convention on
the Rights of All Migrant Workers 292
Nicola Piper

Index 311

List of Tables

3.1 GDP per capita in selected Southeast Asian countries,
     1995   28
3.2 Unemployment rates in selected Southeast Asian
     countries, 1985–95   28
3.3 Estimated stocks of migrant workers before, during
     and after the economic crisis, major crisis-affected
     countries, 1996–99   30
3.4 Emigration from Indonesia, 1969–94   32
3.5 Total employed and number of foreign workers
     in Singapore, 1985–94   37
4.1 Exports from the ASEAN-6 to Other ASEAN-6 countries
     and the rest of the world, 1975–80 to 1995–2000   57
4.2 Estimated temporary labour migration within and
     outside Southeast Asia from the 1970s to the early
     twenty-first century   58
4.3 Main countries of origin and destination for temporary
     migrants within Southeast Asia and abroad   59
4.4 Distribution of skilled and professional migrants by
     country of origin in selected Southeast Asian Countries, 2002   61
4.5 AFAS and GATS (WTO) commitments under Mode 4 by sector   65
4.6 The 'depth' of AFAS commitments under Mode-4   66
4. A1 Key economic indicators in ASEAN, Circa 2001–02   70
5.1 Australia: total student arrivals, 1991–92 to 2003–04   78
5.2 Australia: permanent and long-term arrivals of
     persons born in Southeast Asian countries,
     1991–92 to 2003–04   80
5.3 Australia: refugee-humanitarian settlers from Southeast Asia,
     1996–2004   81
5.4 Australia: Southeast Asia-born settler arrivals by visa
     category, 2003–04   82
5.5 Indonesia: estimated stocks of overseas contract
     workers, c.2000   83
5.6 Number of Indonesian overseas workers processed
     by the ministry of manpower, 1969–2003   84
5.7 Estimates of stock of Indonesian female domestic
     overseas contract workers, 2001–04   86

5.8	Major destinations of official Indonesian female labour migrants 1984–2000	87
5.9	Filipinos legally in selected north countries	89
5.10	Australia: growth of the Philippines-born population	89
5.11	The Philippines: domestic service-workers destinations (New Hires) 1987–94	90
5.12	The Philippines: deployment of newly hired female OCWs by skill category 2003	91
5.13	Vietnamese-born persons living outside Vietnam	92
5.14	Thai-born populations in developed countries	93
5.15	Laos-born communities overseas	97
5.16	Cambodia-born communities overseas	98
5.17	Malaysia: citizenship of population at the 1990 and 2001 censuses	99
5.18	Foreign workers in Malaysia, 1 July 2001	99
5.19	Malaysian-born communities overseas	100
5.20	Singapore-born communities overseas	102
5.21	Restrictions on female workers migration in Southeastern Asian countries of origin	103
5.22	Indonesia: surveyed domestic maids by training received and perceived competency	104
5.23	A suggested list of indicators to measure violence against migrant women	105
5.24	Emigration policy and gender implications	107
6.1	Estimated numbers of OCWs by destination, migration status and occupation, 2001	120
6.2	Adverse conditions confronting Asian women migrant domestic workers	122
6.3	Foreign Direct Investment (FDI) and remittances through official channels to the Philippines	124
7.1	Indonesian labour migrants: numbers and destinations, 1999	142
7.2	Indonesian workers employed in selected Asian countries by economic sector, January to June 2003	143
7.3	Indonesian formal worker migrants by gender and destination, 2003	144
7.4	Indonesian workers in the informal sector by gender, 2003	145
7.5	Number of Indonesians forced to undertake excessive work hours in Saudi Arabia, 1995–99	150
7.6	Number of unpaid salary cases involving Indonesians in Saudi Arabia, 1995–99	150

7.7	Number of sexual abuse cases involving Indonesians, 1995–99	150
8.1	Number and percentage of female migrants in comparison to total flow	164
8.2	Countries of destination and skill composition of female migrants	165
9.1	Total population by residential status in Singapore	178
9.2	Resident and non-resident populations in Singapore	178
10.1	Singapore: changes in population categories, 1970–2000	197
10.2	Singapore: total population by residential status, 1990–2000	198
10.3	Singapore: size of foreign labour force, 1970–2000	198
10.4	The Indian population in Singapore, 1821–2000	200
12.1	Number of documented labour migrants and remittances by region, 2001–03	230
12.2	Historical distribution of documented labour outflows from Indonesia to Saudi Arabia and Malaysia	231
12.3	All arrivals and departures of Indonesian citizens to Malaysia, 2000–03	234
13.1	Regular migrant labour in Thailand in 1990 and 2003	250
13.2	Documented migrants in Thailand: by nationality and occupation as on 25 December 2003	251
13.3	Irregular migrants in Thailand, 1992–2004	253
13.4	Location of irregular migrants in Thailand, 1997	254
13.5	Population of Thai provinces bordering Myanmar, 2002	254
13.6	Registration of irregular migrant labour by sector and nationality according to cabinet resolution of 28 August 2001	255
13.7	Irregular migrant labour with work permit extension between 24 February and 25 March 2002	255
13.8	Thailand: labour force and employment growth rates, 1975–91	257
13.9	Socio-economic background of migrant labour	258
13.10	Thai migration indicators, 1990 and 2000	259
13.11	Types of employment prohibited from alien engagement in Thailand	260
13.12	Thai cabinet resolutions on irregular migrant labour, 1992–2002	262
13.A1	Documented migrants in promoted establishment category by nationality and occupation as on 25 December 2003	268

13.A2   Documented migrants in non-promoted category
        by nationality and occupation as on 25 December 2003   269
13.A3   Regular migrants under section 12 of the Alien Employment
        Act by Nationalities and Occupations as on
        25 December 2003   270
14.1   Bangladesh: migrant outflows, 1977–99   280
14.2   Remittance income flows to Bangladesh, 1976–2000   281
14.A1   Top 15 countries with the highest total
        remittances received, 2001   288
14.A2   Top 15 countries with the highest total
        remittances received as a percentage of the GDP, 2001   289

List of Figures

5.1 A typology of female international migration in
Southeast Asia   74
5.2 The Philippines: destination of overseas contract
workers, 1984–2003   90
7.1 Employment situation by employment status, 1998–2003   141
7.2 The recruitment process of Indonesian labour migrants   147
9.1 Approximate populations of migrant workers in Singapore   179
12.1 Sectoral distribution of all overseas migrant workers
officially placed in 2003 by gender and destination   233
12.2 Effects of the 1997–98 crisis on placement of overseas
migrant workers in major destinations, 1995–1999   237
13.1 Thai migrant labour flows by destination, 1975–2003   249
14.1 Bangladesh: remittance receipts, 1976–2000   279

List of Maps

3.1 Malaysia: migrant worker inflows from Bangladesh,
Indonesia and the Philippines, 1990s   40
3.2 Illegal migration from Indonesia to Malaysia: major flows   41
5.1 Southeast Asia: main flows of domestic workers   76
5.2 Southeast Asia: main flows of sex and entertainment workers   77
5.3 Southeast Asia: main flows of marriage migration   79
5.4 Southeast Asia: trafficking of women and children   94

List of Abbreviations

3D	Dirty, dangerous and degrading jobs
AFAS	ASEAN Framework Agreement on Services
AFTA	ASEAN Free Trade Agreement
AIPO	ASEAN Inter-Parliamentary Organisation
ASEAN	Association of Southeast Asian Nations
BAIRA	Bangladesh Association of International Recruiting Agencies
BLA	Bilateral Agreement
BMET	Bangladesh Bureau of Manpower, Employment and Training
BOESL	Bangladesh Overseas Employment Services Limited
CARICOM	Caribbean Community and Common Market
CEDAW	Convention on the Elimination of All Forms of Discrimination against Women
CRC	Convention on the Rights of the Child
DFA	Department of Foreign Affairs, Philippines
DIMIA	Australian Department of Immigration and Indigenous and Multicultural Affairs
DOLE	Philippine Department of Labor and Employment
EDB	Economic Development Board, Singapore
EOI	Export-oriented industrialization
ERC	Economic Review Committee, Singapore
EU	European Union
FDI	Foreign Direct Investment
FOBMI	*Federasi Organisasi Buruh Migran Indonesia*
FTA	Free Trade Agreement
GATS	General Agreement on Trade in Services
GATT	General Agreement on Tariffs and Trade
GCIM	Global Commission on International Migration
GDP	Gross Domestic Product
GNP	Gross National Product
ICRM	International Convention on the Protection of the Rights of All Migrant Workers and Members of Their Families
IDA	Infocomm Development Authority, Singapore
ILM	International Labour Migration
ILO	International Labour Organisation
IMF	International Monetary Fund
INSTRAW	United Nations International Research and Training Institute for the advancement of Women
IOM	International Organisation of Migration

ISI	Import-substitution industrialisation
KBE	Knowledge-based economy
KOPBUMI	*Konsorsium Pembela Buruh Migran Indonesia*
LDC	Least Developed Countries
MIRAB	Migration, Remittances and Bureaucracy
MNC/TNC	Multinational/Transnational corporation
MOM	Ministry of Manpower, Singapore
MOU	Memorandum of Understanding
MRA	Mutual Recognition Arrangement
MTI	Ministry of Trade and Industry, Singapore
NAFTA	North American Free Trade Agreement
NASSCOM	National Association of Software and Service Companies, India
NEP	New Economic Policy (Malaysia)
NGO	Non-governmental organisation
NIE or NIC	Newly-industrialising economy or country
OCW	Overseas Contract Workers
OECD	Organisation for Economic Cooperation and Development
PJTKI	*Perusahaan Jasa Tenaga Kerja Indonesia*
POEA	Philippine Overseas Employment Administration
PPP	Purchasing power parity
PR	Permanent resident
PTK	Professional, technical and kindred workers
SEWA	Self-employed Women's Association
TFR	Total Fertility Rate
TLM	Temporary Labour Migration
WTO	World Trade Organisation

Acknowledgements

This book grew out of a conference funded by the Japan Foundation, held at UNE, Armidale, in December 2003. We are most grateful to the Foundation for its support. Supplementary funding was provided by the Asia Centre, UNE, the Australian Academy of the Humanities, the Asian Studies Association of Australia, and the Faculty of Economics, Business and Law, UNE. We are also grateful to Dr. Andrew Messner, research assistant to the project, for editorial assistance and help with the final manuscript.

Amarjit Kaur and Ian Metcalfe

Preliminary Note

In Southeast Asia, the Association of Southeast Asian Nations – ASEAN – has given institutional expression to what has been termed an 'essentially declaratory regionalism'. No attempt is made in the book to impose uniformity on the spelling of place names. For example, Cambodia, which became known as Kampuchea, is now again referred to as Cambodia on the ASEAN website. Yet in some official international documents, it continues to be referred to as Kampuchea. Again, while Burma is officially known as Myanmar, both terms continue to be used, and Burmese is more often used than Myanmarese to refer to its nationals.

Notes on Contributors

Rochelle E. Ball is presently based at UNSW @ ADFA, Canberra, Australia. She has written extensively on international migration issues particularly relating to its economic and political impacts, and implications for human and labour rights of migrant workers. She has co-authored a book on international migration and its implications for Australia. Her most recent book examines the impact of international migration on children.

Pradip Bhatnagar is a government civil servant in India. He has worked as an economist at the WTO and in ESCAP. His main research interests are international economic relations and labour migration in particular, and he has published several papers on these subjects, with special reference to South and East Asia.

Melissa Butcher is currently a consultant and researcher at the Research Institute for Asia and the Pacific (RIAP), University of Sydney. Her research focus is the impact of mobility and cross-cultural interactions on transnational corporate professionals. Melissa was an Australian Research Council Post-Doctoral Research Fellow at RIAP from 2002–05.

Carunia Mulya Firdausy is Deputy Minister, Ministry of Research and Technology, Government of Indonesia. His previous position was Senior Researcher at the Research Centre for Economics and Social Science, Indonesian Institute for Sciences (LIPI).

Michele Ford teaches in the Department of Indonesian Studies, School of Languages and Cultures at the University of Sydney. Her main research interests are traditional and non-traditional forms of labour movement organisation in Southeast Asia and cross-border interactions between Indonesia, Singapore and Malaysia. In recent years, she has published on these topics in journals including *International Migration, Journal of Industrial Relations, Australian Journal of Politics and History, Asian Journal of Women's Studies, Asian Journal of Social Sciences* and the *Review of Indonesian and Malayan Affairs*.

Seema Gaur is a Government economist currently based at New Delhi. She is interested in research in the field of international economics, especially issues in international labour migration, including those relating to labour mobility under WTO and regional trading agreements. She has published in these areas in refereed international journals and business newspapers.

Graeme Hugo is Federation Fellow, Professor of the Department of Geographical and Environmental Studies and Director of the National

Centre for Social Applications of Geographic Information Systems at the University of Adelaide. His research interests are in population issues in Australia and Southeast Asia, especially migration. His books include *Australia's Changing Population* (Oxford University Press), *The Demographic Dimension in Indonesian Development* (with T. H. Hull, V. J. Hull and G. W. Jones: Oxford University Press), *International Migration Statistics: Guidelines for Improving Data Collection Systems* (with A.S. Oberai, H. Zlotnik and R. Bilsborrow: International Labour Office), *Worlds in Motion: Understanding International Migration at Century's End* (with D. S. Massey, J. Arango, A Kouaouci, A. Pellegrino and J. E. Taylor: Oxford University Press), several of the 1986, 1991 and 1996 census based *Atlas of the Australian People* Series (AGPS), *Australian Immigration: A Survey of the Issues* (with M. Wooden, R. Holton and J. Sloan, AGPS), *New Forms of Urbanisation: Beyond the Urban-Rural Dichotomy* (with A. Champion, Ashgate) and *Australian Census Analytic Program: Australia's Most Recent Immigrants* (Australian Bureau of Statistics).

Kenneth Jackson is Director of the Centre for Development Studies in the University of Auckland, New Zealand and Associate Professor of Development Studies. He has worked in Malaysia (ACHEM/YPM), and has held visiting appointments at several places including the University of Oregon and Duke University. He has also undertaken consulting and training work many parts of the developing world including China, Kosovo and most recently Samoa on projects funded through international agencies such as NZAID, AusAID, USAID, UNDP, UNESCAP and others. His particular research concentration in recent years has been on South Asia, particularly Bangladesh and India.

Amarjit Kaur is Professor of Economic History at the University of New England. Her research interests include globalisation, the international politics of economic development with a particular focus on labour in Southeast Asia/Asia; labour migration and border controls and the politics of law and human rights policies in Asia. Among her recent books are *The Shaping of Malaysia* (Macmillan: 1999 [co-edited with Ian Metcalfe]), *Wage Labour in Southeast Asia since 1840: Globalisation, the International Division of Labour and Labour Transformations* (Palgrave/Macmillan: 2004) and *Women Workers in Industrialising Asia: Costed, not valued* (ed) (Palgrave/Macmillan: 2004).

Chris Manning is Associate Professor and Head of the Indonesia Project in the Division of Economics, Research School of Pacific and Asian Studies, Australian National University. His main research interests are labour markets and economic development in Indonesia, and labour market issues and international migration in Southeast and Northeast Asia.

Ian Metcalfe is Adjunct Professor and Deputy Director of the Asia Centre at the University of New England. He is an earth scientist who specialises in the geological evolution and natural resources of Asia. He has written extensively on the geology and geological evolution of Southeast Asia and China, and on the palaeobiogeography and palaeogeography of East and Southeast Asia in a global context. His most recent book is *Faunal and Floral Migrations and Evolution in SE Asia-Australasia* (A.A. Balkema, 2001). He is also interested in wider social and economic aspects of Asia, including gender, sustainable development and environmental issues.

Ishrat Shamim is President of the Centre for Women and Children's Studies, University of Dhaka, Bangladesh.

Tessa Morris-Suzuki is Professor of Japanese History in the Research School of Pacific and Asian Studies, Australian National University. Her research interests include frontiers, globalization, and the cross-border movement of people in East Asia. Among her recent publications are: *Re-inventing Japan: Time, Space, Nation* (M. E. Sharpe, 1998); *A View from the Frontier* (in Japanese, Misuzu Shobô, 2000); and *The Past Within Us: Media, Memory, History* (Iwanami Shoten, 2004; Verso, 2005).

Nicola Piper is Senior Research Fellow at the Asia Research Institute, National University of Singapore. She held previous appointments with the Nordic Institute of Asian Studies/Copenhagen and the Australian National University/Canberra. Her research interests broadly revolve around aspects of inclusion and exclusion of migrant workers, with empirical focus of Asia and Europe. Among her recent publications are: *Racism, Nationalism and Citizenship* (1998), and co-edited publications, *Women and Work in Globalising Asia* (2002), *Wife or Worker? Asians, Marriage and Migration* (Rowman & Littlefield, 2003), *Transnational Activism in Asia – Problems of Power and Democracy* (Routledge, 2004), as well as various journal articles. Her current project is on the topic of political organizing of migrant labour and transnational activism to promote the rights of migrants.

Diana Wong is Associate Professor at the Institute for Malaysian and International Studies (IKMAS) at Universiti Kebangsaan Malaysia. Her previous position was at the Institute of Southeast Asian Studies, Singapore. She has written widely on labour migration in Malaysia and Singapore.

Patcharawalai Wongboonsin is an Associate Professor at the Institute of Asian Studies, Chulalongkorn University, Thailand. She has written widely on migrant labour in Thailand.

Part I

Divided We Move: Migration Challenges in Asia

1
Introduction

Amarjit Kaur and Ian Metcalfe

Migration is regarded as the earliest form of globalisation and human migrations have been a constant theme throughout history. Because there were no political boundaries, the movements of people were usually referred to as migration. According to Bohning (1984) the international migration of human beings dates back only to when the 'nation-state' took hold in Europe during the Industrial Revolution, and as a result of colonialism spread in all directions throughout the world. The nation state brought along with it a 'we–they' or 'in–out' distinction and people become identified with a particular nation. Movement from one nation to another or international migration required a change in allegiance and citizenship.

In Asia and elsewhere colonial powers carved out new states with precisely delineated boundaries but kept borders open to trade, investment and labour flows in keeping with the growth of the international economy. In the post Second World War period, decolonisation and the dissolution of empires resulted in the emergence of independent nation states in the Asian region. The East Asian states embraced the 'new' globalisation via trade liberalisation strategies and export-led growth. Concurrently, a new form of the international division of labour brought opportunities for export-oriented industrialisation in East Asia. These countries' comparative advantage lay mainly in lower labour costs, and the labour market thus became one of the main channels through which globalisation impacted on the Asian economies.

Paradoxically though, as the East Asian economies moved up the development ladder, their development objectives become increasingly dependent on foreign labour. The increased internationalisation of capital, growing intra-firm linkages and the demands of the knowledge-based economy requiring professional and highly skilled technical workers, coupled with the need to maintain international competitiveness, are adding to this process. Additionally, the redistribution and reorganisation of production which earlier led to the export of labour-intensive manufacturing to East Asia, is now also evident in the relocation of higher-end production and services as well as

3

outsourcing to cheaper cost locations. This is happening on a much wider scale than before when 'foreign experts' went routinely as 'expatriates' to take up top-level positions. East Asian states thus face the dual challenge of rising structural unemployment due to economic restructuring on the one hand and the need to provide knowledge workers on the other. The level of disparity among the countries within the region is also relatively high and the process of convergence slow. These developments have resulted in migration assuming new features in the region in the contemporary globalisation period.

The growing economic complexities highlighted the diversity of ethnic, cultural and religious forces in the region. In these modern nation states, identities based on ethnic and religious allegiance became the norm, unlike earlier periods when people tended to forge ties based on self-interest and personal connections. Policies were also created to categorise earlier migrant settlers as non-indigenous races and to restrict cross-border movements through new immigration regulations. Moreover, as the racial origins of migrants grew in scale and scope, the rights of migrants to reside in the host countries also disappeared (Castles 2000; Castles and Miller 1998). The previous form of settlement migration for less-skilled migrants has thus given way to a new form of temporary migration, and temporary worker or contract worker schemes. Most of these schemes were also designed with little regard to any impact beyond the destination countries.

There are differences however, in the treatment of foreign workers. Since states are interested in maximising the contribution of labour while minimising social costs, skilled foreign workers are both needed and wanted, but unskilled workers, while needed are unwanted. This has resulted in the implementation of separate recruitment policies for skilled workers, which include higher salaries and an array of perks including residency.

Returning to the issue of sovereignty, most analysts theorise that as the state's sovereignty became increasingly reduced under the weight and authority of international institutional structures – the International Monetary Fund, the World Bank, the World Trade Organisation – and global collective measures, one central role of the state remained: territorial control and the regulation of populations. Since people are 'less' mobile than goods, capital and ideas, the globalised state's role essentially centres on the regulation of populations and the control of cross-border movements. This policy is manifested in evolving border-control strategies, more stringent restrictions on the cross-border movements of unskilled workers and disease containment through epidemiological surveillance.

Nevertheless, evolving border control regimes must be viewed in the context of global governance norms and civil society activism. International migration has become entwined with the issue of human rights and has thus become a major domestic and international political issue, principally in Europe and North America, but also in Asia. Emphasis on the quality of governance and issues of transparency demonstrate how transnational agencies and civil society activism are pushing forward changes to override national sovereignty, particularly in relation to international law determining human rights. This global bureaucracy, that seeks to develop new policy frameworks through non-state actors in the global system, is thus attempting to address the complexity in international labour migration processes.

These issues however, continue to be debated mainly in the context of western nations, and migration challenges and population movements in Asia are less well understood. Many countries in East Asia – Japan, Taiwan, South Korea and Hong Kong (except China) – are now mainly countries of destination, while South Asia continues to consist principally of countries of origin of migrants. In the Southeast Asian region, the pattern is more diverse. The Philippines, Indonesia, Myanmar, Vietnam, Laos and Cambodia are countries of origin; Brunei and Singapore are predominantly countries of destination, while Malaysia and Thailand are both countries of origin and destination of migrants. Skilled migrants from India and Australia now also comprise a new migratory stream in the Southeast Asian region, with Singapore, Malaysia and Thailand the principal destinations. There are also increasing South to North and North to South flows, involving students, refugees and contract workers.

All the labour flows in turn have resulted, for example, in the design of specific schemes for temporary workers, residency policies and schemes for the facilitation of financial flows or remittances by migrant workers. Migration regularisation is also being combined with tighter border controls, employer sanctions and law enforcement measures. At the same time, the rights of unskilled migrant workers have captured the attention of civil society organisations (see, e.g., Human Rights Watch 2004), which now provide a constraint on harsh restrictive measures in conformity with human rights standards and international norms, such as the Universal Declaration of Human Rights, and the United Nations 1990 Convention on the Rights of Migrant Workers and Members of their Families.

Generally, research on international migration in Asia has largely been fragmented between varieties of disciplines, and/or is country-specific. The work of authors such as Hugo (1993, 2002) has focused on migration streams from Indonesia, and detailed studies of the feminisation of Indonesian migration, while Manning (2002) and Athukorala and Manning (1999) have written from the perspective of structural changes in the East Asian labour markets. Regional and/or country studies have also focused on labour categories, settlement migration and state regulation of labour migration (Kaur 2004a, 2004b, 2004c).

There are also gaps in our accounts of key transnational processes impacting on international labour migration in Asia and their economic, political and social contexts. These include the intensification of population regulation and control of international migration; governance of recruitment; legislative frameworks and international treaties on the rights of migrants; enforcement of migrant workers' rights; the facilitation of remittance flows; and the role of civil society activism and global governance norms.

The contributions in this book examine these migration challenges, the regulation of population movements and the issue of agency, focusing on three main themes. The first is the rapid expansion of international labour migration since about the 1970s, against the wider context of the 'new' globalisation and consistent with the globalisation and reorganisation of production. The second is the expanding range of migratory streams – unskilled temporary workers, skilled professional and technical workers, students, refugees and illegal or irregular migrants – and migratory regimes; the growth of a migration industry and networks and kinship relationships among migrants. The third is the gendered dimensions of international migration in Asia and the correlation between gender inequalities in the region and migration. The contributions, however, do not specifically address trafficking in women. Trafficking is a specific form of migration that is linked to exploitative gender relations, and although it is undeniably a key aspect of the gender dimensions of international migration, the contributions focus on the gendered nature of international labour migration more generally.

The chapters in this book detail the main state actors and state policies, migration streams, civil society interests, structures and institutions involved in an understanding of mobility, labour migration and border controls in Asia. The material is organised in the context of a thematic argument that gives a pattern to understanding mobility and international labour migration in Asia. With the territorial role of the state in mind and border control regimes, the book is organised into three parts. Part I introduces the broad issue of migration challenges in the region – economic and legislative frameworks and the diversity of states and state actors whose policies shape cross-border outcomes in the region. Special attention is given to the gendered nature of migration which has become an important migration stream. This broad framework is necessary to comprehend continuity and change as well as the reorientations in the region. Part II focuses on states, development policies and how these impact on migration policies. A key focus is how Asian states enhance their economic performance through specifically designed policies. Part III looks at how states respond to challenges, governance of migration and security, regional cooperation, and the facilitation of financial flows (remittances). It also scrutinises the issues raised earlier, of global governance and the role of non-governmental organisations in penetrating state sovereignty in the area of international law determining human rights.

References

Athukorala, P. and C. Manning (1999) *Structural Change and International Migration in East Asia* (Melbourne: Oxford University Press).

Bohning, W.R. (1984) *Studies in International Labour Migration* (London: The Macmillan Press).

Castles, S. (2000) *Ethnicity and Globalization: From Migrant Worker to Transnational Citizen* (London: Sage).

Castles, S. and M.J. Miller (1998) *The Age of Migration: International Population Movements in the Modern World* (New York: Guilford Press).

Hugo, G. (2002) 'Women's International Labour Migration', in K. Robinson and Sharon Bessel (eds) *Women in Indonesia: Gender, Equity and Development* (Singapore: ISEAS) pp. 158–78.

—— (1993) 'International Labour Migration', in Chris Manning and J. Hardjono (eds) 'Indonesia Assessment 1993 – Labour: Sharing in the Benefits of Growth?', *Political and Social Change Monograph* (Canberra: RSPAS) pp. 108–26.

Human Rights Watch (2004) *Help Wanted: Abuses against Migrant Female Domestic Workers in Indonesia and Malaysia*, Vol. 16. No. 9 (B)(July):1–91(and Appendix).

Kaur, A. (2004a) *Wage Labour in Southeast Asia since 1840: Globalisation, the International Division of Labour and Labour Transformations* (Basingstoke: Palgrave/Macmillan).

—— (2004b) 'Economic Globalisation and the "New" Labour Migration in Southeast Asia', in Tisdell, Clem and Raj Kumar Sen (eds) *Economic Globalisation, Social Conflicts, Labour and Environmental Issues* (London: Edward Elgar) pp. 244–66.

—— (2004c) 'Crossing Frontiers: Race, Migration and Border Controls in Southeast Asia', *International Journal on Multicultural Societies (IJMS)* Vol. 6, No. 2:111–32 www.unesco.org/shs/ijms [Special issue, Managing Migration and Diversity in the Asia Pacific Region and Europe, Eds Christine Inglis and Matthias Koening].

Manning, C. (2002) 'Structural Change, Economic Crisis and International Labour Migration in East Asia', *The World Economy*, Vol. 25, No. 3 (March): 359–85.

2

Changing Border Control Regimes and their Impact on Migration in Asia

Tessa Morris-Suzuki

On 22 January 1954, Australia became one of the first countries to ratify the United Nations Convention Relating to the Status of Refugees (the Geneva Convention) – an agreement which commits Australia to providing asylum to those on its territory, or people arriving at its borders, with a well-founded fear of persecution on the grounds of race, religion, nationality, membership of a particular social group or political opinion.

On 5 November 2003, Australian authorities turned away a boatload of Kurdish asylum seekers from Turkey who had reached Melville Island, forcing them first to remain at sea in a small boat for four days, and then to return to Indonesia, a country which has not ratified the United Nations Convention, and whose economic and social circumstances make it far less able to deal with asylum seekers than Australia's does. In a press statement released at the time, the Foreign Minister Alexander Downer stated that the Kurds had not expressed a wish to seek asylum in Australia. A week later, after the press gained access to other sources of information, the government was forced to modify this statement, and admitted that the boat people had indeed used words such as 'refugee' in their appeals to the Australian authorities.

The forced expulsion of the Turkish Kurds, which under any reasonable interpretation appeared to be in violation of Australia's commitments to the Geneva Convention, was shocking for several reasons. But perhaps the most shocking thing about it was that most people in Australia do not find it shocking. Somehow, they seemed to have become accustomed to the fact that, at least as far as the rights of migrants and refugees are concerned, the government only feels obliged to abide by the international treaties it has signed when these treaties coincide with its political interests. Somehow, they (we) had grown used to the fact that in relation to asylum seekers, our political leaders make statements that later turn out not to accord with the facts. In the first decade of the twenty-first century, such events have ceased to be surprising.

The polling booth and the border post

The fall of the Berlin Wall and the so-called end of the Cold War (although in Northeast Asia it still continues) were seen by many people as marking a decisive stage in the global triumph of democracy. Totalitarian regimes had crumbled from within; the 'Free world' had triumphed. Meanwhile, outside the former Soviet bloc, moves towards democratisation were occurring in many parts of the world, from South Africa to South Korea. Yet, since the start of the twenty-first century, a growing shadow has been cast over this so-called triumph of democracy. The apparently increasing ability of the richer nations of the world to ignore international treaty commitments and flout the authority of the UN with impunity raises new questions about the meaning of democracy and justice in our globalised world. Meanwhile domestically, in many countries including Australia, and particularly in the past two years, the substantive content of democracy appears to be being hollowed out by a repeated process in which political leaders evoke fear of the 'other' through alarming statements (including statements about refugees) which later prove to have a strange lack of congruence to the truth.

Nowhere are the dilemmas of twenty-first century democracy more evident than in relation to migrants – including migrant workers and asylum seekers (and later I want to argue that the distinction between these two groups is becoming increasingly difficult to sustain). Nineteenth and twentieth century ideals of democracy were always firmly embedded in the conceptual framework of the nation state. The subjects of democracy were citizens, and citizens acquired citizenship by virtue of full membership in the national community in which they lived. The system thus possessed an inherent blind-spot which allowed frontiers and those who crossed them to disappear into a 'democracy-free zone'.

Let me elaborate that point a little further by contrasting two key physical sites for the encounter between the individual and the nation state. In most conventional theories of liberal democracy, the crucial encounter between the individual and the state takes place at the polling booth – in that all-important sanctum of democracy where citizens, having listened to the debates of the election campaign, cast their secret ballots for the candidates of their choice. Needless to say, whatever the dilemmas of contemporary democracy, I nonetheless believe that preserving and expanding the right of citizens to participate in such electoral action is a vitally important task.

However, today more and more people cross national boundaries and spend at least part of their lives outside the bounds of the state of which they are citizens. According to the United States Central Intelligence Agency (CIA) (which takes a keen interest in the subject) today some 140 million people live outside the countries of their birth, and more than 50 countries of the world have populations in which migrants constitute over 15 per cent of the population. This represents a striking recent expansion in cross-border mobility: at the start of the 1990s, the number of people living outside the countries of their birth was thought to be about 80 million, just over half the current level (Central Intelligence Agency 2001).

As such mobility increases, for many people – even those who come from or live in formally 'democratic' states – the crucial encounter with the state occurs not in the polling booth but at the border post – that little booth at which one's right to cross the frontier is decided. Here, the relationship between individual and state is radically different from the relationship which is established in the polling booth. Within the polling booth, the state and individual are bound together, in theory at least, by a contract governed by rules set out in the constitution. The constitution promises the people the right to choose those who will govern them, and the people in turn agree to abide by the laws instituted by their rulers. Though the practice of democracy seldom fully accords with the contractual ideals set out in most constitutions, the ideal of the contract remains a powerful force in contemporary society.

At the border post, however, the encounter is inverted. Here it is not the people who choose the government, but the state which chooses people – selecting those who will be allowed to enter its territory, and determining the terms of entry. This relationship is almost entirely non-contractual. Nation states generally have laws defining, in rather broad terms, which categories of people may or may not cross the border, but the way in which the laws are applied to each individual is determined by the officials on the spot. Even in the most democratic of societies, the power of these officials is generally arbitrary and almost absolute. There is no need for them to justify their decisions. The ways in which they exercise their power are not open to public scrutiny and can seldom be challenged. Decisions are made on the basis of the official's personal judgment as to whether potential migrants represent a 'risk' – whether they are likely to violate the conditions of their entry or to break other laws. This 'risk assessment', in turn, is shaped by a mass of information, preconceptions and prejudices about race, nationality, class, language, appearance and so on, which each official brings to the task of judging each individual border-crosser. This arbitrary world of border politics, in other words, is part of what Susan Buck-Morss in her study *Dreamworld and Catastrophe* calls the 'wild zone' of state power – the zone where 'power is above the law' (Buck-Morss 2000:2–8).

The development of modern border control regimes might be viewed as a (so far rather neglected) form of politics. How has the politics of border controls emerged and evolved since the start of the twentieth century? How is the present-day transformation of border control regimes – the radical transformation taking place as part of the so-called 'global war on terror' – affecting the practice of border politics? And ultimately, in the twenty-first century, is it possible to begin to address the blind-spot of conventional democratic theory – is it possible to democratise the border?

To address these questions, I want here to look, in rather broad and general terms, at the rise of modern border control regimes from the first part of the twentieth century onwards. I draw a number of my examples from the areas on which I am mainly focusing in my current research – Australia and Japan – but believe that these also have resonances between events in other parts of Asia. In the final section of this chapter I return to the present, and try to address some possibilities for the future of border controls in our region.

Race and migrant labour at the start of the twentieth century

The border control system which we now take for granted to today is really a surprisingly recent invention. As John Torpey points out in his study of developments in Europe, it took shape mainly in the first two decades of the twentieth century, and particularly around the time of the First World War, when many nations introduced laws requiring people entering the country to be in possession of a passport (Torpey 2000).

Though there have, of course, been large-scale movements of people in earlier phases of history, the nineteenth century rise of corporate capitalism and the creation of global empires was accompanied by particularly significant cross-border and intercontinental migrations. Up to the end of the nineteenth century, however, few international borders were heavily guarded, and travellers rarely carried passports, let alone visas, work permits or residence permits. The rise of the modern border control regime was very closely linked to the evolution of the modern nation state itself. From the late nineteenth century onwards, new measures such as conscription laws, national education systems and (in some countries) the first steps towards the creation of social welfare policies made states far more deeply involved than ever before in the lives of citizens.

In this context, it became increasingly important, from the state's perspective, to draw clear dividing lines between 'citizens' and 'foreigners'. Foreigners were to be excluded from conscription for fear that they might become 'fifth columnists', while the emergence of national education and welfare systems in the richer countries of the world brought growing fears of influxes of immigrants arriving to 'take advantage' of systems meant for citizens alone. These developments, occurring simultaneously with very large-scale exoduses of migrants from countries such as China and Russia, evoked a wave of 'panics' surrounding immigrants, and provoked the introduction of restrictive migration laws in several countries. These laws were deeply embedded in the contemporary structures of empire and empire-building, and were therefore often explicitly or implicitly based on racial discrimination.

One of the most striking examples of this was Australia's Immigration Restriction Act of 1901, a law which today may be seen as one of history's remarkable monuments to political sophistry. Designed specifically as a measure to exclude 'coloured' (particularly Chinese) immigrants, early drafts of the law included references to race. These however, provoked protests, not least from the Japanese government, whose objections to the law were rather intriguing. Japan's political leaders had no objection to Australia's introducing a law which kept out 'lower class' migrant workers from Japan (pearl divers, plantation workers etc.) but they were deeply troubled by the idea that 'well educated' Japanese would be subject to the indignity of exclusion (Japanese Legation to Australia 1901). Above all, the Japanese government conveyed to Australia its strong exception to the idea that 'Japan should be spoken of in formal documents ... as if the Japanese were on the same level of morality and civilisation as the Chinese, or other less advanced populations of Asia'. What they wanted therefore was 'not the modification of the laws by which a certain part of the Japanese population was excluded from Australia and New Zealand, but the abandonment of the language which classed them with others to whom they bore no real similarity, and inflicted upon the nation an insult which was not deserved' (Secretary of State 1901).

As a result, the law as passed nowhere mentioned the words 'race' or 'colour'. Instead, the purpose of maintaining a 'White Australia' was pursued by introducing a 'dictation test', nominally designed to assess the 'literacy' of immigrants. In fact, confidential instructions issued to customs officers (who administered the test) made it quite clear that this test was to be administered only to so-called 'coloured' immigrants. The instructions baldly stated that 'it is intended that the dictation test shall be an absolute bar to admission. Officers will therefore take means to ascertain whether, in their opinion, the immigrant can write English. If it is thought that he can, the test must be dictated in some other European language, one with which the immigrant is not acquainted' (Anon. 1909). The test was not to be administered to Japanese, Indians or Hong Kong Chinese who held passports issued by their governments. However, as we shall see, at this stage passports were generally issued only to officials and other members of the social elite in these countries. Thus migrant workers from Japan, India and Hong Kong were still subject to exclusion by means of the dictation test.

Meanwhile in Japan itself, at the very time when Australia's restrictive immigration laws were being drawn up, the government had introduced the Immigration Ordinance of 1899, which was similarly aimed at keeping out other Asian (particularly Chinese) migrant workers from Japan. This law too made no reference to race, but instead imposed sweeping restrictions on the entry of migrants for the purpose of employment, with the exception of a very small number of specified skills and professions. Although Japan in fact came to rely very heavily on immigrant labour (including forced labour) from its colonies during the Second World War, this restrictive approach to foreign immigrants (i.e., immigrants who did not possess Japanese imperial nationality under Japanese law) remains in place to the present day.

Passports, subversion and mobilisation – The First World War and after

It is worth emphasising here that restrictions on migrant labour began to take shape before the widespread introduction of passport inspections as the main instrument of border controls. At this stage, the bureaucracy of immigration officials did not exist, and border control functions (including the multi-lingual administration of Australia's dictation test) were often carried out by customs officers. A further transformation, however, took place at the time of the First World War.

As John Torpey shows, various types of passports and other travel documents had come into use around the world during the nineteenth century, but these were used only in certain circumstances and by certain groups of people, and were not a universal requirement for cross-border travel. Indeed, possession of a passport was often a *privilege* designed to help travellers from the social elite to obtain favourable treatment on their journeys. The outbreak of the global conflict in 1914, however, evoked new fears of the cross-border movement of 'subversives' or 'enemy agents', and led in one country after another to the introduction of laws requiring entrants to be in possession of a valid passport. Like Britain's Aliens Restriction Act of 1914, these were often intended as emergency measures to last only while 'a state of war exists' (Torpey 2000:108–12).

However, once they were in force, many of the measures remained (one suspects that the 'emergency' border controls introduced as part of the contemporary 'global war on terror' are likely to acquire a similar permanence). One reason for this continuation was undoubtedly the Bolshevik Revolution of 1917 and the rise of communism, which created fears of subversion that would last long after the signing of the Treaty of Versailles. Another factor was the deepening integration of state and society associated with what some scholars have called the 'total war system': the mid-twentieth century process of national economic, social and cultural mobilisation (Yamanouchi *et al.*, 1995). The creation of military, educational and welfare systems associated with national mobilisation intensified the need of the state to distinguish 'nationals' from 'foreigners', even though, in the pre-war colonial empires, the category of 'national' was in turn often divided into ethnically based hierarchies.

New border control systems like those described by Torpey also took shape outside Europe. In Australia, for example, the government in 1915 issued an ordinance requiring those entering the country to be in possession of a current passport, and in 1920 this was permanently enshrined in the Commonwealth Passports Act. Similarly, in January 1918, Japan introduced a directive on the 'entry of aliens', which empowered local authorities to prohibit the landing of a rather long list of categories of foreigners: people who lacked a passport or other evidence of citizenship [*ryoken mata wa kokuseki shômeisho*]; those suspected of working for interests of an enemy nation or against the interests of Japan; people liable to disturb public order or subvert morality; people suspected of being vagrants or beggars; anyone suffering from an infectious disease or thought to be a risk to public health; and the mentally ill, poor people and others deemed likely to require public assistance (Hômushô Nyûkoku Kanrikyoku 1964:8). Interestingly, however, passport-free travel between China and Japan was allowed until 1939 (by which time the two countries were already at war).

Refugees and 'guest workers': from the Second World War to the cold war

Just as the First World War led to the widespread establishment of systems of passport control, so the events surrounding the Second World War precipitated further transformations in the global border control system. Political turmoil in Europe and elsewhere from the late 1930s onwards generated huge 'displacements' of populations, as people were involuntarily driven across frontiers by war and by the genocidal policies of the Nazi government and its allies. In response to these issues, international institutions for the recognition of refugees began to develop, culminating in the signing of the 1951 Geneva Convention on the Status of Refugees. It is interesting to note that this convention was at first specifically limited to assisting the refugees displaced by the events of the Second World War and its immediate aftermath. The Convention's definition of refugees was restricted to those affected by events which occurred before the beginning of 1951. However, with the emergence of new refugee problems associated with the Cold War, it soon proved necessary to widen the scope of the definition, and in 1954 the Convention was revised to cover ongoing displacements of people.

But post-war recovery also generated another and quite different cross-border flow of population. As global economic growth gathered pace in the 1950s, many of the world's wealthier countries experienced labour shortages which they sought to fill by expanding migrant labour programmes. Australia, for example, developed energetic policies to encourage the inflow of permanent migrants, not just from the traditional sources nations – Britain and Ireland – but also from Southern and Eastern Europe. France adopted a rather more cautious and complex approach, retaining restrictions on migration while de facto recruiting migrant labour from poorer parts of Europe, and periodically legalising large groups of *sans papiers*.

Meanwhile, the Evian Accord of 1962 which ended Algeria's war of independence also established the right of Algerians to migrate to France (Togman 2002). At the same time, West Germany initiated the *Gastarbeiter* system, aimed at bringing migrant workers into the country on a short term basis. *Gastarbeiter* programmes were developed through a series of bilateral agreements signed from 1955 onwards with Italy, Spain, Greece, Turkey,

Portugal and Yugoslavia. At this stage, the political and economic circumstances of the global order meant that, in Europe at least, the refugee and migrant labour systems generally remained conceptually distinct. Refugees arriving in Western Europe, the United States, Canada and Australia were mostly Eastern European and often from middle-class backgrounds, while migrant labourers were largely working-class and came from Southern Europe of former colonies in Asia, Africa and elsewhere.

The parallel development of new refugee and migrant labour policies led to the creation of increasingly complex systems under which migrants were sifted into a hierarchy of different categories with varying civic and social rights: foreign permanent residents, refugees, business migrants, *Gastarbeiter*, those on student visas and others. In this age of decolonisation, the crude racial categories which had characterised pre-war migration policy were increasingly discredited. However, the hierarchical sorting of migrants by post-war border control regimes has aptly been described by Etienne Balibar as 'differential racism' (Balibar 1991). In other words, the category into which a particular migrant was placed was determined by migration officials on the basis of a whole range of personal characteristics including nationality, class, education, age and others. But it is certain that preconceived racial stereotypes, inherited from the colonial era, were among the important factors shaping official perceptions of the category in which each migrant belonged. Equally, the fact that people from certain ethnic groups came to be disproportionately represented amongst those groups of migrants with the least rights tended to reinforce racially prejudicial practices and attitudes in the host country.

One further point to note is the crucial place of illegal migrants, who occupied the bottom of the hierarchy in terms of the protection of their human rights. As the post-war migrant labour system took shape, many countries developed what can best be described as 'illegal migration policies': that is to say that (as we saw in the case of France) governments selectively turned a blind eye to – or even covertly encouraged – the entry of 'illegal migrants' whose presence served the economic needs of the nation. After all, 'illegal migrants' are in a sense the ideal workforce: they receive no welfare benefits, hardly ever attempt to demand pay rises, and can be 'disposed of' (deported) whenever their presence is no longer needed.

The cold war and the control of 'subversives'

While post-war shifts in border controls were influenced by the emergence of UN humanitarian schemes and (more importantly) by the need for labour they were also profoundly shaped by the security concerns of the Cold War. In this respects, there are interesting continuities between the policies introduced by the United States and elsewhere in the 1950s, and the new schemes being introduced around the world today as part of the 'global war on terror'.

Early in 1950, the US Senate embarked on a major inquiry into the nation's immigration policies. The inquiry's report provided the basis for a law, enacted in 1952, which would define US immigration policy for the next decade or more. Debate surrounding the new Immigration and Naturalisation Law took place against the background of the Korean War and of a wave of anti-Communist sentiment in the United States reflected in the 1947 investigations of well-known Hollywood figures by the House Committee on Un-American Activities, and in the controversial Alger Hiss case of 1950. In September 1950, the US Internal Security Law – also known as the MacCarran Law, after its chief sponsor, Democrat Senator Pat McCarran – was passed. This, amongst other things, banned the entry of aliens of whom 'there is reason to believe that they would be subversive to national security' (quoted in Bennett 1963:81).

In this context, mainstream US political opinion on immigration rapidly polarised around two positions. The first, held by President Harry S. Truman and others, called for a relatively far-reaching liberalisation of US immigration policy. Racial-based laws which had excluded the entry of many 'Asian' immigrants, and tightly restricted the entry of others should, it was argued, be abolished; plans should be made for a major increase in immigrant numbers; and some care should be taken in balancing human rights considerations and national security concerns. The opposing, more conservative, position accepted the need to abolish overt racial exclusions, but was much more cautious about other areas of reform. Conservatives argued that a quota system (limiting the entry of particular nationalities to a level determined by their ratio in the existing US population) needed to be retained in order to preserve the ethnic 'balance' of the US population. Above all, tight migration controls should be enforced to prevent the possible entry to the US of Communists and other subversives.

The most eloquent exponent of this second view was Congressman Francis E. Walter, Chair of the House Committee on Un-American Activities, who regarded Communist subversion and immigration as inseparably connected. In the confrontation between the two approaches to immigration, the conservative side was unequivocally the winner. The Senate's 1950 inquiry into immigration was chaired by Senator Pat McCarran and (echoing McCarran's security concerns) one of the three sections of its 900-odd page report was wholly devoted to the topic of 'Subversives' (Bennett 1963:100). The 1952 Immigration and Naturalisation Law (more commonly known as the McCarran-Walter Law) was the product of two very similar bills introduced in the Senate and House of Representatives, the first by Senator McCarran, architect of the Internal Security Law, and the second by Francis Walter, Chair of the House Committee on Un-American Activities. The law retained the quota system, and although it abolished overt forms of racial exclusion, it maintained more subtly discriminatory elements (Bennett 1963:153–4). The law also reaffirmed and strengthened the 1950 McCarran Law's stringent measures to exclude and deport 'subversive' aliens.

'Illegal migration policies': the case of Japan

US post-war border control policy is important not only in the context of American history but because it exerted an important influence elsewhere. In many parts of the world, Cold War security concerns were central to post-war changes in migration policy. In Australia, for example, the 'opening of doors' to greatly expanded European migration in the 1950s was partly driven by the demand for labour, but even more by a desire to expand the size of the population for security reasons: the events of the Pacific War had (in the eyes of Australia's leaders) demonstrated all too clearly the risks of being a sparsely populated nation adjacent to large and densely populated neighbours.

In Japan's case, too, the new Migration Control Ordinance introduced in 1951 (and transformed into the Migration Control Law in 1952) was profoundly shaped by fears of the entry of 'subversive' immigrants from Korea, China and elsewhere. This law was in fact based on a draft drawn up at the request of the US occupation forces (who controlled Japan until 1952) by Nicholas Collaer, a retired official of the US Immigration and Naturalisation Service. Collaer based his draft closely on early versions of the US McCarran-Walter Law, which was being debated in Congress while he was working for the Occupation authorities in Japan.

Collaer's understanding of the cross-border movement of people in the Cold War world is well illustrated by the report he wrote for the Occupation authorities, which reads in part:

> While the vast international conspiracy referred to glibly by enemies of true democracy as 'the revolutionary movement' has and will continue to pose serious problems for all democratic nations, Japan can logically anticipate all-out, well coordinated and well-timed efforts on the part of her internal and external enemies to subvert her economy and overthrow her constitutional government. I am convinced that important plans and underground activities with these ends in view are well under way. The efficient control of both legal and illegal immigration therefore transcends in importance many other governmental functions for which more adequate provision has heretofore been made and more efficient enforcement provided. (Collaer 1951:4)

It is not surprising, then, that the law he helped to draft focused very strongly on the task of giving the government all the powers it needed to keep out or deport 'subversive' immigrants from other parts of Asia.

Japan's tight border control system had a particularly severe effect on some 700,000 former 'colonial subjects' – mostly Koreans – who remained in Japan after the end of the Second World War. During the 1950s and 1960s, legal immigration from Korea became virtually impossible, even for those people whose closest family were living in Japan. Partly because of this, despite the stereotypical image of post-war Japan as a country without immigration, a small but steady flow of illegal migration from Korea continued throughout the 1950s and 1960s, with authorities at times apparently turning a blind eye to the phenomenon, and at other times rounding up 'illegals', incarcerating them in the notorious Ômura detention centre near Nagasaki, and shipping them back to Korea. Numbers are very difficult to estimate, but it seems certain that there were tens of thousands of undocumented foreign residents in Japan in the 1960s and early 1970s, and a plausible estimate puts the number at around 100,000 (Taniguchi 1979). This cross-border movement has so far been almost entirely ignored by scholars of Japan's migration history, who continue to insist that 'Japan's economic boom after the Second World War did not lead to the recruitment of foreign workers, as it did in western Europe' (Weiner 1998:9). This inflow of migration between the late 1940s and the 1970s is important, however, not least because it helped to create a system of bureaucratic discretion and selective official acquiescence towards 'illegal entry', which continues to the present day.

From the 1980s, the shortage of labour which accompanied the rise of the 'bubble economy' and the aging of the Japanese population led to a sharp increase in levels of 'illegal' migration. In 2000, according to official figures, there were 224,067 'illegal migrants' in Japan, the largest numbers from South Korea (24.6 per cent), followed by the Philippines (13.2 per cent) and China (12.3 per cent) (National Police Agency website, Japan, http://www.npa.go.jp, accessed 9 September 2003). The official figures, however, mainly refer to visa overstayers, and are surely an underestimate. This situation has led to repeated calls for the introduction of a new migration policy which would allow higher numbers of migrant labourers to enter Japan legally. However, resistance to any 'opening of the doors' is still strong in some sections of Japanese society. Although measures have been introduced to allow the 'return migration' of ethnic Japanese from Latin America and elsewhere, more wide-ranging measures to move beyond the 'illegal migration policy' remain a task for the future. Japan has thus become a good example of a country which operates a large-scale 'illegal migration policy': a policy under which governments tacitly accept, and sections of industry come to depend upon, the presence in the country of substantial numbers of illegal migrants.

Border controls in the 'post-cold war' world

The collapse of the Soviet Union and the accelerating globalisation of the economy since the end of the 1980s have been accompanied by major changes in the international border control regime. As many commentators have pointed out, shifts in the structure of the global economy and the ageing of the population in many of the richer countries of the world have not only encouraged cross-border migration, but also led to radical changes in the direction and nature of migration. One of the most important transformations (noted by scholars like Saskia Sassen in the United States and Iyotani Toshio in Japan) has been a 'feminisation' of the migrant workforce. The globalisation not only of production but also of reproduction, in other words, has been accompanied by increased migration of women workers in areas such as domestic labour, nursing and aged care (Sassen 1998; Iyotani 2002).

Here I want to focus particularly on two further shifts in the border control regime: shifts which have become increasingly visible and controversial in the context of rising concerns about national security since the events of September 11, 2001. The first phenomenon is a blurring of the distinction between 'refugees' and 'economic migrants'. Since the break-up of the Soviet Union, the binary confrontation between the Communist and the Capitalist worlds has been replaced by a more complex multiplicity of conflicts, often occurring within (rather than between) nation states, and often taking place in the poorer nations of the world. These have generated large flows of migrants fleeing a combination of political, social and economic sufferings: civil war, genocide, human rights abuses by military or police, famine, economic disruption, unemployment and poverty. Many individual migrants cross borders to escape a combination of several of these circumstances, and it becomes very difficult to determine whether their main reason for migration is 'economic' or 'political'. Moreover, the Geneva Convention does not extend protection to refugees fleeing civil war, however genuine their need for protection may be.

As many experts acknowledge, the changed circumstances of the twenty-first century world require a rethinking of the definition of 'refugee', and of the best ways of offering international protection to those who cross borders in search of a safe future for themselves and their families. At the same time, however, populist politicians in Europe, North America, Australia and elsewhere increasingly play on public fears of an influx of 'queue jumpers' or 'bogus refugees'. The heated media rhetoric which surrounds the refugee issue in many parts of the world today tends to reinforce the misleading notion that there is a clear and simple line between good 'genuine' refugees and bad 'illegal migrants' who masquerade as refugees to pursue their own economic self-interest. In many cases, however, things are much more complicated than this. The line between people who flee a war torn country with a 'justified fear of persecution' and the people who flee the same country in the desperate hope of obtaining a roof over their heads and an education for their children can be very fine indeed. Rather than addressing this genuine dilemma with imagination, perception and understanding, however, all too many governments are using it as an occasion for raising the barricades against the entry of migrants, in the process sometimes grotesquely compounding the sufferings of people who are attempting to escape the trauma of war, civil strife, imprisonment or torture.

A second important new phenomenon of the past decade or so has been the growing 'despatialisation' of border controls. The US-led international 'war on drugs' and, more recently, the 'war on terror' have promoted the development of a battery of new and sophisticated technologies of border control. These included the introduction of biometric techniques such as digitised fingerprints, iris scans and face recognition, which are increasingly being used to establish the identities of those crossing borders. It is not only the technology that has changed, however. In the European context, Michel Foucher has observed that border control functions, including customs work, the checking of suspected illegal migrants and so on are increasingly being distributed right across the territory of the nation state. Within the European Union, then, the trend is not so much towards the disappearance of borders. Rather, 'in certain respects, the entire national territory is now being treated as an expanded frontier zone' (Foucher 1998:238).

While some border control functions are now taking place within the nation, rather than at the physical border, others are taking place outside the territory of the nation. Perhaps the most extreme example of this is John Howard's 'Pacific Solution', in which foreign territory is used for the incarceration and processing of detained asylum seekers. However, a growing number of countries (including Australia and Japan) are also moving towards the offshore processing of migrants, so that entry procedures are completed at foreign airports or ports well before would-be migrants reach the frontiers of the nation. In the long run, these trends may be seen as part of a profound shift in the very notion of territorial sovereignty: a shift in which the territorial boundaries of the nation coincide less and less with the boundaries of the state's power to bestow rights on individuals, or to withhold those rights. The current Australian government has once again offered us a bizarre foretaste of the future 'virtual nation' through its invention of something called a 'migration zone', a concept previously unknown to national or international law, but something apparently different from the zone of national sovereignty, almost infinitely flexible and susceptible to retrospective reshaping by administrative decree.

Democratising the frontier

In response to a world where governments are so endlessly creative in inventing new ways to keep migrants out, I should like to end by suggesting the need for some political creativity of a different sort by proposing that we take seriously the issue of democratising the frontier. This means first of all reaffirming the fact that migrants, though lacking the status of citizenship in the countries where they live, work or seek asylum, still have human rights which must be protected under international and domestic law.

Beyond this, however, it also means seeking a new form of international collaboration on issues concerning migrant labour, border controls and the recognition of refugees. At present, we are witnessing a rapid erosion of UN-based systems for the protection of human rights, accompanied by an expansion of bilateral and multilateral cooperation between governments intent on tightening border controls and keeping out unwanted border crossers.

NGOs and others concerned with this trend might, I would suggest, seek to initiate a trend towards a different sort of international cooperation, one particularly appropriate to the countries of the Asia-Pacific region. This alternative model of cooperation would bring migrant 'sending' and 'receiving' countries together, not in an effort to build more strongly protected borders, but in an effort to ensure that the cross-border flows of people, which will inevitably form an important part of twenty-first century life, occur in a way that causes as little human suffering as possible. A key feature of such regional forums of 'sending' and 'receiving' countries would be the inclusion, not just of representatives of central, but also of NGOs involved in migration issues. Since migrants often originate predominantly from specific regions of the sending country and settle in specific cities or regions of the receiving country, the involvement of local government in such forums would be particularly valuable. More importantly, such forums would also include representatives of the relevant migrant communities themselves. In this way, it might finally begin to be possible to give migrants some say in the shaping of the migration and border control policies which directly so affect their lives.

At first sight such proposals for 'democratising the border' may sound improbable or utopian, particularly in the current context of the obsessive pursuit of 'national security'. But in an age when national governments so readily and drastically rewrite the rules surrounding key issues of sovereignty, and so enthusiastically cooperate with one another in tightening border controls, it is time for non-state, non-corporate actors to put forward some radical proposals for restraining the expanding powers of the 'wild zone'.

Acknowledgement

The research on which this chapter is based was assisted by the generous support of the Australian Research Council.

References

Anon. (1909) 'Immigration Restriction Acts 1901 and 1905: Notes for the Guidance of Officers'. Held in Australian Archives, Canberra, File A1/15, 1909/10853.

Balibar, E. (1991) 'Is There a Neo-Racism?', in Etienne Balibar and Immanuel Wallerstein (eds) *Race, Nation, Class: Ambiguous Identities* (London: Verso).

Bennett, M. T. (1963) *American Immigration Policies: A History* (Washington DC: Public Affairs Press).

Buck-Morss, S. (2000) *Dreamworld and Catastrophe: The Passing of Mass Utopias in East and West* (Cambridge Mass.: MIT Press).

Central Intelligence Agency (2001) *Growing Global Migration and its Implications for the United States*, Washington DC, National Intelligence Estimate NIE 2001–02D.

Collaer, N. D. (1951) 'Progress of Efforts to have Japan Implement SCAPIN No. 2065 of 20 February 1950 through Adoption of "Effective" Controls on Immigration in Agreement with Generally Accepted International Practice', in GHQ/SCAP archives, box no. 1447, folder no. 7, 'Alien Control in Japan 1951', National Diet Library, Tokyo, microfiche no. LS-26003.

Foucher, M. (1998) 'The Geopolitics of European Frontiers', in Malcolm Anderson and Eberhard Bort (eds) *The Frontiers of Europe* (London: Pinter) pp. 235–49.

Hômushô Nyûkoku Kanrikyoku (1964) *Shutsunyûkoku kanri to sono jittai* (Tokyo: Ôkurashô Insatsukyoku).

Iyotani, Toshio (2002) *Gurôbarizêshon to wa nani ka* (Tokyo: Heibonsha).

Japanese Legation to Australia (1901) Letter from Hayashi, Japanese Legation, to Marquis of Landsdown, 7 October 1901, in the records of the Senate of the Commonwealth of Australia, 14 November 1901, Australian Archives, Canberra.

Sassen, S. (1998) *Globalization and its Discontents: Essays on the New Mobility of People and Money* (New York: New Press).

Secretary of State, Commonwealth of Australia (1901) 'Dispatch from the Secretary of State, of 20th October, 1897, relating to the attitude of Japan towards restrictive legislation as to coloured immigration' in the records of the Senate of the Commonwealth of Australia, 14 November 1901, Australian Archives, Canberra.

Taniguchi, Tomohiko (1979) 'Senzai kyojûsha ni zairyûken o!', *Chôsen kenkyû*, 190, (June): 25–35.

Togman, J. M. (2002) *The Ramparts of Nations: Institutions and Immigration Policies in France and the United States* (Westport, Conn.: Praeger).

Torpey, J. (2000) *The Invention of the Passport: Surveillance, Citizenship and the State* (Cambridge: Cambridge University Press).

Weiner, M. (1998) 'Opposing Visions: Migration and Citizenship Policies in Japan and the United States', in Myron Weiner and Tadashi Hanami (eds) *Temporary Workers or Future Citizens? Japanese and US Migration Policies* (New York: New York University Press) pp. 3–27.

Yamanouchi, Yasushi, J., Victor Koschmann and Ryûichi Narita (eds) (1995) *Total War and 'Modernization'* (Ithaca: Cornell University Press).

3
Order (and Disorder) at the Border: Mobility, International Labour Migration and Border Controls in Southeast Asia

Amarjit Kaur

Labour migration was a dominant feature of Southeast Asian labour history from the 1870s, consistent with open borders, colonial migration goals and the region's increased integration into the global economy. After the Second World War and decolonisation, restrictive legislation was introduced to halt unskilled labour migration into the region. Since about the 1970s labour migration has assumed 'new' regional patterns, coinciding with changing patterns of labour market demands. Migration goals and migratory streams have also changed and emphasise the nationality, race, geographical origins, gender and skills of migrants. Free migration has thus given way to restrictive migration policies and intensified border controls, more sophisticated internal enforcement measures, and a swathe of bureaucratic regulations and procedures. Paradoxically, although the economic incentives for people to move have become stronger, immigration restrictions and intensified border controls in labour-exporting countries now constitute the principal barrier to international labour migration in the region.

Introduction: empires and labour migration in Southeast Asia, 1870–1940

In the second half of the nineteenth century, industrialisation and economic growth in Europe and the expansion of the international economy resulted in European political and economic advances in Southeast Asia. As Europe turned to Southeast Asia for raw materials and new markets, Southeast Asian states were obliged to open up their resources to western enterprise and capital. The imperial drive, which was also driven by an agenda of competitive state building overseas, subsequently resulted in the transformation of the Southeast Asian states into colonies, protectorates, or as part of the informal empire of European powers. This process, which began around 1850, climaxed between 1870 and 1914, resulting in the establishment of six major states, namely, Burma, Indonesia, Indochina, Malaya, the Philippines and Thailand.

The creation of these states with their 'defined' boundaries represented new departures within the region. Previously, a ruler's territory extended as far as his coercive sway and military might was accepted by weaker rulers. The new states had an internal dynamic and possessed a 'permanency' that indigenous states had lacked and a new style of administration and institutional structures to oversee the various aspects of government. Their integration in world commodity and capital markets coincided with an accelerated demand for their products, particularly those associated with industrial processing and manufacturing and greater investment in agricultural and mineral production in the region. This had profound implications for the growth of the labour market in the region.

During this period Southeast Asia had a markedly low population growth relative to the extent of its cultivable area. From a comparative perspective, the region could broadly be divided into 'labour-scarce' and 'labour-surplus' countries. There were two extremes to this division – Malaya (including Singapore) and Java. In sparsely populated Malaya, landlessness and rural deprivation among the Malays was practically non-existent. By comparison, Java had a huge, poor population, and non-farm employment was crucial for survival strategies. Javanese workers shifted or moved around to eke out a living. Using this framework, the other Southeast Asian countries fitted somewhere in a continuum between the two.

Around 1870 the population was estimated at about 55 million and rose to about 69 million in 1900. Moreover, it is estimated that the region had an average annual growth rate of approximately 1.3 per cent between 1870 and 1930. The population was also distributed very unevenly and population densities were relatively low (Kaur 2004a:35). The colonial administrations consequently had to source labour from elsewhere and the large-scale and systematic labour immigration into the region began with European expansion in Southeast Asia. The British colonial administrations in Malaya and Burma turned to labour recruitment principally from China and India, while the Dutch and French administrations in Indonesia and Indochina organised the recruitment of labour from large population reserves in their territories. The region's demographics therefore had important implications both for the location of colonial economic activity and the destination of migrant workers. Moreover, the concentration of migrant workers in specific sectors and countries, and their racial origin, must thus also be viewed through this lens.

The fact that this migration owed its origins to the contract labour systems under which migrants travelled allows it to be distinguished from other previous movements of people into the region. It involved mass migrations; long-distance and short movements; organisation of travel arrangements and the availability of employment in the receiving countries. It also involved two other groups in the migration process apart from the migrants. These were the private labour brokers and other intermediaries who organised travel arrangements and employment, and public officials. Moreover, in the receiving countries, the process involved the establishment of labour depots, and other agencies to manage migrant labour groups.

Transnational labour migration in Asia during this period – the movement of contract workers across borders – was largely dominated by Chinese and Indian migrants. The majority of migrants from both countries were impoverished, and were pushed into migration by factors such as agrarian overpopulation, natural calamities, landlord exploitation, and in China, disruption arising from major rebellions in the nineteenth century. Pull factors in Southeast Asia included the growing economic opportunities in the region, the opening up of hinterlands, and the expansion of mineral and agricultural export production. Unrestricted migration policies, improvements in transportation technology and falling transport costs facilitated this migration. Since most migrants were in no position to meet their travel and related costs these were either met by labour recruiters or future employers. An important element in the contract labour schemes was the promise of a return passage. This was largely because of the distances between China, India and Southeast Asia. More significantly, there were legally enforceable ties between the migrant workers and their future employers.

The recruitment of overseas contract workers was consistent with a rather elastic use of labour. The workers had many characteristics in common. They were young, predominantly unskilled adult males who emigrated as individuals and thus had no dependents. They also primarily comprised illiterate peasants who had spent hardly any time away from their villages. They were involved mainly in the physical production of goods – mineral and agricultural commodities – or in the construction and maintenance of transportation systems and public undertakings, and in the ports. Their sojourn in the host countries/provinces was dependent on the market demand for the principal export commodities. After periods of employment, they usually, but not always, returned to their countries of origin.

Labour migration within the Southeast Asian countries during the colonial period was of relatively lesser significance compared to labour migration from outside the region principally because the majority of the Southeast Asian countries were fairly lightly populated, as noted previously. Migration within the region was basically of four types: migration into empty land; migration from rural areas to town and industry; migration to government-sponsored agricultural settlement projects outside densely populated areas; and migration from the poorer, and overpopulated regions to 'richer' countries. While the first three types largely involved 'free' migrants, the fourth consisted predominantly of contract or indentured labour migrants.

By the first decade of the twentieth century, indentured contract labour had come to be regarded as a form of 'new' slavery and was ended for Indian contract labour in Malaya in 1910. It was ended for the Chinese in Malaya in 1914, and for the Javanese in the 1930s. Concurrently, free migration expanded rapidly during the first four decades of the twentieth century and there was greater individual agency in migration.

Against the backdrop of the current feminisation of labour migration in the Southeast Asian region, it needs restating that women comprised a not insignificant proportion of the labour migration from India and China, particularly in the 1920s and 1930s. Women's migration was striking in two main ways. First, Indian women's migration to Malaya was regulated under the terms of the Indian *Emigration Act* (Act VII of 1922): Rule 23 of the Act stipulated that unaccompanied males were not to exceed one in five of the emigrants. Recruitment under the *kangani* system too, where the *kangani* intermediary was paid a higher commission for recruiting couples and women resulted in an increase in women migrant workers. Moreover, the job classification system on the plantations, where tasks were remunerated on the basis of the 'work' involved, meant that it was cheaper to hire women workers for tasks such as weeding. Indian women workers earned less than male workers, normally between 70 to 80 per cent of the male wage.

With increased female migration, more children also arrived in Malaya, and by the 1920s Indian women accounted for 30 per cent of all arrivals from India. More children were also born in Malaya and raised locally contributing to the transition towards permanent settlement, and the availability of a pool of workers. Thus job possibilities for women on plantations and elsewhere, the provisions of the 1922 *Emigration Act*, the *Emigration Rules 1923* and the establishment and reconstitution of families led to greater permanent Indian settlement in Malaya (Kaur 2004a:ch.4).

Second, the migration of Chinese women to Malaya largely took place when the British established a basic framework for border controls in the 1930s. During this period while restrictions in the form of a quota system were used to limit male Chinese migration, no restriction was placed on the entry of Chinese women and children under 12 years of age (Saw 1988:15). The encouragement of Chinese women was consistent with colonial government policy of improving the gender ratio in the Chinese community (this exemption was revoked in 1938 with worsening economic conditions). A large number of the Chinese women were *dulang* workers or panners, an occupational category reserved solely for women to provide employment opportunities for them. Though not in the same league as the male miners, *dulang* workers made an important contribution to the mining industry and contributed to an improvement in the sex ratio of the Chinese community and the reproduction of the mining labour force (Kaur 2006, forthcoming). In both these cases, the migration of women facilitated the transition from sojourning to settlement for migrant workers.

The ending of colonial rule in Southeast Asia had a major impact on unrestricted cross-border movements in the region for two reasons. First, in the area of immigration policy, more restrictive legislation was implemented to halt unskilled Asian immigration and this was largely dictated by socio-economic and political reasons. Second, border controls and internal enforcement measures assumed greater importance coinciding with decolonisation and the emergence of new independent states in the region.

Global labour markets and labour transformations in Southeast Asia since the 1970s

By about the 1970s, following the various problems of decolonisation and post-war readjustment in Southeast Asia, there had emerged two broad groups of countries in the region. There were those that, under Communist or Socialist regimes, withdrew from the international economy to a large extent. These included Vietnam, Cambodia, and Laos, whose trading relations were concentrated on Eastern-Bloc countries, and Burma, which remained politically neutral and became economically isolated. This group of countries experienced economic stagnation and continued to have per capita incomes among the lowest in the world. The other countries, Thailand, Malaysia, Singapore and the Philippines (and later Indonesia) maintained open economies under various regimes. These experienced significant, though uneven, economic development. Most impressive was Singapore, which was the first Southeast Asian country to become a newly industrialising country (NIC), alongside the other East Asian countries, Taiwan, South Korea, and Hong Kong.

The record of the Southeast Asian countries that embraced globalisation since the 1970s and 1980s has been remarkable. Their economic growth was based on three interconnected factors. First, all of them had access to the North American markets, particularly that of the United States. This market access provided, and continues to provide, the demand for their products, which enabled them to make the economic advances and sustain growth. Closer ties through strategic and security relationships between them and the United States also helped. Second, the strengthening of regional ties through the Association of Southeast Asian Nations (ASEAN) and co-operation on the creation of growth triangles, or sub-regional economic zones, also facilitated the emergence of a regional economy. Also important has been the fostering of Asia-Pacific ties through the Asia Pacific Economic Co-operation (APEC) forum, which embraces Australia, New Zealand and other countries like Japan. Third, the capitalist Southeast Asian countries benefited from trade liberalisation policies and investment flows, consistent with the international economic environment. Not all have benefited equally, of course, as shown in Table 3.1.

Moreover, this growth was accompanied by job expansion in all the countries though not at the same rate.

Table 3.1 GDP per capita in selected Southeast Asian countries, 1995 (at 1995 PPP equivalents)

State	GDP per capita (US$)
Singapore	22,600
Malaysia	10,400
Thailand	8,000
Indonesia	3,800
Philippines	2,800

Source: World Bank (2000).

Table 3.2 Unemployment rates in selected Southeast Asian countries, 1985–95 (%)

	1985	1995
Thailand	3.7	1.1
Malaysia	6.9	3.1
Singapore	4.1	2.7
Indonesia	2.1	7.2
Philippines	7.1	8.4

Source: Asian Development Bank (2002).

At the same time there were striking demographic differences between these countries. Singapore and Malaysia had undergone demographic transition (followed by Thailand later) and experienced significant tightening of their labour markets. In 1995 the population of the five countries was as follows: Singapore, 3.3 million; Malaysia, 20.1 million; Thailand, 58.2 million; Indonesia, 166.5 million and the Philippines, 67.8 million. The demographic differences between the five countries were crucial to changing labour circumstances in the region. In Singapore, Malaysia and Thailand moreover, the increase in labour market participation by women was a source of workforce expansion in the short and medium term.

Unemployment rates for the five countries for the period 1985 to 1995 are listed in Table 3.2.

Indonesia also had low levels of development in terms of specific social indicators such as education. The problems of a high proportion of employment in low-productivity agriculture, rural poverty and land scarcity in Indonesia and also in the Philippines led to varying labour market conditions in the region, and labour thus had an incentive to move from Indonesia and the Philippines (and, to a lesser extent, Thailand), to labour-scarce countries.

Against this backdrop, migration assumed new regional patterns since the 1970s and Southeast Asia may be viewed from the perspective of a two-tier world in which low-wage jobs and lower standards of living are assigned to the poorer countries in the region.

The question then arises, have these labour processes become more and more part of a chain of interconnecting links in Southeast Asia's development experience? Is the Asia-Pacific region the 'newest migratory pole' (OECD 1992; Salt 1992)? The historical record clearly indicates this. By the mid 1990s foreign migrant workers accounted for almost a quarter of Singapore and Malaysia's labour force (Kaur 2004a:ch.9). Crucially, certain occupations or types of economic activity rely on foreign workers for their continued operation. Jobs at the lower rungs of the skill and wage distribution categories are shunned by locals and are filled by foreign migrant workers. Consequently, this reliance on foreign workers is due to structural factors rather than being cyclical in nature (Athukorala and Manning 1999:2; Manning 2002). Indeed, Southeast Asian economies appear to function in a complementary sense, arising from inter-country demographic contrasts; the incidence of labour surplus or shortage; disparities in demand and wages; and worker education and skills, all of which have created strong incentives for intra-Southeast Asian migration.

The Asian economic crisis and ILM

How did the Asian economic and financial crisis of 1997–98 impact on ILM in Southeast Asia? Indonesia, Malaysia and Thailand were particularly hard hit by the economic crisis. Of the three, Indonesia was a major labour-sending country. In Malaysia, capital outflows, business failures and rising local unemployment and worker layoffs impacted on foreign worker employment. The construction sector was badly affected and the Malaysian government deported undocumented workers and stopped the renewal of work permits for documented workers. Thus unemployment rates increased more sharply among foreign migrant workers, particularly undocumented workers.

Nevertheless, as noted by Manning (2002) and Battistella and Asis (1999), these policies had limited success. According to the latter, the reparations and deportations were 'not as high as expected'. Malaysia sent back about 200,000 Indonesian workers who had been employed in the services and construction sectors in 1998 while Thailand also repatriated about 200,000 Myanmar workers by the end of 1998. Foreign worker permit fees were also raised. The Philippines was largely unaffected by the crisis. These observations and the statistics provided in Table 3.3 underscore the structural change within the region.

However, even though unemployment rose in Malaysia and Thailand, labour shortages were reported in some sectors and there was opposition to the migrant flows cutbacks (Kaur 2004a:ch. 9).

Table 3.3   Estimated stocks of migrant workers before, during and after the economic crisis, major crisis-affected countries, 1996–99[1]

	1996	1997		1998	1999[2]
Malaysia					
Legal/with permits	745	1,470		1,130	900
Illegal/apprehended	(590)	(460)		(60?)[3]	(55?)[3]
Total	1,535	1,930		1,190?	955?
Repatriated/Deported			188		
Thailand					
Legal/with permits	n.a.	n.a.		294	89
Illegal/apprehended	n.a.	n.a.		693	563
Total	710	940		987	652
Repatriated/Deported			334		

Notes
1. The number of illegal/apprehended workers is a very rough estimate and probably is a minimum estimate of the total number of illegal workers in each country except Hong Kong. The figures on illegal migrants to Malaysia are based on official data on registration of migrants during amnesties in 1996–97 as well as special operations to apprehend illegal immigrants each year. Data for South Korea and Hong Kong exclude professional and managerial workers.
2. Data are for August–September in both Malaysia and Thailand.
3. Data on the numbers of illegal/apprehended migrants for 1998 and 1999 refer to the number of illegal migrants apprehended only, and understate the total number of illegal migrants.

Source: Chris Manning (2002) p. 374.

On the move: mobility, international labour migration (ILM) and the state

Introduction: setting the scene

ILM in Southeast Asia since the 1970s has coincided with reduced barriers to trade and investment and emphasises the inequality between groups that can cross international borders (owners of capital, skilled workers) and those that cannot (unskilled and semi-skilled workers). Globalisation has also made the demand for the services of unskilled and semi-skilled workers more elastic and workers from other countries can more easily substitute this category of workers. Much of the labour migration in the region does not operate spontaneously, but takes place within networks, both within the source and receiving countries. Chain migration, for example, within family, extended kinship, or close-knit village-based groups, plays a key role in disseminating information about opportunities available in Malaysia, Singapore and Thailand. Moreover, it minimises both financial and removal disruption costs that migrants face.

This cost minimising factor is critical for two reasons. First, unlike the colonial period, ethnicity and social class have become even more pronounced in migration patterns, and there is both overt and covert hostility to migrants by governments and some segments of the population in receiving countries. Additionally, migrants are forced into segmented labour markets that are characterised by wage discrimination, and this has led to social tensions. Second, migrants, their families and prospective employers have to bear the bulk of the financial and social costs associated with migration.

Two dominant migration systems are currently identifiable in the region: the archipelagic ASEAN system and the Mekong sub-regional system. In the first, Malaysia, Singapore and Brunei are the major destination countries importing workers from mainly Indonesia and the Philippines. In the second, Thailand has emerged as the main destination for migrant workers from countries through which the Mekong River flows, namely, Myanmar, Cambodia, Laos and Vietnam. In both these systems, the influence of mass media – radio, television and news media and returned migrants' tales play a key role in disseminating information about job opportunities and influencing the decision to move. At the personal level, migration is also dependent on networks within family, extended kinship, or close-knit village-based groups.

A third system, 'the Asia-Pacific' system, which is largely shaped by the magnitude of income and wage differentials between the nations in the larger Asia-Pacific region and the financial costs of transportation and communication between them involves mainly skilled migrants. The economies of Singapore, Malaysia and Thailand in particular have been transformed beyond recognition in the last decade or so, and these states' need for workers with specific professional and technical skills has determined the composition and magnitude of these skilled migrants and also reflect changing national priorities. This has implications not only for who is permitted to enter but also the conditions under which they could achieve the rights of citizens.

The regulation of migration

The growth in ILM in the last four decades is due to a number of related factors. First, strong economic growth and the ending of major conflicts in the region have made it easier for people to emigrate. Since migration is primarily an economic phenomenon, shaped by the magnitude of income and wage differentials between countries and the financial costs of transportation and communication, there is strong incentive for people to move. Second, although a large percentage of emigrants from Indonesia, the Philippines and Myanmar come from very poor areas, poverty is not the principal determinant of migration. These migrants are also not from the 'poorest' category, as they have to put up substantial amounts of money to get to their destinations. They also have access to loans in their local communities and also from intermediaries involved in the migration industry.

Third, the growth of a regional economy, and establishment of growth triangles and sub-regions designed to facilitate trade, capital and labour flows, has meant that many labour markets now overlap national borders, both for skilled and unskilled labour. These sub-regions, such as, for example, the Brunei-Indonesia-Malaysia-Philippines East ASEAN growth area (BIMP-EAGA) and the Northern ASEAN region have assisted in the emergence of distinctive migration systems. Notably, the dynamics of demography and development between Sarawak and Kalimantan have resulted in the governments of these states co-operating in the establishment of a number of large projects at the Entikong-Tebedu Border post area (Agustiar 2000:235). The pattern of daily commuting workers has also existed on the Singaporean-Johor border (since colonial times) and the Malaysian-Thailand border since the 1950s at least.

Fourth, the specific overseas labour deployment policies of countries like Indonesia and the Philippines have also led to increased ILM in the region. For these countries (and Thailand to a lesser extent), the export of labour has become an important strategy for addressing poverty, easing domestic unemployment pressures, generating foreign exchange and fostering growth. Both Indonesia and the Philippines include targets for the number of workers they hope to send abroad in their economic development plans. These targets have increased over time. Indonesia's targets for exporting migrant workers since 1969 are captured in Table 3.4.

These targets rose to 1.25 million workers in the 1994–99 economic development plan and 2.8 million in the 1999–2003 economic development plan (Human Rights Watch 2004:9).

In the Philippines, the state has developed a highly regulated overseas contract workers management system through the Philippine Overseas Employment Administration (POEA). The POEA provides oversight over recruitment, deployment, and monitors the working conditions of migrants.

Table 3.4 Emigration from Indonesia, 1969–94 (numbers)

Destination	Plan I 1969–74	Plan II 1974–79	Plan III 1979–84	Plan IV 1984–89	Plan V 1989–94
Middle East	–	4,752	60,093	226,030	390,556
Saudi Arabia	–	3,817	55,976	223,573	384,822
Southeast Asia	21	3,008	16,461	49,251	215,492
Malaysia	12	536	11,441	37,785	156,312
Singapore	8	2,432	5,007	10,537	48,896
East Asia	473	1,748	2,681	2,308	21,569
Europe	3,794	7,083	14,020	7,543	10,118
Holland	3,332	6,637	10,104	4,375	5,515
United States	146	176	2,981	6,897	13,993
Others	1,190	27	164	233	544
Total	5,624	17,042	96,410	292,262	652,272

Source: Nayyar, Deepak cited in Rashid Amjad (1996) p. 345.

Outstanding migrants are regarded as *Bagong Bayani* (New Heroes) and receive awards on Migrant Workers' Day. In 1975 some 35,000 Filipino migrant workers left the country. By 1995, 760,091 had left the country. In 2001, there were 7.3 million Filipinos overseas, of whom 1.7 million were in Malaysia, Hong Kong, Japan, Korea, Singapore and Taiwan (*Migration News* 2002).

Finally, the growth of a migration industry, which has coincided with the institutionalisation of ILM by both labour-exporting and labour-importing countries, has resulted in an increase in migration and also its perpetuation. The migration industry comprises several layers of intermediaries: official recruitment agencies, private entrepreneurs (licensed and unlicensed), and labour contractors and brokers. It also rests on network-creating and network-dependent relationships in sending and receiving countries. Consequently, the risks of migration are reduced owing to the varied forms of assistance from intermediaries in matters such as documentation, transportation, and assistance with accommodation. Not surprisingly, the various layers and the fees involved have also led to irregular migration.

Gender dimensions of international migration

In the last three decades of the twentieth century, women's migration grew in importance as a larger percentage of women migrated independently for work purposes. Indeed, a feminisation of the labour force has occurred in the Asian region in response to the gender-selective policies of labour-importing countries and the emergence of gender-specific employment niches. This in turn has resulted not only in the self-sustaining feature of this migratory stream, but also in the emergence of particular female migratory linkages between groups of countries.

This feminisation of the new migrant labour may be attributed to three main factors. The first relates to general changes in the labour markets in Southeast Asia. The newly industrialising countries' trade liberalisation strategies resulted in the emergence of specific production niches (electronics, textiles, garments), consistent with the New International Division of Labour. These developments facilitated the increased labour force participation of women in the formal sector of these countries and was associated with the modernisation of the agricultural sector and rural–urban migration, principally of women. There was also a trend towards migration abroad since women's employment in the urban labour market was often impermanent, irregular, and insecure (Kaur 2004c:ch.8).

The second factor is linked to the maturing of the labour markets in Singapore and Malaysia, associated with relatively high labour force participation rates of women, and general labour shortages in these countries. This in turn created an increased demand for housekeeping and childcare services, which has been met by migrant women workers from the lower-income Southeast Asian countries. Thus the specific labour needs in the destination countries for domestic workers largely shaped and continue to shape women's migration in Southeast Asia. According to Human Rights Watch more than 90 per cent of domestic workers in Malaysia are Indonesian (2004:4).

The third factor influencing women's migration may be traced to individual and family decisions. Although a number of women make autonomous decisions to migrate for work purposes abroad, a large number do so as part of family survival strategies. Women domestic workers have more possibilities of legal employment in West Asia, Taiwan, Hong Kong, Malaysia and Singapore. The state's encouragement of this migration stream also influences their decision. In the Philippines, for example, women migrants are regarded as the new heroes who bring in much needed foreign exchange through their remittances.

Migration goals, temporary worker schemes and regional patterns in Southeast Asia

Issues of labour migration and temporary worker schemes have raised two sets of questions for destination countries in Southeast Asia. The first relates to the number of migrants to be allowed to enter, or the magnitude of immigrants. The second relates to the specific composition of migrants, particularly with respect to occupation, skills, nationality, religion and gender. Both these questions underpin migration goals and are not completely independent, since concerns with composition affect the overall number of migrants permitted to enter.

While the goals of migration policy of the different destination countries are often contradictory, the following regional migration streams have emerged and are consistent with labour market segmentation: skilled labour flows; unskilled and semi-skilled labour flows (including gendered labour flows); and undocumented labour flows. The most important shift in values that underscores these migratory streams is that this migration is the migration of free persons, whether dependent on networks or organised through intermediaries. Nevertheless, they must also be viewed from the perspective of racialised hierarchies in the region.

Skilled migration flows: Workers who enter under this category are considered professionals whose skills are in great demand and who earn high salaries. These workers, who may be from the United States, Europe, Australia, Japan, India, Malaysia or Hong Kong are at the high-end of the labour market. They take up specialised technical or management jobs either on their own initative, through specialised recruitment agencies, or are recruited in their home countries for overseas postings. In this category are included the managers, engineers, and other technicians who work for multinational organisations. They are closely associated with the expanding international trade in services, including financial services and communications. Workers in this category are a 'privileged' group. In Singapore, they are employed on the basis of a re-entry permit, are eligible for permanent residency, and are allowed to bring their families with them (see below).

Unskilled/semi-skilled migration flows: Workers who are recruited under this category are employed on temporary worker schemes to perform a specific job and are employed on work permits. They cannot access the labour market directly and are recruited through private agencies and under specific bilateral agreements between the main labour-exporting and labour-importing countries. Unlike the colonial period, when this category of migrants was largely channelled into the highly capitalised western plantation and mining sectors, these workers are also employed in the tertiary sector in manual (construction) and service employment, with little direct foreign capital involvement. In Malaysia and Thailand they are also employed in the agricultural (plantation), and forestry (logging) sectors and their recruitment/ deployment is decided in consultation with large national employer associations, and in co-operation with governments of sending countries.

In both these categories Southeast Asian countries like Malaysia, Thailand and Brunei permit foreign workers to enter the country temporarily to work at specified pre-approved jobs for which local workers are not available.

Domestic worker flows: Domestic workers are recruited under a system of sponsorship and the sponsor is normally a national citizen. Unlike the other unskilled workers discussed above, who are employed in the regulated spheres and who come under the various employment regulations, the sponsors of domestic workers have a monopoly over the domestic workers' activities in the host country. The International Labour Organisation contends that these workers come under a new category of 'forced labour' (ILO 2005:9–10). Labour Laws are ignored by employers, the pay is low, and working hours may extend up to 18 hours, and they often have no days off. They are unable to complain, are prisoners in the unregulated homes of their employers; are often physically and sexually abused by their employers and protests by them result in deportation without any payment. Thus employers of domestic workers effectively control their employees' residence status which makes for a powerful disincentive to seek redress from employer mal-practice. To remedy this situation, the Philippines has included clauses in bilateral agreements that provide for a minimum wage for domestic workers, as well as for working hours and benefits similar to those for workers in other sectors. The ILO is also working with the Indonesian government for an improvement in working conditions for domestic workers employed in Indonesia as a first step.

All 'documented' semi-skilled and unskilled workers have to pay hefty fees – agency fees (including a one way air ticket); insurance fees, a bank guarantee – in both countries of origin and destination. They are not allowed to remain in the host countries on completion of their contracts, though most return on new contracts. They are therefore not allowed to make the transition from sojourning to settlement under the complex unskilled worker recruitment system. Employers pay their return tickets and face heavy fines if workers are not sent back. In Singapore and Malaysia, workers who overstay are physically punished (caned) and in recent years this form of punishment has been extended to errant employers as well.

Illegal/undocumented/irregular flows: The strong incentives for people to migrate from low-income to higher income countries in Southeast Asia; the high administrative costs of migration, including payments to intermediaries and labour agencies (in, e.g., Indonesia and Malaysia), and the insertion of quotas especially for unskilled contract labour intakes has resulted in illegal migration constituting an important migration stream. There is no accurate data on illegal migration in the region. In Malaysia, it is estimated that there are between 600,000 to a million illegal migrant workers (*Asian Migration News*, 31 May 2002; 30 June 2002; Battistella and Asis 2003). It is also noteworthy that many employers accept illegal workers even though there are strict regulations, fines, goal terms and physical punishment. This is principally because the illegal migrants are concentrated in labour-intensive industries shunned by local workers; paying very low wages. Consequently, illegal workers end up in certain low-paying segments of the labour market where they do not compete with local workers.

The management of foreign labour in Singapore and Malaysia

Both Singapore and Malaysia have restricted labour immigration by attempting to enforce a complex set of criteria for allocating a variety of employment permits. There were also quotas for many categories of labour immigrants – defined by race, gender, skills and need. Singapore has been the most successful of the Southeast Asian countries in managing its foreign labour flows. Malaysia on the other hand, appears to have had a 'reactive' approach. The discussion below summarises the main foreign labour management regulations in these countries.

Singapore

Singapore's real gross national product increased thirteen-fold between 1960 and 1992 and full employment was attained from 1973. From 1970 to 1979, manufactured exports became the engine of the country's growth. Manufacturing's share in total output grew from 16.6 per cent in 1960 to 29.4 per cent in 1979. In 1992 manufacturing contributed 27.6 per cent of GDP and accounted for 27.5 per cent of employment. Singapore offered a cheap labour force, a de-politicised labour movement and government control over workers. However, by the late 1960s, Singapore already faced a labour shortage and the state allowed the recruitment of migrant workers to alleviate the upward pressure on wages. The state also encouraged the entry of married women into the labour market to augment the workforce. Additionally, a policy of encouraging skilled foreign workers to settle in Singapore was adopted to enable the state to better its economic performance. In the 1990s Singapore had an unemployment rate of less than 3 per cent and in 1993 the retirement age in the country was raised from 55 to 60 to ease pressure on the labour market.

Singapore's expatriate workforce may be divided into two categories: guest workers and immigrant labour. Guest workers were categorised into two groups. The first comprised blue-collar unskilled or semi-skilled workers employed on work permits and who earned under S$2,000 per month. The second consisted of skilled professional staff or skilled work-permit holders who held professional passes for employment in supervisory, managerial and professional positions. Immigrant workers were those who had secondary education, were employed on employment passes, earned more than S$2,000 per month, and qualified for permanent residency.

In 1994, there were 300,000 migrant workers in Singapore, as shown in Table 3.5, representing a threefold increase from 1985.

By 1995, migrant blue-collar workers on work permits totalled 300,000, while there were 50,000 foreign workers on employment passes (*Business Times*, 5 January 1996). The largest percentage of migrant workers in Singapore thus fell into the unskilled category and was employed on work permits in low-paying jobs, such as domestic service and factory production. They were prohibited from marrying Singaporeans without prior permission from the state and were generally not allowed to bring their dependents with them. They thus occupied the ranks of the cheap labour force, held two-year work permits

Table 3.5   Total employed and number of foreign workers in Singapore, 1985–94

Year	Total employed	Number of foreign workers
1985	1,135,000	100,000
1988	1,332,000	150,000
1992	1,576,000	200,000
1994	1,680,000*	300,000

Notes: Data for the period prior to 1985 are not available.
* Estimated number.

Source: Ministry of Labour, Singapore, cited in Chew and Chew (1995) p. 197.

(renewable for another two years but not transferable), and could be dismissed or repatriated in times of economic downturn (Chew and Chew 1995).

Malaysia

Malaysia has been selected as case study to explore the various migration issues outlined above since it was the 'largest employer of foreign labour in Asia' in 1999 (Jones 2000:3). The foreign workers comprised both legal and illegal (undocumented) workers employed in the plantation, construction and service sectors. According to several sources, half the foreign workers were undocumented workers (Pillai 1992:14; Kassim 1997:50).

Malaysia's migration transition is noteworthy for several reasons. First, Malaysia is both an exporter and importer of labour. Second, within a relatively short period – 1987 to 1993 – Malaysia was transformed from a net labour exporter to a labour importer. This transition was also very rapid. Third, unlike other countries in the Asian region – Japan, Korea and Taiwan – the migration transition occurred long before Malaysia achieved full employment and when its GNP per capita was only about US$1,800 (Lim 1996:319, 327). Malaysia's dependence on migrant labour also occurred and is occurring against the background of a pro-natalist population policy and a domestic labour force growth rate of between 2 and 3 per cent. This domestic labour force growth rate was significantly higher than in most other Southeast Asian countries.

Most observers attribute the labour shortages in Malaysia to the implementation of the New Economic Policy (NEP) in 1970. The NEP was formulated by the state following the May 1969 race riots in the country (see Kaur 2001:165, 220–1). The two principal objectives of the NEP were the reduction and eventual eradication of poverty irrespective of race and the elimination of the identification of race with economic function. The second objective primarily implied reducing the concentration of Malays in subsistence agriculture and increasing their employment in the modern rural and urban sectors of the economy. Consequently, the state enlarged the bureaucracy, creating white-collar jobs for Malays, increased state participation in the economy and created a whole range of occupations for Malays. The NEP coincided with an expansion in educational facilities, and the tightening up of the labour market. The prospect of better-paid urban jobs also led to changes in attitudes among the Malays towards remaining in rural areas and working in '3D' jobs (dangerous, dirty, and degrading jobs) upon marriage. For the Chinese and Indians, these policies had two major consequences. First, there was a growing trend towards smaller family size, partly as a reaction to a perceived cut in their slice of the cake. Second, those who had the means chose to migrate overseas, to countries like Japan, Singapore, or Taiwan, where there were better employment opportunities. Others went to Western countries such as Canada and Australia as permanent migrants.

Turning to the number of foreign workers in Malaysia, the most commonly quoted figure at the end of the second millennium was two million workers (Jones 2000:3). This represents approximately 9.5 per cent of the total population of 21 million and a quarter of the total labour force of 8 million. Migrant workers in Malaysia are concentrated mainly in the following sectors: construction (30 per cent); agriculture and forestry (30 per cent); nongovernmental services including domestic service and retail trade (30 per cent) and manufacturing and others (10 per cent) (Pillai 1992:9–10, 14). Where distribution by state is concerned, foreign workers are concentrated in four Malaysian states: Selangor, Johor, Pahang and Sabah. In Selangor (and Kuala Lumpur) the real estate and infrastructure boom also absorbed a large percentage of migrant workers. Selangor and Johor also had, and continue to have, huge numbers in the plantation sector, while in Sabah migrant workers were found mainly in the agricultural and forestry sectors.

Race, gender and migration flows

Labour migration flows to Malaysia are consistent with both the growing cross-national income inequality between nations in the region and the historical and political links between source and receiving countries. The major foreign labour flows are shown in the following Map 3.1.

These labour flows are briefly summarised below.

Indonesian migrant flows

Indonesian migrant workers have dominated the labour flows to Malaysia. While this labour migration is predominantly demand-driven, it nevertheless operates within informal and formal networks and has strong historical precedents. During the colonial period, Javanese were recruited as contract *coolies* for the plantation rubber sector in the western Malayan states and Sabah. There was also spontaneous migration to Malaysia during that period. Consequently, informal networks linking Malaysia and Indonesia were already in existence before the 1970s. These historical and cultural linkages have played and continue to play an important role in facilitating migration from Indonesia to Malaysia (Kaur 2004c).

The Peninsular Malaysia migration system draws workers from East Java, Bawean, Aceh, West Sumatra, Central Java, South Sulawesi and West Nusa Tenggara. Lombok is another source. East Malaysia draws workers mainly from South Sulawesi and Flores in East Nusa Tenggara. In the case of illegal (irregular) migrants, the migration routes are from East Java and northwest Sumatra to Peninsular Malaysia and Flores-South Sulawesi to Sabah, as shown in Map 3.2.

Reliable details are unavailable on the age composition of the Indonesian migrant workers. According to one study, about 84 per cent of the illegal immigrant contract workforce on the Malaysian Federal Land Development Authority Scheme (land settlement) plantations were aged between 20 and

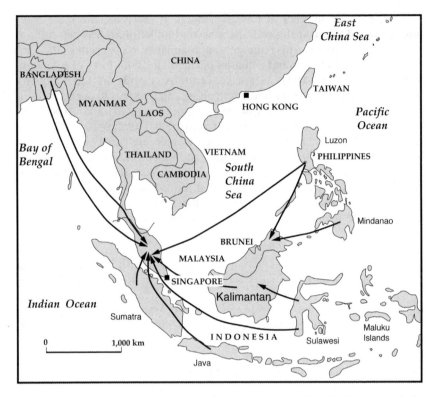

Map 3.1 Malaysia: migrant worker inflows from Bangladesh, Indonesia and the Philippines, 1990s

Source: Kaur 2004a, p. 212.

30 years. The workers were generally unskilled and had limited education (Hugo 1993:45–9).

Indonesian labour outflows coincided with the various development plans in Indonesia instituted since 1969. These labour flows were generated from regions where modernisation, mechanisation of agriculture and foreign investment flows encouraged trends towards rural–urban migration and towards migration abroad. Concurrently, demand for unskilled labour in Malaysia emerged after 1979 arising from labour shortages in the plantation sector, government land settlement schemes and the construction sector. Subsequently, following repeated calls from the Malaysian Agricultural Producers Association (plantation sector), the construction industry (associated with the property boom) and some state governments (notably Johor) for foreign labour recruitment, the Malaysian government allowed the entry of foreign labour into the country. This step was taken despite strong opposition from the Malaysian Trades Unions Congress (MTUC), which stated

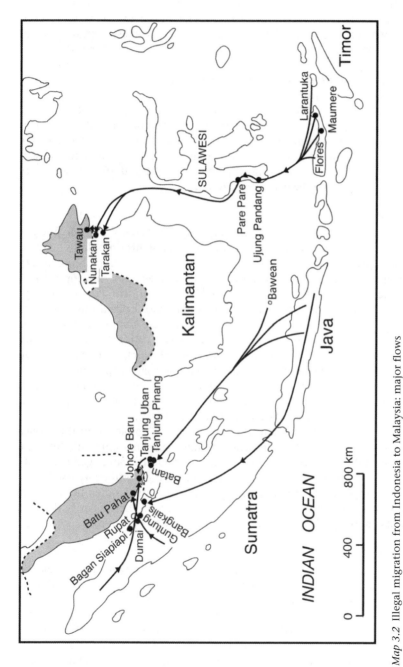

Map 3.2 Illegal migration from Indonesia to Malaysia: major flows

Source: G. Hugo, 'Indonesian Labour Migration to Malaysia: Trends and Policy Implications', *Southeast Asian Journal of Social Science*, 21, 1 (1993): 43.

that migrant worker recruitment would contribute to depressed wage levels in these sectors. In 1993 the manufacturing sector was also allowed to recruit skilled workers from abroad and to hire unskilled workers from the pool of foreign workers already in the country. At the same time, labour demand in the tertiary sector, comprising the entertainment, hotel and restaurant sector and domestic service also increased rapidly, consistent with the rising affluence in the country.

Turning to the gender dimension in Indonesian migrant labour flows, Hugo states that while women dominate some undocumented flows, women outnumber men among documented migrant flows (Hugo 2002:161–2). A report in *Migration News* also states that of the 1.5 million Indonesian migrants who went abroad officially between 1994 and 1999, 'about two-thirds were women' *(Migration News*, 2002).

Filipino migrant flows

Filipinos originally formed the second largest group of Southeast Asian migrant workers in Malaysia. Like Indonesia, there were close historical links between the east Malaysian state of Sabah and Mindanao and Jolo. Filipinos migrated to Peninsular Malaysia and Sabah from 1985 and Filipino migrant workers accounted for almost 1.5 per cent of the total migrant worker population in Peninsula Malaysia in 1994. The majority of Filipinos in Peninsular Malaysia were recruited as domestic workers, while others were employed as musicians and entertainers at holiday resorts, restaurants and petrol stations. In Sabah, most Filipinos were employed either in the plantation or forestry sectors. There were (and are) a large number of illegal migrants as well and in 1990 an official Sabah government estimate put the number of undocumented workers (principally Filipino) at 700,000 against a total state population of 1.7 million (*National Report on Filipino Migrant Workers,* 1994:16–17).

The typical Filipino migrant is a woman who is employed in the service sector, mostly in domestic work. These women were predominantly from the Luzon area (80 per cent). Most of them were educated, and aged below 30. Following reports of abuse, in 1995 the Malaysian government passed legislation raising the age of entry, and subsequently only women between the ages of 35 to 50 were allowed to work in Malaysia. Their security deposits were also raised (*Philippine Daily Enquirer*, 16 September 1995).

Thai migrant flows

The third largest group of Southeast Asian migrant workers in Malaysia comprised Thais from southern Thailand, and their seasonal migration to the northern states of Peninsular Malaysia coincided with the rice cultivation cycle. Close cultural links between south (Muslim) Thailand and the northern states on Peninsular Malaysia have existed for centuries. The Muslim provinces are relatively poor, and during the agricultural slack period, the Thais migrated to Malaysia to work on a temporary basis. The shared border between the two countries, which was a colonial creation, facilitated this labour flow. The Thais were employed predominantly as agricultural workers (on padi farms, rubber and oil palm plantations), as construction labourers and domestic workers (Taneerananon 1997:2).

South Asian migrant flows

Apart from these three countries, the Indian sub-continent re-emerged as a major labour exporter to Malaysia in the 1990s. Most of the workers were predominantly from Bangladesh, which is one of the least developed countries in the world. The Bangladesh government followed development strategies similar to those of the Southeast Asian NICs – modernisation of agriculture and a shift to export-oriented industrialisation. Bangladesh became a major exporter of readymade garments, and of the 1 to 1.2 million workers employed in the textile and apparel industries, 80–90 per cent were women (Wright 2000:226). However, as more women moved into the formal sector, which was consistent with the country's production niche, there was wide unemployment among men. These men thus migrated abroad in search of employment. Moreover, women were disallowed from leaving the country as migrant workers. Undocumented migration was also common, particularly via Bangkok and on through southern Thailand. The Bangladeshis were mainly employed in the plantation and construction sectors and in the service sector in urban areas.

Labour outflows from Malaysia

The inflow of migrant labour must be viewed in the broader context of the outflow of migration from Malaysia. Generally, the outflow of skilled and semi-skilled Malaysian workers was initially confined within the region, principally to Singapore. In 1991, for example, an estimated 100,000 Malaysians, including professionals, were employed in Singapore. About 24,000 of them commuted daily across the causeway linking the two countries (*Star*, 13 February 1991). Again, historical, geographical and economic factors largely determined this migration flow. Since the mid-1970s, following the implementation of the NEP in 1971, and a positive discrimination policy in favour of Malays, there has been a continuous outward migration of Malaysians to areas outside the ASEAN countries. This migration was largely to the United States, Canada, Australia and New Zealand and the migrants, who comprised skilled and semi-skilled workers, were predominantly Chinese Malaysians. Japan and Taiwan in East Asia were two other recipient countries.

Border control regimes and immigration policies in Singapore and Malaysia

The evolving border control regimes in Singapore and Malaya/Malaysia in the twentieth century must be viewed in the context of the three phases in these countries' political history: the period of colonial rule; the immediate post-independence period; and the period since the 1970s. Singapore was part of Malaya during the colonial period and developments during that time were applicable to both countries.

Colonial immigration policy has been discussed elsewhere (see Kaur 2004b) and is dealt with only briefly here. Despite an earlier commitment to unrestricted immigration in the first three decades of the twentieth century, the British introduced legislation in the 1930s that placed restrictions on the entry of adult male Chinese. This legislation represented the first attempts towards border control by the colonial state. Essentially, colonial immigration policy was influenced by the general economic conditions in the country; the export demand for Malaya's export commodities; and labour activism. After the Second World War and in the lead-up to independence, the British implemented the *Immigration Ordinance* (IO). This Ordinance resulted in even more restrictive border controls and laid down for the first time the specific composition of migrants allowed entry into Malaya. Unlike the earlier restrictions that were based on nationality and gender, the IO also specified nationality and occupation and thus placed importance on the skills of the migrants. Permanent entry was restricted to persons who could 'contribute to the expansion of commerce and industry', persons who could provide 'specialised services not available locally', families of local residents; and to other persons on 'special compassionate grounds' (Saw 1988:17). Clearly, this legislation was designed to appease Malay nationalists. New immigrants were also required to have a contract with a Malayan firm of at least two years and earn a salary of not less than M$400 a month. The legislation thus spelled the end of unskilled Indian labour migration to Malaya (Kaur 2004c).

In summary, the ending of empire in Malaya saw restrictive legislation and intensified border controls designed to halt Chinese and Indian immigration into Malaya. Overall, colonial immigration policy had largely been dictated by economic and political considerations and the labour requirements of Western enterprise. Border controls, on the other hand were shaped by economic and political considerations and also to satisfy the aspirations of the Malay nationalists.

Singapore – immigration policy and border controls after 1965

When Singapore became an independent state in 1965, the issue of resident and commuting Malaysian workers to Singapore had to be resolved as a matter of urgency. Consequently, the government implemented the *Regulation of Employment Act 1965*, whereby a one-year work permit was introduced for unskilled Malaysian labour in the state. Subsequently, as Singapore embarked on its industrialisation drive and strove to become less reliant on unskilled labour, an amendment was made to the Act in 1975. This amendment provided for the issuance of work permits for a period exceeding one year, and also included a provision for the imposition of a levy on foreign workers, although the latter was not implemented until 1980. The characteristic feature of this early labour migration flow/pattern was that it comprised Malaysians and was based on Singaporean–Malaysian historical, geographical (and former) political ties. Following the racial riots of 13 May 1969, there was another flow of Malaysians (particularly Chinese) to Singapore.

By the 1970s, as Malaysia also embarked on its industrialisation drive and experienced labour shortages, the Singaporean government had to widen its pool of migrant workers. In 1978 the state permitted the recruitment of migrant workers from 'non-traditional' countries. Although termed 'non-traditional' these included countries like India, Bangladesh, Sri Lanka and Indonesia, which had also previously been sources of labour supply during the colonial period. Another source country was Thailand. Labour flows from these countries thus reflected continuity with the past, albeit with some interruption. Concurrently, the state embarked on a policy of encouraging more women into the formal sector and this coincided with the implementation of a domestic workers' recruitment scheme to facilitate the former policy. In 1981 the state also announced that it would phase out all migrant workers by 1991. Subsequently, following the recession of the mid 1980s, the state adopted a comprehensive migrant worker policy and levy scheme (in 1987) that enabled it to regulate both the size and composition of its migrant workforce.

Crucially, in 1988 an amendment was made to the Immigration Act that enabled the Singaporean state to have at its disposal three instruments to secure its borders and regulate the entry of migrant labour. These were the work permits system, the foreign levy scheme and internal enforcement measures. The work permit scheme, which categorised workers on the basis of their skills, race, and gender, allowed the state to manipulate labour supply in accordance with the labour market demands in the country. The foreign levy scheme enabled it to reduce its dependence on unskilled labour, consistent with its goal of becoming a predominantly high-tech country. The internal enforcement measures permitted the state to intensify border controls throughout the state and not just at the frontiers. These instruments thus typified the state's 'stiff deterrent laws, effective immigration controls and stringent enforcement' (*Straits Times*, 28 October 1995). More significantly, this policy was associated with the introduction of gaol terms for and caning of illegal migrant workers. At the same time, it allowed for an amnesty for and repatriation of illegal migrants. Interestingly, the levy was also extended to Malaysian migrant workers.

In 1990 the state enacted the *Employment of Foreign Workers Act 1990* which resulted in work permit holders being no longer governed by the provisions of the *Employment Act 1965*. This 1990 legislation was designed to improve bureaucratic procedures for the legalisation and regulation of the foreign workforce through a comprehensive work permit system (Kassim 1997).

This Act also introduced quotas ('dependency ceilings') for the following sectors: construction, marine, manufacturing and service, which were designed to allow for adjustments to the changing labour market.

In summary, Singapore's immigration policy and border control regime evolved in response to its changing labour needs. These were consistent with the adoption of a trade liberalisation policy and export-oriented industrialisation strategy after its accession from Malaysia. In stark contrast to Malaysia, the Singaporean state's Employment Acts, comprehensive levy scheme and the imposition of quotas in the various sectors acknowledged the state's dependence on migrant workers. Inevitably, this has resulted in the sifting of workers into complex, racialised hierarchies, and has provided the state with various mechanisms and the bureaucratic administration to regulate and manage migrant labour flows and control its borders (Sullivan *et al.*, 1992; Pang 1994; Chew and Chew 1995).

Malaysia – immigration policy and border controls

Compared to Singapore, an island state, Malaysia shares land borders with Indonesia and Thailand. During the colonial period, borders between the three countries and the Philippines were essentially porous. Moreover, although the long-standing dispute with the Philippines over the Malaysian state of Sabah has flared intermittently, at the same time, there has been some support for the Muslim separatist movement in Mindanao in the past. This has now changed, following incursions into Malaysian territory and has resulted in the 'securitising' of the Filipino illegal migrant worker problem in Sabah. The illegal entry of Indonesian workers, and more alarmingly for the state, rioting by Indonesian construction workers and workers in a textile factory and in a detention camp has also been seen as a security issue. Additionally, there are about 28,000 refugees currently in Malaysia. While the Malaysian government has granted permission to about 10,000 members of Burma's Rohingya Muslim minority to remain in the country, the plight of about 10,000 refugees from Aceh in Indonesia remain uncertain (Human Rights Watch 2004; Liow 2002).

Thus the possible influxes of both documented and illegal migrants, the potential erosion of national sovereignty, and, since 11 September 2001, fears of terrorism have now raised concerns for the Malaysian state. While Malaysia's attempts and policy to manage and regulate foreign workers was earlier regarded as ad hoc, and reactive, ILM has now become a major domestic and international political issue, and there are now intensified border controls and a more stringent immigration policy in place. These in turn have been met with resistance from local and international humanitarian organisations (Human Rights Watch 2004).

Like Singapore, changing labour market demands shape, and have shaped government migration goals and labour recruitment policies. Essentially, the Malaysian state has alternated between tightening immigration controls and loosening them through bilateral agreements and amnesties. Four distinct phases may be distinguished since the 1970s. During the first phase, 1970–80, the Malaysian government followed a liberal policy towards foreign worker recruitment. Employers either hired Indonesians who were domiciled in the country (in squatter settlements) or from Indonesia through private labour brokers, for the plantation and construction sectors. During the second phase, 1981–88, foreign labour recruitment was legalised, an official channel was created for labour recruitment and bilateral agreements signed with governments of sending countries. Thus in 1982 a Committee for the Recruitment of Foreign Workers was established and in 1984 the Malaysian government signed a bilateral agreement (the Medan Agreement) with the Indonesian government for the government-to-government regulated supply of Indonesian workers for the plantation sector and for domestic work. Following this, in 1985, the Filipino and Malaysian governments signed a memorandum of understanding for the importation of domestic helpers. In 1986 employers in the plantation and construction industries in Malaysia were permitted to recruit labour from Bangladesh and Thailand for the plantation and construction sectors, following agreements between Malaysia and Bangladesh and Thailand respectively (Kaur 2000). Nevertheless, migrant workers continued to enter the country as irregular chain migrants using network-dependent and network-creating relationships.

During the third phase, 1989–96, a legalisation programme was commenced to halt illegal immigration. Growing public disquiet against the more pronounced visibility of Indonesian migrant workers fuelled this programme, which had its origins in the economic recession of 1985–86. Thus public sentiment and 'societal borders' led to a change of policy and in 1989 the further importation of foreign labour was frozen. Concurrently, a programme to legalise/regularise the status of Indonesian migrants was implemented. Employers of undocumented workers were encouraged to legalise their workers. However, this programme had limited success since not many employers were willing to change the status of their undocumented workers. During this phase too, the Malaysian government implemented an amnesty programme that was targeted initially at domestic workers and then extended to workers in the plantation and construction sectors. Under this programme all undocumented ('illegal') workers were required to register themselves at special registration centres in order to remain in the country as legal workers (Kaur 2004d).

The intensification of border controls throughout the country during this period was consistent with new internal enforcement measures. For example, the state deployed the Police Field Force to patrol borders and guard against illegal landings on Malaysia's coastlines. This third phase was also marked by the final eradication of on-site illegal recruitment of labour and the implementation of an official migrant labour recruitment system based solely on offshore recruitment. During this period too the Indonesian government established a single company (*PT. Bijak*) to oversee the labour recruitment business and to provide a measure of control over recruitment arrangements (Hugo 1995).

The fourth phase, since 1997, is distinguished by two important developments. First, the financial and economic crisis of 1997–98 marked a turning point in state policy towards foreign labour recruitment. Further efforts to control undocumented migration were implemented; an amnesty programme was introduced that permitted illegal migrants to depart without penalty. Second, a work-permit system based solely on offshore recruitment was enforced resulting in workers being categorised more rigidly than before. Crucially, employment permits have become both location and employment specific, and legislative and police action to combat irregular migration has been strengthened. Detention camps were also established to hold undocumented workers. Furthermore, an amendment was made to the 2002 Immigration Act that resulted in harsh punishments for immigration violations. It is now a criminal offence for foreign workers to work without a work permit or visa, and punitive measures including caning of workers have been implemented. Errant employers who employ more than five illegal workers, are also subject to fines, imprisonment and caning (*New Straits Times*, 12 October 2003). Citing humanitarian reasons, an amnesty period was also granted to all illegal workers who registered themselves at repatriation stations.

But the major change has been in the origin of migration workers. The Malaysian government has enacted new legislation introducing a diversified recruitment policy to reduce dependence on any one racial group, reminiscent of the colonial period. Further, just like during the colonial period, employers are required to provide segregated housing and separate transport facilities for their workers (Kaur 2004d).

Issues of global health and epidemiological surveillance have also assumed greater relevance in Malaysia (and Southeast Asia). During the colonial period, the driving force behind public health policy was the eradication of disease at its source and the survival of the workers through a reduction of mortality and morbidity rates. Costs were borne by both employers and the state. The public health dimension of geographic mobility, which resulted in international co-operation on quarantine and international sanitary regulations, has now been transformed by the use of improved technologies for increased cooperation on the spread of communicable diseases. Against this backdrop, the control of the spread of diseases, linked to the broader currents of trade liberalisation and national sovereignty, has resulted in an abstracting of the disease process and the association of migrant workers with contagion. Moreover, with the emergence of Southeast Asia as the epicentre of new infectious diseases, the public health policy of Malaysia at the border is increasingly being used to practise racial profiling and exclusion.

Indeed, Malaysia's public health policies are increasingly being used to define a major parameter of the state's sovereignty vis-a-vis migrant workers. The government established the Foreign Workers' Medical Examination and Monitoring Agency (FOMEMA) to supervise and monitor the medical examinations of all legal foreign workers from 1997 (Peninsular Malaysia). Prior to this date, employers were entrusted with the responsibility of ensuring that their employees had undergone medical examinations in their home countries at designated heath centres or clinics. Once in Malaysia migrant workers were selected at random to undergo medical checks. But this system of random checks has now been replaced with annual medical examinations for all workers, an exercise involving a vast number of general practitioners. Medical fees are also borne by the workers. The workers are required to undergo examination for sexually transmitted disease, hepatitis B, HIV-Aids, malaria and tuberculosis, and are also tested for drugs.

Women migrant workers' bodies and reproductive rights are also subject to surveillance and control by the state. They are required to take pregnancy tests in addition to the other tests. If found pregnant they are deported immediately, without any redress. Not surprisingly, many choose to undergo termination of pregnancy. Foreign women who marry local men and become pregnant are also deported, despite the work of NGOs like Tenagita (Malaysia), Migrant Care and Federasi Organisasi Buruh Migran Indonesia (FOBMI), a migrant workers trade union (interviews with Migrant Care and FOBMI staff).

Finally, border controls have become diffused in Malaysia in the face of intensified global economic pressures and problems associated with the integration of migrant workers. A shortage of staff to patrol the territory (as distinct from frontier controls) has resulted in the Malaysian state authorising voluntary, neighbourhood security associations to conduct immigration raids and arrest undocumented workers. These civilians receive minimal training and are given cash awards for each illegal immigrant apprehended (see Human Rights Watch 2004). Clearly the undocumented migrant workers have become the 'enemy within' and no effort is made to differentiate between 'undocumented' workers and workers fleeing oppressive employers. Nation state sovereignty is thus equated with border inviolability and the issue of labour migration is thus viewed from the perspective of sovereignty and security.

Acknowledgement

The author would like to acknowledge the Australian Research Council's support of this research.

References

Agustiar, M. (2000) 'Indonesian Workers in Sarawak: The direction of the daily commuting workers via Entikong-Tebedu Border Post', in Michael Leigh (ed.) *Borneo*

2000: Language, Management and Tourism (Kuching: Universiti Malaysia Sarawak and Sarawak Development Institute) pp. 235–44.

Amjad, R. (1996) 'Philippines and Indonesia: On the Way to a Migration Transition', *Asian and Pacific Migration Journal*, Vol. 5, Nos. 2–3: 339–66.

Asian Development Bank (2002) *Key Indicators of Developing Asian and Pacific Countries, 2002* (ADB).

Asian Migration News, 30 June 2002.

—— 31 May 2002.

Athukorala, P. and C. Manning (1999) *Structural Change and International Migration in East Asia* (Melbourne: Oxford University Press).

Battistella, G. and Asis, M.B (1999) *The Crisis and Migration in Asia* (Quezon City: Scalabrini Migration Center).

—— (2003) 'Southeast Asia and the Specter of Unauthorized Migration', in G. Batistella and Maruja M.B. Asis (eds) *Unauthorized Migration in Southeast Asia* (Manila: Scalabrini Migration Center) pp. 1–34.

Business Times, 5 January 1996.

Chew, Soon-Beng and R. Chew (1995) 'Immigration and Foreign Labour in Singapore', *ASEAN Economic Bulletin*, Vol. 12, No. 2 (November): 191–200.

Hugo, G. (2002) 'Women's International Labour Migration', in Kathryn Robinson and Sharon Bessell (eds) *Women in Indonesia: Gender, Equity and Development* (Singapore: ISEAS).

—— (1995) 'Labor Export from Indonesia: An Overview', *ASEAN Economic Bulletin*, Vol. 12, No. 2: 275–98.

—— (1993) 'Indonesian Labour Migration to Malaysia: Trends and Policy Implications', *Southeast Asian Journal of Social Science*, Vol. 27, No. 1: 36–70.

Human Rights Watch (2004) *Help Wanted: Abuses Against Migrant Female Domestic Workers in Indonesia and Malaysia* (July) Vol. 16, No. 9 (B) (July).

ILO (2005) *A Global Alliance Against Forced Labour* Report 1B.

ILO, Director-General's Message on International Migrants Day, 18 December (http://www.ilo.org/public/english/bureau/inf/pr/2000/50.htm).

ILO, Laborsta database, http://laborsta.ilo.org.

Jones, S. (2000) *Making Money off Migrants: The Indonesian Exodus to Malaysia* (Hong Kong and Wollongong: Asia 2000/CAPSTRANS).

Kassim, A. (1997) 'Illegal Alien Labour in Malaysia: Its Influx, Utilisation and Ramifications', *Indonesia and the Malay World*, Vol. 71:50–82.

Kaur, A. (2006) 'Women Miners in Malaya: Gender, Race, and the Tin-mining Industry, 1900–1950', in Kuntala Lahiri-Dutt (ed) *Women Miners in Developing Countries: Pit Women and Others* (London: Ashgate).

—— (2004a) *Wage labour in Southeast Asia since 1840: Globalisation, the International Division of Labour and Labour Transformations* (Basingstoke: Palgrave Macmillan).

—— (2004b) 'Crossing Frontiers: Race, Migration and Border Controls in Southeast Asia', *International Journal on Multicultural Societies (IJMS)*, Vol. 6, No. 2: 111–32. www.unesco.org/shs/ijms [Special issue, Managing Migration and Diversity in the Asia Pacific Region and Europe, eds Christine Inglis and Matthias Koening].

—— (ed.) (2004c) *Women Workers in Industrialising Asia: Costed, not Valued* (Basingstoke: Palgrave Macmillan).

—— (2004d) 'Mobility, Labour Mobilisation and Border Controls: Indonesian Labour Migration to Malaysia Since 1900' http://coombs.anu.edu.au/ASAA/conference/proceedings/asaa-2004-proceedings.html.

—— (2001) *Historical Dictionary of Malaysia*, 2nd edition (New Jersey: Scarecrow Press).

—— (2000) 'Changing Labour Relations in Malaysia, 1970s-1990s', *Journal of the Malaysian Branch, Royal Asiatic Society*, Vol. 73, Pt.1 (June): 1–16.

Lim Lin Lean (1996) 'The Migration Transition in Malaysia', *Asian and Pacific Migration Journal*, Vol. 5, Nos. 2–3: 319–37.

Liow, J. (2002) *Desecuritising the 'Illegal Indonesian Migrant Worker' Problem in Malaysia's Relations with Indonesia* (Singapore: IDSS).

Manning, C. (2002) 'Structural Change, Economic Crisis and International Labour Migration in East Asia', *The World Economy*, Vol. 25, No. 3 (March): 359–85.

Migration News (2002) Vol. 9, No. 12 (December).

Nayyar, D. (1996) 'International Migration and Structural Change in Indonesia' (Manila: ILO/SEAPAT) cited in Rashid Amjad, 'Philippines and Indonesia: On the Way to a Migration Transition', *Asian and Pacific Migration Journal*, Vol. 5, Nos. 2–3 (1996): 339–366.

New Straits Times, 12 October 2003.

Organisation for Economic Cooperation and Development (OECD) (1992) *Trends in International Migration* (Paris: OECD).

Pang Eng Fong (1994) 'An Eclectic Approach to Turning Points in Migration', *Asian and Pacific Migration Review*, Vol. 3, 1: 81–92.

Philippine Daily Enquirer, 16 September 1995.

Philippines Government (1994) *National Report on Filipino Migrant Workers 1994* (Manila: Philippines Government).

Pillai, P. (1992) *People on the Move: An Overview of Recent Immigration and Emigration in Malaysia* (Kuala Lumpur: Institute of Strategic and International Studies [ISIS]).

Salt, J. (1992) 'The Future of International Labour Migration', *International Migration Review*, Vol. 6, No. 4: 1077–111.

Saw Swee-Hock, S. (1988) *The Population of Peninsular Malaysia* (Singapore: Singapore University Press).

Star, 13 February 1991.

Straits Times, 28 October 1995.

Taneerananon, S. (1997) 'Cross Border Migration from Southern Thailand to Malaysia'. Paper presented at the second Asia Pacific Conference of Sociology, Kuala Lumpur, 18–20 September.

World Bank (2000) *World Development Indicators 2000/2001: Attacking Poverty* (New York: Oxford University Press).

World Wide Web References http://www.library.uu.nl/wesp/populstat/ populframe.html

Wright, D. (2000) 'Industrialization and the Changing Role of Women in Bangladesh', in Amarjit Kaur and R. Saptari (eds) Women Workers in Asia, *Asian Studies Review* (Special Issue) Vol. 24, No. 2 (June): 231–42.

4

Coping With Cross-Border Labour Flows Within Southeast Asia

Chris Manning and Pradip Bhatnagar

Introduction

By the early twenty-first century Southeast Asia had emerged as a significant hub for the temporary migration of labour – both on an intra-regional and international scale. The shock of the Asian economic crisis in 1997–98 did not put a significant dampener on flows that had increased significantly in the last two decades of the twentieth century. If anything, structural relationships facilitating migration have become more entrenched. At the same time, most governments have sought to exert more control over cross-border labour movements through national policies and bilateral agreements. They have also facilitated certain kinds of movement through regional and multilateral trade agreements. Against this backdrop, this chapter discusses patterns of temporary labour migration, their impact on labour markets and policy initiatives to deal with migration in the region.

A great deal has been written on the international migration of Southeast Asians, especially Filipinos and Vietnamese, to the Middle East and developed countries. Much less is known of labour movements across national borders *within* Southeast Asia. This chapter focuses on the latter subject. It deals with the magnitude and regulation of movements of migrant workers within Southeast Asia, leading up to and since the Asian economic crisis. We examine the scope of national policies as well as the coverage of regional agreements, such as the Association of Southeast Asian Nations (ASEAN) Framework Agreement on Services (AFAS), which seeks to encourage temporary labour migration for services, trade and investment within the region. The chapter draws attention to some of the difficulties of both regulating and encouraging labour migration, in seeking to move towards an ASEAN Economic Community by the year 2020, the stated goal of ASEAN governments (articulated at the Bali Summit meeting in 2003).

In the second section, we start with a discussion of patterns and trends of international labour movement, and some dimensions of the multilateral framework for regulating mobility. The third section provides a brief overview of economic growth and structure in Southeast Asia, the framework for regional trade and investment relationships, and intra-regional economic ties. We then look at both trends and policies in labour mobility, including 'Mode 4' relationships associated with services trade in Southeast Asia, in the following two sections. This is followed by a brief concluding section.

The international context

Recent studies by Dani Rodrik (2002) and Alan Winters *et al.* (2003) have drawn attention to the large potential economic gains from liberalisation of temporary labour migration (TLM), both for developed and developing countries (OECD 2002a; World Bank 2003). These studies have been undertaken at a time when TLM has assumed a more prominent role in major multilateral forums for trade liberalisation, such as at the 2003 Cancun Ministerial Meeting, in the Doha round of trade negotiations. Together, they are part of a new impetus in discussions of international labour movement at a multilateral and regional level, in relation to broader patterns of trade liberalisation and globalisation – even if few informed observers are optimistic regarding the prospect for significant broad-based reform at these levels, in the immediate future.

The last two decades of the twentieth century witnessed only a very modest rise in world TLM, in contrast to ambitious, albeit carefully phased, plans for expansion envisaged by Winters *et al.*, and Rodrik. The increase has been on a much smaller scale and different to migration patterns experienced in the last decades of the previous century (Stalker 1994, 2000; OECD 2001, 2002b). Now, flows are dominated by temporary migrants, in contrast to the prevalence of permanent settlers to the 'new world' a century ago (Hatton and Williamson 1998). Many more have come from less developed countries (LDCs) seeking a growing number of low wage jobs in the developed world, principally western Europe and the United States, as well as in the capital abundant Middle Eastern countries.

Two points are worth noting with regard to recent developments in international TLM. Flows have been asymmetric between developed and developing countries. Labour 'exports' from developed countries have tended to be 'easier', consisting of a smaller number of movements of professionals and business people accompanying both foreign direct investment (FDI) and other capital outflows to LDCs. Labour 'imports' by the same group of countries (and 'exports' from the developing countries), on the other hand, have consisted of the much larger number of unskilled workers, many employed on contract in domestic firms in declining industries. Such workers have also been prominent in seasonal jobs and non-tradable industries (health care, construction and household services), as well as in tradable industries.

Second, while the focus of much public debate on the economic gains from TLM has been on these South–North movements, an equal if not greater number of movements of temporary workers have occurred between LDCs (or between poorer countries and their neighbours, which have now graduated to middle or high income status). Official and anecdotal evidence suggests increasing flows of contract and undocumented or illegal migrants *between* LDCs, as intra-regional income differentials have widened in many parts of the developing world in the last decades of the twentieth century (see Stalker 1994). This has especially been the case in East Asia, and specifically in Southeast Asia, where several countries have been transformed from low to middle or high income countries in less than one generation. In Southeast Asia, these intra-regional flows have been particularly large and had become a stable feature of labour markets in many countries from the 1980s and early 1990s.

TLM policies: Mode-4

What policies have countries adopted to deal with increased temporary movements of workers across national boundaries? Both policies towards and the regulation of these migrant flows has been primarily a matter of policy for individual states, even in Europe. Several regional agreements have had migration clauses, such as NAFTA, the Common Economic Relations between Australia and New Zealand and the Caribbean Community and Common Market (CARICOM), where 15 member states have committed to near-free movement of skilled workers in the region. Nevertheless, migration has generally been a minor subject in such agreements. There have been no stand-alone, multilateral agreements on TLM to mirror those in trade, largely because of the political sensitivity and different dimensions of the issue across countries and regions. Unlike in the case of trading arrangements, the more developed north has had less interest in negotiating agreements on TLM that would result, mainly, in opening their labour markets to workers from LDCs.

Nonetheless, there has been some attempt to establish rules for TLM through regulations regarding multilateral trade in services. The GATS – General Agreement on Trade in Services – found it necessary to incorporate a set of clauses on TLM (the movement of 'natural' persons) to facilitate trade and especially investment in services (Chanda 1999). Mode-4 in services trade agreements was thus created to regulate temporary travel for a limited period – usually up to two years – by workers to perform specific services abroad in connection with trade or foreign investment. Its main focus is on the employment in service areas such as tourism, telecommunications, air and sea transport, in which foreign capital and trade are prominent. In particular, Mode-4 does not cover workers seeking permanent jobs in a foreign country. Nor does it encompass work outside the service industries, for example, in mining, manufacturing and agriculture.

In promoting more temporary migration, it has been argued that two sets of issues need to be addressed: the architecture (framework) on which Mode-4 is based and, second, fears regarding the predicted or even sometimes imagined impact on the labour markets of receiving and sending countries (Chanda 1999; Winters *et al.*, 2003; World Bank 2003). Regarding the *architecture*, developing country objections to Mode-4 have highlighted restriction in negotiations largely to professional and highly skilled manpower, thus limiting opportunities for mobility of other middle-level skill groups – such as computer software analysts and nurses – and especially semi-skilled and unskilled workers. Limiting negotiations to the international mobility of workers to the service sector means the exclusion of the important group of migrant workers in agriculture (especially seasonal workers), major mining projects and manufacturing.

Discussion of *labour market effects* has centred on the potential for wage-depressing effects of the movement of temporary workers into permanent status and creating low-wage pockets in the host country economy. Developing countries, on the other hand, have been more concerned about the treatment of nationals working overseas and the 'brain-drain' effects of their professionals – especially scarce doctors and highly skilled engineers – seeking high-wage jobs abroad. At the same time, several studies have pointed out the benefits of reverse flows to countries ('brain circulation') that have industrialised quickly and encouraged their nationals to return home (Korea, Taiwan and Singapore deserve special mention; [World Bank 2003:160]).

Given these concerns, the question arises as to whether such TLM flows related to trade in services might be better regulated through regional negotiations rather than through multilateral arrangements. Before dealing with this subject, however, we first look at trends in migration and the policies adopted to cope with increased pressure from migrant workers in neighbouring states in Southeast Asia.

Development and economic integration in Southeast Asia

Marked intra-regional differences in per capita income and economic structure, combined with dispersed land areas and populations, have encouraged migration within Southeast Asia in recent decades.

GDP per capita, and economic structure and growth. Substantial differentiation in terms of per capital income, living standards and economic structure underpin labour supply pressures for substantial TLM in Southeast Asia. Table 4. A1 indicates some the key variations. The wide range in per capita incomes between countries probably best captures the differences in living standards and economic structure. Per capita income was some 50 times higher in the mainly service sector economies of Singapore and Brunei, and some ten times higher in Malaysia and Thailand, compared with the low income, mainly agricultural-based countries the region (differences in PPP [cost of living] adjusted per capita income were smaller but still substantial).

All the high-income economies grew rapidly from the 1970s. Rising incomes in turn, are associated with substantial and growing absolute wage differentials over time, acting as a powerful incentive for cross-border movements of labour (Manning 2002).

The ratio of trade and investment to GDP ratios are high and foreign investment flows substantial, especially in the major migrant receiving areas in Southeast Asia, such as Singapore and Malaysia, and to a lesser extent in Thailand. In these relatively open economies, there is a strong incentive to maintain international competitiveness. As we shall see, temporary migration has been one strategy adopted in pursuit of this goal.

Nevertheless, trade and foreign investment links developed by Southeast Asian countries continue to focus on Northeast Asia, North America and Europe. Table 4.1 indicates, for example, that the share of intra-ASEAN exports have been small, although they did rise in most countries from the 1970s (see column 1, bearing in mind that much of the trade through Singapore was likely to consist of transhipments). According to officia data, intra-ASEAN investment flows were similarly small, and in this case a declining share (falling from 13 to 9 per cent) of all investment in the latter half of the 1990s (ASEAN Statistical Yearbook 2003).

Economic and migration ties within ASEAN. In thinking about the forces that link trade, investment and migration flows within ASEAN, it is useful to divide the economies of the region into two geographical groups. First, there are the Mekong River states consisting of relatively developed Thailand (per capita income of close to $2000 in 2001–02), and the four lower income countries, Burma, Lao PDR, Cambodia and Vietnam (per capita income of around $200–400). Three of the above countries – Burma, Lao PDR and Cambodia have common borders with Thailand, and both Lao PDR and Cambodia share borders with each other and Vietnam.

The second group consists of two high per capita income states, Singapore and Brunei Darussalam, middle income Malaysia and the lower-income island states of Indonesia and the Philippines. Singapore and the three other 'Malay' states have a common history of interaction through trade and migration. Similarly, the Philippines has long had close economic interaction with East Malaysia, and also with the northern provinces of Sulawesi and the Moloccus (Maluku), and East Kalimantan of Indonesia.

Cross-border labour flows

Like much of the Third World, the economies of Southeast Asia were first exposed intensively to international migration during the colonial period,

Table 4.1 Exports from the ASEAN-6 to Other ASEAN-6 countries and the rest of the world, 1975–80 to 1995–2000* (in percentage)

Year/ exporting country	All ASEAN excl. Singapore	Singapore	Sub-Total	Japan	Other East Asia	North America	Rest of the world	Total
			Destination country/region					
1975–80								
Brunei	4.9	2.6	7.6	71.9	0.0	8.8	11.7	100
Indonesia	1.5	10.5	12.0	44.4	2.4	23.7	17.5	100
Malaysia	3.3	17.8	21.2	21.6	5.0	17.8	34.5	100
Philippines	3.0	1.8	4.8	26.6	6.1	32.5	29.9	100
Singapore	26.8	–	26.8	9.1	9.9	15.0	39.2	100
Thailand	9.0	7.8	16.8	20.4	7.9	11.6	43.4	100
1985–90								
Brunei	13.1	6.8	19.9	61.6	8.3	4.5	5.7	100
Indonesia	2.1	8.2	10.4	43.3	8.5	17.7	20.1	100
Malaysia	5.8	19.9	25.7	18.4	9.6	17.5	28.8	100
Philippines	4.5	3.4	7.8	19.2	7.7	38.2	27.0	100
Singapore	24.6	–	24.6	8.8	10.5	23.7	32.5	100
Thailand	4.5	7.8	12.3	16.0	8.6	22.2	40.9	100
1995–2000								
Brunei	13.2	7.7	20.9	49.3	16.1	6.5	7.1	100
Indonesia	5.7	10.1	15.8	23.2	13.7	14.6	32.7	100
Malaysia	6.9	18.7	25.6	12.3	10.6	21.0	30.4	100
Philippines	6.9	6.8	13.7	15.1	8.6	33.5	29.1	100
Singapore	27.6	–	27.6	7.4	14.7	18.9	31.3	100
Thailand	6.8	10.5	17.3	15.2	10.3	21.2	36.1	100

* The ASEAN-6 countries include the six original ASEAN countries, Singapore, Malaysia, Brunei, Thailand, Indonesia and the Philippines.

Source: IMF, Direction of Trade Data, various years.

when unskilled immigrants from China and India worked mainly in plantation agriculture and mining projects (Kaur 2004). Many of the migrants returned to their home countries in the early post-colonial period and it was not until the 1980s that TLM began to have a significant impact on most of the economies of the region, both in terms of worker flows within the region and to and from the rest of the world.

Table 4.2 assembles data from a variety of sources to provide an estimate of migration trends since the 1970s. The number of temporary migrants working in Southeast Asia from other countries in the region, or from abroad, probably peaked on the eve of the Asian crisis at around four million. As already noted, this is a sizable number by international standards, especially in relation to a total labour force of major receiving (host) countries of around 120 million. Although in relation to the rest of the world Southeast Asia as a whole has been become a significant labour exporter – mainly from the Philippines and Indonesia to the Middle East – several *countries*

Table 4.2   Estimated temporary labour migration within and outside Southeast Asia from the 1970s to the early twenty-first century (approximate stocks)[1]

	Early 1970s	Early 1980s	Early 1990s	1996–97	2001–02
Within Southeast Asia (1,000 persons)	300–500	500–1,000	2,000–2,500	3,000–3,500	3,000–3,250
To/from countries outside Southeast Asia					
1. *Out-migrants* (1,000 persons)	500–750	1,000–1,500	2,500–3,000	3,000–3,500	3,500–4,000
DISTRIBUTION (%)					
Other East Asia	10	15	25	30	20
USA	30	20	15	10	10
Europe	20	15	10	10	15
Middle East	10	25	40	35	45
Australia	25	20	10	10	5
Other	5	5	5	5	5
	100	*100*	*100*	*100*	*100*
2. *In-migrants* (1,000 persons)	50–100	100–200	500–750	750–1,000	500–750
DISTRIBUTION (%)					
Other East Asia	15	30	40	35	25
South Asia	10	10	20	25	30
USA	40	20	15	10	5
Europe	25	20	15	15	15
Other	10	20	10	15	25
	100	*100*	*100*	*100*	*100*
Net Labour Emigration from SEAsia (1,000 persons)[2]	450–600	900–1,200	2,000–2,250	2,250–2,500	3,000–3,250
Ratio of Intra-regional SEAsian Migrants to Out-migrants[3]	0.6–0.7	0.5–0.7	0.8	1.0	0.8.–0.9
Memo Item: SEAsian Population (millions)[4]	275	350	430	490	530

Notes

1. Refers to the estimated number of migrants working in each country. Includes an estimate of the number of undocumented or illegal migrant workers.
2. Numbers of emigrants working outside Southeast Asia minus the number for immigrant workers from outside the region employed in Southeast Asia.
3. The number of migrants from destinations within Southeast Asia employed in the region, divided by the estimated number of Southeast Asians employed abroad.
4. Rounded to the nearest five million, for years 1970, 1980, 1990, 1997 and 2002.

Sources: Based on official sources and estimates from Ministries of Labour/Manpower for 2001 and 2002, and various estimates of illegal migration cited in Stahl (1999), Athukorala and Manning (1999), Manning (2002), OECD (2001, 2002a), Battistella (2002) and Hugo (2003), and numbers reported in various numbers of *Asian Migration News* (Manila: Scalabrini Migration Centre); Population data are from the ASEAN Statistical Yearbook (2003).

within the region are large labour importers, principally from elsewhere in Southeast Asia.

From the supply side, the Philippines, Indonesia and Burma have been the dominant countries of labour out-migration since the Vietnam war ended and peace was restored to Indochina in the second half of the 1970s (Table 4.3). Filipino migrant flows have been much larger outside than within the region (earlier focusing on the United States and more recently the Middle East), whereas both Indonesians and Burmese have moved mainly to neighbouring countries within Southeast Asia.

Table 4.3 Main countries of origin and destination for temporary migrants within Southeast Asia and abroad (Estimated stocks, circa 2000–01. (Thousands)[1]

Country of origin	Main destination countries within Southeast Asia				Outside SE Asia
	Malaysia	Thailand	Singapore	Sub-total[2]	
Indonesia	1,500	n.a.	200	1,700	1,000
Burma	5	500	5	505	100?
Philippines	300	10	*150*	460	2,000–2,500
Thailand	30	n.a.	30?	60	200
Malaysia	n.a.	5	*300*	305	200
Indochina states	25	*75*	5	105	50
Total	1,860	590	660	3,135	3,550–4,000

Notes
1. As with Table 2, includes an estimate of undocumented migrant workers.
2. Excludes workers from each of the main sending countries working in another main sending country, or in Brunei. These numbers are likely to be quite small (almost certainly less than 100,000 overall), with the exception of a large number of 'temporary', undocumented Vietnamese workers resident in Cambodia.
n.a. = not available.
Sources: See Table 4.2.

Unskilled migrants

As noted, TLM among unskilled workers *within the region* has been associated with an interaction between geographical proximity, on the one hand, and contrasting economic structure and labour force deployment, related to different levels of per capita income, on the other (Pang 1993; Athukorala and Manning 1999; Athukorala *et al.*, 2000).

As shown in Table 4.2, intra-regional migrant stocks are estimated to have peaked during the boom years preceding the Asian economic crisis. One or several countries acted as magnets for unskilled labour migration, both in the Mekong region states, and among the remaining ASEAN countries. At the same time, major host countries for migrants tend to export capital and skilled and professional manpower to the other countries in the group. Thailand has played this role in the Mekong River states. Three relatively small countries – Singapore, Malaysia and Brunei – are in a similar position in relation to the poorer and more populous countries of Indonesia and the Philippines in the second group. Two large bilateral flows, mainly of unskilled and undocumented workers within Southeast Asia – from Indonesia to Malaysia and Burma to Thailand – predominate, and have been one of the causes of tensions between source and destination countries in recent years.

Given low levels of intra-regional trade and investment, one would not expect a close relationship between trade and investment flows and international labour migration (ILM) within Southeast Asia. 'Non-tradable' activities in which foreign investment plays a minor role, especially construction and domestic service, have been a major source of employment for migrants. Women from the Philippines and Indonesia dominate domestic service in Malaysia and Singapore. Similarly, Indonesians have played a major role in the construction industry in Malaysia. In Thailand, migrants from Burma were significant in both the latter occupations in 2001–02 (Chalamwong 2002).

Alternatively, among tradable industries, agriculture and fisheries attracts large numbers of migrant workers in Thailand, and plantation agriculture in Malaysia. However, unlike in other parts of East Asia (especially South Korea and Taiwan) migrant workers have not been concentrated in 3-D jobs in labour-intensive and sometimes 'sunset', manufacturing, industries (Athukorala and Manning 1999). Participation of migrant workers in electronics in Malaysia and in small-scale manufacturing in Thailand and Singapore are an exception, allowing firms to remain competitive in low-wage, niche markets.

Business, skilled and professional workers

In contrast to the patterns for unskilled workers, skilled and business migrants have tended to be much more heavily engaged in tradable industries where FDI is prominent in the region. Many fewer skilled than unskilled workers migrate temporarily within the region. They probably accounted for only around 5 per cent of all TLM in 2000–01, although skilled and business workers accounted for a much higher share (probably around 30–40 per cent) of all migrants who came from outside the region to work in Southeast Asian countries.

Perhaps surprisingly, it appears that Southeast Asia has been a net importer of skilled manpower in recent years despite the lure of high wage jobs in developed countries. Singapore, Malaysia and Thailand hosted some 60,000–70,000 migrants; Indonesia and the Philippines permitted entry of 10,000–20,000 workers; and the other countries a smaller numbers of business, skilled and professional temporary workers from abroad in 2001–02 (Unpublished data, Ministry of Manpower, Jakarta). Foreign professionals employed by FDI firms by domestic investors were increasingly recruited from a wider range of countries, including North East Asia and India, prior to the crisis in the 1990s (Table 4.4).

Skilled manpower movements were more affected by the slow-down in FDI flows in several countries after the economic crisis, especially in Indonesia where numbers dropped from close to 60,000 in 1996–97 to less than 20,000 in 2001–02. At the same time, foreign takeovers and asset sales

Table 4.4 Distribution of skilled and professional migrants by country of origin in selected Southeast Asian Countries, 2002

	Malaysia	Thailand (Number)	Philippines	Malaysia	Thailand (Percentage)	Philippines
Japanese	10,791	13,675	3,576	18.0	23.3	33.3
Taiwan	2,739	3,681	506	4.6	6.3	4.7
Korean	n.a.	n.a.	1,900	n.a.	n.a.	17.7
Sub-total	13,530	17,356	5,982	22.5	29.6	55.7
Chinese	4,050	4,593	1,098	6.7	7.8	10.2
Indian	12,864	5,135	589	21.4	8.8	5.5
Sub-total	16,914	9,728	1,687	28.2	16.6	15.7
Filipino	2,938	2,337	x	4.9	4.0	
Singaporean	4,177	n.a.	144	7.0	n.a.	1.3
Sub-total	7,115	2,337	144	11.8	4.0	1.3
British	3,990	5,148	584	6.6	8.8	5.4
American	2,079	4,099	515	3.5	7.0	4.8
Australian	2,354	2,089	226	3.9	3.6	2.1
German	n.a.	1,783	301	n.a.	3.0	2.8
Sub-total	8,423	13,119	1,626	14.0	22.4	15.1
Other	12,649	14,513	1,300	21.1	24.8	12.1
Total	60,069	58,597	10,739	100.0	100.0	100.0

Source: Unpublished data provided by the Government Immigration Offices/Labour Ministries in each country, July–December 2003.

to overseas investors (despite strong nationalist opposition to 'fire-sales') have tended to increase opportunities for foreign managers and professionals in Korea and to a lesser extent also in Thailand and Malaysia. In these countries, the net effect is likely to have been only a slight change in the number of skilled foreign workers employed.

Migration policies in host countries and Mode-4

Although contrasting economic performance and associated income and wage differentials have been strong facilitating factors, the policies adopted by host economies have also played a role in migration outcomes. We look briefly at how migration has been influenced by development policies and strategy first, before turning to policies specific to migration and, in particular, at Mode-4 in the regional context of AFAS.

National policies and bilateral agreements

The three major labour-importing countries – Singapore, Malaysia and Thailand – have adopted differing policy approaches to foreign workers. These have sought to balance the tension between achieving longer-term goals of industrial-upgrading and technological change, on the one hand, and maintaining competitiveness in the shorter-term, on the other. Key areas of policy have focused on four areas: employment of workers in low-wage 'non-tradable' industries; prolonging the life of labour-intensive, export-oriented industries; FDI flows; and the promotion of education and health. We deal briefly with each in turn.

Maintaining competitiveness in non-tradable industries. The three labour-importing countries have promoted (or turned a blind eye to) the entry of unskilled workers mainly domestic helpers and construction workers, which have often been left by nationals, either because of low wages or the unsavoury nature of jobs. The presence of foreign workers in these activities has enabled Singapore, Malaysia and Thailand to slow the increase in domestic labour costs.

Maintaining competitiveness in labour-intensive tradables. As touched on above, the objective of migration policy in tradable industries has similarly been to control wage costs. In this case, the aim has been to maintain competitiveness in some potentially declining industries, as wage rates rose and countries began to lose their competitiveness in labour-intensive processes. Plantation agriculture would probably not have remained internationally competitive from the 1980s if the government had forced the sector to depend on domestic workers in Malaysia. Similarly difficult and dangerous coastal fishing in Thailand has remained internationally competitive partly because the government has permitted a large inflow of migrants from Burma. Government policies also targeted some low-wage, manufacturing activities in all three countries (Athukorala and Manning 1999).

Promoting FDI flows. In contrast to Japan and Korea, the major importing countries in Southeast Asia have long had open-door polices to FDI. Permitting the entry of foreign business and professional workers to accompany investment from abroad has been one element in this strategy (Athukorala and Hill 1998). Singapore has gone well beyond this, more recently articulated in its 'foreign talents' policy of attracting foreign workers in a range of service and manufacturing industries (Low 2002).

Meeting skilled labour shortfalls in health and education. In health and education, several countries have sought to improve and extend services to domestic and international consumers through permitting the entry of professionals from abroad. Both Singapore and Malaysia import doctors and nurses from other countries in the region. Singapore has adopted an open door to overseas academics for several years. Malaysia has begun to liberalise work in this sector and has begun to promote English much more widely at tertiary level. Twinning arrangements between domestic and overseas universities has inevitably involved greater movement of professionals. Other countries in the region – in particular the Philippines which has a relatively well-educated workforce chasing limited job openings at home – have been more wary of competition from foreign service providers and professionals. The labour-importing countries differ significantly in the breadth and focus of TLM policy, and also in the extent to which it has been integrated into the broader economic and social policy-making framework (Manning and Bhatnagar 2004b: Table 4 A1). Singapore stands at one extreme in developing a set of policies that are closely integrated into national development strategy through a sophisticated set of migrant levies on less-skilled workers, incentives for highly skilled manpower and strict policing. In regard to unskilled workers, policies adopted by the Thai government lie at the other extreme. Regular registration and repatriation has sought to stem the inflow of unrecorded migrants from neighbouring states, since the mid-1990s. Malaysia lies somewhere in between.

Bilateral agreements between neighbours have also been one means of negotiating rules governing cross-border movements (e.g., recruitment and repatriation policies, and protection of workers in host countries). For example, Thailand initiated a set of bilateral talks with neighbouring countries of Cambodia, the Lao PDR and Burma in 2002–03, in an attempt to regularise the recruitment of migrant workers in places of origin (rather than after undocumented arrival in Thailand). In May 2004, after a longer period of conflict over undocumented migration, Malaysia and Indonesia signed a memorandum of understanding (MOU) to provide more safeguards in the recruitment, placement, repatriation and the treatment of migrant workers. While it is too early to assess the impact of these arrangements, they face strong vested interests in favour of illegal recruitment and placement of migrant workers in both receiving and sending countries.

Mode 4 and migration policy

Historically, ASEAN negotiations on international economic relations have kept away from sensitive migration issues within the region. No separate agreements have been made within ASEAN in some 35 years. Building on a framework set out by the World Trade Organisation, a liberalisation agenda in services has been pursued through the ASEAN Framework Agreement on Services (AFAS), signed in 1995 (Manning and Bhatnagar 2004b:16–26). However, improving the flow of professional manpower within ASEAN including mutual recognition of qualifications (or MRAs) have been mentioned in the context of achieving the ASEAN Economic Community by 2020, although mechanisms for achieving this goal have yet to be put in place (Soesastro 2003). For several years, negotiations have been under-way to extend MRAs for selected occupations, including surveyors, accountants, engineers and health care workers in the region, although it seems likely that most progress will be made on a bilateral basis, at least initially. AFAS can thus be considered the first step towards a region-wide agreement on migration issues. Removal of restrictions on temporary labour migration in services has been viewed as one means of facilitating a more open market in services trade in the region. We look briefly at progress made in this area since 1995.

AFAS commitments by sector.   One goal of AFAS was to go beyond commitments made by member countries under the General Agreement on Trade in Services, or GATS, at the World Trade Organisation. Seven priority sectors were selected from the 12 included within the GATS umbrella, including business services, communications, construction, financial services, sea and air transport and tourism/travel. The sectors not included in for negotiation in the AFAS context include distribution, education, health, the environment, recreation and 'other'. Notably, health and education services, two areas with potential for multilateral and regional freeing up of labour movements among professionals, are not included in the original list (although the movement of healthcare workers has subsequently been given higher priority).

In general, commitments towards freeing up labour mobility among ASEAN countries, over and above those made through GATS, have been limited (Table 4.5). Up to late 2003, the core ASEAN-6 (excluding Burma and the former Indochina states) had made very few extra commitments, and those that have been made were in the relatively easy category of business services. Among this group of six countries, no additional commitment was made for migrant participation in financial services, and only one undertaking was given in three of the other sectors. Perhaps surprisingly, the other four less-developed nations are recorded as having made more commitments under AFAS. However, this is mainly because two are not members of the WTO, Cambodia only joined very recently and Burma which has been a member of the WTO for some time had initially made only one commitment to liberalisation of TLM (in tourism) under GATS. Comparing countries within the region, the largest number of commitments to Mode-4 movements of skilled manpower were made by Singapore and Malaysia, followed by Indonesia and Thailand, under GATS and AFAS combined.

The Depth of AFAS Commitments.   In addition to limited Mode-4 commitments in AFAS beyond that achieved through the WTO, pledges made up to late 2003 carried a large number of restrictions on the movement of skilled manpower. In GATS terminology, there was little 'depth' to undertakings made by ASEAN countries to a freer regional labour market. Table 4.6 indicates that the large majority of commitments were of a partial nature, that is some

Table 4.5 AFAS and GATS (WTO) commitments under Mode 4 by sector[1]

	Business services (46)		Telecommunications services[2] (24)		Construction and related eng. services (5)		Financial services[3] (17)		Air transport services (35)		Maritime transport services (12)		Tourism/travel services (4)		Total[4] (104)		Grand total (104)
	WTO	AFAS	WTO	AFAS	WTO	AFAS	WTO	AFAS	WTO	AFAS	WTO	AFAS	WTO	AFAS	WTO	AFAS	WTO + AFAS
ASEAN-6																	
Singapore	22	1	9	1	5	0	16	0	0	0	3	0	3	0	58	2	60
Malaysia	27	2	12	0	5	0	15	1	0	0	3	1	3	1	65	5	70
Brunei	7	4	8	3	0	5	4	1	1	1	0	2	0	1	20	17	37
Thailand	14	2	8	0	3	2	13	0	1	1	4	2	3	1	46	8	54
Indonesia	9	3	9	0	4	1	14	0	0	0	2	0	3	1	41	5	46
Philippines	0	5	4	0	0	5	14	0	3	0	4	0	3	0	28	10	38
ASEAN-4																	
Burma	0	5	0	9	0	5	0	0	0	0	0	0	1	1	1	20	21
Vietnam	–	5	–	13	–	5	–	4	–	2	–	4	–	1	–	34	34
Cambodia	–	4	–	7	–	5	–	0	–	1	–	2	–	1	–	20	20
Lao PDR	–	7	–	12	–	5	–	1	–	1	–	2	–	1	–	29	29

Notes

1. Includes both commitments made in GATS and extended to non-WTO ASEAN members, as well as additional commitments made under AFAS. Numbers in brackets in each column refer to the total number of sub-sectors.

2. May be understated on account of additional commitments made under the Agreement on Basic Telecommunications signed after the conclusion of the GATS negotiations.

3. May be understated on account of additional commitments made under the Financial Services Agreement (Fifth Protocol) signed after the conclusion of the GATS negotiations.

4. May be understated as the table has been constructed using the GATS service classification list that mainly uses the 4-digit CPC. It therefore excludes the commitments made by some countries at the 5-digit level.

Source: Constructed from specific schedules of commitment under the ASEAN Framework Agreement on Services, www.aseansec.org.

Table 4.6 The 'depth' of AFAS commitments under Mode-4

	Number of services[1]	Number of services with commitments[2]	Number of services with commitments mode 4	Depth of mode 4 commitments	
				% 'None'[3] (No restrictions) 6	% partial commitments 7
Singapore	104	62	60	7	93
Malaysia	104	81	70	2	98
Brunei	104	39	37	8	92
Thailand	104	57	54	28	72
Indonesia	104	48	46	0	100
Philippines	104	49	38	25	75
Vietnam	104	41	34	0	100
Cambodia	104	20	20	0	100
Lao PDR	104	30	29	0	100
Burma	104	31	21	18	82

Notes
1. Number of services contained in the seven sectors under which ASEAN countries made commitments in the first two rounds of negotiations.
2. Implies commitments under any mode of supply.
3. Any commitment that has specified 'None' under either the market access or national treatment column has been counted. Only Burma has unconditionally liberalized both market access and national treatment for two kinds of Business services and for amusement parks. However, as *all* countries have placed horizontal limitations that apply across all sectors, there is really no unconditional liberalisation of Mode 4 by any country in any service at all under the AFAS.

Source: Manning and Bhatnagar (2004b: Table 8). Constructed from the 'Specific Schedules of Commitments' under AFAS.

limitations were placed on each country's pledges, usually related to some aspects of special access given to domestic workers (or quotas) to work in a particular sub-sector.

While Thailand and the Philippines had made unqualified commitments (referred to as 'none' – no restrictions) in 25 per cent of their pledges, undertakings of this category were limited in other countries in Southeast Asia. Thailand, for instance, has committed to unrestricted national treatment (i.e., no discrimination between nationals and foreigners) for employment of non-nationals in a range of services. These included foreign suppliers of aircraft repair and maintenance, engineering, computer related services, construction, maritime transport, telecommunication, tourism and other business services related to agriculture and mining. Similarly, Singapore, Brunei and Malaysia had made a few commitments without restrictions whereas Indonesia, Vietnam, Cambodia and Laos have placed restrictions on all of their Mode 4 commitments.

What kinds of limitations have been imposed by ASEAN countries? In all, some 13 main restrictions have been imposed by countries on their Mode 4 commitments for the employment of foreign workers in 2003 (Manning and Bhatnagar 2004a:Table 9). Most importantly, nearly all countries have restricted their commitments to entry of skilled workers like specialists or senior managerial personnel, they have imposed restrictions on the duration of stay and required employers of foreign labour to undertake a programme for upgrading the skills of local workers. This, of course does not mean that the country will not import unskilled workers. Singapore for instance, allows a significant number of seafarers from the Philippines to enter on a temporary basis every year but it reserves the right to refuse their entry.

A third of the countries have also made entry subject to labour market/economic needs tests, or linked entry to commercial presence. A similar proportion of countries has placed pre-employment conditions or has made entry contingent upon the recognition of qualifications.

Across countries, the widest range of restrictions were used by Malaysia (10 out of 13) followed by Vietnam (9) in 2003. Singapore imposed the least number of restrictions (5). Cambodia, Laos and Burma each used just 3 out of the 13 restrictions listed in the table. But along with Indonesia, they subsumed all or many of their undertakings under a catch-all clause 'domestic regulations', which effectively dilutes the impact of their commitments to employment of overseas employees in the specific sectors.

In addition, entry of foreign workers is hampered by a plethora of administrative constraints. There have been large variations in visa and work-permit arrangements and fees. For example, the issue of work permits is given only after potential employees have entered under a different visa status in some countries. Similarly, the direct financial costs imposed on the employers of foreign workers differ substantially across countries.

Conclusion

Temporary labour migration (TLM) across national borders rose significantly with globalisation in Southeast Asia in the 1980s and 1990s. In this respect, Southeast Asia appears to have gone against international trends, at least in the 1990s. TLM increased partly in response to challenges posed by rapidly rising living standards and wage rates in labour-receiving countries in the region. Most migrants were unskilled or semi-skilled, and by the 1990s the numbers moving to destinations within the region, seems to have matched the number seeking jobs outside Southeast Asia. A large share of intra-regional migrants was undocumented or illegal, and hence largely unprotected by labour legislation in receiving countries. We have highlighted the movement of many migrant workers into non-tradable, service industries, in addition to finding work in low-wage manufacturing. Greater integration of trade *within* Southeast Asia had had a relatively minor impact on cross-border labour flows.

Overall, host countries have found it difficult to cope with labour supply pressures that underpinned migration from neighbouring countries. What was their policy response? Regulations dealing with temporary migration were mostly introduced unilaterally, although some countries had entered into bilateral ties with neighbours, seeking to control the seemingly unrestrained movement of less-skilled workers. It was also noted that while Singapore, in particular, had made major progress, the other major 'importing' countries, Malaysia and Thailand, were still grappling with major problems of undocumented migration. Multilateral and regional arrangements played a much smaller role in regulating migration flows. Even in services, most workers who sought temporary jobs abroad moved outside the guidelines set out in multilateral and regional trade agreements.

The migration of skilled, professional and business people tended to be more organised and integrated with trade and investment, mostly with countries from outside Southeast Asia. Some of these flows were regulated through 'Mode-4' in the international and regional agreements in services trade – GATS and AFAS – although a significant number of migrant workers were unaffected. We also found that regional arrangements under ASEAN did not lead to significantly more commitments than had already been made in multilateral trade negotiations through the WTO. Thus despite the potential for substantial economic gains (especially for poorer countries) highlighted by trade reformers, the AFAS process might have been expected to achieve more after having already completed three packages of commitments from two rounds of negotiations. Those sectors opened beyond GATS still imposed many restrictions on potential migrants.

Not surprisingly, the more open and developed economies Singapore, Malaysia and Thailand took a more liberal approach than other countries in the region. Nevertheless, many of the restrictions which effectively limit the movement of unskilled workers will need to be reviewed even in these countries, if cross-border migration is to increase further and to be conducted on a more orderly manner. The same applies to labour market, pre-employment and economic needs tests, and limitations on the duration of stay in visa arrangements that now apply to skilled workers.

Note

Both authors were attached to the Australian National University at the time this research was undertaken.

Empirical research was supported by an AusAID funded research project administered by the Regional Economic Support Facility at the ASEAN Secretariat in Jakarta. Of course, the authors alone are responsible for the views expressed in the paper.

Appendix

Table 4. A1 Key economic indicators in ASEAN, Circa 2001–02

Country	Population 2001 (m.)	GNP per Capita 2001 ($US)	GDP Growth 1999–2002[1] % p.a.	Total GNP 2002 $b.	% of GDP in agriculture 2002 %	% of GDP in manufact. 2002 %	International Trade in goods as a % of GDP 2001 (% p.a.)	Gross Domestic Investment 1999–2002[1] (% of GDP)	Foreign Direct Investment 1995-96[1] ($m., p.a.)	1999–2000[1] ($m., p.a.)
The ASEAN-6										
Singapore	4	24,740	3.9	86	0.2	19	278	27	9,580	6,794
Brunei	0.3	12,245	2.3[2]	5[3]	2	(56)[4]	n.a.	n.a.	619	598
Malaysia	24	3,640	4.8	88	9	32	184	24	4,628	1,607
Thailand	63	1,970	4.0	115	9	34	111	23	2,202	4,790
Philippines	80	1,050	3.9	71	15	23	89	17	1,498	1,301
Indonesia	214	680	3.2	145	16	26	60	15	5,270	−3,648
The (mekong) ASEAN-4 states										
Vietnam	79	410	4.9	33	24	21	94	26	2,366	1405
Lao PDR	5	310	6.1	2	51	18	50	21	128	76
Cambodia	13	270	6.4	3	39	17	92	16	223	135
Burma	51	n.a.	n.a.	n.a.	57[3]	8[3]	n.a.	12	294	254
Other selected countries in Asia										
Taipei, China	22	13,380	3.2	309	2	25	n.a.	20	1,712	3,927
Korea	47	9,400	7.4	421	4	30	69	27	2,051	9,309
China	1,271	890	7.6	1,063	15	(44)[5]	44	38	41,777	38,576
India	1,018	460	5.1	455	25	15	20	24	2,285	2,241

Notes

n.a. = not available; data for Burma is not available or not reliable according to conventional measures.

1. Unweighted mean of annual rates and levels.

2. 1999–2001.

3. 2001.

4. All industry (manufacturing plus mining, utilities and construction).

5. Includes mining and utilities.

Source: Asian Development Bank, *Development Indicators*, various years; ASEAN Secretariat (2002) *ASEAN 2001 Statistical Yearbook 2001*: World Bank, *World Development Indicators*.

References

Athukorala, P. and C. Manning (1999) *Structural Change and International Migration in East Asia* (Melbourne: Oxford University Press).

Athukorala, P. and H. Hill (1998) 'Foreign Investment in East Asia', *Asian Pacific Economic Literature*, Vol. 12, No. 2: 23–50.

Athukorala, P., C. Manning and P. Wikramasekera (2000) *Growth, Employment and Migration in Southeast Asia: Structural Change in the Greater Mekong Countries* (London: Edward Elgar).

Battistella, G. (2002) 'Unauthorised Migrants as Global Workers in the ASEAN Region', *Southeast Asian Studies*, Vol. 40, No. 3: 350–71.

Chalamwong, Y. (2002) 'Thailand', in OECD and Japan Institute of Labour (eds) *Migration and the Labour Market in Asia: Recent Trends and Policies* (Paris: OECD) pp. 289–308.

Chanda, R. (1999) *Movement of Natural Persons and Trade in Services: Liberalising Temporary Movement of Labour under GATS*, Indian Council for Research on International Economic Relations, New Delhi.

Hatton T. and J. G. Williamson (1998) *The Age of Mass Migration: Causes and Economic Impact* (New York: Oxford University Press).

Hugo, G. (2003) 'Labour Migration Growth and Development in Asia: Past Trends and Future Directions'. Paper delivered at the *Tripartite Meeting on Challenges to Labour Migration Policy and Management in Asia*, Bangkok, 30 June –July 2.

Kaur, A. (2004) *Wage Labour in Southeast Asia since the 1840s: Globalisation, the International Division of Labour and Labour Transformations* (Basingstoke: Palgrave Macmillan).

Low, L. (2002) 'Migrant Worker Policy in Singapore', in Y.A. Debrah (ed.) *Migrant Workers in Pacific Asia* (London: Frank Cass) pp. 95–118.

Manning, C. (2002) 'Economic Crisis and Labor Migration in East Asia', *The World Economy*, Vol. 25, No. 3: 359–85.

Manning, C. and P. Bhatnagar (2004a) '*The Movement of Natural Persons in Southeast Asia: How Natural?*', Working Paper in Trade and Development 04/01, Division of Economics, Research School of Pacific and Asian Studies, Canberra.

—— (2004b) *Liberalizing and Facilitating the Movement of Individual Service Providers under AFAS: Implications for Labour and Immigration Policies and Procedures in ASEAN*, Final Report, REPSF Project 02/004, ASEAN Secretariat, March.

OECD (2002a) *Service Providers on the Move: The Economic Impact of Mode 4*, Working Party of the Trade Committee, Paris, March 19.

—— (2002b) *Trends in International Migration: Continuous Reporting System on Migration*, Annual Report 2002 Edition, SOPEMI Report, Paris.

—— (2001) *Trends in International Migration: Continuous Reporting System on Migration*, Annual Report 2001 Edition, SOPEMI Report, Paris.

Pang, E. F. (1993) *Regionalisation and Labour Flows in Pacific Asia* (Paris: OECD Development Centre).

Rodrik, D. (2002) *Feasible Globalizations*, NBER Working Paper W9129, National Bureau of Economic Research, Mass., Cambridge, August.

Soesastro, H. (2003) ASEAN Economic Community: Concepts, Costs and Benefits, Paper prepared for the ASEAN Roundtable 2003 on 'Roadmap to an ASEAN Economic Community' (Singapore: ISEAS) August 20–21.

Stahl, C. (1999) 'International Labour Migration in East Asia: Trends and Policy Issues', Paper presented at the APRMN Symposium, *New Trends in Asia Pacific Migration and the Consequences for Japan*, Waseda University, September 23–27, 1999.

Stalker, P. (2000) *Workers Without Frontiers: The Impact of Globalization on International Migration* (Boulder, Colorado: Lynne Rienner).

—— (1994) *The Work of Strangers* (Geneva: International Labour Organisation).

Winters, A., T. L. Walmsley, Z. K. Wang and R. Grynberg (2003) 'Liberalising Temporary Movement of Natural Persons: An Agenda for the Development Round', *World Economy*, Vol. 26, No. 8: 1137–61.

World Bank (2003) *World Economic Prospects*, Washington [chapter 4: 'Labor Mobility and the WTO: Liberalizing Temporary Movement', pp. 143–76].

5

Women, Work and International Migration in Southeast Asia: Trends, Patterns and Policy

Graeme Hugo

Introduction

In the massive expansion of international migration in Southeast Asia over the last two decades a striking feature has been the feminisation of that movement. In several countries of origin of international migrants, females are a major element in the movement, if not the majority of out-migrants. Similarly, in the countries which are the main destinations of international migrants, all have a significant in-movement of women. Yet this movement remains little understood in the region. Indeed its measurement is problematic because data collection systems in Southeast Asia are under-developed, much of the movement occurs outside official migration systems and there is an inbuilt bias in existing census and surveys which leads them to not detect female immigrants. Nevertheless, women are involved in the full gamut of international movement in Southeast Asia. It is important to study the movement of women separately from those of men for a number of reasons:

- the patterns differ from those of men;
- the causes and consequences of movement can differ from those of men;
- the policy implications of movement can differ from those of men.

International migration in Southeast Asia is very definitely a gendered process and interlinked closely with changes in the age and status of women in Southeast Asia.

Much of the increasing international mobility of women in the region is associated with work. While labour is usually only associated with the bur-geoning flow of overseas contract workers (OCWs) in fact, much of the other mobility has an important work dimension. Accordingly, this chapter begins by identifying the major significant types of international migration of women in Southeast Asia. This will be the basis for making an assessment of the major patterns and scale of the various types of female international migration in the region insofar as it can be established using the limited data and research available. The next part of the paper addresses the main policy issues which relate to female international migration in the region. This will involve consideration of the female migrants themselves, their communities of origin and the destination. It is impossible to consider the policy aspects of female migration without considering the relationships between this movement and such important issues as economic development and social change and the empowerment of women.

Types of female international migration in Southeast Asia

Female migration in the Southeast Asian context has taken some distinctive forms and there is a great deal of segmentation into specific types of migration. I have attempted to summarise the major types of contemporary female migration in the region in Figure 5.1.

In the diagram the Y-axis differentiates the type of *migration* by two key features:

* The movements are differentiated between permanent and non-permanent movements. Both types have increased greatly in significance in recent years. Contract labour migration, whereby women undertake to work in the destination nation for a specified period of time is the fastest growing type of migration in the region. Of course in some cases such movement merges into permanent movement and permanent migration turns out to be temporary. Indeed one of the major fears in destination centres in Southeast Asia and elsewhere is that temporary migrant workers may eventually settle in the region as occurred in Europe with guest workers in the 1950s and 1960s (Castles *et al.*, 1984).
* Another important dimension of difference relates to whether the migrations occur through official channels at origin and destination. As is pointed out elsewhere in this volume an increasing proportion of international

Nature of migration		Characteristics of migrant			
		Low skill	High skill	Family	Refugee
Migration through official channels	Permanent				
	Non-permanent				
Migration not through official channels	Permanent				
	Non-permanent				

Figure 5.1   A typology of female international migration in Southeast Asia

migration is undocumented. This applies equally to men and women and exposes the migrants to a range of additional uncertainties at the destination that documented migrants face.

It is also important to distinguish important dimensions not only of the migration itself but also among the migrants. Here we have made a distinction between those who migrate for work-related reasons and those migrating for other reasons. One of the key elements in the feminisation of international migration in Southeast Asia has been the fact that more and more women are migrating autonomously and not as the 'non-decision maker dependants' of fathers and husbands. Traditionally most female migration in the region has been dismissed as family migration in which women are not decision makers but are the passive followers of male migrants. Traditionally many Southeast Asian cultures have placed great restrictions on the independent mobility of women, although these are generally breaking down. However, even in family migration, it is apparent that the non-autonomous nature of migration of women has been greatly exaggerated in the past and certainly is not the case at present.

A distinction must be drawn in the employment related migration of women (and men) in the Southeast Asian situation between migration of non-skilled or low-skilled migrants on the one hand, and highly skilled migration on the other. These types of movement differ not just with respect to the characteristics of the migrants, but also to the circumstances, destination, nature and experience of the migration. There is a little overlap with some more-skilled migrants accepting some 'occupational skidding', whereby they accept an unskilled occupation in order to migrate and earn money. Hence there are many examples whereby Filipino women who have tertiary level education have become domestic workers overseas in order to be international labour migrants (e.g., see Battistella 1995).

It is apparent, however, among female migrants from Southeast Asia who move to work, that unskilled women predominate. Indeed much of the migration involves women, like men, taking up low wage, low status 3D (dirty, dangerous, difficult) jobs that are eschewed by local women at the destination. With women, however, there needs to be even greater occupational segmentation among this group than is the case with men. There are a relatively small number of occupations among which unskilled female international labour migrants from Southeast Asia are concentrated. Paramount here is the occupation of domestic workers. Southeast Asia is one of the world's greatest suppliers of female international migrants who become domestic workers, not only elsewhere in Southeast Asia but also in other regions especially the Middle East, Europe and elsewhere in Asia. The following Map 5.1 shows the major patterns of international movement of domestic female workers originating in Southeast Asia.

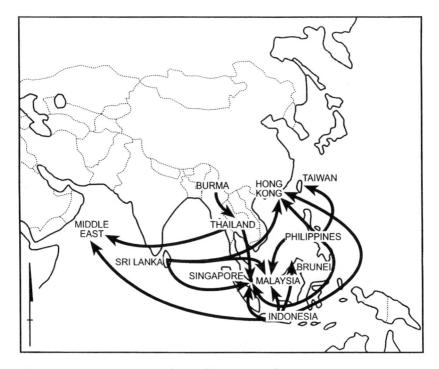

Map 5.1   Southeast Asia: main flows of domestic workers

This movement involves at least more than two million women, mainly from the Philippines, Indonesia, Sri Lanka (into Southeast Asia) and Thailand. Since this job is located in the homes of employers in the destination, it is open to greater exploitation than people working in a factory or other workplace.

Some of the other main occupations which unskilled female migrant workers take up in the destinations also make them vulnerable to exploitation. One of the most significant of these is the movement of women in the so-called entertainment or sex industry. Map 5.2 shows the main patterns of movement of Southeast Asian women who are involved in the sex and entertainment industry at the destination. The main origins of women in this industry are in the Philippines and Thailand but there are also flows from Indonesia to Malaysia and Singapore and from Myanmar and Laos into Thailand as shown in Map 5.2. Other important occupations for unskilled migrant women include factory work and a range of informal sector activities.

Females in many Southeast Asian countries have not enjoyed equal access to higher education compared with their male counterparts. Accordingly, they have not been as much part of the movement of skilled workers in the region as males. Nevertheless, females have been a significant component of

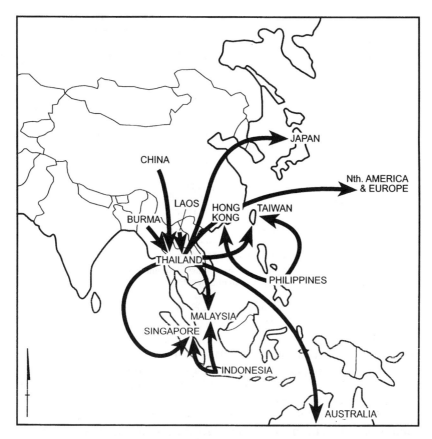

Map 5.2 Southeast Asia: main flows of sex and entertainment workers

the skilled migration to more developed, north countries which is sometimes characterised as a 'brain-drain'. The Philippines has been particularly significant with the movement of, for example, a large number of female nurses (Ball 1990) to the Middle East, North America and elsewhere. With the increasing shortage of nurses and other medical workers in more developed nations (Aiken *et al.*, 2004) it is likely the outflow of health workers from less developed countries will increase. It is estimated that in 2004 around 40,000 Filipino nurses were working abroad with an annual outflow between 7000 and 10,000 (*Asian Migration News*, 16–31 August 2004).

One significant dimension of the skilled outflow of women is the increasing number of women in the increasing outflow of students travelling for education to More Developed Countries (MDCs). Table 5.1 shows the gender breakdown of students from Southeast Asia travelling to Australia. It clearly indicates that overall there is little difference between male and female student numbers from Southeast Asia.

Table 5.1   Australia: total student arrivals, 1991–92 to 2003–04

Country of origin	Total Male	Female	Sex ratio
Brunei	5,467	5,294	103.3
Myanmar	1,226	961	127.6
Cambodia	1,469	912	161.1
East Timor*	432	327	96.2
Indonesia	120,305	119,340	100.8
Laos	1,260	1,124	112.1
Malaysia	98,970	104,651	94.6
Philippines	7,559	7,512	100.6
Singapore	78,169	88,693	88.1
Thailand	43,963	53,119	92.9
Vietnam	14,549	11,767	123.6
Total	378,669	393,700	132.1

* Included with Indonesia prior to 1999–2000.

Source: Australian Department of Immigration and Indigenous and Multicultural Affairs (DIMIA), unpublished data.

Another classification along the X-axis of Figure 5.1 of female migrants is related to family migration. While the stereotype of non-autonomous migration does not apply, there is significant movement of Southeast Asian women as the dependants of males. This occurs mainly in the case of more permanent migration, especially that from south to north, developed countries. A particularly significant type of this movement is marriage migration. There are substantial numbers of Southeast Asian women, especially from the Philippines and, to a lesser extent, Thailand who move to northern countries as part of the mail order bride schemes. Hence, there are significant numbers of Filipino brides in Japan, Australia, North America and Europe. The main flows of Southeast Asian women involved in marriage migration are shown in Map 5.3.

It will be noted that Taiwan has become an important destination of Southeast Asian female marriage migrants. Tsay (2004:180) reports that in 2003 there were 16,600 women with a Southeast Asian nationality who married a Taiwanese man (9.6 per cent of all marriages). Piper and Roces (2003) maintain that the distinction between labour and marriage migration is by no means a complete one and there is considerable overlap. Many women involved in marriage migration move to improve their own or their families' economic situation and many also work at their destination (Hugo and Nguyen 2004). It is apparent that much of the south–north migration of Southeast Asian women is via the family migration categories in their immigration programmes. This is especially the case in Canada, the United States, Australia and New Zealand. In Australia, for example, Table 5.2 depicts the numbers of permanent and long term arrivals from Southeast Asian nations,

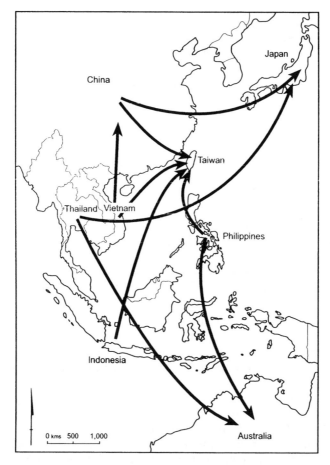

Map 5.3 Southeast Asia: main flows of marriage migration

and it is interesting that women outnumber men substantially among permanent settlers. Moreover, only in the small flows from Myanmar, Brunei and Laos is there a balance between males and females. It will be noticed that the Philippines and Thailand have especially low sex ratios indicating a dominance of women among settlers. This reflects the particular importance of marriage migration from these two countries. The inflow of fiancées and wives often as a result of introduction, so called 'mail order', bride schemes whereby an Australian man is introduced to a Southeast Asian woman via companies and other intermediaries is an increasing element in south–north migration. It is a major cause of women outnumbering men among Southeast Asian permanent settlers arriving in Australia but there are also important flows to other developed countries. It is interesting to see in

Table 5.2   Australia: permanent and long-term arrivals of persons born in Southeast Asian countries, 1991–92 to 2003–04

Country of birth	Persons		Sex ratio		
	Settler arrivals	Long-term arrivals	Settler arrivals	Long-term arrivals	Settler and Long-term arrivals
Brunei Darussalam	614	4,569	112	108	109
Cambodia	8,304	2,396	73	141	84
Indonesia	28,610	105,222	84	102	98
Laos	833	2,256	67	110	97
Malaysia	23,737	115,337	88	95	94
Myanmar	3,519	2,313	92	119	102
Philippines	46,517	21,767	57	69	61
Singapore	13,314	77,707	88	94	93
Thailand	9,886	39,166	40	80	70
Vietnam	46,595	22,983	58	118	74
Total	181,929	393,716	67	95	85

Source: DIMIA, unpublished data.

Table 5.2 that women substantially outnumber men among settlers moving from Vietnam to Australia. This reverses a pattern of male dominance in the previous decade (Hugo 1991) when this flow was dominated by Vietnamese entering Australia under the refugee-humanitarian category. Now family migration accounts for most Vietnamese settlers. Vietnam has become and important country of origin of brides for men in Taiwan, Japan and Southern China (Hugo and Nguyen 2004).

Turning to migrant women who have left Southeast Asian countries because of force. There is an international regime of refugees whereby only people who fit the UN definition of a refugee qualify for the UN protection and immigration privileges. The 1967 United Nations protocol on refugees considers as refugees 'every person who, owing to a well-founded fear of being persecuted for reasons of race, religion, nationality, membership of a particular social group or political opinion, is outside the country of his *(sic)* nationality and is unable or, owing to such fear is unwilling to avail himself *(sic)* of the protection of that country' (Keely 1981:6). Females have made up an important part of the major refugee movements in Southeast Asia in the post-war period. This includes the movement out of Indo-China beginning in the mid-1970s and extending for two decades and the smaller movement from the southern Philippines to Sabah, Myanmar to Thailand, Irian Jaya to Papua-New Guinea, North Sumatra to Malaysia and out of East Timor. However, in general, males have outnumbered females in refugee flows, although refugees tend to send for their wives, female children and other female relatives to join them once they are established at a destination.

Table 5.3 Australia: refugee-humanitarian settlers from Southeast Asia, 1996–2004

	Male	Female	Sex ratio
Myanmar	426	344	123.8
Cambodia	170	158	107.6
Laos	2	4	50.0
Thailand	25	41	61.0
Vietnam	917	755	121.5
Brunei	–	–	–
Indonesia	54	53	101.9
Malaysia	7	4	175.0
Philippines	31	32	96.9
Singapore	–	–	–
East Timor	43	46	93.5
Total	1,675	1,437	116.6

Source: DIMIA, unpublished data.

In recent years refugee flows out of Southeast Asia have declined. Table 5.3 shows the number of refugee-humanitarian settlers from Southeast Asia. It will be noticed that the numbers are relatively small compared to earlier years and that the flows tend to be male dominated with the largest numbers coming from Cambodia, Vietnam and Myanmar.

The representation of women in migration streams is influenced by the visa categories under which they enter their destination countries.

Table 5.4 shows the balance of males and females arriving in Australia as settlers in 2003–04 according to the visa category order which they entered. Only in the smallest flow from Brunei which is dominated by skilled migrants are males more numerous overall. Also, in the nations from which skill migration is most significant (Malaysia, Singapore and, to a lesser extent, Indonesia) is there only a small dominance of females. In other nations where family migration is the main form of movement, women outnumber men by 2 to 1 or more. This is especially the case for the Philippines – the largest Southeast Asian source of settlers to Australia. Marriage migration of one kind or another is the dominant element in the migration system.

Patterns of female international migration in Southeast Asia

Indonesia

Indonesia has one of the largest flows of female international migration in the Southeast Asian region. There are two main international flows of Indonesians and a number of smaller flows. Table 5.5 shows the main estimated stocks of Indonesian contract workers overseas and estimating these is difficult because

Table 5.4 Australia: Southeast Asia-born settler arrivals by visa category, 2003–04

Country of birth	Family migration		Skill migration		Humanitarian		Total		Sex ratio
	Male	Female	Male	Female	Male	Female	Male	Female	
Brunei Darussalam	6	1	26	24			32	25	128.0
Myanmar	31	74	17	18	16	23	64	115	55.7
Cambodia	179	299	6	16	1	1	186	312	59.6
Indonesia	251	612	801	860	13	9	1,065	1,481	71.9
Laos	8	19	2	4	1	2	11	25	44.0
Malaysia	88	172	1,655	1,746			1,743	1,918	90.9
Philippines	611	1,580	843	855	12	16	1,466	2,451	59.8
Singapore	69	135	973	1,006			1,042	1,141	91.3
Thailand	155	732	45	81		1	200	814	24.6
Vietnam	576	1,366	84	74	26	27	686	1,467	46.8
Total	1,974	4,990	4,452	4,680	69	79	6,495	9,749	66.6

Source: DIMIA, unpublished data.

Table 5.5   Indonesia: estimated stocks of overseas contract workers, c.2000

Destination	Estimated stocks	Source
Saudi Arabia and Kuwait	1,200,000	*Migration News*, April 2004
United Arab Emirates	35,000	*Asian Migration News*, 30 April 1999
Malaysia	1,200,000	*Migration News*, October 2004
Hong Kong	77,000	Schloss 2002
Singapore	40,000	*Jakarta Post*, 17 March 2004
Taiwan	90,739	*Migration News*, April 2003
South Korea	25,473	*Asian Migration News*, December 2002
Japan	4,000	DEPNAKER
Philippines	26,000	*SCMP*, 10 December 1998
Brunei	2,426	Scalabrini Migration Center, 2001
Other	20,000	DEPNAKER
Total	2,720,638	

the vast majority of movement occurs outside legal channels, especially that to Malaysia, the main flow out of Indonesia.

Table 5.6 shows the annual changes in the number of *official* Indonesian Overseas Contract Workers (OCWs) which have occurred over the last quarter century. Two features of the table stand out. First, there is a general pattern of growth in the numbers deployed overseas over the last two decades, and second, the movement has been consistently dominated by women. There also have been some apparent fluctuations in numbers.

1. The apparent downturn in movement in 1995–96 was due to the exclusion of some workers from the data while the exceptional numbers in 1996–97 includes a large number of workers already in Malaysia who received an amnesty (Hugo 2000).
2. The downturn in recent years is partly due to the expulsion of Indonesia workers in Malaysia following efforts by the then Prime Minister of Malaysia to replace Indonesians with other international workers (Inglis 2002). However, following the devolution of power following the fall of President Suharto in 1998, it is apparent that provincial reporting of statistics to Jakarta became less complete than it had been previously.

The second major feature of the table is the dominance of women involved in official international labour migration and it is apparent that domestic workers make up the majority of this flow. While there are not accurate data available, Table 5.7 presents some estimates of the stocks of Indonesian domestic OCWs in the main countries of origin.

Much controversy has surrounded this movement since these women, especially those moving to Saudi Arabia have a high risk of being exploited by their employees (Wijaya 1992). NGOs suggest that the many of these women are exploited through over work, extended hours, poor conditions

Table 5.6 Number of Indonesian overseas workers processed by the ministry of manpower, 1969–2003

Year (single year)	Middle East		Malaysia/Singapore		Other		Total No.	% Change over previous year	Sex ratio (males/ 100 females)
	No.	%	No.	%	No.	%			
2003*	116,018	65	51,022	29	11,832	7	178,872	na	35
2002	241,961	50	168,751	35	69,681	14	480,393	+42	32
2001**	121,180	36	144,785	43	73,027	21	338,992	−22	80
2000	129,165	30	217,407	50	88,647	20	435,219	+2	46
1999	154,636	36	204,006	48	68,977	16	427,619	na	41
1999–2000	153,890	38	187,643	46	62,990	16	404,523	−2	44
1998–99	179,521	44	173,735	42	58,153	14	411,609	+75	28
1997–98	131,734	56	71,735	30	31,806	14	235,275	−55	20
1996–97	135,336	26	328,991	64	52,942	10	517,269****	328	79
1995–96	48,298	40	46,891	39	25,707	21	120,896	−31	48
1994–95	99,661	57	57,390	33	19,136	11	176,187	10	32
1993–94	102,357	64	38,453	24	19,185	12	159,995	−7	36
1992–93	96,772	56	62,535	36	12,850	7	172,157	15	54
1991–92	88,726	59	51,631	34	9,420	6	149,777	74	48
1990–91	41,810	48	38,688	45	5,766	7	86,264	3	73
1989–90	60,456	72	18,488	22	5,130	6	84,074	37	35
1988–89	50,123	82	6,614	11	4,682	8	61,419	1	29
1987–88	49,723	81	7,916	13	3,453	6	61,092	11	35
1986–87	45,405	66	20,349	30	2,606	4	68,360	23	61
1985–86	45,024	81	6,546	12	4,094	7	54,297	21	44
1984–85	35,577	77	6,034	13	4,403	10	46,014	57	79
1983–84	18,691	64	5,597	19	5,003	17	29,291	38	141

1982–83	9,595	45	7,801	37	3,756	18	21,152	18
1981–82	11,484	65	1,550	9	4,570	26	17,604	11
1980–81	11,231	70	564	4	4,391	27	16,186	56
1979–80	7,651	74	720	7	2,007	19	10,378	
1977							3,675	

Five Year Planning periods		Target	Total deployed
	1999–2004	2,800,000	1,201,830***
Repelita VI	1994–99	1,250,000	1,461,236
Repelita V	1989–94	500,000	652,272
Repelita IV	1984–89	225,000	292,262
Repelita III	1979–84	100,000	96,410
Repelita II	1974–79	none set	17,042
Repelita I	1969–74	none set	5,624

* To September 2003.

** From 2001 the Ministry of Manpower was decentralised and there was less compulsion for regional offices to report the numbers of overseas contract workers deployed to the central office.

*** 1 January 1999 to 30 September 2003.

**** Year in which 300,000+ Malaysian labour migrants were regularised (194,343 males and 127,413 females).

Note: In 2000 the Indonesian government transferred to a calendar year system of accounting from previously using 1 April–31 March.

Source: Suyono (1981); Singhanetra-Renard (1986), p. 52; Pusat Penelitian Kependudukan, Universitas Gadjah Mada (1986), p. 2; Departemen Tengara Kerja (1998), p. 14; Soeprobo (2003 and 2004).

Table 5.7   Estimates of stock of Indonesian female domestic overseas contract workers, 2001–04

Country	Number	Source(s)
Saudi Arabia	450,000–500,000	Sherry, 2004
Malaysia	216,000–240,000	Varia, 2004
Hong Kong	80,000	*Asian Migration News*, 1–15 February 2003
Singapore	55,000	*Asian Migration News*, 16–31 October 2002
United Arab Emirates	33,000	*Kompas*, 17 March 2001
Taiwan	85,677	Loveband, 2003, p. 2
Bahrain	6,000	*Asian Migration News*, 1–15 September 2004

and sexual harassment and assault from male members of their household. Indonesia actually encourages women to migrate as domestic workers, in contrast to a number of countries in Asia which at different times have attempted to ban the movement of women to work as maids in the Middle East. This is despite some intense opposition in Indonesia especially from Muslim groups and leaders and a significant number of NGOs. Much of the movement includes women who do not go through official channels and many who travel to the Middle East do so not as labour migrants but under an *umroh* visa to make the pilgrimage to Jeddah.

While domestics dominate among legal female migrant workers, increasingly more educated women are migrating legally to Malaysia and South Korea to work in factories. There are also significant movements of sex workers from Indonesia to Sabah (predominantly from East Java and from Sumatra to Singapore and Peninsula Malaysia (Jones 1996). In general, however, the major illegal movement, that of Indonesians to Malaysia, both Peninsular and East Malaysia, is dominated by males. Nevertheless, it is clear that the significance of females in this movement is increasing (Hugo 1998) over time. This is evident in a number of surveys undertaken of Indonesian migrants in Malaysia:

- Paramasivam (1996:70) found that 10.3 per cent of respondents in a study of illegal Indonesian migrants in Malaysia were female.
- A survey by Haris (1997:85) found that 8 per cent of 115 illegal migrants from West Nusatenggara were women.
- In Nasution's (1997) study of Indonesian migrants in Jakarta no analysis is made of gender but 397 out of 2720 were female household domestics (14.6 per cent).
- Official migration from East Flores to Malaysia over 1987–93 was 2176 persons of whom 23.8 per cent were female (Kapioru 1995:73).
- In a survey of a village in East Flores 24 per cent of migrants were females (Hugo 1998:42).
- Of the Indonesian migrant workers expelled from Sabah in East Malaysia to East Kalimantan in Indonesia between 1994–96, 29.5 per cent were female (Hugo 1998:42).

Table 5.8 Major destinations of official Indonesian female labour migrants 1984–2000

Destination		Number of female migrant workers	Sex ratio of total movement
Malaysia	1999–2000	174,094	107.3
	1994–99	283,822	96.1
	1989–94	52,754	196.3
	1984–89	6,606	422.0
Singapore	1999–2000	54,608	10.9
	1994–99	119,143	22.9
	1989–94	28,951	68.9
	1984–89	3,602	192.5
Brunei	1999–2000	8,119	33.6
	1994–99	10,943	28.3
	1989–94	9,009	13.2
	1984–89	783	17.5
Hong Kong	1999–2000	34,423	0.1
	1994–99	34,553	1.7
	1989–94	3,615	46.7
	1984–89	40	423.8
Taiwan	1999–2000	68,668	16.3
	1994–99	17,735	152.9
	1989–94	981	704.1
	1984–89	0	–
Saudi Arabia	1999–2000	220,003	11.5
	1994–99	507,113	8.5
	1989–94	342,028	12.5
	1984–89	186,052	20.2
UAR	1999–2000	26,573	2.1
	1994–99	40,710	2.6
	1989–94	2,080	11.7
	1984–89	0	–

Source: Indonesian Manpower Department, unpublished tabulations.

Many of these migrants move into domestic service jobs but there is evidence of increased diversity in the types of work being taken up by Indonesian women in Malaysia. Surveys such as those quoted above are showing increased numbers involved in factory work, tailoring/dress making, petty trade, cleaning, clerks, office workers and sales workers.

In recent years the destinations of Indonesian female OCWs in Asia have diversified. Table 5.8 indicates that the migration of Indonesian women to work as domestics in Asia is more recent.

In 1984–89 there were only 11,031 Indonesian women who moved as labour migrants to the five major Asian destinations compared to 186,052 going to Saudi Arabia. By 1999–2000, however, they numbered 339,912 compared to 220,003 going to Saudi Arabia. The largest outflow to Asia is currently to neighbouring Malaysia where the legal movement of labour migrants until the 1990s was very male dominated. The second half of the 1990s saw a massive increase in the number of women moving to Malaysia to work and in this period there was a more or less equal number of males and females in the flow. Singapore has been the second major destination but Indonesian labour migration to the island has been dominated by women since the late 1980s. Currently, 9 out of 10 Indonesian labour migrants to Singapore are female domestic workers. The oil rich small country of Brunei has had a significant inflow of Indonesian domestic workers for more than two decades.

A feature of the last decade in Table 5.8 has been the extension of the countries to which substantial numbers of female Indonesian domestic workers have gone to – Hong Kong and then Taiwan. This has occurred to such an extent that in 1999–2000 Taiwan was the third largest single destination of Indonesian female migrant workers. Table 5.8 indicates that in Hong Kong virtually all of the Indonesian migrant workers were female domestic workers. In Taiwan, the initial movement of Indonesian workers was overwhelmingly male until the late 1990s when the flow of domestic workers increased greatly.

Philippines

The Philippines is one of the world's major sources of international migrants and this is especially the case for female permanent and non-permanent female international migrants. There are over 7 million Filipinos overseas at any one time. This includes around 3.4 million temporary workers overseas in 2003, some 2.8 million permanent migrants and 1.5 million irregular migrants (Philippines Overseas Employment Administration, Department of Labour and Employment, Republic of the Philippines, http://www.poea.gov.ph/). These must be considered the lower bounds of movement which is almost certainly substantially higher. Among the temporary labour migrants women represent around half of officially deployed workers (Shah and Menon 1997:11) and probably more than half of those illegally migrating. Moreover, they make up more than half of those moving permanently to other countries, especially those in the north, the countries of Canada, United States, several European nations, Australia, New Zealand and Japan. Table 5.9 shows the officially resident Filipino populations in the major destination countries around the early and mid 1990s. It is clearly dominated by the United States where Filipino migration has a long history but also Japan, Australia and Canada have also been important destinations. Table 5.10 shows the growth of the Filipino population in Australia over the last two decades and the predominance of females in that migration.

The destinations of Filipino migrant workers are quite different. Figure 5.2 shows the distribution of destinations of official Filipino workers. Over the period 1984–2003 the numbers annually officially deployed increased from 299,278 to 651,938. The number going to the Middle East was over a quarter of a million and the share going to other Asian countries has greatly increased over the last decade.

Table 5.9   Filipinos legally in selected north countries

Country	Year	Total	Source
Japan	2000	93,662	Japan, Statistics Bureau, Population Census, 2000
Austria	2001	8,881	Statistics Austria
Denmark	2003	3,849	Statistics Denmark
France	1993	1,900	Neymarc and Cervantes (1996, p. 85)
Italy	1993	46,300	Neymarc and Cervantes (1996, p. 85)
Netherlands	2003	7,959	Statistics Netherlands
Norway	2002	6,446	Statistics Norway
Spain	1993	8,400	Neymarc and Cervantes (1996, p. 85)
Sweden	2001	5,740	Statistics Sweden
United Kingdom	1993	17,000	Neymarc and Cervantes (1996, p. 85)
USA	2003	1,346,000	US Bureau of Census, Current Population Survey 2003
Canada	2001	239,160	Statistics Canada, 2001 Census
New Zealand	2001	10,137	New Zealand 2001 Census
Australia	2001	115,800	ABS 2004
Total		1,911,234	

Table 5.10   Australia: growth of the Philippines-born population

Year	Males	Females	Females (percentage)
1981	5,392	10,039	65.1
1986	10,380	23,347	69.2
1991	25,633	48,027	65.2
1996	32,326	60,623	65.2
2001	35,807	68,135	65.6
2002	40,300	75,500	65.2

Source: ABS 1981, 1986, 1991, 1996 and 2001 censuses; ABS 2004.

Female migrants from the Philippines fill many categories shown in Figure 5.1. Among labour migrants Filipino women take up a wide range of jobs but probably domestic work accounts for the largest number. The stock of Filipino domestic workers overseas was conservatively estimated in the mid 1990s to be half a million (Vasques, Tumbaga and Soriano Cruz 1995). The destinations of new hire official maids is shown in Table 5.11 and this indicates that the majority go to other Asian countries, especially Hong Kong which is considered to have around 100,000 Filipino maids (*Asian Migration News*, 16–30 September 2004) while Malaysia, Singapore and Taiwan are other important destinations. The involvement of Filipino women in the so-called entertainment industry is somewhat more controversial but it probably would be the largest supplier of entertainment workers. Filipinos are the largest group of entertainers entering Japan illegally (Miki 1995).

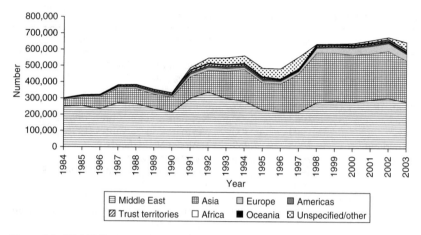

Figure 5.2   The Philippines: destination of overseas contract workers, 1984–2003

Source: Drawn from data in Battistella 1995; Scalabrini Migration Center 2000; Philippine Overseas Employment Administration, Department of Labour and Employment, Republic of the Philippines, http://www.poea.gov.ph/

Table 5.11   The Philippines: domestic service-workers destinations (New Hires) 1987–94

Region	1987		1994	
	No.	%	No.	%
Asia				
Hong Kong	10,731	21.5	23,779	31.0
Taiwan	1	–	9,399	12.2
Malaysia	2,040	4.1	5,875	7.7
Singapore	14,792	29.6	2,443	3.2
Others	1,490	3.0	1,462	1.9
Total	29,054	58.2	49,958	56.0
Middle East				
Saudi Arabia	6,484	13.0	17,755	23.1
UAE	6,958	13.9	6,970	9.1
Others	4,178	8.4	7,142	9.3
Total	17,620	35.3	31,867	41.5
Others	3,283	6.6	1,919	2.5
Total	49,957	100.0	76,744	100.0

Source: Hugo 1998, p. 113.

However, Filipino women overseas have a wide range of occupations. Table 5.12 shows a large proportion in the services category which demonstrates the predominance of maids and entertainers among the female migrants from the Philippines. Nevertheless other groups are represented. Filipino nurses both male and female have been an important migrant group

Table 5.12 The Philippines: deployment of newly hired female OCWs by skill category 2003 (%)

Skill category	%
Professionals and technical workers	38.46
Administrative and managerial workers	0.06
Clerical workers	1.26
Sales workers	0.80
Service workers	43.57
Agricultural workers	0.02
Production workers	10.72
For reclassification	5.13
Total	100.0

Source: Philippine Overseas Employment Administration 2004, p. 13.

(Ball 1990) and they predominate in the professional category. Indeed many nurse training organisations in the Philippines are oriented specifically to training nurses to work overseas. With respect to more permanent migration, the movement of Filipinos to more developed countries has been significant. There have been substantial movements of women who have married men via introductory agencies and pen pal clubs. Marriage migration has become significant to all of the major destinations shown in Table 5.9, but there have been particularly significant movements to Australia (Iredale 1994; Cahill 1990) Japan, North America and Europe. The movement of Filipino women to Australia has been dominantly in the family migration category comprising marriage migrants and the families they have subsequently brought to Australia.

The Philippines has been pro-active in developing policies to protect its female migrants. At different times it has placed bans on the deployment of female domestics to Saudi Arabia, Hong Kong and Singapore due to unacceptable treatment of Filipino women. Although the bulk of Filipino female migrant workers go into domestic or entertainment jobs, many are well educated with college degrees. The out-migration of nurses is increasing apace with the global shortage of trained medical professionals. The Philippine Nurses Association estimates that close to 40,000 Filipino nurses are now working in foreign hospitals and between 7000 and 10,000 more are leaving each year. They are especially directed to North America, Europe and Australasia (*Asian Migration News*, 16–31 August 2004). In the United Kingdom it was reported that of 27,171 foreign nurses recruited in 2003, some 12,000 were from the Philippines. The loss is increasingly being felt in Filipino hospitals many of which are experiencing nurse shortages (*Asian Migration News*, 1–16 June 2004). A growing group of emigrants are trained caregivers who will be in increasing demand in developing countries where the ageing of populations is leading to rapid increases in the numbers of aged people dependent on some form of care.

Vietnam

Vietnamese migration in the 1970s and 1980s mainly involved the more-or-less permanent dislocation of refugees and their families who moved initially to nearby countries in Southeast Asia but subsequently settled in more developed countries. While men may have predominated in the initial movement of refugees, women were very important and outnumbered men in the subsequent family migration and the Orderly Departure Program by which refugees brought out family members to join them in the United States, Canada, and Australia and others. Table 5.13 shows the numbers of Vietnamese-born recorded as living in a number of 'north' countries. As indicated earlier, in recent years, much of this movement has been of the family reunion kind and involves an over-representation of women. Many of the Vietnamese women settling in 'north' nations face difficulties with language and suffer discrimination and exploitation in the work place. Vietnamese women are often involved in outworking, especially in the government industry where they are often subject to exploitation (Cuc, Lieu and Cahill 1989).

An increasing area of concern in Vietnam is with the increasing involvement of Vietnamese women in marriage migration. One of the largest flows is to Taiwan where some 60,000 brides have gone in recent years (Hugo and Nguyen 2004). This involves intermediaries in both Vietnam and Taiwan and involves Taiwanese men coming to Vietnam and selecting a bride.

Table 5.13   Vietnamese-born persons living outside Vietnam

Country	Year	Number	Source
Australia	2002	171,600	ABS 2004
United States	2003	865,000	US Bureau of Census Current Population Survey, 2003
Canada	2001	150,135	Statistics Canada, Census of 2001
New Zealand	2001	3,948	New Zealand 2001 Census
Japan	2000	12,965	Japan Statistics Bureau, Population Census of 2000
Austria	2001	2,376	Statistics Austria
Denmark	2003	8,577	Statistics Denmark
Finland	2002	3,020	Statistics Finland
France	1993	33,700	Neymarc and Cervantes 1996, p. 85
Germany	1993	95,500	Neymarc and Cervantes 1996, p. 85
Netherlands	2003	11,656	Statistics Netherlands
Norway	2002	11,500	Statistics Norway
Sweden	2001	11,126	Statistics Sweden
Switzerland	1993	7,300	Neymarc and Cervantes 1996, p. 85
United Kingdom	1993	11,000	Neymarc and Cervantes 1996, p. 85
Total		1,399,403	

Currently, around a quarter of births occurring in Taiwan are to foreign women among whom Vietnamese women are important (Tsay 2004). Many of the Vietnamese women experience difficulties associated with language problems, cultural clash and the expectations of husbands (Hugo and Nguyen 2004). There are increasing flows of Vietnamese brides to Southern China and other destinations.

Turning to non-permanent international labour migration, there has been an increasing involvement of the Vietnamese in recent years. It is estimated that some 75,000 OCWs were sent abroad in 2003, when there was a stock of 350,000 Vietnamese migrants abroad (*Migrations News*, October 2004). While there are no data available it would seem that this movement is male dominated. The main destinations are Korea, Japan, Libya, Czech Republic, Yemen, Singapore, Laos and Malaysia (*Saigon Times Daily*, September 17, 1997). There was much more substantial migration in the 1980s to the then USSR and on the break up of the USSR many moved to Europe. Accordingly, in Germany there are estimated to be 40,000 undocumented Vietnamese who had applied for asylum. These were said to be among the 100,000 Vietnamese workers who once lived in East Germany (Atkinson 1995).

Thailand

Thailand differs from the countries considered so far in that it is both a significant origin and destination country of international migrants in the destination region. First, considering Thailand as an origin of permanent migrants, Table 5.14 shows the stocks in some 'north' countries. Females dominate among Thai immigrants and most of them arrive under the family migration category. Thailand is second only to the Philippines in the mail order bride system in Australia. Moreover, Thai sex workers are significant in Australia. Brockett (1996) has shown how there is a circuit for Thai sex workers moving into Australia whereby women work in other Asian destinations such as Japan. Brockett (1996) estimates that there are 250–300 Thai women working in the Sydney sex industry at anyone time. O'Connor's (1995) survey of 214 sex workers in Sydney found that 60 had been born in Thailand.

Table 5.14 Thai-born populations in developed countries

Country	Year	Number	Source
USA	2003	174,000	US Bureau of Census, Current Population Survey 2003
Canada	2001	8,770	Statistics Canada, Census of
New Zealand	2001	5,154	New Zealand 2001 Census
Australia	2002	27,000	ABS 2004
Japan	2000	23,967	Japan Statistics Bureau, Population Census of 2000

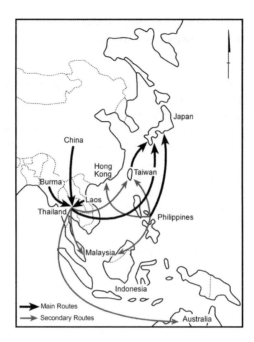

Map 5.4   Southeast Asia: trafficking of women and children
Source: *Far Eastern Economic Review*, 14 December 1995, p. 26.

Thai women are heavily involved in the migration of women within Asia in the so-called entertainment and sex industry. Map 5.4 shows that the dominant movement has been to Japan. One insidious element here has been the increased scale of trafficking of women from Thailand. The main routes for trafficking women and children in Southeast Asia and the centrality of Thailand in this pattern is evident in the map.

This trade is largely in the hands of organised crime, some of it involving diversification from the drug trade. There are an estimated 150,000 foreign sex workers in Japan alone, most of them Thais and Filipinos (Sherry *et al.*, 1995:24). It is clear that Southeast Asian women, especially Thais are living in virtual slavery in Japan. Miki (1995:21) found in a study of one of many shelters for foreign wives of Japanese men that of the 160 women helped by the shelter, 142 of them were Thais and 132 of them had been the victims of slavery. Skrobanek *et al.* (1997) have made a study of the trafficking of women in Thailand, and have graphically shown the misery experienced by women involved in this movement which dates back to the nineteenth century. However, this modern form of movement developed out of the expansion of the sex industry in the 1980s due to the basing of many US military men in Thailand. It grew in the 1980s and many thousands of Thai women were trafficked to Europe and Asia. The main routes of these women are identified as follows:

* Europe, especially Germany;
* Malaysia and Singapore;
* Hong Kong and Taiwan;
* Japan (in 1993 the Thai embassy in Japan estimated there were 80,000 to 100,000 Thai women working in Japanese industry).
* Smaller flows are to the United States, Australia, New Zealand, Canada and China.

The movement of OCWs out of Thailand involves both documented and undocumented migrants. Many of the women who are trafficked are undocumented migrants. The numbers officially leaving Thailand to work overseas have increased from 3851 in 1977 to 117,341 in 1982 and 123,054 in 1989 (Sussangkarn 1995:248). In more recent years they have increased to 185,436 in 1995, 202,296 in 1996 and 287,071 in the first ten months of 1997 (*Bangkok Post*, 12 December 1997) however, by 2003 they had declined to 147,769 (Janta_ Po 2004). Women make up a minority of these, accounting for only 20.2 per cent of the numbers leaving between 1990 and 1993 (43,902 – Skrobanek *et al.*, 1997:24) the main countries they are moving to include Hong Kong (44.4 per cent) Japan (22.3 per cent) and Germany (1.6 per cent). As is the case with Filipino women, the bulk of these women are involved as domestics and the entertainment industry, although at different times the Thai government banned the export of women to work as domestic labourers.

There is also a significant movement of people into Thailand especially from Myanmar, the other neighbouring countries of Cambodia and Laos and from South Asia. The ILO (2004) estimates that in 2002 there were around 1.1 million Burmese, 111,000 Laotians and 88,000 Cambodians living in Thailand. They also estimate that over 80,000 women and children from Myanmar, Laos and Yunnan (China) have been trafficked into Thailand. A great deal of this movement is undocumented. There has been a substantial refugee presence in Thailand for the last twenty years. The bulk of Vietnamese, Laotian and Cambodian movement has been restricted to countries from which the bulk of people have either been resettled in Third World nations or repatriated to their homeland. More recently there has been an influx of around 115,000 refugees from Myanmar many of whom have been settled near the Myanmar border in northwest Thailand (Elegant 1997). This movement has included more females than males.

More numerous in recent times has been an influx of around 780,000 to a million undocumented workers from Myanmar (*Bangkok Post*, 10 December 1997) although estimates of the total number of undocumented workers go up to 2 million (*International Herald Tribune*, 8 April 1996). Burmese are the largest group accounting for 60–70 per cent of illegal labour migrants. The others came from Cambodia, Laos, Southern China and South Asia (Stern 1996:100). Most work in jobs eschewed by the Thais, including construction, agriculture, fishing, warehouses, small factories and restaurants among men and women in domestic service and in the sex industry. There are estimated to be at least 20,000 Burmese girls working as prostitutes in Thai brothels (*Manila Chronicle*, 1 February 1994). Female sex workers are also bought in from southern China and even Europe (Skrobanek *et al.*, 1997:50–51). Bangkok has an Indian population of around 100,000, many of them living in a 'Little India' (Lintner 1995). The involvement of women in the illegal migration is not known but they would make up at least a third of such migrants.

Myanmar

Little is known about Burmese international migration. The major flow referred to in the last section involves illegal movement of up to a million people into neighbouring Thailand. Many of the migrants are drawn from minority groups like the Karen, Shan and Mon (*South Morning China Post*, 17 December 1997). It is apparent that females are well represented among the migrants from Myanmar to Thailand but males make up a majority of the migrants. The movement of Burmese out of the country to work in formal work contracts is minuscule despite the vast pool of excess labour in the country (2188 workers in the 1990–96 period – ILO 1997:26). Migration on a permanent basis out of Myanmar is quite small. As Table 5.12 shows, the movement to Australia, for example, is relatively small and much of the total 10,973 Burmese in Australia in 2001 is of relatively long standing. In 2003 there were 49,000 Burmese born in the United States (US Bureau of the Census, Current Population Survey 2003).

Between 1988 and 1991 it is estimated that 100,000 people left Myanmar because of the political repression (Lintner 1995). These tended to be drawn from among the most educated groups creating a brain drain effect. Most went initially to Bangkok and while many stayed on there, others were able to arrange legal, or more often illegal, entry to other countries (Lintner 1995). Some ended up working in the sweatshops of Taiwan, in the United States or Europe but Japan was a major destination of choice, so that by 1991 it had around 10,000 Burmese. Most of them are former University students whose university was closed down in 1988. Trafficking of Burmese women into Pakistan and Thailand has also increased substantially in recent years.

Laos

Laos has experienced both in- and out-migration. Currently out-migration of workers from Laos is largely seasonal movement of agricultural workers to neighbouring provinces of Thailand. The ILO (1997:27) has estimated that there are around 11,000 workers in Thailand. Trafficking of women and children into Thailand has also increased. There are also significant Lao

Table 5.15   Laos-born communities overseas

Country	Year	No. of Lao born	Source
USA	2003	127,000	US Bureau of Census, Current Population Survey 2003
Canada	2001	14,315	Statistics Canada, Census of 2001
New Zealand	2001	1,017	New Zealand 2001 Census
Australia	2001	9,565	ABS 2001 Census
France	1990	50,000	Neymarc and Cervantes 1996, p. 84
Japan	2000	1,433	Japan Statistics Bureau, Population Census of 2000

communities established in more developed countries based on the refugee movements out of Laos during the long Indo-Chinese war. Many Hmong and Lao people who were displaced went to camps in Thailand and subsequently settled elsewhere, especially North America. Table 5.15 shows the number of Lao people in each of the main destination countries. In Australia the sex ratio is 100.1 and this would suggest that women are well represented in these flows.

In addition to the out-movement of Lao there are some movements into the country. In 1996 there were some 12,832 foreign workers officially in the country. Some 40 per cent were from Vietnam, 22 per cent from China and 20 per cent from Thailand (ILO 1997:26–7). The bulk of these are males involved in construction (63% of workers) 12 per cent in services and 10 per cent in manufacturing.

Cambodia

Cambodia experienced substantial out-movement of refugees associated with the tragic upheavals of the two decades following the mid-1970s. Most moved initially to Thailand and the bulk of these have been repatriated back into Cambodia. Nevertheless, there was significant third country settlement of refugees as Table 5.16 shows.

The largest numbers were resettled in North America but Oceania and France were also significant. Females were important in this movement, with the pattern in Australia being indicative. In 2002 there were 25,500 Cambodian-born people in Australia with a sex ratio of 91.7. In mid-1991 there were more than 400,000 Cambodians in Thailand (Hovy 1991) in the refugee camps many of whom were repatriated to Cambodia subsequently. There was a refugee movement of 60,000 Cambodians into Thailand in 1997 following fighting between Hun Sen and Ranariddh forces (*The Straits Times*, 8 January 1998). There also have been reports of trafficking of women and children out of Cambodia into Thailand (*Hong Kong Standard*, 20 December 1997). The Cambodian government in the late 1990s developed a programme to send 300,000 Cambodian workers overseas to create an inflow of remittances (*Far Eastern Economic Review*, 3 August 1995). Some 100,000 Khmers fled across

Table 5.16   Cambodia-born communities overseas

Country	Year	No. of Cambodia born	Source
USA	2003	136,000	US Bureau of Census, Current Population Survey 2003
Canada	2001	18,965	Statistics Canada, Census of 2001
New Zealand	2001	4,770	New Zealand 2001 Census
Australia	2001	25,500	ABS 2004
France	1990	66,000	Neymarc and Cervantes 1996, p. 84

the Vietnamese border during the Khmer Rouge period and returned after the invasion of the Vietnamese Army (Desbarats 1995:101).

There has been a long-standing migration of Vietnamese into Cambodia. At the time of the coup against Sihanak in 1970 there were 500,000 Vietnamese in Cambodia. Subsequently there was much killing of Vietnamese and many of the rest returned to Vietnam but they began filtering back when Pol Pot was ousted by Hanoi. This was given a boost by the expansion of UN and other foreign activity in Cambodia which initiated a building boom in Phnom Penh. 'The majority of construction workers are Vietnamese. Hundreds of Vietnamese bar girls and prostitutes have flocked to 'brothels and dance halls' (Chanda 1992:15). The estimate is that their numbers have increased again to half a million, although statements range from 100,000 to 1 million (Desbarats 1995:102, Huguet 1997; Chanda 1992). Huguet estimates that there is an equal balance of males and females in incoming migrations into Cambodia (Huguet 1997:19). It is apparent that there is trafficking of women both into and out of Thailand (ILO 2004).

Brunei

Brunei is the smallest nation in Southeast Asia and is an oil-rich state with around 300,000 people. There is a substantial in-movement of workers to Brunei with 62,326 of the nation's 100,000 workers being foreigners. The main countries of origin are neighbouring ASEAN countries, especially Indonesia, Malaysia, Thailand and the Philippines. Males dominate in the movement and the bulk of migrants work in construction, manufacturing and the oil industry and in services (Gunasekaran 1994:45–56; Mani 1995:441–55). There are reports of women being trafficked to Brunei for sex work. The bulk of female in-migration, however, is of domestic workers, especially from Indonesia.

Malaysia

Like Thailand, Malaysia is both a significant importer and exporter of migrants. Its role as a major target for labour migrants, especially from Indonesia has already been discussed. Nevertheless, it is a significant target

Table 5.17 Malaysia: citizenship of population at the 1990 and 2001 censuses

	1990		2000	
	No.	%	No.	%
Citizens	16,812,300	95.72	21,889,946	94.05
Non-citizens	751,700	4.28	1,384,744	5.95

Source: Kassim 1998, p. 274 and 2002, p. 29.

Table 5.18 Foreign workers in Malaysia, 1 July 2001

Nationalities	%
Indonesia	77.64
Bangladesh	17.54
Filipinos	1.90
Thais	0.80
Pakistan	0.40
Others	5.80
Total %	100.00
Total Number	807,984

Job sectors	%
Manufacturing	30.08
Plantations	25.59
Domestic helpers	20.40
Construction	8.57
Services	7.32
Total %	100.00
Total Number	807,984

Source: Kassim 2002, p. 31.

of migrants from other Asian countries. Table 5.17 shows that at the 2000 Census less than 6 per cent of the population had non-Malaysian citizenship. However, Table 5.18 shows there were almost a million legal foreign workers in Malaysia in 2001 and this did not include illegal workers who were officially estimated at around 40,000 to 500,000 but almost certainly exceeded this figure (Kassim 1998:273 and 2002:31). The representation of females among this inflow is not known but it is believed that males outnumber females and the latter probably make up between a quarter and a third of immigrants.

However, as indicated earlier, there has been a substantial outflow in the opposite direction. One element in this has been the movement on a more or less permanent basis of Malaysians to a number of more developed countries (Tasker and Aznam 1987). Table 5.19 shows that Australia has been dominant among these destinations. The sex ratio of Malaysian settlers in Australia in 2002 was 88.6. This would suggest that there is probably a relatively balanced sex ratio among these migrants. There has also been a major outflow of students from Malaysia to study in these countries. Again a relative balance in the number of males and females is in evidence.

It is not only the more permanent migration which is important in the movement out of Malaysia but there are significant temporary outflows of labour migrants. The movement to Brunei has been mentioned but the movement to closer Singapore has been more significant. Pang (1994:79–94) estimates that in the late 1980s there were 100,000 Malaysians working in Singapore, predominantly in the manufacturing, construction and shipyard industries and there were around another 20,000 who commute daily from Johore to work in Singapore. In Japan, in addition to a small number of permanent settlers, there has been a significant movement of labour, much of it undocumented. The significance of this arises from the fact that in 1993 some 29,840 Malaysians were detected in Japan as visa overstayers. Female migrant workers make up about one third of Malaysian migrants in Japan (Kassim 1998). Sazaki (1994:565–77) indicates that Malaysian workers are confined to low-status jobs as construction, production, transport, and other such manual work; cooks, dishwashers, hosts and hostesses, waitresses or bartenders, prostitutes and other services. Of the 29,840 Malaysian overstayers in Japan in May 1993, 9590 were women (Shah and Menon 1997:13).

It is clear that Malaysian women are, like the Thais, engaged in the international trafficking of women. For example, on 27 September 1997, Canadian and US police co-operated in raids in California and Toronto rescuing more than 20 Thai and Malaysian women from brothels where they were being forced to work and live in debt-bondage. Similarly, in Australia well-organised crime gangs are smuggling women from all over Asia to work as prostitutes in Sydney, Melbourne and Brisbane where they are starved, have no freedom,

Table 5.19 Malaysian-born communities overseas

Country	Year	No. of Malaysianborn	Source
USA	2003	34,000	US Bureau of Census, Current Population Survey 2003
Canada	2001	21,485	Statistics Canada, Census of 2001
New Zealand	2001	11,460	New Zealand 2001 Census
Australia	2002	89,600	ABS 2004
Japan	2000	5,849	Japan Statistics Bureau, Census of 2000

have unprotected sex and have to service debts of between $A40,000 and $A50,000. Some 67 were deported in the last half of 1997 (*Australian*, 23 February 1998). Taiwan is an important destination, again predominantly for illegal migrants. Tsay (1995:13–19) notes 2186 legal Malaysian workers in Taiwan but there were many more of them. Many of these are clearly women and they are employed in the entertainment/tourist industry and, to a lesser extent, in manufacturing. In Hong Kong, Skeldon (1994:543–54) indicated that there were 11,700 Malaysians in the early 1990s.

Singapore

Singapore is one of the major destinations of migrants in Southeast Asia but in recent years government sensitivity about migration of workers has prevented them from publishing details of migrant workers in the island republic. The country does have a policy of accepting highly skilled foreigners as settlers (Hiebert 1996). While the country has draconian measures, including beating as punishment for illegal migrants, it is apparent that illegal migration is significant. Much of it occurs from Malaysia and Indonesia which are visible from the shores of Singapore. Singapore in 1996 had 3 million residents and about 500,000 foreigners who are blue-collar workers and 53,000 who are skilled professionals with about 30,000 new permanent residents in 1996 short of the governments goal of 35,000 per year (*Straits Times*, 27 October 1997). Migrants make up between a quarter and a third of workers in Singapore. Detection of illegal migrants is increasing, averaging 580 per month in 1996 (*Straits Times*, 12 October 1996). As indicated earlier, Malaysians and Indonesians make up a major part of the foreign workforce. Filipinos make up a major part of the foreign population numbering around 75,000 in 1996 (*Philippine Daily Inquirer*, 5 February 1996) the Thais 40,000 (*Straits Times*, 6 May 1995) and the Indians and Bangladesh 30,000. The fact that Singapore regards foreign workers as a stop-gap solution to meeting labour demands is reflected in the fact that in the 1984–85 recession 200,000 foreign workers were sent home (Salaff 1990:113).

One of the major elements in the overseas migration is domestic maids, increasing from 20,000 in 1987 to 40,000 in 1988 and 80,000 in 1995 (Huang and Yeoh 1996:484) with the number probably currently being around 100,000. Filipinos make up around three quarters, one-fifth from Indonesia and most of the rest from Sri Lanka. Women, hence, do make up a major part of the overseas migration to Singapore since they are not only overwhelmingly dominant among domestic maids but also are significant among other skilled and unskilled migrants. The role of the maids is seen as being to release Singaporean women for work outside the home and the government insists that employers of maids pay a substantial monthly levy to the government.

Singapore also experiences permanent out-migration to MDCs and Table 5.20 shows that the movement to North America and Oceania has been

Table 5.20   Singapore-born communities overseas

Country	Year	No. of Singapore-born	Source
Australia	2002	37,900	ABS 2004
New Zealand	2001	3,912	New Zealand 2001 Census
Canada	2001	9,635	Statistics Canada, Census of 2001
USA	2003	33,000	U.S. Bureau of Census, Current Population Survey 2003

small. Nevertheless, it is significant that they tend to be highly educated and some have argued that this represents a brain drain to Singapore (Teng 1993).

Policy issues

A number of policy issues arise in the discussion of female migration in Southeast Asia. There is a lack of policy development in this area except in the case of the Philippines which has been more pro-active in taking steps to protect its overseas migrants than many other countries of the region. For example, the Philippines is the only country in the region to ratify both the

- United Nations Convention on the Protection of the Rights of All Migrant Workers and Members of their Families;
- ILO conventions:
  - 97. Migration for Employment 1949;
  - 86. Migration for Employment 1949;
  - 143. Migrant Workers 1975;
  - 151. Migrant Workers 1975.

Despite the significance of migration in the region until recently there has been little attempt to develop a regional Southeast Asian agreement on migration at all, let alone female migration specifically. This is despite some, but limited progress in liberalising trade between countries of the region through AFTA – the ASEAN Free Trade Agreement (Hugo 1998). There are signs, however, that since the events of September 11, co-operation in the migration area is increasing (Hugo 2004).

In considering policy aspects of female migration I need to differentiate policy aspects relating to all migration and those which are specifically relating to women. Lim and Oishi (1996, p. 32) have suggested that the policy aspects of female migration are best approached through consideration of

- Issues relating to the country of destination.
- Issues relating to the country of origin.
- Issues relating to the female migrants themselves.

I examine the third of these first. An issue of paramount significance relates to the *protection* of female migrants. It is apparent from what has been considered so far that many female migrants are put into a very vulnerable situation by virtue of being both female and a migrant and on occasion, their jeopardy is increased by being illegally present at the destination. The abuse and exploitation of Southeast Asian migrant women remains substantial and policies and programmes regarding women are largely ineffective. Countries of origin of course find it difficult to protect their nationals overseas, especially when those nationals are not documented.

One of the ways in which Southeast Asian countries have attempted to protect female migrant workers is to place restrictions on their movement. Table 5.21 lists some of the restrictions placed on female migration by authorities in the main Southeast Asian countries of origin of migrant workers. However, placing bans and restrictions of movements of women has generally been counterproductive. Bans on movement results in the migration being driven underground so the migrant women have to be undocumented and even more vulnerable to exploitation and abuse. Restrictions also tend to lead to lying and bribery of officials. The forging of birth, marriage, nationality certificates, identify cards and passports has become an industry in the region.

One of the major ways in which migrant women can be effectively protected in destinations is through thorough preparation. The countries vary in the preparation given to women. For example, domestic workers leaving Indonesia for Saudi Arabia are supposed to receiving training in

- basic Arabic;
- basic Arab culture;
- training in a mock up of a Saudi Arabian house with appropriate appliances and so on.

Table 5.21 Restrictions on female workers migration in Southeastern Asian countries of origin

Country	Restrictions
Myanmar	Ban on recruitment of female workers except in the case of professionals.
Indonesia	Women must be at least 22 years of age; restrictions regarding place of employment for household workers and male/female ratio recruited by authorised agents may be lifted under certain conditions.
Malaysia	None
Philippines	Selective ban on the employment of female domestic workers according to country of employment; women intending to work as entertainers must be certified by Professional Entertainers Certification Centre. *April 1996:* Ban on migration of female domestics to Kuwait since 1988. Domestic workers must be 25 years of age and performing artists must be 21.
Thailand	Ban on recruitment of women except in the case of selected countries of employment.

Source: Shah and Menon 1997, p. 19, Lim and Oishi 1996, p. 41.

Table 5.22 Indonesia: surveyed domestic maids by training received and perceived competency

Subject	Receiving practical training				Perceived competent	
	Rural (n = 28)		Urban (n = 23)			
	no.	%	no.	%	Rural	Urban
Arabic	7	25.0	16	69.6	5	4
Cooking	2	7.1	21	91.3	2	0
Child caring	18	64.3	5	21.7	3	1
Table arrangement	15	53.6	19	82.6	1	2
Laundry	6	21.4	13	56.5	1	2
House cleaning	16	57.1	18	78.3	0	1
Ironing	16	57.1	18	78.3	0	0
Bed-making	15	53.6	16	69.6	0	1
Pancasila/P4	5	17.9	4	17.4	5	1
Self protection in case of being harassed	2	7.1	2	8.7	11	2
Contact the embassy	2	7.1	1	4.3	7	7
Posting letter	6	21.4	4	17.4	1	4
Sending remittance	2	7.1	4	17.4	1	7
Using public transport	9	32.1	4	17.4	1	4
Contact labour recruiting company	2	7.1	1	4.3	11	6

Source: Wijaya 1992, p. 110.

The reality is that the training is often perfunctory and ineffective. For example, few take Arabic because they have learned the Koran but find they have little effective proficiency in Arabic when they get to Saudi Arabia (Wijaya 1992:100). The training is predominantly undertaken by recruiting companies in the major cities especially Jakarta. A study in Indonesia found that not all female migrant domestic workers received training in all areas relevant to their work and as Table 5.22 shows few considered themselves competent in a number of areas.

Clearly, female workers need to be carefully trained in how to deal with problems at the destination and this is not happening in an effective way. There are no regulations which protect such workers abroad and ways have to be developed to provide protection. The most promising avenues appear to be self-help organisations and NGOs which have been developed to protect migrant women. Religious-based groups have in some cases been effective in this. However, the sending country needs to have the political will and commitment to support such activities.

Shah and Menon (1997:7) have listed the types of exploitation and violence which have been perpetuated against migrant women workers from Asia and these are listed in Table 5.23.

NGOs in Indonesia report that abuse of Indonesian domestics is commonplace but is rarely reported because of a lack of effective mechanisms and because women fear that they may lose their husbands in the home village and have their reputations damaged. Suicide and deaths of women in Saudi Arabia are surprisingly high. A number have been executed in Saudi Arabia for killing their employers (e.g., *Jakarta Post*, 17 October 1997). The execution of Flor Contemplacion, a Filipino domestic worker in Singapore led to a major rift between Singapore and The Philippines (Battistella 1995).

Table 5.23 A suggested list of indicators to measure violence against migrant women

A. Economic violence

In home country	– Overcharging for visas and processing
	– Excessive amounts of interest charged by money lenders used for raising money for the move
	– Misuse of remittances by husband or other relatives (contrary to migrant's wishes)
In host country	– Non-payment of wages
	– Violation of the salary agreement in contract
	– Delay in wage payment
	– Difficulties in sending remittances

B. Social/psychological violence

In home country	– Ill treatment of children left behind
	– Extra-marital affairs, or alcoholism of husband
In host country	– Living conditions in terms of space, holidays, free time, working hours, and type of work
	– Access to friends and social network from home country
	– Social isolation and somatic and psycho-somatic illnesses

C. Physical/sexual violence

In home country	– Abuse and abandonment by agents
In host country	– Verbal abuse and ridicule
	– Beating
	– Sexual abuse including rape
	– Imprisonment and deportation (legality of this, proof required, and ability for defence)
	– Delay in deportation
	– Illegal pregnancy, treatment of mother and child
	– Murder

Source: Shah and Menon, 1997, p. 7.

The obvious need is for bilateral and multilateral agreements between countries which protect female workers and indeed all migrant workers. The need to develop an international regime for migrant workers as has been done for refugees is important. Lim and Oishi (1996, pp. 43–50) have given some highly relevant indications of how this can be done. They conclude that the following needs to be done

- the regulation of recruitment agencies;
- legal, social and educational outreach to migrant women;
- training female police officers and protection from male officers;
- better enforcement of existing laws;
- involvement of trade unions;
- implementation of relevant UN resolutions and reporting mandates, and;
- enforcement of national labour standards for all workers that conform to international guidelines.
- the international community, including the United Nations, the specialised agencies such as the ILO, intergovernmental organisations and non-governmental organisations should take advantage of this momentum of growing concern to promote more concerted actions for the protection of this highly vulnerable group.

Within countries of origin of female migrants several of these steps are relevant. Lim and Oishi (1996:34) point out that the policies of labour export countries have three main and interrelated objectives

- the promotion of labour exports;
- the protection of migrant workers;
- the maximisation of the developmental impact of migration.

Many of the initiatives taken in these areas are gender neutral but several in fact have an important gender dimension. The range of policy intervention are presented in Table 5.24 and it appears that many of these policies are in fact gender sensitive.

Much of this discussion with respect to policy has focused on Southeast Asian women's involvement in international contract labour migration since it is in this area that most exploitation tends to occur. Nevertheless, there are a number of issues relating to more permanent movement. In many cases, the policy issues are the same for both men and women but some relating specifically to women need to be mentioned.

- In the area of marriage migration there is a need to protect the rights and interests of the women involved.
- The rights of all migrants should be respected and protected especially those in the workplace and in the community more generally.

Table 5.24 Emigration policy and gender implications

Goals	Policy interventions	Gender implications
Promote employment	*Foreign market development*	
	1. Establishment of diplomatic relations	gender-neutral
	2. Strengthening placement services, public and private	gender-selective/selective
	3. Promotions and marketing missions	gender-selective
	4. Market information and research	gender-selective
	5. Bilateral agreements	gender-sensitive
	Manpower supply management	
	1. Manpower registry	gender-selective
	2. Corporate export of services	gender-selective
	3. Restrictions/policies against brain drain	gender-selective
Protect and promote well-being of migrants	*Standard setting and enforcement*	
	1. Minimum standards for employment contracts	gender-neutral
	2. Exit control measures	gender-selective/sensitive
	3. Social security arrangements	gender-selective
	4. Restrictions on exit of selected categories of workers especially minors and young women	gender-sensitive
	Supervision of private recruitment	
	1. Licensing of firms in recruitment	gender-neutral
	2. Performance guarantees and penalties	gender-neutral
	3. Limits to recruitment fees	gender-neutral
	4. Measures against illegal recruitment and clandestine migration	gender-neutral
	Welfare services	
	1. Information and counselling services prior to departure	gender-sensitive
	2. Labour Attaché services on site	gender-sensitive
	3. Community facilities/centres for workers abroad	gender-sensitive
	4. Support services to families left behind	gender-sensitive
	5. Returnee training and employment assistance	gender-sensitive
	6. Emergency evacuation or repatriation	gender-sensitive
Maximise developmental impact of labour migration	*Remittances of migrants' earnings*	
	1. Foreign exchange market policies	gender-neutral
	2. Remittance policies and services	gender-neutral
	Migrants' savings and investments	
	1. Special financial instruments	gender-neutral
	2. Information and support services to small investors	gender-neutral
	3. Housing programmes for migrants	gender-neutral
	Return of talents and skills	
	1. Special placement services and incentives	gender-sensitive
	2. Bilateral training agreements	gender-sensitive

Source: Lim and Oishi, 1996.

- Migrants should not be impeded in maintaining strong linkages with their country of origin and in their cultural and language maintenance and religious observance activities.
- Many women migrants are in vulnerable occupational and living situations and need access to resources and awareness of empowerment to overcome this vulnerability be made available.

Overall, in immigration countries there is a need to inject gender sensitivity into policies and programs relating to female migrants. This involves taking account of the initiatives presented above but taking account of the particular needs of migrant women (United Nations 1995).

Conclusion

The migration of women in Southeast Asia remains under-studied in the region and the policy interventions related to them are limited and ineffective. There is evidence that migration can, but not necessarily does, enhance the position of women in the region (Hugo 1997) but migrant women remain more vulnerable to exploitation and abuse than their male counterparts. There is a pressing need to move towards a regime which recognises the inevitability and increasing size of this movement and influences it so that its benefits can be maximised to the migrants themselves and their families, as well as to their countries of origin and destination.

Acknowledgement

The author would like to acknowledge the Australian Research Council's support of this research. He would also like to thank Ms Janet Wall, Ms Margaret Young and Ms Maria Fugaro for their help in preparing this article.

Permanent movement is defined by DIMIA as persons migrating to Australia and residents departing permanently; *Long term movement* is defined by DIMIA as temporary visa holders arriving and residents departing temporarily with the intention to stay in Australia or abroad for twelve months or more, and the departure of temporary visa holders and the return of residents who had stayed in Australia or abroad for twelve months or more.

References

Aiken, L.H., J.Buchan, J.Sochalski, B. Nichols, and M. Powell (2004) 'Trends in International Nurse Migration', *Health Affairs*, Vol. 23, No. 3: 69–77.

Atkinson, R. (1995) 'Cold War Bell Tolls for Berlin's Little Hanoi', *Washington Post*, 16 June.

Australian Bureau of Statistics (ABS) (2004) *Migration Australia 2002–03*, Catalogue No. 3412.0, ABS, Canberra.

Ball, R. (1990) 'The Process of International Contract Labour Migration: The Case of Filipino Nurses', Unpublished PhD thesis, University of Sydney.

Battistella, B. (1995) 'Philippine Overseas Labour: From Export to Management', *ASEAN Economic Bulletin*, Vol. 12, No. 2: 257–74.

Brockett, L. (1996) 'Thai Sex Workers in Sydney: A Study of Labour and Migration', Unpublished MA Thesis, Department of Geography, University of Sydney.

Cahill, D. (1990) *Intermarriages in International Contexts: A Study of Filipino Women Married to Australian, Japanese and Swiss Men* (Quezon City: Scalabrini Migration Centre).

Castles, S., H. Booth, and P. Wallace (1984) *Here for Good: West Europe's Ethnic Minorities* (London: Pluto Press).

Chanda, N. (1992) 'Wounds of History', *Far Eastern Economic Review*, 30 July: 14–16.

Cuc, L.T., L.T. Lieu and D.Cahill. (1989) 'Vietnamese Female Outworkers in Melbourne's Western Suburbs', *Asian Migrant*, Vol. 2, No. 3: 95–98.

Departemen Tenaga Kerja, Republic of Indonesia (1998) *Strategi Penempatan Tenaga Kerja Indonesia Ke Luar Negeri* (Jakarta, Departemen Tenaga Kerja) Republic of Indonesia.

Desbarats, J. (1995) *Prolific Survivors: Population Change in Cambodia 1975–1993* (Tempe: Arizona State University).

Elegant, S. (1997) 'Wasted Days of Their Lives', *Far Eastern Economic Review*, 22 May: 66.

Gunasekaran, S. (1994) 'Cross National Flows within Asean: Patterns and Problems', in W. Gooneratne, P.L. Martin and H. Sazanami (eds) *Regional Development Impacts of Labour Migration in Asia* (UNCRD) Research Report Series, No. 2, Nagoya, Japan.

Haris, A. (1997) *Mobilitas Ilegal Orang Sasak Ke Malaysia Barat: Proses dan Dampaknya Bagi Daerah Asal*, Kepada Program Pasca Sarjana, Universitas Gadjah Mada, Yogyakarta.

Hiebert, M. (1996) 'Help Wanted', *Far Eastern Economic Review*, 6 June: 67.

Hovy, B. (1991) 'Southeast Asian Refugees: Tide Set to Turn?', *Population*, Vol. 17, No. 12: 2.

Huang, S and B.S.A Yeoh (1996) 'Ties that Bind: State Policy and Migrant Female Domestic Helpers in Singapore', *Geoforum*, Vol. 27, No. 4, pp. 479–93.

Hugo, G.J. (2004) 'Regional Patterns of International Co-operation on Migration Issues in Asia, Present and Future: Australia'. Paper prepared for the Workshop on International Migration and Labour Markets in Asia organised by the Japan Institute for Labour Policy and Training (JILPT) supported by the Ministry of Health, Labour and Welfare, Japan (MHLW) Organisation for Economic Cooperation and Development (OECD) and the International Labour Office (ILO) Tokyo, Japan, 5–6 February.

—— (2000) 'Labour Migration from East Indonesia to East Malaysia', *Revue Européene des Migrations Internationales*, Vol.16, No.1: 97–124.

—— (1998) 'International Migration in Eastern Indonesia'. Paper prepared for East Indonesia Project, ANU, Canberra.

—— (1991) 'Knocking at the Door: Asian Immigration to Australia', *Asian and Pacific Migration Journal*, Vol.1 No.1: 100–144.

Hugo, G.J. and Nguyen Thi, H.X. (2004) 'Marriage Migration Between Vietnam and Taiwan: A View from Vietnam'. Paper presented at 12th Biennial Conference of the Australian Population Association, Canberra, 15–17 September.

Huguet, J.W. (1997) *The Population of Cambodia, 1980–1996, and Projected to 2020* (Phnom Penh, Cambodia: National Institute of Statistics, Ministry of Planning).

Inglis, C. (2002) 'Malaysia Wavers on Labor Crackdown', *Migration Information Source*, http://www.migrationinformation.org/feature/print.cfm? ID = 63.

International Labour Office (ILO) (2004) 'Mekong Sub-Regional Project to Combat Trafficking in Children and Women', International Programme on the Elimination of Child Labour (IPEC) Thailand, http://www.ilo.org/public/english/region/asro/bangkok/child/trafficking/wherewework-thailanddetail.htm.

International Labour Office (ILO) (1997) *Cooperation in Employment Promotion and Training in the Greater Mekong Subregion.* Interim Report TA No. 5681-REG, The ILO East Asia Multi-disciplinary Advisory Team (ILO/EASMAT) Bangkok, Thailand.

Iredale, R. (1994) 'Patterns of Spouse/Finance Sponsorship to Australia', *Asian and Pacific Migration Journal*, Vol. 3, No. 4: 547–66.

Janta_ Po, A. (2004) 'Forced Migration in Thailand: Problems Involving Trafficking of Thai Workers Abroad', Presentation to International Conference on 'Toward New Perspectives on Forced Migration in Southeast Asia' organised by Research Centre for Society and Culture (PMP) at the Indonesian Institute of Sciences (LIPI) and Refugee Studies Centre (RSC) at the University of Oxford, Jakarta.

Jones, S. (1996) 'Women Feed Malaysian Boom', *Inside Indonesia*, No. 47, July–September: 16–18.

Kapioru, C. (1995) *Laporan Penelitian – Mobilitas Pekerja Yang Berstatus Suami, dan Dampaknya Terhadap Perubahan Status Wanita dan Kondisi Sosial Ekonomi Rumah Tangga*, Pusat Studi Kependudukan Universitas Nusa Cendana.

Kassim, A. (2002) 'Economic Slowdown and its Impact on Cross-National Migration and Policy on Alien Employment in Malaysia', Malaysia Country Report 2002 presented at Workshop on International Migration and Labour Market in Asia organised by the Japan Institute of Labour (JIL) supported by Ministry of Health, Labour and Welfare, Japan, OECD and ILO, held at JIL, Tokyo, 4–5 February.

—— (1998) 'International Migration and its Impact on Malaysia', in M. J. Hassan (ed.) *A Pacific Peace: Issues and Responses* (Kuala Lumpur: ISIS) pp. 273–304.

Keeley, C.B. (1981) 'Global Refugee Policy: The Case for a Development Oriented Strategy', The Population Council Public Issues Papers on Population, New York.

Lim, Lin Lean. and Oishi, N. (1996) 'International Labor Migration of Asian Women: Distinctive Characteristics and Policy Concerns', in G. Battistella and A. Paganoni (eds) *Asian Women in Migration* (Quezon City: Scalabrini Migration Centre) pp. 23–54.

Lintner, B. (1995) 'Bangkok's Little India', *Far Eastern Economic Review*, 16 March: 50–51.

Loveband, A. (2003) *Positioning the Product: Indonesian Migrant Women Workers in Contemporary Taiwan*, Southeast Asia Research Centre Working Paper Series No. 43, City University of Hong Kong.

Mani, A. (1995) 'Migration in Brunei Darussalam', in O. Jin Jui, C. Kwok Bun and C. Soon Beng (eds) *Crossing Borders – Transmigration in Asia Pacific* (Singapore: Prentice Hall) chapter 25.

Miki, E. (1995) 'Foreign Women in Japan: Victims of Slavery', *Asian Migrant*, Vol. 8, No. 1: 20–23.

Nasution, M.A. (1997) *Aliran Pekerja Indonesia Ke Malaysia: Kes Tentang Pekerja Indonesia Dalam Sektor Pembinaan Di Kuala Lumpur, Malaysia*, Fakulti Sains Kemasyarakatan dan Kemanusiaan Universiti Kebangasaan Malaysia, Bangi.

Neymarc, K. and Cervantes, M. (1996) 'Asian Migration to OECD Countries', in OECD, *Migration and the Labour Market in Asia: Prospects to the Year 2000* (France: OECD) pp. 75–96.

O'Connor, C. (1995) *Predictors of Sexually Transmitted Infections and Condom Usage in Local and International Sex Workers in Sydney*, Masters Treatise, Master of Medicine (Sexual Health) University of Sydney.

Pang, E.F. (1994) 'Foreign Workers in Singapore', in W. Gooneratne, P.L. Martin and H. Sazanami (eds) *Regional Development Impacts of Labour Migration in Asia*, UNCRD Research Report Series No. 2, Nagoya, Japan, pp. 79–94.

Paramasivam, S.R.S. (1996) 'The Dynamics of Indonesian Illegal Immigration to Malaysia: A Case Study of Kuala Lumpur and its Periphery', M.A. Thesis, Population Studies Programme, University of Malaya, Kuala Lumpur.

Philippine Overseas Employment Administration (2004) *Annual Report 2003*, POEA, Republic of the Philippines.

Piper, N. and Roces, M. (eds) (2003) *Wife or Worker? Asian Women and Migration* (Maryland, USA: Rowman and Littlefield).

Pusat Penelitian Kependudukan, Universitas Gadjah Mada (1986) *Mobilitas Angkalan Kerja ke Timur Tengah*, Gadjah Mada University, Yogyakarta.

Salaff, J.W. (1990) 'Women, the Family and the State: Hong Kong, Taiwan, Singapore – Newly Industrialised Countries in Asia', in S. Stichter and J. L. Parpart (eds) *Women, Employment and the Family in the International Division of Labour* (Basingstoke: Macmillan) pp. 98–136.

Sazaki, S. (1994) 'Clandestine Labour in Japan: Sources, Magnitude and Implications', in W. Gooneratne, P.L. Martin and H. Sazanami (eds) *Regional Development Impacts of Labour Migration in Asia*, UNCRD Research Report Series No. 2, Nagoya, Japan, pp. 151–62.

Scalabrini Migration Centre (2000) *Asian Migration Atlas 2000*, http://www.scalabrini.asn.au/atlas/amatlas.htm.

Schloss, G. (2002) 'A Growing Army of Southeast Asian Domestic Helpers is Enabling More Mothers to Work', *South China Morning Post*, 9 December.

Shah, N.M. and Menon, I. (1997) 'Violence Against Women Migrant Workers: Issues, Data and Partial Solutions', *Asian and Pacific Migration Journal*, Vol. 6, No. 1: 5–30.

Sherry, A., Lee, M. and Vatikiotis, M. (1995) 'For Lust or Money', *Far Eastern Economic Review*, 14 December: 22–23.

Sherry, V.N. (2004) 'Bad Dreams: Exploitation and Abuse of Migrant Workers in Saudi Arabia', *Human Rights Watch*, Vol. 16, No. 5(E) (July).

Singhanetra-Renard, A. (1986) 'The Middle East and Beyond: Dynamics of International Labour Circulation Among Southeast Asian Workers', Mimeo.

Skeldon, R. (1994) 'Turning Points in Labour Migration: The Case of Hong Kong', *Asian and Pacific Migration Journal*, Vol. 3, No. 1: 93–118.

Skrobanek, S., Boonpakdee, N. and Jantateero, C. (1997) *The Traffic in Women: Human Realities of the International Sex Trade* (London and New York: Zed Books).

Soeprobo, T.B. (2003) 'Recent Trends of International Migration in Indonesia'. Paper presented at the Workshop on International Migration and Labour Markets in Asia, Japan Institute of Labour, Tokyo, Japan, 6–7 February.

Soeprobo, T.B. (2004) 'Recent Trends of International Migration in Indonesia'. Paper presented at the Workshop on International Migration and Labour Markets in Asia, Japan Institute of Labour, Tokyo, Japan, 5–6 February.

Stern, A. (1996) 'Thailand's Illegal Labor Migrants', *Asian Migrant*, Vol. 9, No. 4: 100–03.

Sussangkarn, C. (1995) 'Labour Market Adjustments and Migration in Thailand', *ASEAN Economic Bulletin*, Vol. 12, No. 2: 237–54.

Suyono, M. (1981) 'Tenaga Kerja Indonesia di Timur Tengah Makin Mantap', *Suara Karya*, h.v.k.:2–6.

Tasker, R. and Aznam, S. (1987) 'Voting With Their Feet', *Far Eastern Economic Review*, 26 November: 21–23.

Teng, M.Y. (1993) 'Brain Drain or Links to the World: Views on Emigrants from Singapore', Paper prepared for the Asia-Pacific Migration Affecting Australia Conference organised by the Bureau of Immigration and Population Research, Darwin, 14–17 September.

Tsay, C.L. (1995) 'Taiwan', *ASEAN Economic Bulletin*, Vol. 12, No. 2: 175–90.

Tsay, C.L. (2004) 'Marriage Migration of Women from China and Southeast Asia to Taiwan', in G.W. Jones and K. Ramdas (eds) (*Un)tying the Knot: Ideal and Reality in Asian Marriage* (Singapore: Asia Research Institute, National University of Singapore) pp. 173–91.

United Nations (UN) (1995) *International Migration Policies and the Status of Female Migrants* (New York: United Nations).

Varia, N. (2004) 'Help Wanted: Abuses against Female Migrant Domestic Workers in Indonesia and Malaysia', *Human Rights Watch*, Vol. 16, No. 9(B) July.

Vasquez, N.D., Tumbaga, L.C. and Cruz-Soriano, M. (1995) *Tracer Study on Filipino Domestic Helpers Abroad* (Geneva: International Organisation for Migration).

Wijaya, H. (1992) 'Trade in Domestic Helpers-Indonesia', Report for Asian and Pacific Development Centre and ISS, Colombo, Sri Lanka.

Part II

Crossing Borders: The State, Migration Strategies and Temporary Migrant Worker Schemes

6

Trading Labour: Socio-economic and Political Impacts and Dynamics of Labour Export from the Philippines, 1973–2004

Rochelle Ball

The international labour migration of temporary and contracted foreign workers has become one of the most important contemporary labour supply systems for labour-deficit nations and a critical source of foreign exchange earnings for labour-exporting nations. No region in the world has been more profoundly affected by the rapid growth of global demand for migrant workers than in South East Asia. Since the early 1970s, the Philippines has been the dominant labour exporter in the region in terms of the magnitude of its labour trade. Both ordinary Filipinos and the Philippine State have increasingly embraced labour export as a palliative against an ailing economy and extensive poverty, to the extent that even contemplating a future without exporting workers would be untenable for the livelihoods of millions of people, and for national economic and political security. In fact, the Philippines has actively globalised and transformed its economy and society through labour export as a quasi-development strategy, despite the fact it is highly contentious and fraught with political difficulties for the Philippine state resulting from wide-ranging levels labour and human abuse of its nationals working overseas.

Introduction

The Philippines is one of the major contemporary countries of migration – perhaps even the largest migrant nation with Filipino migrants found in more than 181 countries. As a labour-exporting nation the Philippines ranks second in the world, next only to Mexico (Carlos 2002:81). For over thirty years now, since the OPEC oil crisis of 1973, the Philippines has been a labour-exporting nation that has supplied workers to labour-deficit and/or capital-rich nations. While the export of labour was promoted by the state as a temporary measure for over twenty-five years, this phenomenon has not only persisted but greatly expanded over the last three decades. In fact, this migration has experienced sustained growth for almost the whole period from 1973 to 2002, except for the years 1984–86 when significant changes in the demand for workers began to occur, and in 2003 (see below).

This chapter examines international labour migration from the Philippines primarily from the 'supply side'. The overall context of the labour trade from the Philippines is provided through a brief history of contract labour migration beginning with the OPEC oil crisis of early 1970s. The chapter then turns to examine the globalisation of labour from the Philippines in terms of its historical and contemporary magnitude, its highly gendered nature, and occupational segregation by destination. The importance of remittances from overseas workers for the Philippine economy is then discussed in terms of the massive dependency of the Philippine state on labour export for economic survival. The final section of the chapter examines some of the transformative impacts that labour migration has had on Philippine society and polity, and inter-state relations between labour-exporting and importing nations.

The magnitude of labour export

The growth of the overseas employment industry has been remarkable. International contract labour migration from the Philippines has wrought substantial changes on Philippine society and economy. Exactly how many Filipinos are working abroad is unclear. In 2001, the Commission on Filipinos Overseas and the Philippine Overseas Employment Administration (POEA) (http://www.poea.gov.ph) estimated that almost seven and a half million (7.4 million) Filipinos live abroad. Of these the majority (3.1 million) are temporary overseas contract workers, followed by 2.7 million permanent migrants and 1.6 million undocumented migrants (such as overstaying tourists working illegally in Japan or Sabah).

Since the OPEC oil crisis of 1973, which catalysed the Philippine government's labour export programme, the Middle East has been a major Filipino labour-importing region, although its relative dominance in the early 1990s (employing 300,000 or 60 per cent of the 500,000 workers deployed in 1993) has been weakened due to the expansion of other markets for Filipino labour. So while the volume of workers being deployed to the Middle East has remained steady with between 280,000 and 300,000 being deployed there annually, this number now accounts for about a third of the Philippines' annual labour export (2002). Since the late 1980s, the first and second tier newly industrialising nations have been increasingly experiencing serious labour shortages due to their high economic growth rates. For example, Taiwan emerged as a new market in the 1990s, but recently recruitment declined because of the transfer of industries to mainland China (Battistella 2002:114). Overall however, East and Southeast Asia, particularly

Japan, the tiger economies of Hong Kong, Singapore, Taiwan, South Korea and more recently Brunei and Malaysia, has become an increasingly significant labour-importing region to the extent that this region rivals the Middle East as the premier labour-importing region. In fact, in the years 1998, 1999 and 2000, the Asian region exceeded the Middle East as the major labour-importing region, although by 2001, 2002 and 2003 the Middle East had edged past Asia once again.

In terms of annual worker outflow, more than 600,000 have been leaving for overseas employment each year since the early 1990s, and 866,590 left in 2001 (Tan 2001:380). From 1999 to 2002 the overall trend of the country's overseas employment increased at an annual average rate of 2 per cent (POEA 2003, http://www.poea.gov.ph). This annual increase in the outflow of overseas contract workers (OCWs) was also part of an established pattern of considerable annual increases in worker outflow throughout the 1990s and, for 2001 and 2002 for both the Philippines and all countries of origin in Asia. In the case of the Philippines, migration increased by 52 per cent in the 1990s (Battistella 2002:112). Graziano Battistella (2002:114) provides an important qualifier to these statistics. He argues that the overall number of deployed persons has been a steady rather than spectacular increase. The big jump in 1998 figures was due to changes in counting procedures, rather than a real increase, so that current figures are more reflective of multiple departures, rather than an increase in persons going abroad.

Against the established long-term trend, in 2003 there was a slowing down of total deployment of overseas foreign workers by an overall 2.7 per cent to 867,969 from 891,908 in 2002 (POEA Annual Report 2003, http://www.poea. gov.ph). According to the POEA (2003) thousands of job opportunities were lost due to global economic recession, exacerbated by the US-Iraq war and the SARS outbreak, which further weakened the economies of major markets of OCWs in the Middle East, Asia, and the Pacific, Europe and Americas, and the increasing competition by other labour-sending countries. As a result, deployment of workers in major labour-importing regions decreased by varying degrees. In Asia, the total number contracted by 11.8 per cent to 254,520 (from 288,481 in 2002) (POEA 2003). In the Middle East, deployment declined by seven per cent (to 285,564 in 2003 from 306,939 in 2002). This was due to efforts of host countries in the Gulf States to intensify the employment nationalisation policy due to increasing unemployment of nationals (POEA 2003). Europe and the Americas also showed a declining trend in 2003 (down respectively 16.3 per cent and 4.2 per cent from 2002) as depressed economic conditions and restrictive immigration policies arising from increased security concerns since the 9/11 attack slowed down recruitment of workers (POEA 2003). As part of the Philippines resilience and determination to maintain labour deployment levels through POEA's marketing capabilities, deployment of workers to Africa increased by 26.5 per cent from 2002 levels (POEA 2003).

The overall trend for migration flows from the Philippines has been of great resilience over the past thirty years. For example between 1997 and 1998 the deployment of Filipino workers to Asia increased significantly despite the Asian financial crisis. Battistella attributes this resilience to the nature of the jobs the migrants hold, the shift between countries to compensate for downtrends, and the devaluation of the monetary value of (Battistella 2002:112).

Skill composition

The deployment of Filipino workers, and the skill composition of labour exports reflect the changing labour requirements of the principal employment markets for Filipino labour. Several features of the skill composition of Filipino workers employed abroad are notable.

One of the most outstanding historical trends is the rapid growth of demand for construction and transport labour in the early to late 1970s, and the gradual shift from the construction to service and professional sectors after that time. The OPEC oil price hike in the early 1970s created an unprecedented need for construction workers to meet the demand created by extensive infrastructural development in the Gulf States, particularly in Saudi Arabia. By the early 1980s labour demand in the Middle East began to broaden to include both production and construction workers as well as the demand for professional and service workers. The proportion of professional workers increased from 10 per cent to 21 per cent of total Filipino workers in the Middle East, and the proportion of service workers rose from 12 per cent to 25 per cent between 1983 and 1986. In contrast, the proportion of construction workers declined from 72 per cent to 47 per cent. The proportion of workers involved in the service industry rose even more dramatically in Asia than in the Middle East (from 40 per cent to 60 per cent), to become the major area of employment for Filipinos outside the Middle East in 1986. In the early to mid-1980s employment as entertainers has also increased in relative importance (from 29 per cent to 35 per cent) making it the second most important employment sector for Filipinos in Asia.

By the early 1990s, the skill categorisation of overseas workers no longer treated entertainers by a separate classification. Rather, the entertainer category was treated under the 'professional and technical skill' classification. This classification obscures what is really happening in overseas labour markets, as nurses are also a major occupational group within this professional category. It is impossible to know exactly what proportions of professionals are entertainers, nurses, or of other occupations. However, it is well known within the POEA that numbers of entertainers working overseas constitute the majority of professional workers, although there is a sense that calling these workers 'professionals' obscures both the vulnerability of their occupations and the variety of entertainment practices that constitutes their employment.

From POEA statistics available on newly hired workers from 1992 until 2002, three major skill categories dominate over 93 per cent of worker export from the Philippines: professional and technical workers; service workers; and production workers. Although the relative balance between these three groupings has varied over this period, what is striking about these three categories is just how highly gendered each of these skill categories are with the first two groupings being largely women, and third category being primarily men. The increased demand for service and professional workers has been accompanied by a dramatic rise in the participation of women in the international employment industry. As a result, a central and controversial feature of labour migration from the Philippines since the mid-1980s has been its highly gendered nature.

Gendered migration

By the mid-1980s a combination of several key factors increased the global demand and employment of Filipino women. Briefly these key factors were escalating economic decline in the Philippines; a rise in labour demand in the international service sector in both Asia and the Middle East; declines in (male) labour demand in the Middle East construction sector; and aggressive global labour marketing campaigns by the Philippine state (Ball 1997). Thus, within a relatively short period the gender structure of the global Philippine migrant labour force was remarkably transformed. In the early 1980s, men comprised the majority of land-based Filipino labour migrants, and by 1994 Filipino women constituted 60 per cent of migrant workers leaving the Philippines (Go 1997). While male workers still typically dominate in the construction and shipping industries, Filipino women are employed in all tiers of service sector employment ranging from entertainment and prostitution, domestic service through to nursing in Southeast Asian, North American, European and Middle Eastern labour markets (Ball 2004; Barber 2000). Within the broad categorisation of 'service sector' there are wide-ranging employment vulnerabilities related to the intersection of occupation and country of employment. In addition, most Philippine women who are employed legally are generally overeducated for the forms of employment that they take on overseas, resulting in both a brain drain and a significant de-skilling of the globalised and gendered Filipino labour market, and constitute a net loss of human capital from Philippine domestic labour markets (Ball 1996, 2004).

There are two major characteristics of women's participation in contract labour and irregular migration from the Philippines. First, women are most often employed as unskilled or semi-skilled workers, such as domestic servants, whilst often possessing professional qualifications such as in teaching and accounting.

In 1994, domestic servants constituted 13.6 per cent of total worker deployment and entertainers 10.2 per cent (White Paper 1995:2). By 1992

Table 6.1 Estimated numbers of OCWs by destination, migration status and occupation, 2001

Country	Permanent	Temporary	Irregular	Total	Main occupations of Filipinos in a regular status
World Total	2,736,528	3,099,940	1,566,426	7,402,894	
Africa	271	31,530	10,103	41,904	
Asia (East and South)	70,349	826,782	360,527	1,257,658	
Brunei	26	20,240	1,500	21,766	Domestic workers, production workers
Hong Kong	404	171,485	2,000	173,889	Domestic workers, electrical and electronics workers
Japan	65,647	138,522	36,379	240,548	Entertainers, production workers, permanent residents
Korea	1,510	12,018	13,000	26,528	Industrial trainees, production workers, entertainers
Malaysia	310	58,233	167,936	226,479	Construction/production, domestic workers, professional, hotel staff
Singapore	152	56,377	71,917	128,446	Domestic workers, entertainers, supervisors,construction workers
Taiwan	1,901	116,480	4,300	122,681	Domestic workers, construction/ production workers
Others	399	253,427	63,495	317,321	
Asia (West)	1,546	1,233,325	123,332	1,358,203	
Kuwait	92	53,067	10,000	63,159	Engineers, nurses, domestic, production and construction workers
Saudi Arabia	239	897,000	18,000	915,239	Production and construction workers, nurses, domestic and service workers
UAE	373	128,604	38,000	166,977	Engineers, domestic worker, nurses, construction and production workers
Others	842	154,654	57,332	212,828	
Europe	152,851	420,232	203,249	776,332	
France	925	4,804	26,121	31,850	Service workers
Germany	41,321	7,005	4,392	52,718	Permanent residents
Italy	2,431	69,998	78,000	150,429	Domestic workers, service workers
Spain	33,643	5,687	4,000	43,330	Permanent residents
United Kingdom	45,889	15,767	8,344	70,000	Permanent residents, nurses
Others	28,642	316,971	82,392	428,005	
Americas	2,291,311	286,793	848,879	3,426,983	
Canada	338,561	21,146	4,000	363,707	Permanent residents, domestic workers, nurses
United States	1,910,844	60,373	532,200	2,503,417	Permanent residents, nurses
Others	41,906	205,274	312,679	559,859	
Oceania	220,200	46,009	20,336	286,545	
Australia	204,075	687	2,041	206,803	Permanent residents, IT professionals
New Zealand	16,045	236	100	16,381	Permanent residents
Others	80	45,086	18,195	63,361	

Source: Commission on Filipinos overseas (2001), Department of Foreign Affairs, Philippines; http://www.poea.gov.ph/html/statistics.html

and 1999, respectively, the proportion of total deployment of contract migrants that were women increased from 50 per cent to 64 per cent. By 2002 professional and service workers comprised the majority of newly hired overseas workers (35 per cent and 34 per cent respectively), and over two-thirds (69 per cent) of migrant workers from the Philippines were women. These figures indicate that the Philippines has been increasingly reliant on the export of women for its labour export programme and alleviation of its large foreign debt. Second, women are typically employed in extremely vulnerable occupations and workplaces as domestic servants and entertainers. Table 6.1 details estimated numbers of OCWs by destination, migration status and occupation for 2001.

The major destinations for domestic helpers are mainly in Asia – primarily Hong Kong and Singapore. Other important countries of employment for domestic helpers are Italy, Saudi Arabia, and the United Arab Emirates (UAE). The principal destination for entertainers is Japan, and to a much lesser extent, South Korea. The major job opportunities for Filipino men are in the construction and production oriented occupations. The major destination for construction and production workers is the Middle East – principally Saudi Arabia, the UAE, and Kuwait. Outside of the Middle East, Malaysia, and Taiwan and, more recently, South Korea import significant numbers of male construction, production and service workers. Table 6.1 indicates that Philippine labour migration is highly gendered by destination, and that the nature of these destinations and the intersection of occupation and gender have a large bearing on worker abuse/wellbeing.

Despite the many problems of sexual and other forms abuse suffered by Filipinos as service workers, the Philippines is increasingly reliant on the export of women for its labour export programme and alleviation of its large foreign debt. Accompanying the significant increases in the numbers of Filipino women working internationally are anecdotal increases in the level of abuse of workers. Table 6.2 outlines the major forms of human rights and labour abuses experienced by domestic helpers by four major groupings – legal, economic, physical and social abuse and difficulties. Some areas of legal and economic difficulty pertain to illegalities in the recruitment process prior to migration such as deceptive contractual arrangements, and excessive recruitment charges. However, most of the abuses of domestic workers occur once they are employed overseas. These are abuses derived usually from both the employment environment of the worker as well as from the socio-legal culture of employment. Common forms of workplace abuse include confiscation of passport; non-payment or cutting of wages; excessive hours of work, including no day-off; sexual harassment and abuse; verbal abuse and racial denigration; substandard accommodation such as no personal living space or bed. Examples of the later broad issues include lack of protective labour legislation for temporary workers and lack of avenues for redress of grievances (Ball and Piper 2002). Illegal workers are all the more vulnerable as illegal migration by definition precludes access to protective labour and human rights mechanisms in the labour-receiving nation.

Table 6.2   Adverse conditions confronting Asian women migrant domestic workers

Legal	Deceptive contractual arrangements: contract substitution infringements of contracts lack of protective labour legislation lack of avenues for redress of grievances confiscation of passport marginalised position re labour and human rights

Economic	Exploitation in relation to:
	recruitment charges
	wages paid
	wages withheld
	excessive work hours
	no day off
	deception in relation to:
	  presented economic benefits
	  hidden charges for worker to cover

Physical	Marginal legal protection against a range of abuses such as: physical abuse sexual abuse substandard accommodation e.g., no bed, private space
Social	Social deprivation: social marginalisation or isolation deprivation of family life deprivation of religious freedom verbal/psychological abuse and harassment

Source: Based on Cox (1997: 70).

Both domestic servants and entertainers are employed under circumstances where they are highly vulnerable to a wide range of abuse. Both sets of workers are generally employed in private spaces (people's homes), or in small-scale public spaces (e.g., nightclubs), which in the latter instance may well be controlled by organised crime syndicates such as the Japanese Yakuza. While there are approximately 140,000 mainly female workers in Japan on temporary work contracts, there are over 36,000 workers who are illegal residents there (Table 6.1). Both domestic servants and entertainers have little opportunity to protest against unfair or abusive work practices, and even more so the case for those who are resident illegally. In contrast, many male Filipino workers are employed in large-scale public workplaces, such as construction sites, where solidarity amongst workers against abuses work practices is more likely to occur, although this definitely is not intended to imply that abuse does not occur.

Many migrant workers are victims of trafficking and abuses, and this is particularly for women. In some cases, they may be legitimately recruited, but end up as prostitutes, entertainers, or bonded labourers. Ralph Boyce, U.S. Deputy Assistant Secretary for East Asia and the Pacific, said human trafficking was the third largest source of profits for organised crime next to guns and drugs. Global turnover was estimated at $16 billion (*Asian Migrant* 2000:3–4). This is considered such a major problem for both individual countries such as the Philippines, and for the region in general, that in March 2000 a three-day meeting of the Asian Regional Initiative Against the Trafficking of Women and Children was held in Manila. It was organised by the United States and the Philippines and was attended by delegates from 23 nations and 18 international organisations. The purpose of the meeting was to 'draw a regional action program that would protect victims and prosecute traffickers' (*Asian Migrant* 2000:3–4). While such initiatives still remain in their infancy, the fact that multilateral initiatives have begun is critical to tackling widespread abuse.

National dependency on hard currency earnings

Remitted income from overseas workers is the premier foreign exchange earner for the Philippines. The 'national' economy of the Philippines has become increasingly dependent on hard currency remittances of OCWs. The high level of Philippine macro-economic dependence on worker remittances is outstanding, as the following statistics and discussion reveal. Central Bank of the Philippines data reveals that in 2002 US$7.2 billion was remitted through formal channels. In 2003, remittances from the migrant sector reached an all-time high of $7.6 billion: an increase of over six per cent from 2002 (POEA 2003). Remittances through formal channels in 2003 accounted for ten per cent of GDP (ADB 2003). The remittances of OCWs have contributed greatly to the country's foreign exchange earnings that averaged 20.4 per cent of exports and five per cent of GNP in 1990–98 (Tan 2001:380).

Importantly, however, monies remitted through the Central Bank constitute only just over one-third of the total volume of remittances as most overseas earnings are remitted through informal channels such as through friends, door-to-door delivery and small agencies (Alburo and Abella 1992). Taking into account the capital being remitted to the Philippines through formal banking and informal channels, remittances could well be estimated to be even more significant as a foreign exchange earner than the above figures indicate. For example, research by Florian Alburo and Manolo Abella (1992) found that in 1989 remittances were approximately US$2.9 billion (equivalent to 54 per cent of total foreign earnings for the Philippines of US$5.4 billion). Alburo and Abella also estimate that from 1980 to 1989 total overseas earnings of OCWs was almost US$40 billion, of which $21.8 billion was probably remitted (Alburo and Abella 1992:36). The above figures indicate that annual remittances through formal channels, alone, have been

Table 6.3   Foreign Direct Investment (FDI) and remittances through official channels to the Philippines (1971–93) (in million US dollars)

	FDI	Remittances	Ratio of FDI to remittances
1971–75	125	n.a.	n.a.
1976–80	340	1,077 (1978–80)	31.6
1981–85	314	3,193	9.8
1986–90	2,775	4,483	62.0
1991–93	1,990	5,932	33.6
1998	2,127	7,368	28.9
1999	608	6,795	8.9
2000	1,348	6,051	22.3

Sources: IMF (1990); *Philippine Statistical Yearbook* (1991), and Central Bank of the Philippines (2001).

critical to offsetting the cost of oil imports, the foreign debt and improving the balance of payments for the Philippines (Vasquez 1992:51).

The important economic contribution of women's overseas employment should not be underestimated, and reflects the dominance of women to overall labour export. By the mid-1990s it was estimated that Filipinas working abroad contributed in legally and illegally remitted earnings nearly $8billion yearly to the Philippines economy (Ball 2004). Table 6.3 reveals that labour export in the Philippines has far exceeded direct foreign investment (FDI) in terms of its foreign exchange generating capacity over the last three decades.

From 1970 to 1979, the average FDI amounted to approximately only US$ 57 million per year. Under the Aquino administration, FDI rose substantially, although unevenly. For example, while FDI in 1984 was only US$9 million, capital investments flows increased to US$936 million in 1988 (Alburo and Abella 1992:34). The recent figures for 1998 and 2000 indicate direct foreign investment accounted only 29 per cent and 22 per cent respectively of the amount of remittances for these years – and as we have noted above, the remittance figures are underestimates. The annual remittances of overseas Filipinos coursed through the Philippine banking channels are used by the government to augment the country's foreign exchange requirements for international transactions. In particular, the remittances of overseas Filipinos is a major source of dollars that is sold to importers. It is also a major source of dollar earnings used to pay the country's external debt. The substantive differences between both forms of foreign exchange generation in actual capital flows into the Philippines is further underscored by the level of state dependence on the hard currency generated from worker remittances for the basic macro-economic functions. These results indicate that the Philippine state and economy is more dependent on the earnings of overseas workers than it is on foreign investments and foreign loans, emphasising the high level of macro-economic and political importance of this industry to the Philippine state.

The importance of labour export to the Philippines goes beyond the macro-economic function of remittances and labour market impacts. The level of dependence of households on remitted income is also very significant. Results from the 1988 household income and expenditure survey indicated that approximately 15.5 per cent of Filipino households receive income from overseas workers (Alburo and Abella 1992:30), which contributed about 30 per cent to their total income (Tan 2001). While these results are now a little dated, they do indicate a high level of household reliance on income generated by labour migration, and a level of reliance that we can only have expected to have increased commensurate with the eight-fold increase in remitted income between 1988 and 2002 (US$857 million versus US$7,189 million in respective years).

Research on internal and international migration has revealed some interesting disaggregation of the types of regions and households involved in, and benefiting from, labour migration versus internal migration. There are dualistic migration processes operating in the Philippines, where domestic migration involves the movement of people from poorer to richer regions, but not abroad, and a separate movement of workers from richer regions seeking overseas employment. Thus throughout the country, the poor are most likely to be reliant on income from internal migration, and the more affluent from international migration. Thus the benefits from overseas employment accrue disproportionately to the richer Filipino households (Cruz *et al.*, 1988; Cruz and Repetto 1992; Costello and Ferrer 1992 and 1993). These results indicate the key role international demand for labour has had on income and employment generation, and in particular in enhancing income-earning opportunities for millions of Filipino workers and the many millions of dependents, and associated with this, increasing class and regional inequalities. Without the advent of contract labour migration however, the pool of the unemployed, overall levels of impoverishment and subsequent levels of social dislocation would have been much larger.

Some Impacts and dynamics between international and domestic labour markets

Labour export and the use of foreign labour is, at its most general level, generated by the requirements of capitalist accumulation, and is highly selective. Even amongst the 'unskilled' it is the most able, highly motivated, fit and of prime working age workers that successfully weave their way through a myriad of obstacles to obtain overseas employment. The role of international labour migration and the large-scale movement of workers from less-developed countries to rapidly expanding economies has relatively recently been acknowledged as significant components of divergent globalisation (Castles 2000; Ghosh 2000; Stalker 2000; Ball 2004). The characteristics of the labour supply and the terms under which that labour is supplied reflects a sending-nation's role in the world economy, the strength of its political ties and dependencies, and the degree of economic necessity to find employment for its nationals abroad. In fact, the globalisation of contract labour migration involves imbalances in the flow of people and the siphoning away of their human capital from developing nations. Thus one aspect of globalisation of labour through contract labour migration that has largely gone unrecognised is that it has involved skill and brain drain from developing nations on a massive scale (Ball 2004).

International demand for Filipino workers has significantly affected the domestic labour market. Between 1977 and 1990 the country's labour force was estimated to have grown from 15 million to 24.5 million or by 730,000 per year, by 2002 the labour force had grown to 33.7 million (ADB 2003:273), which amounts to a more than doubling of the size of labour force in only 25 years. During the same period (1977–2002) the number employed rose from 14.3 to 30.3 million (ADB 2003:273), or an additional 640,000 people entering the labour market each year. In 1998, the stock of emigrants amounted to 10.1 per cent of the population and 23.2 per cent of the labour force; the outflow of workers abroad in 1998 (755,000) as a proportion of the increment to the labour force in 1997–98 was seven and a half per cent (Tan 2001:380). However, there is an important distinction to be made between stock and flow of overseas workers. The flow figures are fairly reliable since they are collected at POEA directly from the record of OCWs it services for employment and migration purposes. The stock figures are estimates made by the Department of Foreign Affairs from its foreign offices and POEA (Tan 2001). However, despite these qualifiers, overseas employment has clearly been a critical source of job creation for annual entrants to the labour market.

International demand for labour has thus been responsible for absorbing a large proportion of the annual growth in employment for the country as a whole during three decades of economic decline and instability. While the impact of the loss of 3.1 million OCWs and 1.6 undocumented workers overseas has not been systematically assessed, research that has been conducted shows that with the exception of the medical and health services, in particular nurses, skill shortages have not been pronounced in spite of the large emigration of skilled workers (Alburo and Abella 1992:28; Ball 1996; Ball 2004). However, data on the ages of the Philippine immigrant population indicate that OCWs are in their prime working years, with the largest percentage of registered Filipino emigrants between the ages of 15–39 years, with 52.17 per cent falling into this category (Commission on Filipinos Overseas 2004). That workers emigrating for employment are in their prime working years, must impact negatively on the quality of the Philippine domestic labour market. However, there is a strong political and social aspect to this labour emigration that must be taken into account. Global demand for Filipino workers, and its absorption of so many labour market entrants, must act as a safety valve against widespread social and political discontent over the long-term failure of the Philippine economy to generate sufficient domestic employment for its citizens.

While the historical trend has been that it is the income differentials between labour-importing countries and the Philippines that has provided the strong impetus for high and sustained levels of both demand for overseas employment and worker outflow, these determinants have significantly changed. Despite general increases in the numbers of workers migrating, there has also been a devaluation of migrant labour, and as a result, the Philippines is deploying a cheaper and more precarious workforce (Battistella 2002:114). For example, in 1998, Hong Kong succeeded in decreasing the salary for domestic workers by five per cent. A second round of wage cuts was stopped through concerted Philippine government action and migrant NGO protests. Wages in Taiwan were decreased when the workers were charged the equivalent for food and lodging, previously provided by employers. More recently, reports of discussions between the POEA and Saudi officials indicate that Philippine minimum wages have been indicated as acceptable wages (primarily for construction workers), prompting a probable downturn in compensation to migrants around the region (Battistella 2002:113). Steadily increasing deployment figures together with the above examples of the devaluation of migrant labour indicate significant shifts in the determinants of migration. Migrants usually leave for higher salaries. Some scholars had theorised that a ratio between domestic and foreign salaries lower than one to three should lead to decreasing migration (Battistella 2002:113). Now it seems that many workers in particular skill groupings, are willing to work abroad simply for a salary, perhaps even as low as Philippine minimum wages.

A rising incidence of worker abuse indicates that the conditions of employment for OCWs are increasingly precarious. NGOs claim that the incidence of worker abuse has increased between 1995 and 2002 (IBON 2004). As some examples of this, *Migrante-International* found that in 2002, 42 OCWs were awaiting beheading in the Middle East, while 36 are facing the death penalty in Saudi Arabia and 6 in Malaysia. Thousands of OCWs are also stranded in Saudi Arabia, 44 domestic helpers in Hong Kong were sexually assaulted and 6 OCWs arrived everyday in the Philippines in coffins as a result of 'mysterious deaths' (Alcuitas 2002). Both NGOs and the POEA report significant increases in worker deportation. Between 2002 and 2003 the number of repatriation cases jumped by 113 per cent to 1562 from only 733 recorded in 2002. In addition the number of welfare cases reported through Philippine government increased by 27 per cent (from 1699 to 2203 cases) in 2003 from 2002 (POEA 2003:29).

The resourcing of government overseas missions is a major obstacle to adequate welfare provision to overseas workers. Most missions provide inadequate training and are understaffed and overworked. Labour attachés and Overseas Worker Welfare Agency (OWWA) staff are on call 24 hours a day (Gonzalez 1998:89). On average, there are less than two labour attachés per labour-importing country – or about one attaché per 16,000 workers. The Department of Labour and Employment (DOLE) has released statistics showing extremely high ratios between the number of labour and welfare officers assigned to a country and the numbers of OCWs in that particular country: in Japan, the ration was 1:26,333 (Gonzalez 1998:89). Understaffing results in overworked and highly stressed staff and inadequately protected workers.

In addition to these indicators of severe under-funding to resource missions and, therefore, welfare provision, there is overwhelming evidence to show that the impacts are clearly gendered. For example, OWWA data for 1994 revealed that DOLE, together with the Department of Foreign Affairs 14,314 reported cases involving OCWs (Gonzalez 1998:92). Cases involving women far exceeded those for men: 94.5 per cent of health and death cases, 80.6 per cent of crime and cultural offences, 78.9 per cent of contract payment cases, and 78.5 per cent of welfare cases (Gonzalez 1998:92). This pattern existed in all world regions, and illustrates how a lack of state resources has an overwhelmingly negative impact on Filipino women.

Migrante International argues that these data reflect increasingly restrictive immigration policies of host countries, themselves a sign of the global economic recession. For example, in Asia the Malaysian government recently cracked down on illegal immigrants and ordered a number of Filipinos to be deported. An Associated Free Press report cited 7000 Filipinos were deported in 2002. In Japan, a new law effectively categorises undocumented workers as 'criminals' (Alcuitas 2002). Thus while host countries exploit migrant labour as a source of cheap and flexible labour in times of labour shortage, in times of economic crisis, migrants are easily disposable and become an easy excuse for slowdowns in the economy. This in turn has lead to an increase in the incidence of racism and discrimination (Ball 1997; Alcuitas 2002).

Recently President Arroyo set a target of increasing deployments to one million OCWs a year (Battistella 2002:114). It is difficult not to think that this target has clear social and political safety valve considerations underpinning its establishment. Given the downward pushes on wages and conditions in the two major labour regions for Filipino labour, Asia and the Middle East, it is hard to imagine that increased deployment could not but further devalue Filipino labour. Given that the Philippines exports workers who are in their prime and who are generally not desperately poor, it is these workers who are most likely to protest the loudest when their survival aspirations are clearly threatened by such downturns. Battistella (2002:114) makes the ominous conclusion: 'It is not difficult to imagine that the country is reaching the limit of its capacity to hold social discontent. What will happen when it will no longer be possible to export such discontent?'.

Social impacts of labour migration

While the impact of international contract labour migration (ICLM) can be examined in a variety of ways such as the absolute value of this industry in hard currency terms; it can also be examined in terms of the extent of dependence by households on income from their family members living overseas; and the wide degree of social dislocation resulting from the absence of OCWs from their spouses, children and, other family members. One need not wander very far in the Philippines to encounter the great variety of examples which indicate that the labour export industry has had a profound material effect on Philippine society such as the thousands of new houses for *balikbayans* (returning workers) and their beneficiaries; the plethora of quick courses to prepare people to work abroad; the deeply entrenched legal and illegal recruitment industry; and the numerous stories of success and victimisation that abound, bearing testament to the widespread positive and negative effects of this industry on Filipinos and their families (Ball 2000).

Due to the massive debt accrued during the Marcos regime, the day-to-day survival ability of Filipino families has declined markedly since the 1970s. The massive growth in overseas employment has transformed family survival strategies from a domestic to an international focus. The very visual degree of financial success that many individuals and families have gained from overseas employment has resulted in many Filipinos more readily seeing the solution to their survival problems as lying overseas rather than domestically (Ball 2000). Millions of Filipinos are increasingly orienting their skill base towards international rather national labour markets, to the extent that now most Filipino women training to be nurses are making their career choice as a highly conscious family survival strategy to enable them to work overseas (Ball 2000), in order to support their families. Research by Rochelle Ball (1996, 2000, 2004) has found that the existence of international employment opportunities for nurses, and national economic decline in the late 1970s and during the 1980s have resulted in highly significant shifts in the nurse labour market in the Philippines. Many nurses are not making professional choices and employment decisions with the aim of working in the Philippines. Rather, the possibility of overseas employment is alarmingly prominent in the ways that nurses think about their future employment. Nurses, in the social context of their families, are making these decisions with the object of meeting the requirements not of the national labour market, but of international employers. The ways that individuals think about themselves and their labour has changed the focus of the nurse labour market in the Philippines away from local needs and it is increasingly directed to meeting international demand, and thereby further globalising labour markets and the Philippine economy.

In fact, the extensive participation and dominance of Filipino women more broadly in overseas migration for employment is not simply due to the nature of international demand, but also the role of women in Philippine society. Within the family, daughters are seen as more likely than sons to fulfil familial obligations (Trager 1988:79). As they become more economically active, daughters are expected to not only contribute financially to the household, but also to support younger siblings, particularly with their education. The investment in education for the migration of young single women and their subsequent payoff in financial assistance to parents and siblings is thus part of a household strategy oriented to the maintenance and improvement of the status of the family as a unit (Trager 1988:83). Not surprisingly, empirical evidence reveals that female migrant workers have stronger commitments and obligations to their households in the Philippines than their male counterparts (Go 2001:107). In the study of Filipino migrants in Rome (Tacoli 1995), on average mothers sent home 6.4 monthly salaries per year, contributing 3.2 times the household income, while fathers sent only 5.5 monthly salaries contributing only 2.3 times the household income. The situation was similar among single migrants where daughters tended to send more money back than sons.

While the strongest social unit in the Philippines may be the family unit from which survival strategies such as migration decisions are made, there is evidence of the great stress that long-term and extensive international migration has placed on Philippine families and society, that paradoxically maybe undermining family structures. Stella Go writes:

> There is a prevailing perception, fuelled by anecdotal accounts in the print and broadcast media, that the institutions of marriage and the family are slowly being eroded by international labour migration. Moreover, the absence of the mother is perceived to have more negative effects on the family, especially young children, than the absence of the father.
>
> Negative national perceptions of the effect of long-term family separation include, both the worker migrant and their spouse left behind may experience psychological distress resulting from homesickness, loneliness, and anxiety over family-related concerns such as the possibility of their spouses' marital infidelity while they are away and the care of their children; and money-related problems, including the possible mismanagement of remitted salaries. (Go 2001:108)

Another issue of widespread concern that has accompanied the feminisation of labour migration is the violence experienced by migrant workers, particularly women migrants. They include various forms of physical exploitation and abuse as well as sexual violence. The sexual harassment and abuse experienced by domestic helpers and entertainers and the trafficking of women and children who have been forced into prostitution by criminal syndicates have been the focus of much public grieving and media attention. The public outpouring over these issues has had political ramifications and has been often been accompanied by calls for the Philippine government to take responsibility for the maltreatment and abuse of its citizens whilst working overseas.

The overwhelming national economic and social dependence on labour migration as an economic and social palliative has profound ramifications. Philippine economy and society and political stability has become dependant on continued labour export and the sustainability of income derived from it. Many Filipinos no longer think of their country as being able to generate the employment needed to secure the survival of the family unit. No wonder the President Arroyo has now shifted the targets for annual labour deployment to one million – but at what cost?

Philippine migration policy: history and critique

The contemporary history of Philippine labour migration (Ball 1997; Gonzalez 1998; Sto. Tomas 2002; Tan 2001) has been well documented. Briefly, the Philippine state has been heavily involved as the dominant institution in the labour export industry for over three decades – since the revolutionary growth in overseas demand for Filipino labour that occurred following the OPEC Oil crisis in 1973. The Philippines has the most well developed apparatus for labour export in Asia, and has become the model for other countries to emulate (Ball and Piper 2002). The POEA and its precursor the Overseas Employment Development Bureau, as part of the Department of Labor and Employment has been the key institution to regulate, administer and promote all aspects of the second largest overseas employment industry in the world. The POEA's multiple functions include a regulator of private sector recruitment practises; a marketer of Filipino labour; an arbiter between workers and recruiters/foreign employers; and to a lesser extent, a recruiter in its own right (Ball 1997). In so doing the Philippine state functions have been developed to mediate and balance between a range of competing stakeholder interests, which in the end has meant that it has occupied somewhat contradictory positions in which its protective functions vis-à-vis Filipino workers have been undermined by the macro-economic dependence of the Philippine economy on the foreign exchange generated by work remittances (Ball 1997).

The need for capital accumulation expressed in the billions of US dollars generated through worker remittances is the major reason for state involvement in the industry. This is clearly expressed in the State's need to actively market and promote Filipino workers as entities for international trade. The dependency on hard currency generated by worker remittances has compromised the Philippine governments effectiveness in strongly negotiating for its workers rights with labour-importing states, lest they lose their market share. Safeguarding worker rights domestically and internationally in real terms is of secondary importance to hard currency generation. As a result, in the Philippines, the general policy approach to labour export has been to maximize the benefits and to minimize the costs (Battistella 1999:231).

That migrant workers, and particularly women, are vulnerable is not contested between stakeholders. What is contested, however, is the extent to which particularly the state should be held responsible for the vulnerabilities of its overseas workers. The most recent major legislation purports to structurally address worker vulnerabilities is *The Migrant Workers and Overseas Filipinos Act of 1995 (RA 8042)*. According to both the Departments of Labor and Employment and Foreign Affairs (DOLE and DFA, respectively), this law

> seeks to institute measures for overseas employment and establish a higher degree of protection for the welfare of migrant workers, their families, and overseas Filipinos. It affirms the State's policy of ensuring full protection of labour, local and overseas, organized and unorganised ... Moreover, the State accepts overseas employment as a present-day reality, and requires assurance for the protection of the dignity and fundamental human rights and freedoms of the (sic) Filipino citizens.
>
> Other salient features of the law include the progressive policy of deregulation of recruitment activities and the eventual phase-out of the regulatory functions of the POEA (http://www.dlsu.edu.ph/pinas/gov/ocwhb.html).

This Act uses the language of human and labour rights to promote 'a new era' of state consciousness over the need to protect migrant workers. However, these two quotes are in essence contradictory. On the one hand, the Act has as its centrepiece the protection of migrant workers, and on the other hand it promotes the deregulation of the labour export industry, through a winding back of the regulatory and protective functions of the POEA (Ball and Piper 2002:1021); and this is the crux of the contradiction that underpins Philippine labour export policy implementation. It is impossible to increase the national and international protective apparatus for workers through stronger government involvement and simultaneously deregulate the industry, wherein conditions of overseas employment are negotiated between workers and foreign employers without government involvement. Graziano Battistella (2002:114) aptly expresses this contradictory approach:

> This contradiction is reflected in the work of the executive, which affirms stronger regulations – but with lower conditions obtained for workers deployed – and at the same time encourages further deployment (now targeted at one million a year). It is not possible to pursue protection and deployment with the same energy. One of the two will be sacrificed, and normally it is protection that is sacrificed.

In many respects migration is the product of the interplay of complex global forces that are often beyond the control of national governments

(Tigno 1997:249). The following quotation, taken from an recent article written by Patricia Sto. Tomas, the Philippine Secretary of Labour, highlights the inter-jurisdictional complexities embodied in the temporary transnational migration of workers

> The rights of overseas workers or any other kind of migrants have understandable political overtones. There are those who view rights as part of a square which is shared by locals and nationals. A line that divides the square might be moved horizontally and vertically. Always, somebody's loss is the other's gain. Governments will find it difficult to move that line if it is seen as increasing the rights of strangers.
>
> But what if there were no line? What if there were overlapping circles instead of a square and the area of overlap defined our responsibility for each other's nationals once they are in our shore? We may deny others those rights reserved for our citizens but we certainly cannot deny responsibility for them once we receive them in our jurisdictions. Conferring rights may be problematic, even if it has been done before. Assuming responsibility is what structures and institutions do to ensure civility and peace in an increasingly globalized world ... The limiting confines of a square might then evolve toward a circle of hope and harmony for the peoples of the world. (Sto. Tomas 2004)

The vulnerability of migrants derives not only from the wrong doings of many agents involved in the process, including recruiters, transport operators, government officials and employers. It is mostly the result of their lack of membership to the state in which they are legally or illegally employed. Worker vulnerability is largely derived from the lack of jurisdiction of the labour-exporting state once they move across the borders of their home nation. The compromised ability of the Philippine state to ensure worker welfare domestically and internationally has been the subject of great controversy and has even resulted in the demise of at least one labour secretary.

One mechanism for overcoming the lack of regulatory capacity that the Philippines has over the conditions of employment for its citizens abroad is through Bilateral Agreements between it and receiving nations. The Philippine government has engaged in a number of Bilateral Agreements (BLAs) and Memoranda of Understanding with several labour-importing nations, which I have detailed elsewhere (see Piper and Ball 2001). In practice, bilateral agreements have been a longstanding means of resolving and managing migration flows between two countries, rather than making significant inroads into safeguarding worker welfare. Overall, the BLAs that are in place are very general in nature. Only five of fifteen BLAs between the Philippines and labour-importing nations refer to the need to strengthen mechanisms to improve worker welfare, and none of these address the particular needs of women. In addition, there are relatively very few BLAs in existence given the overseas employment programme has been in existence for thirty-one years. There has been no ongoing assessment of existing agreements, and no re-evaluation of existing agreements have occurred when each new administration of POEA is appointed. This indicates that while a number of BLAs are in existence, they are not taken seriously enough to be reassessed or expanded when necessary. Another major flaw of existing agreements is that they have been written within the framework of each labour-importing countries' existing laws, rather than bridging the conflict of laws between both countries. As a result of this, the BLAs have not been translated into operational terms, thus relegating them to generalities and making it difficult to assess their effectiveness.

The most controversial aspect of labour export is its human rights violations both prior to migration and once the worker migrates. Despite the existence of regional and subregional organisations, increasing regional integration of labour markets, investment, trade and capital flows, there has been a great deal of reluctance to discuss the labour migration problems, which cuts across national borders in regional forums. Obstacles to the regional approach to migration have been different policies pursued by various countries, the sensitivity of the issue, the fear of compromise in an area which has become the last bastion of national sovereignty, and the avoidance to reach agreements which might limit the flexibility that migration offers to labour-importing nations (*Asian Migrant* April–June 1999:33). Nevertheless, the Philippine State has been very vigorous in promoting issues surrounding worker welfare in multilateral forums.

The Asian financial and economic crisis has exposed the commonality of problems concerning irregular and undocumented labour migration and the ineffectiveness of isolated policies. As an outcome of this understanding *The Bangkok Declaration on Irregular Migration* was adopted by the ministers and representatives from 18 governments of East, Southeast, and South Asia participating in the International Symposium on Migration 'Towards Regional Cooperation on Irregular/Undocumented Migration' held in Bangkok on 21–23 April 1999. The Bangkok Declaration was a promising first step towards meaningful dialogue. However, declarations are fairly easy to adopt, since they imply little commitment. Nevertheless this was a significant move in addressing migration as a regional issue.

In terms of global initiatives to bring the many labour and human rights issues surrounding migrant workers to greater prominence, there has been significant progress recently through the United Nations. In his report on the 'Strengthening of the United Nations: an agenda for further change', Mr Kofi Annan identified migration as a priority issue for the international community (GCIM website, www.gcim.org). Acting on the encouragement of the UN secretary-general, a Global Commission on International Migration (GCIM) was launched by the UN secretary-general on 9 December 2003 in Geneva. It is comprised of 19 Commissioners, one of which is

Patricia Sto. Tomas, Minister of Labour and Employment from the Philippines. It began its work on 1 January 2004 and made available its final report to the Secretary-General, and to other stakeholders, on 5 October 2005. The Commission placed international migration on the global agenda, analysed gaps in current policy approaches to migration and examined inter-linkages with other issue areas and, presented recommendations to the UN secretary-general and other stakeholders (www.gcim.org). This Commission is a highly significant development in the international recognition of migration as a global and inter-jurisdictional issue.

The many difficulties involved in the safeguarding of human and labour rights of temporary migrant workers highlighted by both the quote by Sto. Tomas (2004), and the preceding discussion requires greater development of still fragmentary transnational legal regimes (Sassen 1996) and the various human rights codes, to cope with the insufficiency of regulatory apparatus due to globalisation. The development of new legal and regulatory systems able to ensure migrant workers' rights would require further changes to the nature of the nation state. Rather than sovereignty eroding as a consequence of globalisation and supranational organisations, sovereignty must be transformed in order to accommodate and protect those whose rights are undermined by virtue of their employment outside the country of their citizenship (Sassen 1996; Ball and Piper 2002). The work of the Global Commission, under the auspices of the UN secretary-general, is a major step in developing inter-jurisdictional dialogue and potentially the apparatus for dealing with the complex legal and labour rights issues embodied in the global labour trade.

Conclusion

The advent of extensive labour migration in the early 1970s has been transformative in how the Philippines and Filipinos think about economic growth, national and household survival. No longer conceived predominately in terms of economic growth generated by production and labour within the Philippines, now hopes about household, regional and national growth and national survival are firmly pinned on labour export and labouring overseas. Indeed, one would be pressed to find a community anywhere in the Philippines that has not been significantly affected by the Philippine's state-sponsored international trade in labour. In fact the global trade in labour has become such a deeply embedded economic, social and political feature of contemporary Philippines, that it is hard to imagine a future for this nation without labour export.

Clearly, as seen from this chapter exporting labour from the Philippines has not been without costs to family structures, to worker well-being, to the sustainability of certain labour market segments (such as nurses), as some examples. However, given the downward pressure on wages for some components of the overseas labour market, the heavy reliance on the export of women for the continuation of the labour export programme and the concomitant vulnerabilities and abuse of women, much more substantial gains need to be achieved with respect to worker rights both within the Philippines and multilaterally. While the Philippine state has been vigorous in drawing attention to the many labour and human rights concerns of their transnational labour force, greater momentum for rights recognition needs to be better embraced by both receiving nations themselves, and nations which adopt global leadership in multilateral forums, such as the United Nations. Without doubt, international understanding of the complexities involved in recognising the rights of a permanently circulating and flexible international labour force has increased over the last decade, as the recent establishment of the Global Commission on International Migration, indicates. The well-being a millions of workers and their families – and the continued political stability of the Philippines is at stake here. Let us hope that there is sufficient commitment to make the necessary advances in international labour law to make manifest the labour and human rights of this globalised labour force.

References

Alburo, F. and Abella, M. (1992) *The Impact of Informal Remittances of Overseas Contract Workers' Earnings on the Philippine Economy*, Asian Regional Program on International Migration, Working Paper (Bangkok: ILO).
Alcuitas, H. C. (2002) *Seven years after Flor ... Conditions of Overseas Filipino Workers Worsen [online]*, IBON Foundation Incorporated, http://www.ibon.org/news/if/02/18.htm (accessed 20 May 2004).
Asian Development Bank (2003) *Key Indicators 2003: Education for Global Participation* (Manila: ADB).
Ball, R. (2004) 'Divergent Development, Racialised Rights: Globalised Labour Markets and the Trade of Nurses – the Case of the Philippines', *Womens Studies International Forum*, Vol. 27: 119–33.
—— (2000) 'The Individual and Global Processes: Labour Migration Decision-making and Filipino Nurses', *Pilipinas*, No. 34 (Spring): 63–92.
—— (1997) 'The Role of the State in the Globalisation of Labour Markets: The Case of the Philippines', *Environment and Planning A*, Vol. 29: 1603–28.
—— (1996) 'Nation Building or Dissolution: The Globalization of Nursing – the Case of the Philippines', *Pilipinas*, No. 27(Fall): 67–92.
Ball, R. and Piper, N. (2002) 'Globalization and Regulation of Citizenship – Filipino migrants in Japan', *Political Geography*, Vol. 21: 1013–34.
Barber, P. G. (2000) 'Agency in Philippine Women's Labour Migration and Provisional Diaspora', *Women's Studies International Forum*, Vol. 23, No. 4: 399–411.
Battistella, G. (2002) 'Emerging National and Transnational Issues', *Asian Migrant*, Vol. 15, No. 4: 112–16.
—— (1999a) 'Philippine Migration Policy: Dilemmas of a Crisis', *Sojourn*, Vol. 14, No. 1: 229–48.
—— (1999b) 'Free Movement of Labor in ASEAN: Points for Discussion'. Paper presented at the Beyond AFTA and Towards an ASEAN Common Market Conference, Mandarin Oriental Hotel, Manila, the Philippines,18–20 October.

Battistella, G. and M. Asis (1999) *The Crisis and Migration in Asia* (Quezon City: Scalabrini Migration Center).

Carlos, R. (2002) 'On the Determinants of International Migration in the Philippines: an Empirical Analysis', *International Migration Review*, Vol. 36, No. 1: 81–102.

Castles, S. (2000) *Ethnicity and Globalization: From Migrant Worker to Transnational Citizen* (London: Sage Publications).

Central Bank of the Philippines (2001) Selected Philippine Economic Indications 2002, http://www.bsp.gov.ph/Statistics/stats_SPEIY.htm.

Commission on Filipinos Overseas (2004) *Stock Estimate of Overseas Filipinos*, http://www.cfo.gov.ph/ (accessed 25 May 2004).

Costello, M. and Ferrer, P. (1993) 'Projected Patterns of Labour Force Participation for the Year 2000: The Philippines and its Administrative Regions'. Paper prepared for the project: 'Strategic Approaches Toward Employment Promotion', sponsored by the Japanese Ministry of Labour, executed by DOLE, Manila and ARTEP-ILO, New Delhi (Manila) June.

—— (1992) 'Net Migration in the Philippines, 1980–1990'. Paper prepared for the project: 'Strategic Approaches Toward Employment Promotion' sponsored by the Japanese Ministry of Labour, executed by DOLE, Manila and ARTEP-ILO, New Delhi (Manila) August.

Cox, D. (1997) 'The Vulneribility of Asian Women Migrant Workers to a Lack of Protection and to Violence', *Asian and Pacific Migration Journal*, Vol. 6, No. 1: 59–75.

Cruz, Ma. C, I. Zosa-Feranil, C. and Goce (1988) 'Population Pressure and Migration: Implications for Upland Development in the Philippines', *Journal of Philippine Development*, Vol. 15, No. 26: 1–12.

Cruz, W. and R. Repetto (1992) *The Environmental Effects of Stabilization and Structural Adjustment Programmes: The Philippine Case* (Washington DC: World Resources Institute).

De Guzman, O. (2003) 'Overseas Filipino Workers, Labor Circulation in Southeast Asia, and the (Mis)management of Overseas Migration Programs', http://kyotorview. cseas.kyoto-u.ac.jp/issue3/article_322.html (accessed 29 May 2004).

Ghosh, B. (ed.) (2000) *Managing Migration: Time For a New Regime?* (Oxford: Oxford University Press).

Global Commission on International Migration, www.gcim.org (accessed 29 May 2004, 6 January 2005).

Go, S. (2001) 'International Labor Migration and the Filipino Family: Examining the Social Dimensions', *Asian Migrant*, Vol. 14, No. 4 (October–December): 105–09.

Gonzalez, J. L. (1998) *Philippine Labour Migration: Critical Dimensions of Public Policy* (Singapore: Institute of South East Asian Studies).

Government of Philippines (2001) *Commission on Fillipinos Overseas* (Manila: Department of Foreign Affairs).

IBON (2004) http://www.ibon.org/news/if/02/18.htm.

Philippine Department of Labor and Employment, White Paper (1995) *The Overseas Employment Program* (Manila: DOLE).

Philippine Overseas Employment Administration (POEA) (2003) *Annual Report: On the Path to Global Excellence in Governance* (Mandaluyong City: Philippine Overseas Employment Administration) http://www.poea.gov.ph.

Piper, N. and R. Ball (2001) 'The Globalisation of Asian Migrant Labour: Re-evaluation of State and Regional Dynamics in Human Rights Negotiations: The Philippine-Japan Connection', *Journal of Contemporary Asia*, Vol. 31, No. 4: 533–54.

Republic of the Philippines (1995) 'Migrant Workers and Overseas Filipinos Act of 1995', *Asian Migrant*, Vol. 8, No. 3: 87–94.

Sassen, S. (1996) *Losing Control?* (New York: Columbia University Press).

Stalker, P. (2000) *Workers Without Frontiers: The Impact of Globalisation on International Migration* (Boulder: Lynne Rienner Publishers).

Sto. Tomas, P. (2004) 'The Strangers among us', *Manila Bulletin*, 19 May.

—— (2002) 'Managing the Overseas Migration Program: Lessons Learned and New Directions', *Asian Migrant*, Vol. 15, No. 4: 94–98.

Tacoli, C. (1999) 'International migration and the Restructuring of Gender Asymmetries: Continuity and Change among Filipino Labor Migrants in Rome', *International Migration Review*, Vol. 33, Fall: 658–75.

—— (1995) 'Gender and International Survival Strategies: A Research Agenda with Reference to Filipina Labour Migrants in Italy', *Third World Planning Review*, Vol. 17, No. 2: 199–212.

Tan, E. (2001) 'Labor Market Adjustments to Large Scale Emigration: The Philippine Case', *Asian and Pacific Migration*, Vol. 10, Nos. 3–4: 379–400.

Tigno, J. (1997) 'ASEAN Labor migration: Strategic Implications for Japan in South East Asia', *Asian Migrant*, Vol. 10, No. 3: 86–89.

Trager, L. (1988) *The City Connection: Migration and Family Interdependence in the Philippines* (Ann Arbor: University of Michigan Press).

United Nations (1990) *International Convention on the Protection of the Rights of All Migrant Workers and Members of their Families*, 1990, Official Records of the General Assembly, Forty Fifth Session, Supplement No. 49(A/45/49).

Valencia, J. (2003) Speech at the Seminar on Philippine Migrants, SASK Solidarity Weekend in Lahti, Finland, 5 April 2003.

Vasquez, N. (1992) *Economic and Social Impact of Labor Migration* in G. Battistella and A. Paganoni (eds) *Philippine Labor Migration: Impact and Policy* (Manila: Scalabrini Migration Centre) pp. 41–67.

7
Indonesian Labour Migration after the 1997–98 Asian Economic and Financial Crisis

Carunia Mulya Firdausy

Introduction

The reduction of unemployment is currently one of the most pressing tasks of government, as the Indonesian economy has not fully recovered from the Asian economic crisis of 1997–98. The export of labour has thus become an important issue as Indonesia confronts the economic and social issues associated with unemployment and the globalisation of labour markets. During the period from 2001 to 2002, 455,879 Indonesian workers went to work abroad. Again, between January and June 2003 the government sent 62,655 workers to East Asia (Department of Manpower and Transmigration 2004). Previously, about 2.5 million Indonesians had worked abroad. However, all these figures exclude undocumented Indonesian migrants. The main regions that recruit Indonesian workers include the Middle East and East and Southeast Asian countries (particularly with the latter's commitment towards economic integration).

However, there have been many instances where Indonesian migrant workers have been abused by employers. Reported cases include sexual harassment, unpaid wages and excessive working hours. The Indonesian government's current policies towards their labour emigrants are considered limited and ineffective, and both previous and current policies have failed to protect Indonesian migrant workers. Accordingly, some policy reforms have been proposed including formulation of a National and Regional Manpower Planning Policy; a national Legal Assistance body; and adequate worker insurance and the formation of Foreign Employment Boards in labour-receiving countries. Additionally, official Memoranda of Understanding (MOUs) between the Government of Indonesia and governments of labour-receiving countries have been formulated. Labour contract agreements between migrants and employment agencies on the one hand, and between employment agencies in Indonesia and receiving countries on the other, are also in the pipeline.

Why did Indonesian labour migration increase after the 1997–98 economic and financial crisis?

Indonesia was hit harder by the Asian crisis of 1997–98 than any other country. In less than a year the country was transformed from an economic miracle into an economic debacle. Annual growth rates that had averaged 7.8 per cent for almost thirty years of economic development (1969–97) under Soeharto's New Order regime suddenly contracted to −13.7 per cent in 1998. Annual growth rates since that year have always been less than 5 per cent. In 2000, for example, the growth rate was only 3.2 per cent, whilst in 2001 and 2002 growth rates were 3.3 per cent and 3.9 per cent respectively. Some improvement was apparent in 2003 (4.5 per cent). However, low annual growth rates of less than five per cent have made it difficult for the economy to absorb an additional two million job seekers annually (ILO 2003).

According to the Central Board of Statistics (2004), the shortfall in employment opportunities in Indonesia was especially apparent between 2001 and 2003. During these years total employment remained static and stood at an average of 90.8 million, leading to an increase in unemployment. According to the Department of Manpower and Transmigration (2004) about 40 million within the workforce in 2003 were under-employed (defined as labourers working less than 35 hours in a week). Unemployment was recorded at about 11 million in the same period.

Unemployment has resulted in increased poverty in Indonesia. The World Bank (2002), citing figures for the Central Board of Statistics (2003), estimated that about 110 million people, or 53 per cent of Indonesia's total population in 2002, had per capita incomes of less than US$2.00 per day. Using official poverty line definitions (average per capita income per month of Rp.110 000 [equivalent US$12.50] or less), about 19.6 per cent of the population fell into this category. The proportion of the poor in Indonesia is significantly higher now than in 1996, when it was estimated at around 11.3 per cent.

Apart from increased unemployment and a rise in the incidence of poverty, the crisis has also changed the employment status situation. Formal sector employment has shown a declining ability to absorb newcomers into the workforce. In 2003 the total number of employees in the formal sector was only 23.3 million, while in 2000 it was about 29.5 million. The declining ability of the economy to absorb formal sector employees appears to be associated with a decreasing number of employers in the country. In 2001 the number of employers was about 2.8 million, and this fell to 2.7 million in 2003.

Within formal sector employment, agriculture and construction are the dominant economic sectors that have shown a declining ability to absorb labour. Between 2000 and 2003 the ability of the agricultural sector to absorb new entrants fell by 61 per cent, while the construction sector's ability fell by 38 per cent. Other major sectors that have also shown a declining ability to absorb new entrants over the same period include transportation and telecommunications (−12 per cent) and manufacturing (−11 per cent).

The declining ability of the agricultural sector to absorb new entrants into the workforce has been associated with falling growth rates in this sector. In 2001 the agricultural sector growth rate decreased by 1 per cent, while in 2003 it decreased by 2.5 per cent. This suggests that the economic crisis has had an adverse impact upon the ability of both agricultural and non-agricultural sectors to absorb new entrants into the workforce.

One major consequence of the declining ability of the formal sector to absorb new entrants into the workforce has been a rise in employment in the informal sector, defined as consisting of self-employed persons, self-employed persons assisted by family members, farmers and unpaid family workers. Employment in the informal sector increased from 57.8 million in 2001 to 64.2 million in 2003 (see Figure 7.1). It is clear, therefore, that

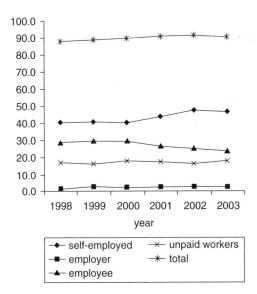

Figure 7.1 Employment situation by employment status, 1998–2003

Source: Central Board of Statistics, Labor Force Survey, various years.

increased Indonesian labour emigration is consistent with the high unemployment rates stemming from low economic growth since 1998. Low economic growth has also led to increased competition between skilled workers and unskilled workers for shrinking employment opportunities. In fact, there have been indications that workers with educational attainments higher than elementary school have sought work in the informal sector. Consequently, both male and female workers with lower educational levels have found it harder to find employment. This predicament has especially impacted upon women in particular. Between 1999 and 2003 female employment decreased by 25 per cent, while male employment decreased by 14 per cent.

Size and composition of Indonesian labour migration

As noted, increasing unemployment has led the government to encourage Indonesians to work abroad. In 2001, for instance, the government sent 217,555 workers to work abroad. In 2002, and between January and June 2003, the government sent 238,324 and 62,655 workers abroad respectively to East Asia (Department of Manpower and Transmigration 2004). Prior to this period, in 1999, there were already about 2.5 million Indonesian labour migrants abroad (Table 7.1).

As shown above, the main destinations of Indonesian labour flows included Saudi Arabia and Malaysia, followed by Singapore, Hong Kong,

Table 7.1 Indonesian labour migrants: numbers and destinations, 1999

Destination	Number of migrant workers
Saudi Arabia	425,000
United Arab Emirates	35,000
Malaysia	1,900,000
Hong Kong	32,000
Singapore	70,000
Taiwan	18,269
Rep. of Korea	11,700
Japan	3,245
Philippines	26,000
Brunei	2,426
Others	20,000
Total	2,543,640

Note: These figures exclude undocumented Indonesian migrants.

Source: Hugo cited in R. Aswatini (2001).

Philippines, Taiwan and the Republic of Korea. The Department of Manpower and Transmigration (2004) has estimated that illegal Indonesian labour migration amounted to about 3.5 million people between 1999 and 2001. Hugo (1998) and Kassim (1998) estimate that the number of Indonesian illegal migrants in Malaysia alone in 2000 stood at about 1 million workers.

Indonesian migrant workers are mainly semi-skilled and unskilled workers (Department of Manpower and Transmigration 2004). However, in terms of the types of jobs undertaken by the migrants, differences exist between receiving countries. In Malaysia, for instance, most of the Indonesian migrant workers are engaged in the agricultural sector (especially the plantation sector), while the remainder are employed in the construction sector, manufacturing and certain service sectors (Watanabe 2002). In Taiwan, Hong Kong and Singapore most of the Indonesian migrants are engaged in the '3D' (dirty, dangerous and degrading) occupations. These include domestic work, construction work and jobs in the manufacturing, marine and service sectors (Hui 2000; Athukorala 2003). Apart from the large number of Indonesian migrants who migrated to East Asia, there has been a

Table 7.2 Indonesian workers employed in selected Asian countries by economic sector, January to June 2003

| Countries | Sector | Months | | | | | | Total |
		Jan	Feb	Mar	Apr	May	June	
Malaysia	Estate	1,286	6,164	6,967	1,558	4,258	767	21,000
	Construction							28,825
	Manufacturing							28,073
	Service							740
	Domestic work							2,180
	Domestic work	2,295					250	2,545
	Industry	170		50				220
Hong Kong	Domestic work	1,760					80	1,840
Brunei Darussalam	Industry			1,450	260			1,710
Singapore	Domestic work					2,923	3,234	9,395
Rep of Korea	Formal							
Saudi Arabia	(e.g. nurses)	3,238				48	140	188
Kuwait	Domestic work	690					250	2,735
	Formal							
	(e.g. nurses)	500				1,795	54	554
Jordan	Domestic work	1,000				1,000		2,000
Qatar	Domestic work	300					100	400
United Arab Emirates	Domestic work	500		7,049		165	375	8,089
Oman	Domestic work	100						100
Total		23,077	14,568	30,358	15,702	18,095	8,794	110,594

Source: Department of Manpower and Transmigration, Government of Indonesia 2004.

significant number of migrants working in the Middle East, especially Saudi Arabia. These migrants principally comprise female migrants who are contracted for a period of about two to three years, mainly as domestic workers. Table 7.2 shows the type of occupations of Indonesian labour migrants in some Asian countries.

Apart from unskilled and semi-skilled workers, there were also Indonesian professional and technical workers in Malaysia, Singapore, the Republic of Korea, Japan, and Brunei. However, these workers account for a small share of total labour migrant flows and consist predominantly of contract workers (who migrate for a period of around two to three years). These workers went abroad during the period when these labour-receiving countries (especially Japan and the Republic of Korea) had begun to export capital in the process of industrial adjustment and upgrading (Department of Manpower and Transmigration 2004). However, detailed figures for these types of workers are not available. The movement of skilled and professional manpower from Indonesia has gained importance in recent years, a feature

Table 7.3 Indonesian formal worker migrants by gender and destination, 2003

No	Region/State	Male	Female	Total
I.	*Asia Pacific*			
1	Malaysia	27,148	13,543	40,691
2	Singapore	0	0	2
3	Brunei Darussalam	344	293	637
4	Hong Kong	0	3	3
5	Taiwan	1,054	246	1,300
6	South Korea	5,075	929	6,004
7	Thailand	0	0	0
8	Japan	61	0	61
	Total	33,682	15,016	48,698
II.	*Middle East and Africa*			
1	Saudi Arabia	534	224	758
2	United Arab Emirates	73	18	91
3	Kuwait	52	34	86
4	Bahrain	0	0	0
5	Qatar	0	0	0
6	Oman	0	0	0
7	Jordan	0	0	0
8	Yemen	0	0	0
9	Cyprus	0	0	0
	Total	659	276	935

Source: Department of Manpower and Transmigration, Government of Indonesia, 2004.

Table 7.4 Indonesian workers in the informal sector by gender, 2003

No	Region/State	Male	Female	Total
I.	*Asia Pacific*			
1	Malaysia	1,615	6,622	8,237
2	Singapore	5	2,087	2,092
3	Brunei Darussalam	0	447	447
4	Hong Kong	0	2,740	2,740
5	Taiwan	39	287	326
6	South Korea	92	23	115
7	Thailand	0	0	0
8	Japan	0	0	0
	Total	1,751	12,206	13,957
II.	*Middle East and Africa*			
1	Saudi Arabia	9,931	94,009	103,940
2	United Arab Emirate	17	1,400	1,417
3	Kuwait	69	8,765	8,834
4	Bahrain	0	108	108
5	Qatar	0	194	194
6	Oman	0	401	401
7	Jordan	0	189	189
8	Yemen	0	0	0
9	Cyprus	0	0	0
	Total	10,017	105,066	115,083

Source: Department of Manpower and Transmigration, Government of Indonesia, 2004.

associated with greater regional integration through trade and investment (Manning 2002).

In terms of employment by gender, the number of male formal migrant workers in some occupations such as nursing has been approximately twice that of formal female workers (Table 7.3).

In the informal sector, particularly domestic work, female workers have predominated (Table 7.4). These differences appear to be related to the nature of the services demanded by the labour-receiving countries. Female workers tend to migrate to countries where domestic workers are needed, while the large number of male formal workers tend to migrate to countries where jobs are available in the health, construction, transportation, agricultural and estate sectors. Tables 7.3 and 7.4 show the number of male and female Indonesian migrants working in the formal and informal sectors in 2003.

What are the reasons for Indonesian migrant labour demand and recruitment? In the case of the labour-receiving countries in East Asia, for

example, Athukorala (2003) and Stahl (2000) have argued that the two
factors influencing labour migration are changes in demographic patterns
and differences in economic growth. For Japan, migrant worker inflows have
been associated with the rapid decline in fertility brought about by
economic affluence, coupled with an ageing population. The increasing
affluence of the Japanese has made them reluctant to engage in 3-D forms of
employment and other jobs that do not provide an upward career path.

Similarly, in Korea and Taiwan, inflows of migrant workers have risen
due to rapid industrialisation, which has created labour shortages in
non-tradeable goods sectors and small to medium scale manufacturing
firms, as well as the reluctance of domestic labour to undertake 3-D jobs.
Inflows of migrant workers to Hong Kong and Singapore have been
associated with a significant structural shift in the services sector, away from
traditional activities and towards modern, more-skilled intensive operations.
These conditions have also consequently led to the lessening of Hong Kong's
and Singapore's dependence on unskilled migrant workers.

In Thailand and Malaysia, large inflows of migrant workers are due to
labour shortages in self-employed and contract jobs in agriculture and
fishing leading to increased international labour migration. These migrant
workers mostly entered the construction, domestic service and manufacturing
industries in the major urban centres of Malaysia and Thailand.

Therefore, the size and composition of migrant worker flows from
Indonesia are very much subject to the demand for particular types of labour
in the receiving countries. Demand has mostly been for semi-skilled and
unskilled workers. This is mainly because most of the labour-receiving countries in East Asia have labour shortages due to demographic changes and
comparative economic affluence. As these conditions will continue in the
near future – and because of the current large unemployment problem in
Indonesia – the Indonesian government is now working to facilitate and
regulate unskilled and semi-skilled migration. This is necessary to minimise
the exploitation of migrant workers, reduce illegal migration, and deflect
negative publicity aired by the media.

Recruitment procedures and practices

The recruitment procedures of the recruitment agency locally known as
Perusahaan Jasa Tenaga Kerja Indonesia (PJTKI) are not that simple.
Moreover, according to an officer at PT Sukma Karja Sejati (employment
agency) in Jakarta, most of the potential labour migrants are not directly
recruited by this company (PJTKI). The recruitment process starts at the village level, where a local village sponsor's permission has to be sought by
potential emigrants. In fact, these local village sponsors scout around to seek

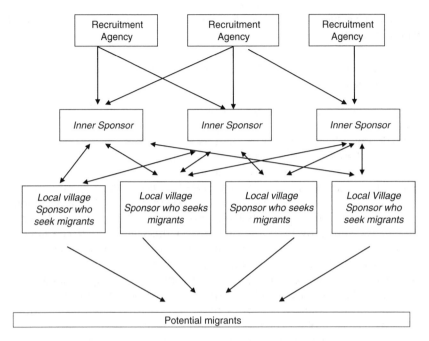

Figure 7.2 The recruitment process of Indonesian labour migrants

potential migrant workers by visiting villages where unemployment is rife. The local village sponsors then take the potential migrants to other sponsors who work for the urban-based employment recruitment agencies. These 'inner' sponsors then take potential migrants to employment recruitment agencies (see Figure 7.2).

Labour migrants do not register directly with employment recruitment agencies for two reasons. First, most of the employment recruitment agencies are located in large cities and potential labour migrants have to incur transport and accommodation costs. Second, local village sponsors are usually known to the migrants, and some of them also offer financial assistance. Therefore, local village sponsors play an important role in labour recruitment at the village level.

I was informed by a resource officer at PT Sukma Karya Sejati that the local village sponsors are also important sources of information on employment opportunities abroad, information on registered places, emigration costs and other administrative matters. However, information on travel procedures is obtained from the employment recruitment agency. In sum, local village sponsors have many roles in providing assistance and information to potential labour migrants.

Economic and social effects of labour migration on the economy

It is true that the increasing number of international labour migrants from Indonesia have made positive contributions to the economy. Apart from the reduction of domestic unemployment, labour migration also contributes to foreign exchange earnings and reduces poverty. In terms of unemployment reduction, for instance, Indonesian labour migration provided employment opportunities for about 1.4 million workers between 1999 and 2001. In the case of foreign exchange earnings, the Department of Manpower and Transmigration (2004) estimated that migrant workers increased foreign exchange earnings by US$3.145 billion over the same period. The largest remittance contributions came from the Asia Pacific region, followed by the Middle East. This is not surprising as the number of Indonesian workers working in the latter region is very small compared with the Indonesians working in East Asian countries. However, this particular contribution did not take into account remittances made by 3.5 million illegal migrants (*Kompas*, 17 June 2004). The exact amount of the exchange earnings attributable to illegal migrants is not known, but it clearly makes a significant contribution to Indonesian foreign exchange earnings.

Unfortunately there is no data available on the contribution of Indonesian labour migration to poverty reduction. Apart from difficulties arising from the lack of data, it should be noted that not all of the workers who migrate abroad fall into the lowest income-earning categories. Many labour migrants have been able to remit their salaries to their families providing for daily family needs, house renovation, educational fees, and other purposes.

On the other hand, international labour migration has resulted in an increase in marriage dissolution rates. This is particularly so for migrants who work abroad for extended periods. Also, male domination of migration flows has caused a decline in fertility rates. High rates of male out-migration have also increased the burden of women in the family since they have to (with the help of children) perform tasks traditionally performed by men (Aswatini 2001). The absence of men, nevertheless, has tended to increase the self-reliance of those women charged with providing for their families.

Similarly, female out-migration also has had profound social impacts, particularly among younger female workers. Yayasan Pengembangan Pedesaan's study (1996) reveals that the social impact of female out-migration on the family includes the following: first, many husbands' respect for their wives has increased; second, men took on more childrearing roles during the absence of their wives, and there was a breaking down of the traditional division of family tasks along gender lines; third, there was little evidence of negative effects on children during their mother's absence; fourth, the extended family covered many of the tasks usually undertaken by the absence of women; and fifth, most women returning to the family home considered their main role to be house wives.

However, these findings are difficult to verify as they are not quantifiable. Generally, women's involvement in migration may create numerous problems for the migrants themselves and the family left behind, particularly young children. In the short term, the absence of mothers involves potential health costs for children. Separation of mothers from young children may cause emotional deprivation that in turn could result in stunted emotional growth. However, in the long run the children may also benefit from economic gains (Purwaningsih 1994 cited in Aswatini 2001). Also, because of the low educational and work experience attainments of the majority of labour migrants, migration can have a positive effect on the workers' performance after they return from abroad. Work experiences gained through labour migration are believed to stimulate economic growth. Therefore, it is quite clear that Indonesian labour migration has economic and social effects upon the economy as well as individual migrants and their families.

Problems and constraints faced by migrant workers

Mistreatment and sexual abuse

Working abroad is not without problems. There is much evidence that many international labour migrants (especially unskilled workers) have been mistreated not only by the employers, but also by the employment recruitment agencies in both the home and host countries. However, the forms of mistreatment and abuse appear to vary from country to country. In Saudi Arabia, where data is available, it was reported that mistreatment included sexual harassment, excessive working hours, unpaid salary and other mistreatment and abuse. In relation to excessive working hours, in 1995 the number of reported cases amounted to 544 while in 1999 it was 1589. Of the total number of cases in the respect, it appears that a number of cases are as yet unresolved (see Table 7.5). The increase in mistreatment and abuse of labour migrants can be attributed to the increase in Indonesian migration flows from 1997.

Similarly, in relation to cases of unpaid salary and sexual abuse, it can be seen in Tables 7.6 and 7.7 that there were a number of workers who were abused on a continuous basis. Whilst most of these cases have been resolved, some remain unresolved. Some workers also suffered during the recruitment

Table 7.5 Number of Indonesians forced to undertake excessive work hours in Saudi Arabia, 1995–99

Year	Number of workers	Overwork cases	
		Cases	Cases solved
1995–96	43,521	544	424
1996–97	127,137	1,602	1,276
1997–98	121,965	1,524	1,203
1998–99	161,063	2,013	1,672
1999–2000	127,165	1,589	1,526

Source: Manpower Department, Government of Indonesia, 2000.

Table 7.6 Number of unpaid salary cases involving Indonesians in Saudi Arabia, 1995–99

Year	Number of workers	Unpaid salary	
		Cases	Cases finalised
1995–96	43,521	470	401
1996–97	127,137	1,374	950
1997–98	121,965	1,318	907
1998–99	161,063	2,741	2,563
1999–2000	127,165	1,374	106

Source: Manpower Department, Government of Indonesia, 2000.

Table 7.7 Number of sexual abuse cases involving Indonesians, 1995–99

Year	Number of workers	Sexual abuse	
		Cases	Cases finalised
1995–96	43,521	212	142
1996–97	127,137	640	573
1997–98	121,965	659	537
1998–99	161,063	988	697
1999–2000	127,165	927	503

Source: Manpower Department, Government of Indonesia, 2000.

process, particularly those forced to pay exorbitant application and administrative fees. Others were forced by Indonesian companies to take jobs they would not normally consider. Mistreatment and abuse by employers and by recruitment companies in Indonesia and overseas encouraged the Minister for Women's Empowerment, together with many non-governmental organisations (NGOs), to call for a stop to the government's policy of exporting Indonesian workers overseas.

One consequence of worker mistreatment is that migrants seek to change employers. If they cannot find a different employer, they usually seek assistance from friends or the local Indonesian embassy. However, these migrants almost never return to Indonesia, particularly if they cannot pay their travel costs. Consequently, government protection at both ends is an issue that needs to be resolved.

Migrant fee charges

Apart from mistreatment and sex abuse, potential migrant workers also face problems and constraints in relation to non-standardised overseas fee charges. Generally, these charges range between Rp. 2.5 million (equivalent to US$290) and Rp. 5 million (equivalent to US$550). Fees usually cover five cost components, namely transportation and accommodation costs from the village to the domestic recruitment agency; accommodation and subsistence costs during the waiting period for placement abroad; administrative costs for education and training; fees for employment agency or brokers; other related costs such as levies, work permit fees, passport fees and the like.

However, migrants who apply through non-registered brokers are charged higher fees. Also, overseas placement fees vary according to the employment sector. Higher overseas fees are generally charged in the construction, fishing and other services sector. In respect of Malaysia, labour migrants have to pay at least RM1800 for jobs in these industries, whilst in the estate sector Indonesian migrants usually have to pay RM500.

Labour migrants (especially those who rely on brokers) thus spend considerable amounts of money to obtain employment, and most have to minimise their spending abroad if they are to repay their debt to the employment agency. Those migrants who can restrict spending to basic living expenses can usually repay their debt in a year. Working abroad is no easy matter either. Apart from the fees that have to be paid to obtain employment, migrants also have to wait long periods for job approvals by recruitment agencies abroad. During this period labour migrants have to find work through local employment recruitment agencies. Some migrants (especially domestic workers) even work in local households in Jakarta before they go abroad. Perhaps due to this time consuming and uncertain process, many migrants decide to work abroad illegally.

Other problems and constraints

Indonesian labour migrants face considerable adjustment processes in terms of foreign culture and languages. There is a need for the employment recruitment agencies to provide information upon weather conditions, cultural environments and language training prior to migrant workers travelling abroad. Migrant workers also face problems associated with sub-standard accommodation and restrictions placed upon their ability to communicate with friends and family. The latter problem is usually faced by domestic helpers, while those who work at the construction, estates and other services sectors often have to cope with crowded and un-sanitary living conditions abroad.

Despite these problems, it is quite surprising to find that almost all the labour migrants interviewed are eager to return overseas. The main reason for this is simply the higher wages that can be obtained abroad as opposed to earnings in Indonesia. This eagerness to continue working abroad suggests that the attraction of comparatively high wages is one of the primary factors behind Indonesian labour migration.

Current policies towards labour migrants

Government policy relating to Indonesian labour migrants (especially low-skilled migrants) in both Indonesia and labour-receiving countries is very limited. In Indonesia, Ministerial Rule No. 4/1970 deals generally with the management of domestic and international migration. Another rule, the Minister of Transportation and the Minister of Manpower, Transmigration and Cooperative Units No. KM 136/S/PHB and No. Kep-59/men/1977, deals directly with international migration. However, currently there is no regulation to protect Indonesian labour migrants abroad. This situation can be contrasted with the Philippines, where the government has protected migrants working abroad under the Migrant Workers and Overseas Filipinos Act of 1995.

The Indonesian government has not ratified the International Labour Organisation (ILO) Convention protecting rights of migrant workers and their families, and has no pertinent bilateral agreements with any of the labour-receiving countries. These arrangements are important not only to protect migrants from various types of exploitation, but also to discourage illegal labour migration. As such, they need to be formulated, and moves for protective legislation are currently afoot.

International migration will become an even bigger issue for Indonesia in the future, as the national government attempts to address unemployment problems and the globalisation of labour markets. Efforts to reduce unemployment are now critical as the Indonesian economy has not fully recovered from the 1997–98 Asian economic crisis. Countries that have the potential for accepting Indonesian workers are now not limited to the Middle East, but also include East and Southeast Asian countries such as Taiwan, Malaysia, Singapore, Brunei Darussalam, Hong Kong, and the Republic of Korea. In the Middle East region, Kuwait, Qatar and Bahrain and Saudi Arabia are potential destination countries for future Indonesian migrants. Indonesian workers overseas have suffered sexual harassment, are not paid on a regular basis (some not at all) and work excessive hours. Illegal migrants have also been exploited being forced to pay high administration fees and low wages. For these reasons, the Indonesian government is working to establish strong bilateral relationships with governments of destination countries to minimise these problems. The present policies towards labour migrants from Indonesia have been considered limited and ineffective. There is much evidence that previous and present policies are failing to protect labour migrants, and that much more needs to be done.

References

Aswatini, R. (2001) *Indonesian Female Labor Migrants: Experiences Working Overseas (A Case Study among Returned Migrants in West Java)*, Working Paper No. 32, Research Centre for Population-Indonesian Institute of Sciences, Jakarta.

Athukorala, P. (2003) 'International Labor Migration in East Asia: Patterns, Determinants and Policy Issues'. Paper presented at ISEAS meeting, University of Singapore.

Central Board of Statistics (2004) 'Indonesian Labour Force Survey' (Surve angkatan kerja nasional-SAKERNAS), Jakarta.

—— (2003) 'Jumlah penduduk Miskin di Indonesia', (The Poor in Indonesia) monograph, Jakarta.

Department of Manpower and Transmigration (2004) 'The employment situation and labour migration in Indonesia', (Kondisi Ketenagakerjaan dan Migrasi Tenaga kerja Indonesia) Jakarta.

Hugo, G. (1998) 'Undocumented International Migration in Southeast Asia', in C.M. Firdausy (ed.) *International Migration in Southeast Asia: Tends, Consequences, Issues and Policy Measures* (Jakarta: Toyota Foundation-Southeast Asian Studies program-Indonesian Institute of Sciences).

Hui, W.T. (2000) 'Foreign Manpower and Development Strategy in Singapore'. Paper presented at the international workshop on International Migration and Structural change in the APEC member economies, Taipei, 19–20 October 2000.

ILO (2003) 'Employment Challenges of the Indonesian Economic Crisis' (Jakarta: ILO).

Kassim, A. (1998) 'Household Study on Indonesian Immigrants in Malaysia: An Insight Into the Consequences of their Migration and their Problems', in C.M. Firdausy (ed.) *International Migration in Southeast Asia: Tends, Consequences, Issues and Policy Measures* (Jakarta: Toyota Foundation-Southeast Asian Studies program-Indonesian Institute of Sciences).

Kompas (17 June 2004) 'Problems faced by Indonesian migrants' (Masalah pekerja Indonesia di luar negeri).

Manning, C. (2002) 'Structural Change, Economic Crisis and International Labor migration in East Asia', *World Economy*, Vol. 25, No. 3: 359–84.

Stahl, C.W. (2000) 'The Impacts of Structural Change on APEC Labor Markets and Their Implications for International Migration'. Paper presented at the International

Workshop on International Migration and Structural Change in the APEC Member Economies, Taipei, 19–20 October 2000.

Watanabe, M. (2002) 'The Labour Market and International Migration in Thailand', in Y. Hayase, (ed.) *A Study on Trade, Investment and International Labor Migration in the APEC Member Economies* (Japan: APEC Study Centre, Institute of Developing Economies-JETRO).

Yayasan, Pengembangan Pedesaan (1996) 'The Impact of Women's Migration to the Family in Rural Areas' (Dampak dari Migrasi terhadap Keluarga di Pedesaan). Paper presented at the workshop on Women's Migration in Indonesia, Hotel Indonesia, Jakarta, 11–13 September 1996.

8

The Feminisation of Migration: Gender, the State and Migrant Strategies in Bangladesh

Ishrat Shamim

Introduction

At the start of the twenty-first century, one out of every 34 persons worldwide is an international migrant. The Population Division of the United Nations estimates the total number of international migrants at approximately 175 million (United Nations 2002). This number includes refugees and displaced persons, but does not capture irregular migrants who escape official accounting. Almost half of the estimated 175 million migrants worldwide are women.

Based on a world population of 6.057 billion (2000 estimate), migrants represent some 2.9 per cent. This percentage has changed in recent decades and has been rising steadily over the past fifteen years. Migration is difficult to quantify both at the national and international level because of the large number of undocumented migrants and the lack of established governmental systems in most countries for collection of migration related data. However, it is generally agreed that the number of movements has increased significantly over the past ten years, particularly through the emergence of 'new' groups of migrants, such as women migrating individually and highly qualified migrants (International Organisation of Migration [IOM] 2003:4–6).

Over the last few decades, the number of women who migrate for work has increased sharply: worldwide, the proportion of women in the migrant labour force rose from roughly 15 per cent in the 1970s to over 50 per cent in many countries by 1996 (International Labour Organisation [ILO] 1996). Women now move around far more independently and no longer in relation to their family position or under a man's authority. This reflects women's growing participation in all aspects of modern life. While many women migrate as spouses or family members, more are migrating independently of family, often to work abroad as principal breadwinners. IOM estimated that

48 per cent of all migrants are women (IOM 2003). In some regions, this proportion is even higher.

Most migration-related policies and regulations, both at the country of origin or the country of destination, have not adjusted to this new phenomenon of female migration. Policies are either non-existent or do not recognise the gendered nature of migration, which has unforeseen consequences for women, as we find that the feminisation of migration is not always a progressive development. Compared to men, more women often choose to migrate because of poverty and the lack of professional prospects, and are therefore more exposed to forced labour and sexual exploitation than men. They are also more likely to accept precarious working conditions and poorly paid work (IOM 2003).

With limited legal migration opportunities in some parts of the world, women resort to irregular forms of migration involving agents and traffickers, falling prey to various forms of violence and exploitation. Where regular migration has declined, illegal migration has increased – as has the recent trend of the trafficking in women. Trafficking for commercial sexual services is the most common form of exploitation in both Asia and Europe, although trafficking for other purposes like domestic labour, factory work, mail order bride services, begging, adoption and drug trafficking may be more common in Asia. Women become helpless victims of violence when they are trapped in situations from which they cannot escape. In Bangladesh, trafficking takes place by a variety of means including promises of jobs or marriages, and at times even by physical violence and abduction. But employment promises often prove false, and in some cases children of extremely poor families have been sold to brokers by their own parents or guardians simply to evade poverty and hunger. These victims often also become unwitting and unwilling subjects of sexual exploitation (Shamim and Kabir 1998).

Destination countries view trafficked women as undocumented migrants who entered or worked illegally. These women are vulnerable to arrest, detention and deportation because destination countries are unwilling to recognise that they are victims of crimes. They often do not have the chance to lodge complaints, seek damages, assess whether it is safe to return home, collect their belongings, or apply for asylum. Many laws and emigration management practices fail to distinguish between prostitutes and the victims of forced trafficking, treating the latter as criminals rather than those who deserve temporary care (Shamim 2002). The increase in tourism in recent decades has led to an escalating demand for entertainment and sex services. As the sex industry grows, so does the market for trafficking.

This paper explores the recent phenomena of female migration in Asia, and Bangladesh in particular – its nature and magnitude, contributory factors, employment and working conditions in destination countries, economic impacts upon households, women's empowerment, and lastly government policies regarding female migration. The paper is based on data collected from various secondary sources such as government agencies, private institutions and research organisations, as well as empirical research based on the findings of a field survey of 200 sample households.

Women in the migrant labour force in Asia

The main migrant labour-sending countries in Asia include the Philippines, Sri Lanka, Pakistan and Bangladesh (Wickramasekera 2002). On the other hand, the main labour-receiving countries are in the Middle East and other parts of Asia (Waddington 2003). Female labour migration is largely economically driven. The poorer countries are faced with rapidly increasing numbers of unemployed persons while the developed and newly industrialising countries (NICs), have an ever-increasing shortage of labour, especially in '3-D' (dirty, difficult and degrading) categories of work, due largely to affluent economies and low population growth rates. As such, labour migration, especially of women, is generally perceived as a convenient solution to the human resource problems of both sending and receiving countries.

The Asian Migrant Forum identified three basic types of female migrant workers in Asia. The first is the sex worker; the second is the domestic worker or 'maid'; and the third is the manufacturing worker. There are other service workers such as nurses and other health workers but the first three are the most dominant. Sex workers are the most desperate and the most vulnerable to exploitation, and are usually recruited by criminal syndicates after having worked in the prostitution industry for some time. They are hired under various guises as 'culture' workers, 'students', or 'trainees', or they enter as 'tourists'. Because sex workers eventually overstay their legitimate visas in order to continue to work, they are the most vulnerable to abuse not only by the criminal groups, but also by the employers and clients.

Domestic workers are very much in demand in Asia. They are hired primarily to free local women from house work. Domestic workers are generally oppressed by the nature and the environment of their work. Their work involves taking care of babies and infants, the elderly or ailing members of the family, or disabled people. It involves cleaning, cooking, laundrying, and sometimes 'massaging' employers. Domestic workers are 'on call' twenty four hours a day and have no specific working hours.

Manufacturing workers also face many problems, especially if they are undocumented workers. They live and work in substandard conditions. They are prone to industrial accidents because equipment operational instructions often are not supplied in their language. Others acquire work-related diseases and since most are not legally employed they are not entitled to any compensation (Migrant Forum in Asia 1995).

Over the years, the role of women in labour migration has been very much overshadowed by the attention given to certain other sectors like undocumented/illegal workers. Even in the Asian region, where women overwhelmingly outnumber male migrant workers, there is lack of sensitivity to the impact of female migrants on labour forces, economies and societies. However, recent incidents such as the execution of a Filipino maid, Flor Contemplacion, in Singapore and the sentencing of another Filipino maid, Sarah Balabagan, in Abu Dhabi for the murder of her rapist, have focused the spotlight on the plight of migrant women.

In Asia, women now make up the majority of expatriates working abroad: in 1986, female migrants represented 33 per cent of all Sri Lankan migrant workers overseas, increasing to 65 per cent by 1999. In the Philippines, women accounted for 70 per cent of migrant workers abroad in 2000, most living without their families and providing for those who stayed behind (IOM 2003). However, the majority of Sri Lankan women migrants perform low-wage occupations such as domestic work, which accounted for 66 per cent of Sri Lanka's total flow in 1995 (Waddington 2003).

In both sending and receiving countries, Asian women face two forms of discrimination and exploitation: as women, and as migrant workers. As women, they are discriminated against and considered inferior to men and, therefore, are predominantly limited to low-wage job categories. Given the high illiteracy rate among Asian women, they are also more likely to be deceived by unscrupulous employment agencies and employers. Semi-literate and illiterate women often sign work contracts without knowing the terms and conditions of their employment. Often they are also underpaid whilst being compelled by employers to sign receipts for higher amounts. As migrant workers, women are more vulnerable to physical and sexual harassment. Moreover, employers know that Asian women, because of their cultural backgrounds, tend to be more submissive and hence are less likely to complain about their living and working conditions, or physical or sexual harassment (Migrant Forum in Asia 1995).

Many female migrants are more vulnerable to human rights abuses since they work in gender-segregated and unregulated sectors of the economy such as domestic work, entertainment and the sex industry – all largely unprotected by labour legislation or policy. Many women are employed in unskilled jobs with limited prospects for upward mobility: they earn low wages, work long hours, and have little or no job security or rights to social benefits. They are frequently unaware of their rights and obligations (IOM 2003:7). Wickramasekera (2002) contends that the most important trend in terms of protecting the rights of migrants is the rising number of irregular migrants who, without legal status, are subject to frequent abuse. This phenomenon is certainly true of many Asian women migrants who are unable to avail themselves of legal migration channels.

The Bangladeshi state and migration policy

The Bangladeshi state promotes employment of its human resources abroad as part of its development plans as migration generates significant financial flows in the form of remittances. Moreover, the migration of workers also has helped reduce the unemployment rate, one of the country's major problems. Bangladesh's labour market dynamics have changed in the context of a globalised labour market. Since the mid-1970s Bangladesh has exported around 3 million people, of which more than 80 per cent went to the Middle East (Afsar *et al.*, 2002). But policies, legislation and institutions for managing the outflow of labour have lagged behind the flow, primarily due to a lack of resources and skills.

After Bangladesh's independence, migration was regulated and controlled by legislation inherited from the British colonial period. With the gradual increase in the flow of temporary labour migrants from Bangladesh to Middle-eastern countries, the inadequacy of these laws was felt and major policy changes were envisaged. A new legal instrument, the Emigration Ordinance of 1982, was promulgated. This dealt with the process of recruitment, the licensing of recruiting agents, emigration procedures, minimum standards for wages and employment conditions, charges for recruitment, malpractice, enforcement machinery, and so on. Labour recruitment from Bangladesh has involved various ministries and agencies of government, private recruiting agents, their local and international intermediaries, and potential migrants and their families – making it a complex process. Until 2001, the Ministry of Labour and Employment had charge of international labour migration. The current government, responding to the demand of expatriate Bangladeshis and migrant workers, formed a new ministry in December 2001. Since its inception, the Ministry of Expatriates' Welfare and Overseas Employment has undertaken various steps for managing labour migration, including the implementation of rules framed in 2002 under the 1982 Emigration Ordinance. The leadership of the ministry has made several visits abroad to expand the labour market for Bangladeshi workers. New agreements have been signed with Italy, Greece, Korea and Malaysia. The ministry is also organising inter-ministerial meetings to coordinate welfare programmes for migrant workers (Siddiqui 2003).

The Bureau of Manpower, Employment and Training (BMET), established in 1976, is the primary agency of the Ministry Expatriates' Welfare and Overseas Employment. BMET is currently involved in the regulation of recruitment agents, collection and analysis of labour market information, the registration of job seekers for local and foreign employment, development and implementation of training programmes in the light of specific labour needs both in national and international labour markets, designing apprenticeship and other educational programmes in the existing industries, organising pre-departure briefing sessions and resolving legal disputes.

Since 1980, private agencies have recruited workers for overseas employment under a government license. These agencies collected information on demand for foreign employment, recruited workers and then processed cases for deployment. By 2002, 45 per cent of the total number of labour migrants went through such agencies. The latter eventually organised themselves under the auspices of the Bangladesh Association of International Recruiting Agencies (BAIRA) in 1983, and by 2002 the association had a membership of around 700 agencies. In 1984 the government also set up BOESL to undertake direct recruitment. Since its inception up until February 1999, BOESL has recruited 8909 workers. This is 0.31 per cent of the total number of those who went overseas through official channels. Nonetheless, a substantial portion of those who went abroad through BOESL were skilled or professional women (Siddiqui 2001).

In spite of the above initiatives, about 55 to 60 per cent of recruitment is conducted through individual initiatives and social networks (Siddiqui 2001). Usually persons already deployed in the host countries arrange visas for their friends and relatives through their own contacts. Sometimes these visas are sold to interested parties. The cost of migration is less when work visas are obtained through individual migrants working abroad. Though Bangladesh has been a major source of labour, civil institutions have done little to provide services and protect migrant workers' rights. That said, during the last few years some human rights organisations and research bodies have initiated limited ameliorative activities (Siddiqui 2003). The Christian Commission for Development in Bangladesh (CCDB), for example, was involved in a collaborative project with the Kuala Lumpur-based CARAM Asia on HIV AIDS and mobility. To reach its target group, it funded SHISUK, an NGO, to establish an association of migrant workers. Currently SHISUK provides pre-departure orientation for Bangladeshi migrant workers going to Malaysia. Ain O Shalish Kendra (ASK), Bangladesh Legal Aid and Services Trust (BLAST) and Bangladesh Society for Enforcement of Human Rights (BSEHR) have on different occasions also provided legal aid to migrant workers cheated by recruiting agents.

Some returnee migrants have also developed their own organisations. Over the last few years, three such organisations have emerged. The Welfare Association of the Bangladeshi Returnee Employees (WARBE) has been

---

CARAM Asia

Coordination of Action Research on AIDS and Mobility (CARAM) is a partnership of seven NGOs from Bangladesh, Cambodia, Indonesia, Malaysia, Philippines, Thailand and Vietnam. CARAM Bangladesh carries out pre-departure briefing and training of migrant workers going to Malaysia. The organisation relies on migrants who have already returned from working in Malaysia to help in the training. Women attending the sessions are given information on where they can go in Malaysia if they have difficulties. Upon arrival, CARAM Malaysia takes over handling their cases and offers them medical support. CARAM Malaysia also encourages Bangladesh migrants to participate in the post-orientation programmes. CARAM Bangladesh, in turn, involves return migrants in reintegration programmes.

Source: UNAIDS (2001).

organising returnee migrants since 1997 and acts as a pressure group for promoting and protecting migrant worker rights. The Bangladesh Migrant Centre (BMC) focuses its activities on returnees from Korea. The Bangladeshi Women Migrants Association (BWMA) is campaigning to lift the ban on female economic emigration.

The regulation of female migration

During the 1970s the Bangladesh government did not have any concrete policy on female migration. In early 1981, through a Presidential order, certain categories of women workers were barred from migrating overseas for employment. The order stated that professionals and skilled women could migrate as principal workers, but semi-skilled and unskilled women could not go overseas without a male guardian. It has been claimed that in 1980 the then association of Bangladeshi migrant workers of Kuwait presented a case to a visiting Bangladesh government minister wherein they demanded that the government should ban the migration of women for employment purposes. Subsequently the government imposed the ban on the migration of unskilled and semi-skilled women, arguing that it would protect their dignity (Siddiqui 2000).

The Bangladesh government later decided to ban women migrating abroad to work as housemaids and nurses due to complaints of abuse (*Daily Star*, 22 July 1998). After protests, the ban was partly lifted, but maintained for domestic workers (*Daily Star*, 26 September 1998). This decision led to a major campaign by different civil organisations. BAIRA, the trade body of the recruiting agents, became very active in the movement to rescind the decision. It presented its point of view primarily through newspaper advertisements. In an open letter to the Prime Minister, the BAIRA president argued that such a ban would lead to the loss of a major market in the Middle East including the Gulf region. The Association stated that some of the labour-importing countries of that region had embarked on an undeclared policy of recruiting women from predominantly Muslim countries. BAIRA regretted that while Indonesia and other predominantly Muslim nations were developing strategies to take advantage of such a policy, the Bangladesh government had not done so. The Association claimed that the decision of the government would not only work against women's progress, but that it was also contrary to women's rights and would undermine their empowerment.

BAIRA met with the Prime Minister, and a decision was taken by the Labour Ministry to lift the ban on migration of all other categories of women workers except domestic workers. However, a further revision allowed women to work as domestic workers if the employer belonged to any of the following three groups: (a) Bangladesh embassy staff; (b) financially solvent Bangladeshis such as doctors and engineers; and (c) foreign passport holders of Bangladeshi descent. Permission for these positions would only be granted by the Ministry of Labour and Employment following verification by the Bangladesh missions in the countries concerned. It is interesting to note that when the ban affected the organised sections of the female labour force (such as nurses and garments workers) they were able to place effective pressure upon the government to amend restrictions in their favour. Although there exists a major demand in the international labour market for female labour in the domestic service sector, this unorganised group of women could not mobilise similar support (Siddiqui 2000).

In a recent notification dated 9 December 2003, the Bangladesh government intends to control the migration of female workers to Saudi Arabia to ensure their rights and to protect them from adverse exploitation (GOB Notification 2003). All concerned in the recruitment process must adhere to terms and conditions laid down by the government. For female workers

- All able-bodied workers not below the age of 35 who wish to volunteer are entitled to be recruited as household workers;
- Female workers have to obtain 'No Objection Certificates' from their legal guardians;
- All workers have to undergo a training programme of not less than 30 days (but preferably 60 days). This will enable them to gain sufficient knowledge in the operation of all kinds of household equipments and electronic apparatus including televisions, vacuum cleaners, washing/drying machines, air coolers, conventional/microwave ovens, juicer/blender/grinders etc. The workers will also have to learn skills such as answering telephone calls, ironing clothes, serving tea and coffee, baby sitting and taking care of the elderly;
- Only women who are in good health and physically fit are eligible for selection;
- Women having experience in beauty parlour and physical fitness programmes will be given preference.

Again we find that there are inherent restrictions for female migrant workers; these regulations are also only applicable to Saudi Arabia – the ban on domestic workers going to other countries remains.

Women and migration in Bangladesh: a gendered perspective

Traditionally, men migrated for work to urban centres while women remained in rural areas. For women, *purdah*, or the exclusion of women from men's space, meant that women rarely migrated alone for work outside their village homes, let alone abroad. Thus female migration is a new phenomenon that poses challenges to traditional rural social structures. Women are emerging from their traditional household roles by seeking employment abroad. On the question of whether female migration abroad has made any significant difference to the existing gender roles and identities can be assessed in terms of:

- whether migration has played a positive role in the empowerment of women, especially their socio-economic status, and freedom from exploitation and violence;
- whether women's capacity for decision-making and that of their family members has been strengthened
- whether migration had been gainful for women and their families in the context of employment, earnings and savings.

The global shift towards a service and labour intensive economy has increased the demand for female labour. Thus gender analysis is crucial to understanding the institutions that structure female migration processes. Development policy debates need a clear understanding of the feminisation of migration, including trafficking. The emergence of women in large numbers into the migrant labour force has brought about their 'empowerment' in a developing country like Bangladesh, but ongoing and progressive policies need to be implemented to address the dark side of female labour migration.

The nature and magnitude of female migration

Until the 1980s, there was an overwhelming domination of male workers in the migration of labour from Bangladesh. Women migrated mostly as spouses or other family members of male migrants. In the 1990s, however, scope for employment of Bangladeshi women was created in some Asian countries, and a significant section of the female labour force of Bangladesh has responded to such opportunities. Within a short span of time Bangladeshi women have become quite visible in the short-term labour market in the Middle East and in Southeast Asian countries (Siddiqui 2001).

The Government of Bangladesh has signed the UN Convention on the Protection of the Rights of all Migrant Workers and Members of their Families (1990), but it has still not been ratified. In 1998 the Bangladeshi government decided to prohibit the sending of women abroad as domestic workers and nurses due to complaints of abuse. After protests the ban was partly lifted but maintained for domestic workers. However, such restrictions have not stopped women from migrating.

According to the Ministry of Labour and Manpower, about 12,000 female workers were employed abroad as nurses, housemaids, cleaners and garment workers (*Daily Star*, 22 July 1998). Table 8.1 indicates that in the nine-year period, from 1991 to 1999, a relatively low figure of 13,544 women migrated. Nonetheless, BMET claimed that all those who officially went overseas for employment by obtaining clearance from BMET were accounted for in this data. However, BMET could not provide a year-by-year breakdown of women migrants up to 1995.

Table 8.1 Number and percentage of female migrants in comparison to total flow (1991–99)

Year	Female migrants (%)	Total number
1991–95	9,308 (0.98%)	953,632
1996	1,567 (0.74%)	211,714
1997	1,389 (0.36%)	381,077
1998	960 (0.36%)	267,667
1999	320 (0.12%)	268,182
Total	13,544 (0.65%)	2,082,272

Source: Siddiqui compiled from BMET database (2000) p. 91.

The annual figures indicate that female migration from Bangladesh is negligible. However, Siddiqui (2000) contends that official figures are rather unrealistic. First, they contradict the recent global trend of the feminisation of the temporary labour force. Second, they deny the reality that female migration involves lower cost. Third, in different pockets of the country, sub-agents of recruiting agencies are strongly involved in the recruitment of female migrants. Areas were also located from where thousands of women had migrated, returned and are still migrating (United Nations International Research and Training Institute for the Advancement of Women [INSTRAW]/ IOM 2000).

The inadequacy of these annual figures can also be understood from the number of returnees from the Iraq–Kuwait war. After the war ended a compensation package was drawn up for war-affected people. About 72,000 Bangladeshis registered for compensation, and of them 2000 were women. On these figures 2.8 per cent of the total returnees were women. It may also be noted that these women migrated before 1990, at a time when the flow of women migrants had just begun. In other words, it is expected that the percentage share of women would be more in the years after 1990. The Association of Iraq–Kuwait Returnees claimed that their organisation has 12,500 female members. Only a very small number of them would be spouses of male migrants; the remainder were principal migrants (Siddiqui 2000:93–4).

Contrary to the official statistics, then, a large number of women are migrating from Bangladesh for work. However, the migration of women from Bangladesh has become an irregular operation. That is why most female migrants are not counted in official figures. Various factors have contributed to irregular migration: government restrictions, cumbersome registration and legal procedures; the emergence of illegal channels that are less time consuming and sometimes cost more effective; and lastly, the

Table 8.2 Countries of destination and skill composition of female migrants (1991–98)

Country	Professionals	Skilled	Semi-skilled	Unskilled	Total
Saudi Arabia	496 (71.47%)	23 (3.31%)	13 (1.87%)	162 (23.34%)	694
Kuwait	14 (0.45%)		1,149 (36.85%)	1,955 (62.70%)	3,118
U.A.E.	8 (0.40%)	607 (30.27%)	63 (3.14%)	1,327 (66.18%)	2,005
Malaysia	137 (2.64%)	5,034 (97.35%)			5,171
Bahrain	20 (2.26%)	112 (12.66%)	53 (5.99%)	700 (79.09%)	885
Oman	18 (8.22%)	76 (34.70%)	15 (6.85%)	110 (50.23%)	219
Brunei				21 (100%)	21
Qatar	4 (7.40%)		13 (24.07%)	37 (68.52%)	54
Mauritius		115 (89.84%)		13 (10.16%)	128
Korea		6 (100%)			6
Lebanon			47 (88.68%)	6 (11.32%)	53
Singapore				56 (100%)	56
Others	2 (2.04%)		15 (15.31%)	81 (82.65%)	98
Total	699 (5.59%)	5,973 (47.75%)	1,368 (10.94%)	4,468 (35.72%)	12,508

Source: Siddiqui compiled from BMET database, (2000) 92.

promulgation of the 1998 restriction that allowed only licensed recruiting agencies to operate.

Table 8.2 shows the skill composition of short-term female migrants by the country of destination, classified into four categories by BMET: professionals, skilled, semi-skilled and unskilled. Professionals include doctors, engineers, nurses and teachers, of which the highest number are nurses (647 out of 699). Manufacturing or garment workers are considered skilled and they constitute about 47.75 per cent of that category. Tailors and masons consist of 10.94 per cent of the semi-skilled category. Domestic workers, cleaners and labourers are classified as unskilled (and they constitute 35.72 per cent of that category). It appears that low paid jobs like garment workers, house-maids, cleaners and labourers are dominated by female migrant workers. Malaysia has the highest intake of female migrant workers, the majority of whom are skilled, while the next largest destination countries, Kuwait and United Arab Emirates, have the highest number of unskilled female migrants (who are mostly domestic workers).

Factors contributing to female migration

There are gender-specific factors that uniquely affect the short-term migra-tion of women (INSTRAW/IOM 2000; Siddiqui 2001). However, factors that contribute to migration can be classified as to whether they are 'situational' or 'catalytic' (Mahmood 1996). Situational factors are related to the socio-economic conditions of women such as the prevalence of patriarchal norms and values that are discriminatory; exploitation and gender violence, especially dowry related violence; and the desire for independence and domestic harmony. Catalytic factors refer to foreign demand for labour; proactive policies in labour-exporting countries; the growth of fee-charging private entrepreneurs; and the social networks of migrant workers.

Situational factors

With increased poverty in rural families and the inability of males to provide for basic needs, an increase in the abandonment of wives has occurred as husbands migrate alone to urban areas in search of work. This situation has paved the way to female-headed households, which are on the increase (according to UNDP [1994], about 30 per cent of rural households are female headed). Women have also been compelled to migrate to urban centres, and gradually made their way into the urban labour force in the garment, food-processing and domestic sectors. Rural–urban migration has also empowered many women to seek jobs in the international labour market.

In the INSTRAW/IOM (2000) study of 200 sample female migrants, 52 out of 70 urban migrants had migrated from rural areas to Dhaka city. Among the 130 rural migrants, economic hardship and misfortune were the major causes of migration. Common reasons cited were landlessness, lack of employment opportunities, seasonal unemployment, unexpected death or prolonged sickness of family providers, and poor working conditions as domestic workers. Divorced, deserted and unmarried women went abroad mainly to sustain the patriarchal family. Dowry obligations have been a significant reason for the migration of women who have eligible daughters and younger sisters. The same is true of unmarried, divorced and abandoned women. Women have also migrated to escape domestic violence. In some households, women have to unhappily live with co-wives, a situation in which migration offers a way out. Greater participation in paid employment has also given women a sense of independence, and labour migration has enhanced this factor considerably.

Catalytic factors

Bangladeshi women workers are increasingly preferred in the Middle East compared to women from the Philippines, Thailand and Sri Lanka owing to their religious background. This has been one of the major 'pull' factors responsible for the recent increase of women from Bangladesh to that region, especially with regard to domestic workers. Recent studies have shown that informal social networks play a much wider role in facilitating international labour migration (Grasmuck and Pessar 1991). The importance of these networks is also true in the case of Bangladesh female migrants (INSTRAW/IOM 2003). Of a sample of 200 female migrants, 22 acquired their work permits and visas through informal channels that involved relatives, neighbours or friends. Also, close to half of the 150 returnee migrant women pointed out that they first got information about migration from their neighbours, friends or relatives. In one particular region, the study found that the success of a migrant appears to have been a catalyst in the decision of many others to migrate. Membership in an NGO also appears to have worked as a catalyst for migration, especially in rural areas. Awareness-raising efforts, and NGO credit and training programmes seem to have given many rural women some degree of self-confidence. Thirty-six rural migrant women, or someone from their family, were linked with an NGO in the survey. Access to credit from an NGO also enabled a few families to shoulder the cost of sending women abroad.

Despite government restrictions, and more recently a complete ban on the migration of unskilled women, slightly more than half of the women in the sample were domestic workers. Nearly all had legal work visas, but most went abroad without a BMET clearance. At the airport, immigration officials colluded with fee-charging labour agents to enable the women to leave Bangladesh without the usual necessary documents. Private recruiting agencies have increasingly become an important catalyst in female labour migration. Particularly in rural areas, recruiting agencies persuade the families of potential female migrants that money is better spent sending women to work overseas rather than paying their dowry obligations. Moreover, women who migrate can save for their own dowry while they contribute to the family income. In the same way, agents encourage deserted or divorced women to migrate so that they can be an asset rather than a burden to their family. Almost 30 per cent of the returnee migrant workers had learned about the prospect of migration from such agents (INSTRAW/IOM 2000).

Sources of finance

The average cost of migration for a woman is around Tk. 43,413 (Tk. 51 was equivalent to 1 US dollar at the time of the INSTRAW/IOM study). This fee includes all types of expenses including airfare, passport, visa, insurance, medical check up and other incidental charges like local transport, clothes and others. However, most of the female migrants in the INSTRAW/IOM (2000) study sample lacked sufficient resources to cover their total costs. Only 23 per cent were able to rely on their own resources to finance at least a part of the total cost, 33 per cent received some support from their extended family, while 75 per cent had to borrow part of the total cost from traditional money lenders, friends and relatives.

Conditions of employment in the country of destination: case studies

Two-year contacts were the norm for most migrant workers in the INSTRAW/IOM (2000) study. However, a few nurses had four-year contracts, and about 25 per cent of other workers had three-year contacts. A sizeable minority (24 migrant workers) had to return home in their first year without completing contracts because of improper documents, family and personal problems, while others suffered from poor health or had problems with their employers. The stress of migration often created health problems, eventually forcing some migrant workers to return home. Jaundice, peptic ulcers and temporary insanity were some of the untreated health problems that arose in the study. Some employers, moreover, did not bear medical costs incurred by their workers.

Regarding hours of work, nurses reported that their working hours were regular and that they were also paid overtime for longer working hours. On the other hand, factory workers (especially garment workers) officially worked from eight to ten hours, but they reported also having to work long hours without payment for overtime. The majority of domestic workers worked as long as 15 to 18 hours a day, and few had any holidays. Garment and factory workers had the provision for holidays in their contracts, but found that they could not obtain leave on a regular basis. Women migrants have to deal with additional challenges ranging from substandard working conditions, are deprived of any private space and social life, and are restricted in their movements. Women who worked as domestic workers particularly were subject to physical, social and cultural isolation. On the other hand, a handful of women workers had positive work experiences and faced no serious problems.

About 25 per cent of the returnees reported that they had been subjected to regular physical abuse, sometimes of an extreme form. Frequently reported forms of physical abuse included being struck on the head with shoes and whipped with belts. A few experienced physical torture such as the pressing of red hot metal objects on to their skin, while some were exposed to a risk of physical harm as they had to take care of mentally ill persons without proper training or instruction. Eight women in the sample were subjected to rape or attempted rape. One domestic worker who was raped in Kuwait took up prostitution on her return to Bangladesh.

Economic impact of migration

The 200 families of the UNSTRAW/IOM study (2000) were categorised into three groups in terms of whether the overall economic impact of migration on the household had been positive, negative or mixed, analysed according to the length of time abroad. More than half of the women migrants whose families economically benefited from migration felt a sense of achievement (INSTRAW/IOM 2000). Having made a significant contribution to their families' economic welfare gave them a high degree of self-satisfaction and improved their self-esteem. Some supported their father's family, some their own family, and others both. Remittances enabled family members to enjoy better health care and better educational opportunities, and also helped to support other family members to work abroad. Their achievements elevated their status within the family and earned them respect within the community. In contrast, some women migrants had to return home before they could recover the costs incurred in the financing of their migration. These women were found to suffer from feelings of extreme guilt and were generally blamed by their families for their failure to persevere abroad. One woman in the study had attempted suicide, whilst another was forced to hide from moneylenders and officers of an NGO from whom she had borrowed money to finance her migration. In a couple of instances, where the fraudulent practices of recruiting agencies caused a premature return, women were able to appeal to informal rural courts and, in one case, win restitution. Exploitative work conditions also on occasion pushed women to fight back. Five returnees, with the help of the Bangladesh embassy, brought charges against their employers for non-payment of wages, succeeding in a few of the cases. The cases lodged by another four who had returned from the Maldives are still pending with the involvement of an NGO, the Ministry of Labour, and the Bangladesh Overseas Employment and Services Limited (BOESL).

Women migrants usually had little power over family decisions involving the use of their remittances, as they did not have any bank account of their own in the destination country and most sent all their earnings home. Nurses, however, were an exception. They kept a part of their earnings invested in saving certificates, bonds, and the like and in general had greater control over their earnings. Some who went abroad a second time or those who had stayed relatively longer gradually developed control mechanisms over their earnings. Although land purchased was usually transferred in the name of male member of the family, 16 per cent of these cases were registered in the migrant women's name.

Many women found that their decision-making status regarding children's education and marriages of family members were valued more as remittances flowed home. They concurred that migration had taught them to be self-reliant. It is perhaps not surprising that the vast majority of the women were willing, and about half had already tried, to go abroad again despite its hardships. It can be concluded that the experience of migration had an empowering effect for many female migrants, and enhanced their status and decision-making power, more so where they had brought financial gain to the entire family.

Conclusion and policy recommendations

Globalisation is reshaping the management of female migration. The existing 'migration regime' based on bans/restrictions on female migration cannot effectively manage migration. Rather, it pushes the flow underground, making women easy victims of crime syndicates. Migration can be better managed by progressively regulating outward flows. An urgent need exists for the formulation of a national migration policy that pays proper attention to female migration management. The importance of female migration on the socio-economic development processes, both in origin and destination countries, should also be reconsidered. Female migration needs to be acknowledged as a developmental force. A comprehensive, flexible and balanced mechanism to regulate female migration might also reduce tensions between states and between employers and female migrants.

As a labour-sending country Bangladesh should immediately ratify the UN Convention on the Protection of the Rights of all Migrant Workers and Members of their Families (1990), and frame necessary enabling national legislation. At the same time, bilateral agreements should be fostered between Bangladesh and receiving countries in order to establish minimum working standards and protect female labour migrants. Preventive measures and legal remedies should be put in place to protect female migrant workers' rights. Bangladeshi embassies in the host countries should also play an active role in monitoring the welfare of migrant women workers. Similarly, government agencies should identify the female labour needs of host countries. The private sector and NGOs need to train potential female migrant workers so that women avail themselves of legal channels instead of relying on informal channels and networks. There should be more pre-departure training directed at making Bangladeshi female labour migrants more aware of the working situations they will experience in host countries, particularly in terms of language and financial skills training. Female migration through appropriate interventions can help address poverty reduction, and empower women in both their local and adopted communities.

References

Afsar, R., M. Yunus and A.B.M.S. Islam (2002) *Are Migrants Chasing After the 'Golden Deer'? A Study on Cost-Benefit Analysis of Overseas Migration by the Bangladeshi Labour*, International Organisation for Migration IOM, Regional Office for South Asia and UNDP, Dhaka.

Daily Star, 22 July 1998, Dhaka.

Government of the People's Republic of Bangladesh (2003) 'Notification: Conditions for Recruitment of Bangladesh Females as Household Workers/House Assistants in the Kingdom of Saudi Arabia, Ministry of Expatriates', Welfare and Overseas Employment, Section 5, Bangladesh Secretariat, Dhaka.

Grasmuck, S. and P. Pessar (1991) *Between Two Islands: Dominican International Migration* (Berkeley: University of California Press).

International Labour Organisation (1996) 'Female Asian Migrants: a Growing But Increasingly Vulnerable Workforce', in Watkins (ed.) *Migration in South Asia in Policy and Practice: A Regional Overview* (ILO Database: Scalabrini Migration Center) DFID Report (2002).

International Organization for Migration(IOM) (2003) *World Migration 2003, Managing Migration Challenges and Responses for People on the Move* (Geneva: IOM).

Mahmood, R.A. (1996) 'Emigration Dynamics in Bangladesh: Level, Pattern and Implications'. Paper prepared for the Asiatic Society of Bangladesh, Dhaka.

Migrant Forum in Asia (1995) *Ratifying UN Convention Protecting Migrant Workers Migrant Women Quest for Justice* (Hong Kong: Migrant Forum in Asia).

Shamim, I. (2002) 'Feminization of Trafficking: The Nexus Between Supply and Demand in South Asia'. Paper presented in the International Conference on The Human Rights Challenge of Globalization in Asia-Pacific-US: The Trafficking in Persons, Especially Women and Children, Honolulu, Hawaii, USA, 13–15 November.

Shamim, I. and F. Kabir (1998) *Child Trafficking: The Underlying Dynamics* (Dhaka: Red Barnet).

Siddiqui, T. (2003) 'Migration as a Livelihood Strategy of the Poor: The Bangladesh Case'. Paper presented at the Regional Conference on Migration Development Pro-Poor Policy Choices in Asia, Dhaka, 22–24 June.

—— (2001) *Transcending Boundaries: Labour Migration of Women from Bangladesh* (Dhaka: The University Press Limited).

—— (2000) 'State Policy and Nature of Female Migration from Bangladesh', in Chowdhury R. Abrar (ed.) *On the Margin Refugees, Migrants and Minorities* (Dhaka: Refugee and Migratory Movement Research Unit, University of Dhaka) pp. 83–101.

United Nations (2002) *Activities of the United Nations Statistics Division on International Migration* (New York: United Nations Statistics Division).

United Nations Development Programme (1994) *Report on Human Development in Bangladesh* (Dhaka).

United Nations International Research and Training Institute for the Advancement of Women and International Organisation for Migration (INSTRAW/IOM) (2000) *Temporary Labour Migration of Women: Case Studies of Bangladesh and Sri Lanka*, (Dominican Republic: UN International Research and Training Institute for the Advancement of Women and International Organisation for Migration).

United Nations, Joint United Nations Programme on HIV/AIDS (UNAIDS) (2001) *Population Mobility and AIDS*, UNAIDS Technical update (Geneva).

Waddington, C. (2003) 'International Migration Policies in Asia'. Paper presented at the Regional Conference on Migration Development Pro-Poor Policy Choices in Asia, Dhaka, 22–23 June.

Wickramasekera, P. (2002) *Asian Labour Migration: Issues and Challenges in an Era of Globalization*, International Migration Paper No. 57 (Geneva: ILO).

9
'White-Collar Filipinos': Australian Professionals in Singapore

Melissa Butcher

Not all migrant labour in Asia is regarded with the same complex relationship of need and demonisation as many of the documented cases cited in this book. In Singapore, for example, highly educated and entrepreneurial white-collar professionals are clearly not only wanted by the government, but unlike their domestic and blue-collar counterparts, are encouraged to settle there. Supporting the migration of foreign talent is one of the corner stones of Singapore's economic development strategy, but professional migrants are also impacting on the country's social organisation. The process of migration and settlement of transnational professionals is reflecting the wider dynamics of cultural change that are taking place as a result of global mobility. It is this latter phenomenon that is the focus of this chapter, using Singapore's Australian expatriate community as a case study of how global labour regimes can shift or reinforce personal understandings of identity and belonging.

Processes of cultural change as a result of transnationalism, that is, regular and repetitive mobility, contact and relationships across national borders, have been described and discussed by authors such as Nina Glick-Schiller *et al.* (1992), Arjun Appadurai (1977), Luis Guarnizo and Michael Smith (1998), Alejandro Portes (1999) and Ulf Hannerz (2002). According to them, transnational migration is marked by processes of identity re-evaluation, including aspects of acculturation and hybridisation influenced by local cultural contexts such as socio-economic distinction. The capacity to move has gained in value and become a marker of the divisions in the impact of globalisation – between those with the ability and the means to move, and those without. In a sense, the logic of mobility has become an addition to Frederic Jameson's (1984) logic of consumption in describing contemporary society. This chapter analyses the impact of mobility on identity, highlighting the continuing importance of place, and arguing against the idea that a mobile transnational life creates 'denationalised identities'. It also suggests that while there will be similarities in the process of cultural adaptation, the level of economic and social capital can create different responses to the process of migration.

The circulation of transnational professionals

Studies in transnationalism to date have tended to focus on the movement of people, in particular, less-skilled or unskilled migrants, from developing countries to Europe, North America and wealthier parts of Asia. Portes *et al.*,'s rationale for this tendency is that the field of 'transnationalism from above' is covered by other areas of study such as globalisation and international relations, whereas 'transnationalism from below' 'represent[s] the more novel and distinct development in this area and, hence, the one that deserves greatest attention' (1999:223).

Yet, while undoubtedly outnumbered, the influence of highly skilled transnational professionals circulating the globe commends them as research participants. Russell King, while also focusing his research on lower socio-economic migration, mentions the 'rapid growth of skilled international migration – a new breed of executive nomads who, while quantitively much less important than the mass labour migrations of the past, nevertheless wield enormous influence over the functioning of the global economy' (1995:24). The movement of these professionals and their families is facilitated by better communication and transport technologies. Their circulation, mostly between key global cities and within transnational corporations (TNCs), has influenced the development of national and global labour regimes. The movement of 'natural persons' is covered by the World Trade Organisation's General Agreement on Trades in Services (www.wto.org/english/tratrop_e/ serv_e/gatsqa_e.htm). Bilateral free trade agreements, such as that between Australia and Singapore (2003), streamline professional movement by instituting the recognition of qualifications and allowing easier access to employment passes.

Saskia Sassen (2002) has made the distinction between classes of migrant workers: professionals, incorporated into legal, formal administration, disappearing from the category of migrant, and 'others' – domestic and construction workers, cheap labour who face resistance to their formal recognition. The participants in this research are Sassen's former category. They would probably be labelled by Leslie Sklair (1998) as members of his transnational capitalist class – they share similar life styles, levels of education, and consumption habits, they also generally share an outward-looking perspective that informs their decision to migrate. In the case of the research participants involved in this study, all were actively seeking an experience outside of Australia.

Transnational professionals appear to have a problematic relationship with migration studies. Guarnizo and Smith (1998) go as far as to suggest that expatriate consulting and entrepreneurship does not entail migration.

However, it is necessary to make the distinction between two groups of transnational professionals. First there are those I would describe as transnational itinerants, ostensibly based in a particular home country but moving throughout a region. An example of this would be a businessman who, while based in Australia, spends four out of six weeks travelling throughout Asia. The second group is the more familiar expatriate, who, by the Australian Department of Immigration, Multiculturalism and Indigenous Affairs (DIMIA) definition, has or intends to depart from Australia for more than one year.

If Guarnizo and Smith are referring to the former group, they would be semantically correct that they are not migrants per se, but their transnational movement, particularly if the journeys are repetitive, stimulates intercultural interactions nonetheless. With regard to the second group, into which the participants of this research would fall, their extended stay in country, for some over a period of many years, and their heightened sense of mobility creates a new set of dynamics. For this reason I would argue that 'transnationalism from above' is not adequately explored.

Other writers have suggested that this elite transnational life somehow creates 'denationalised' identities, even contributing to the decline of the nation state (Bauman 1998:58; Sklair 1998; Huntington 2004). Deterritorialisation of capital and corporations is occurring, but for the individuals driving this movement and these corporations, I would suggest that place still matters: geographic place imbued with meaning and shaped by cultural context including identity referents such as history, economic and social organisation. David Fitzgerald's (2004) work, with its focus on the 'transnationalism from below' of Mexican members of a USA union, for example, finds no transcending of nationalism in favour of the uniting of 'workers of the world'. I would argue that all is not so fluid and mobile in the contemporary transnational social field that place can be neglected, even for a highly mobile, highly skilled, labour force. Place is still politically produced and contested according to Gille Zsuzsa and Sean O'Riain (2002:273), and I would add, consumed. The mobilities and flows of globalisation are juxtaposed to the stoppages at local points along the way (Zsuzsa and O'Riain 2002:272). Guarnizo and Smith argue that '[a]ll of these [transnational] relationships are mediated by trans-local understandings' (1998:14), strengthening the idea that the local, with its concomitant set of meanings, still has a role to play in a global world.

Methodology

Transnational research is still grappling with models to effectively explore highly mobile research cohorts. Portes *et al.*, argue that to date transnationalism lacks a theoretical framework; there are 'diverse levels of abstraction' (1999:218) and disparate units of analysis used (e.g., individuals, organisations, states). Guarnizo and Smith (1998:25) question what the appropriate unit of analysis actually is: at the local level there has been a failure to connect human experience to social and historical context; and analysis at the macro level can lead to overarching generalisations. They also point to a lack of comparative studies that can measure the scale, weight, prevalence and intensity of transnational relationships (28). Their conclusion is that qualitative studies are needed to compliment the quantitative. However, in qualitative work there is a need to be cautious of approaching transnationalism 'as a set of abstracted, dematerialised cultural flows, giving scant attention either to the concrete, everyday changes in people's lives or to the structural reconfiguration that accompany global capitalism' (Nonini and Ong 1997:13, cited in Vertovec 1999:456). A high-level abstract approach neglects the capacity of individuals to make sense of the world around them, and to shape it.

Taking into account these concerns, this research is qualitative in nature but maintains a focus on individuals' everyday experiences, for example, the process of 'settling in', adapting to a new workplace and establishing new friendship networks. The research began in 2000, when the author worked for a transnational financial services consulting firm based in Sydney. This included working for short periods of time in the Singapore head office. As well as many informal discussions, from 2002 to 2003 a formal methodology was applied involving the narrative analysis of eleven in-depth interviews and participant observation in the workplace and leisure sites in Singapore (April 2003). Two participants were from Asia-Australian backgrounds, one of whom was born in Singapore but who had migrated to Australia as a child.

While acknowledging that transnationalism involves powerful institutions such as corporations and governments, the focus of this research is on the individual and the social networks within which they are embedded. I would agree with Portes *et al.*, that beginning with the history and activities of individuals is an 'efficient way of learning about the institutional underpinnings of transnationalism and its structural effects' (1999:220). It is individual motivation, interplaying with the acquiescence or rejection of collective norms, which drives decisions to move, to adapt and to resist change, to engage social capital or to mobilise social networks. As members of a community these expatriates find meaning and create places of belonging in their relationship networks, their value recitation and in their everyday practices. In other words, they circumscribe in their activity shared meanings that help to make sense of and interpret their place in a new environment. From this point of view, globalisation can be seen as the accretion of a series of decisions taken by individuals moving transnationally, motivated by their own curiosity, anxieties, ambitions and ideas about pleasure. But before examining participants' responses to the processes of migration more fully, I would like to provide some of the context of the research site of Singapore with which these transnational professionals interacted on a daily basis.

The 'hub'

Singapore is a competitive, energetic city-state, reflected in both work and leisure activities and in the ambitions and curiosities of the research participants. Given the country's geography and lack of natural resources, its main economic strategy has been to develop a highly skilled workforce and high technology industries. In particular, in recent years it has aimed to establish itself as 'the hub of Asia', and a centre for bio- and information technology development. It portrays itself as a point of translation between East and West. The Economic Development Board (EDB) claims that Singaporeans 'have been able to integrate the strengths of diverse Asian cultures to evolve a strong identity of their own'. At the same time they are familiar with 'the business environments and practices of the West (EDB 1995:6, *Regionalisation 2000: Singapore Unlimited*, cited Yeoh and Willis 1998).

Singapore has both a skilled and unskilled foreign labour force but openly prefers the former as its Ministry of Manpower (MOM) states:

> We need to attract foreign talent to become a dynamic global city of excellence. [...] MOM will also review Singapore's foreign worker policy guidelines to reduce unskilled foreign workers. More skilled foreign workers will result in productivity gains without taxing the fabric of the society, and contribute to raising the skills profile of Singapore's workforce. (*Manpower News*, September 1999, http://www.mom.gov.sg/MOM/ManpowerNews/sep_spec/st3.htm)

Strategies to encourage skilled foreign workers or 'foreign talent' include targeting countries such as India and China, and developing grant programmes, recruitment missions and permanent residency schemes (Yeoh 2004). Commercial and technology park facilities for TNCs (of which there were over 18,000 in 2000 according to Sassen 2000:18), have been developed both in Singapore and in nearby regional countries. Singapore has also taken steps to redress its image as a staid, over-regulated city by relaxing some of its entertainment regulations, and instituting a new government policy to promote creative thinking and entrepreneurship in the corporate sector.

Singapore's distinction between skilled and unskilled foreign workers is enforced in its employment regulatory regime. There are three separate foreign employment classes: Employment Pass, S Pass and Work Permits. Employment and S Passes are aimed at professionals, managers, executives, specialists or middle level skilled workers, earning at least S$1800 per month and with prescribed education, professional qualifications or skills. Quotas and levies apply to S Pass holders.

The third category, work permits, is specifically aimed at unskilled or skilled foreign workers in Singapore with a basic monthly salary of less than S$2500. Work permits are generally issued according to industry sector (such as the construction and domestic sectors) and incur more restrictions.

Employers must pay a security bond of S$5000 for each non-Malaysian worker they employ, as well as a levy for all foreign workers per month. All work permit holders must undergo a medical examination and be certified fit for employment. Some industries, such as domestic services, have prescribed employees. Only women from 'Non-traditional Source' countries (including India, Bangladesh, Thailand, Myanmar, Sri Lanka, Pakistan and the Philippines) and Indonesia are permitted to work in the domestic sector. In general the work-permit system ensures that lower or unskilled labour remains transient and subject to repatriation should they no longer be needed in an economic downturn.

According to the MOM, there are more than 590,000 work permit and Employment Pass holders in Singapore (as of 2 December 2003; personal communication, Ms Winnie Chan, Singapore Department of Statistics). The breakdown of this number by nationality is not available as these are not figures that the MOM wishes to make widely known given an undercurrent of resentment towards foreign workers, both skilled and unskilled. According to Velayutham (2003), unskilled foreign workers are generally regarded as being of 'low status' and resented because of their 'social presence'. Large numbers congregate in particular places such as Little India and parts of Chinatown. Skilled foreign workers are perceived as arrogant, and disliked because they are seen as competition for local jobs, earning more than locals and enjoying special privileges (Personal correspondence with Dr Selvaraj Velayutham, 9 August 2004).

The number of foreign workers includes approximately 470,000 unskilled labourers concentrated in the construction industry and domestic services (Yeoh 2004; 140,000 in the domestic sector alone, *SingStats* 1999). In 2000, 'higher skilled' professionals accounted for some 80,000 to 100,000 foreign workers (approximately 15 per cent of the foreign workforce, http://www.usembassysingapore.org.sg/ep/2000/Incli2000.html). Professional migrants may also hold Permanent Resident (PR) status and would therefore be counted as part of the resident population along with citizens (see Tables 9.1 and 9.2). Three of the eleven interviewees in this research cohort held permanent residency.

In comparison to the populations of lower skilled migrant communities, the skilled expatriate contingent is quite small as shown in Figure 9.1. In general, the 12,000 Australians in Singapore (2003), with some four to five thousand engaged in employment (the remainder consisting of accompanying spouses and family members), would generally circulate within the 'higher skilled' categories, that is, Employment Pass or permanent residents. The participants in this research primarily worked in the services sector (law, media, marketing, finances, technology and consulting), had spent at least two years in Singapore, and their age tended to be late 20s to mid 30s. The average length of stay is anecdotally two to three years but some participants had lived there for longer periods, up to 12 years, or followed meandering

Table 9.1 Total population by residential status in Singapore

Residential status	Number		Per cent		Average annual growth 1990–2000 (%)
	1990	2000	1990	2000	
Total population	3,047,132	4,017,733	100.0	100.0	2.8
Resident population	2,735,868	3,263,209	89.8	81.2	1.8
(citizen)	2,623,736	2,973,091	86.1	74.0	1.3
(permanent residents)	112,132	290,118	3.7	7.2	10.0
Non-resident population	311,264	754,524	10.2	18.8	9.3

Source: Singapore Department of Statistics (2002).

Table 9.2 Resident and non-resident populations in Singapore

Census date	Total population	Singapore resident	Non-resident	Growth rates (%) Total population	Singapore resident	Non-resident
1980	2,413,945	2,282,125	131,820	1.5	n.a.	n.a.
1990	3,047,132	2,735,868	311,264	2.4	1.8	9.0
2000	4,017,733	3,263,209	754,524	2.8	1.8	9.3
2001	4,131,200	3,319,100	812,100	2.8	1.7	7.6
2002	4,171,300	3,378,300	793,000	1.0	1.8	−2.4

Source: Cited in Lee and Yeo 2003, p. 10.

trajectories through other Asian countries such as Hong Kong, Thailand or the Philippines for several years beforehand.

Yeoh believes it is inevitable that ethnic relations in Singapore will become more complex as a result of the presence of foreign labour, including highly skilled expatriates.

Foreigners who hail from a number of different continents and countries are not only providers of labour, skill and talent, but also bearers of specific geographies and histories. Not only are they of different nationalities, they carry multiple identities along dimensions of ethnicity, culture, customs and the like. ... As such, the insertion of foreign/ethnic others into Singapore, even if temporary but more so if permanent, will undoubtedly change the complexion of society (2004:10).

However, it is not only Singapore that would appear to change as a result of migration. Their insertion in the city impacted on the expatriates in this study as well, as the following sections will begin to examine.

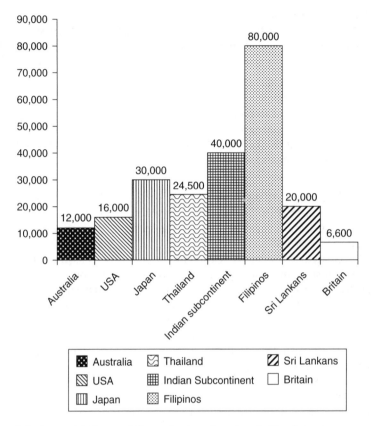

Figure 9.1 Approximate populations of migrant workers in Singapore

Sources: American Chamber of Commerce (2003), Australian Department of Foreign Affairs and Trade (2002), Hewison (2003), Yeoh (2004).

'Expat' life

The expectations of expatriate life are changing: the generous remuneration packages are no longer so freely available, and there is an apparent trend for Australians to actively seek employment in Singapore by first moving there, rather than seeking an offer from a TNC first. There is a segment of skilled professionals who are on 'local packages', that is, local employment conditions and without the housing or other allowances found in traditional expatriate packages. There is a perception within the TNC sector that Australians are hard working and cheap (hence the slang nickname 'White-Collar Filipinos'). With humour, it was also recounted by some participants that New Zealanders are considered to be even cheaper, and so the traditional trans-Tasman rivalry between Australia and New Zealand was relocated transnationally.

Working in Singapore is generally regarded as a 'good lifestyle', with domestic help (one of the few points of intersection between skilled and unskilled foreigners) and a circuit of leisure activities centring around other expatriates' homes, in bars and clubs in particular 'expat' areas, and at sporting events (e.g., rugby and cricket).

> I mean, if you want to party all night, seven nights a week, you can do it. You can go out drinking and you've got plenty of mates you can do it with and plenty of girls that will hang around you while you're doing it. (Lawyer, two years in Singapore)

It could be argued that this is a similar pattern to the rhythms of life in Australia except that in the Singapore context, narratives were marked at times by 'frustration' and at times by a sense of greater 'opportunity'. Frustration was as a result of cross-cultural challenges at work and a sense of restraint created by Singapore itself. There is an air of determination in the act of socialising, in sporting activities and in getting off the island. But while the stereotype of the 'work hard, play hard' expatriate does have an element of truth to it for some, in general there was a conscious decision by participants to maintain a sense of balance. Participants who believed they worked longer hours commented that it was the same as they would have expected to in Australia. For those in middle to senior management longer than average work hours are the norm.

Mobility is very much a part of Singapore life, both for work and leisure. To combat the feeling of being 'island-bound' there is a steady stream of expatriates leaving the country each weekend to shop in Malaysia, play golf or surf in Indonesia, go diving in Thailand or sightseeing in Cambodia. Singapore's access to the rest of Asia is an attractive feature; it is a base from which the region can be explored. In terms of the workplace, senior expatriate positions in Singapore often entail a regional responsibility and can involve regular travel to other countries in the Asia-Pacific corporate division. This mobility is a key factor contributing to the strain expatriate life can have on relationships, particularly for 'trailing spouses' who are not working.

> I got there and a day later [my husband] left on a nine-day trip. And I was like 'Oh OK, what am I supposed to do now?' So I did a Masters. Everyone studies. And I learnt to run marathons, because what else do you do. (laughs) (Human Resources Manager, nine years in Singapore)

On the side of 'opportunity', several interviewees remarked on being able to take part in business or a social life that they would not be able to access in Australia. There is the possibility in Singapore to live a different life.

> The lifestyle here is just fantastic. I can't think of anywhere else I'd rather be ... It's just the opportunities are fantastic here. It just never stops. ... Whatever I've wanted to do here, I can do. (Consultant, seven years in Singapore)

Participants' motivations for leaving Australia (push factors) and relocating to Singapore in particular (pull factors) included this element of tapping into opportunities in Asia, but career development, money, adventure or some sense of excitement, and gaining cross-cultural experience were also notable motivations. There was usually a suite of these factors noted by each interviewee although 'cross-cultural experience' in particular featured strongly. Corporate employment was used as a means to engage with, or at least assuage curiosity about other cultures.

Motivations could also change over time. One participant felt that the people who came to Singapore were either 'misfits, mercenaries or missionaries'. In his case, he was initially a 'missionary', wanting to change, not Asia, but what he perceived as Australia's parochial view of Asia, and for that he felt he needed 'Asia experience'. After seven years, he now saw himself more as a mercenary, 'here for the money', or more precisely, the low tax rate. He questioned how he would be able to return to Australia having become so enmeshed in Singapore; it had become home. In this case, his partner was Singaporean and a key factor in embedding his sense of place in the city.

Singapore was regarded as a safer option for those seeking 'adventure' and 'excitement'. It was often referred to as 'Asia for Beginners' or 'Asia 101'; it was seen as an easy country for those wanting Asia experience without too much hardship. In this scenario the question is raised as to whether this is really migration or more simply temporary relocation. What I would like to propose is that even if the participant had no intention of staying permanently in Singapore, the impact of re-establishing their lives in another country still had an effect at times on their sense of identity and place, even, as will be seen below, if it was to heighten their sense of being Australian.

For some, intercultural interaction was a stressful process, while others thrived under the challenge of making sense of a new environment. More so for the former group, their sense of Australianness was reinforced; in effect they never left Australia as a reference point for their identity and there was a strong longing for home that marked their narratives.

> I always see myself as Australian and going back to Australia. So, for example, my husband subscribed to this journal the other day which has a 'Where people are now' type page, and they've got this 'So-and-so is now working at this Company', and these people go all around the world, and to me it was 'oh, my goodness! You actually can live like that?' You know,

like, you could actually go from one job in one country to another job in another country for your entire working life if you wanted to. And that was like a totally new concept for me. Like, I always knew we'd be going to Singapore for three years and then we'd come back ... and although that expectation has changed to, 'Yeah, we're going to Singapore for three years and we might extend it to do five,' it has always been, 'We'll go back at the end.' So, although ... I feel global in some ways in that I'm sure we could move around the world if we wanted to, I would still feel like the only place we really fit is Australia. (Corporate Communications, three years in Singapore, since returned)

For others, their frames of reference of what it means to be Australian, based on shared understanding of endogenous cultural codes, expected, routinised everyday practices, and networks of relationships, began to change.

Framing the expatriate experience

Shifting cultural codes

Shared understandings of cultural codes marked the boundaries of the expatriate community. These were often based on common experiences encountered in Singapore, for example, the perpetuation of stereotypes about local staff or jokes about the rigidity of the city's regulations. There was an expectation of the repetition of introductory questions when meeting other expatriates: 'Where are you from?', 'How long have you been here?', 'How long are you staying?' This questioning incorporated the process of placing others.

It's such a pecking order. Like you get asked two questions: 'how long have you lived in Asia and have you lived anywhere else?' ... And the longer you're here the greater credibility you get. (Marketing Manager, two years in Singapore)

There is also a hierarchy of credibility in terms of the difficulty associated with particular countries that expatriates may have worked in prior to settling in Singapore. India or China for example, would be considered difficult, Singapore and Hong Kong are at the easier end of the scale. The length of time spent in the country is also important in the eyes of the Singaporeans. In the office of an Australian consultant, every call that was made to a potential local client involved in the initial conversation the question of how long she had lived in Singapore. The fleeting expatriate is viewed with some caution.

Cultural codes are embedded in the shared understanding of the meaning of terms such as 'Sarong Party Girl', 'trailing spouse', 'ladies' night', 'permanent expat'; in knowing that if one is a single man and if the stay is longer than seven years people will begin to wonder 'what's wrong with you?'. The understanding of these vocabularies came with time, and have been passed on from generation to generation, marking out the expatriate community in Singapore.

Everyday practices

The second element of framing the migration experience of these expatriates was centred on the maintenance or establishment of everyday practices. New patterns of socialising were based on routinised leisure activities such as the party circuit, sporting activities such as the Hash Harriers running club that meets every Saturday and/or golf on Sundays, and recreated rituals such as ANZAC Day and the Australia Day Ball. For some participants, what is 'normal' begins to be challenged. An example of everyday practice in Singapore is to employ domestic workers, which did present a moral dilemma for some participants but which was eventually assimilated. There was an impulse to adopt new normalities in the face of challenges to former ways of thinking.

> When we first came out, it wasn't compulsory to wear seat belts in the back of taxis ... [so] nobody else did, and I felt kind of stupid putting my seat belt on, so I kind of stopped after a while. [When a law was passed] I instantly went back to putting my seat belt on, now that it was a norm again, and you didn't feel like an idiot for doing it. So, yeah. ... I guess you kind of adapt to your environment. (Corporate Communications, three years in Singapore)

The workplace was the key learning centre. If adjustments were not made here then the expatriate had a more uncomfortable migration experience. Language was tempered, humour was restrained, but over time it became easier to be understood and to understand as adaptations were made. All participants recognised that they had changed their behaviour to some extent in the workplace at least. There is then perhaps a compartmentalisation of adaptation, divided between public workspace, when interaction with Singaporeans is inevitable, and private space, where contact can be minimised.

In other areas there seemed less suspension of norms. There is the perpetuation of gender expectations – 'sarong party girls' for the men, but gossip about the single Australian woman who may participate in fleeting sexual encounters, or the married woman who has an affair. It could be argued that these norms stem from the relocation of established social custom from 'back home'. When it was perceived that someone had overstepped the boundaries, strategies of social censure, such as gossip, even a degree of ostracisation, could be employed. A manager from an Asian Australian background held a party in her house, to which all her staff, local and expatriate, were invited. Members of the Australian contingent became uncomfortable with the outgoing behaviour of their Singaporean co-workers, who would 'normally' be seen in the office in a quieter mode.

Later on, in the office, the guy said to me, 'Well you're a turn coat because when you're with Westerners you say one thing and when you're with Asians you say another thing!' And I said 'Oh I take that as a compliment!' (laughs). And he said, 'No, you're a turncoat. You need to decide where you are'. (Human Resources Manager, nine years in Singapore)

Her Australian co-worker could no longer place her as belonging to his community circumscribed by the appropriate relationships with local Singaporean staff. She had stepped beyond the limits of expected norms and this behaviour created anxiety and confusion. There was a need expressed in these comments to ensure correct practices that demarcate appropriate relationships, and consequently the identity marked out by those relationships, were upheld.

Reconstituting relationships

The remarks above reinforce the role of relationships, the third element of framing the Australian expatriate in Singapore, as markers of identity and different levels of belonging and status. There are two core relationship networks within which Australians in Singapore are embedded: first, within the expatriate community itself, and second, their relationships with Singaporeans. In the majority of cases both networks are marked by transience.

It is true that up here you have more transient friendships, without a doubt. You don't have as many deep friendships. You have twice ... I would have to say I'd have three times as many friends in Singapore as I do in Sydney, but nowhere near the depth of my friendships, probably, in Sydney, bar say one or two. (Consultant, six years in Singapore)

Among the Australians there was a general trend towards knowing more people, but knowing them less well; they tended to make more of an effort to make friends; they were more likely to include someone they just met in their social activities; and they might even find themselves socialising with someone who 'you wouldn't necessarily hang out with at home' (a phrase repeated often by interviewees).

Most Australians in this research tended towards a social network that was predominantly other expatriates, not necessarily Australian, and including Singaporean 'acquaintances'.

I think there are differences ... [Singaporeans] are happy to go to a *hawker* [food] centre and ... have a beer and watch sport. I'm not saying that's not a fun way to spend a night, but ... I think because there's such a big network of expats there's no real need to sort of start branching out and hanging out with locals. And they're probably ... I would find them as ... what's the word ... like, 'cliquey' as what a group of expats can be.

Like, you know, [...] on a Saturday night, it's all locals. And a lot of times you go down there, and I just don't get a place, because they hang around in big groups of guys, and they find white guys threatening to their ... threaten their, take their girls and stuff like that. (Marketing Manager, two years in Singapore)

Few participants felt they had 'deep' relationships with Singaporeans, but when they did it was often as a result of contact through sporting activities, a connection through business or a Singaporean partner. Some participants, actively seeking to develop local relationships, and seeing it as part of 'the experience', encountered a degree of difficulty because of time and perceived cultural differences.

When we first came we said, 'We don't want to be these kind of expats that only talk to other Australians,' and it was actually difficult because [my husband] works at the Company, so he only ever met other Australians, and I ... when we first arrived I wasn't working, so I wasn't meeting anybody, either. I had one friend, one local friend who I knew already when we came over, and she's remained a friend and has been really good. But for the first few weeks we had her, and that was basically it. We were trying not to, you know, just socialise with Australians, but it got to August and we still hadn't been able to meet anyone yet. We'd been to church and we'd tried to join small groups to meet people, and it just didn't happen. And by August we were going, 'OK! Brain-snap time! We just can't cope with this social isolation!' And then we started forming a group of friends with people at the Company, and that has been really, really lifesaving, because otherwise we'd have just had to go home. You can't survive without a friendship group, and it's better to have an Australian friendship group than no friendship group at all. (Corporate Communications, three years in Singapore)

This interviewee's reasoning focused on both the perceived Singaporean social practice of forming 'tight social groups', and Singaporean perceptions of expats as condescending and 'difficult to get on with'. Other reasons are possibly financial; prices for drinks and meals at expatriate bars are much more expensive therefore local employees are less likely to socialise there. There is also the fact of comfort levels based on shared understanding. The above respondent later stated: 'I do tend to talk a lot more to the English girl and any other Anglo expats in my office than anybody else. That's because I feel more comfortable – it can be fun with her'.

To adjust to their changing environment, the shifting meaning of cultural cues, everyday practices and relationship networks in Singapore, research participants appeared to adopt combinations of three identity strategies, namely recreating Australia; redefining 'home'; and becoming more comfortable with mobile identities.

Recreating Australia

Despite an emphasis on adjectives such as hybridisation and cosmopolitanism to describe the outcomes of contemporary migration, transnational movement does not necessarily guarantee positive engagement. The result of uncomfortable intercultural contact can be the reinforcement of borders, articulated in the participant's stereotyping of both Australia and Singapore. There were also expressions of nostalgia and gentle undertones of homesickness in their narratives. Several of the participants fondly reminisced about brunch at the beach, the weather, the "Aussie larrikin', as well as missing family connections.

In both overt stereotyping and nostalgic reminiscing, there was a reassertion of connection to a geographic place defined by imagined shared national characteristics. Even when increasingly mobile, their cultural identity was given a landscape. Memories of the Australian environment were wrapped up in images of the 'wide brown land' and 'blue seas'.

I miss my concept of what Australia is, but whether I miss Australia, I don't really know. I just have this vision of the beach, the beach, running along the beach at seven o'clock at night after a hard … after a day's work, and the sun going down at about eight and … I miss that element, again, … and the banter thing. Like, the egalitarian feeling of Australia is what I miss. It doesn't matter if the waiter in the restaurant is … you're having a chat and you're having a proper conversation … yeah. It's the egalitarian nature I miss, of Australia. You don't get that here. (Consultant, six years in Singapore)

There are peak bodies in Singapore such as the Australia New Zealand Association (ANZA) and the Australian Chamber of Commerce (AustCham) that can fill the nostalgic gap, organising social events including key functions such as ANZAC Day ceremonies and the Australia Day Ball. These organisations also became points of intercultural contact and networking. AustCham, for example, encouraged Singaporean participation and ran events that were comprised on average of 60 per cent Australian and other expatriate nationalities, and 40 per cent Singaporean participants (personal communication, Philip Forrest, President, AustCham). There are also the pubs and clubs where interviewees knew they could always meet another Australian: the Wombat Football Club, the Wanderers Rugby Club, the cricket club. This circuit circumscribed what was commonly referred to as the 'Western Bubble'; a comfort zone consisting of the familiar, in particular, ways of behaving, language and humour.

There were, however, research participants who deliberately avoided these sites, feeling that they perpetuated the perception of an Australian 'yob', part of their culture they wanted to leave behind.

> Half the time I forget that I've got a white face here. So, no. ... I don't hang out at the real – for want of a better term, 'yobbo' expat bars here. When I do go out, it tends to be in a crowd that's maybe, sort of, half expat, half Asian. Those kind of bars, rather than just full-on whitey bars here. (Consultant, seven years in Singapore)

There was a division among the expatriates who took part in this research, between those who saw themselves outside the western bubble and those who didn't mind being in it, and there was a subtle competition between the two for authenticity. It was also possible that participants moved in and out of the 'western bubble', using the connections within when necessary but also quite comfortable operating in other, more 'local' social networks. This is a core tension that marked some interviewees' narratives: in Singapore there is the opportunity to be history-less, to renew or to reinvent the self. Where a person is unknown when they arrive there are no boundaries created by the expectations of other's familiarity. But there is still that need to feel a sense of belonging, to share humour and common frames of reference. There is still a longing for place that manifested itself in the process of redefining home.

Redefining home

Transnational employees in this research engaged in place making activities, bound in particular by new social relations developed over time and employing imaginative practices which enabled the reconstitution of home. There were Australians who objected to being called 'expats'; they felt they had lived in Singapore for enough time (16 years in one case) to now be regarded as 'local'. Those same markers of their Australian home – family, friends, familiarity, comfort, 'knowing the faces' – had been relocated to their Singapore context.

> Australia's home when there's a rugby test or test cricket or something like that. But my wife always says, 'home is where the dogs are', and that's Singapore. (Businessman, 12 years in Singapore)

If the conditions of comfort as defined by the individual can be met, then, according to Kivisto (2001), rather than simultaneously living in two worlds, a condition of more mobile identities discussed below, the place the migrant is in counts for more and more over time.

> I sort of feel like there's a finite number of home points, and I've sort of transferred some of my home points to Singapore. Singapore feels more

like home than it did before when I first came, and Australia feels less like home than it did when I first left. (*What are the "home points"?*). Home points ... it's very hard to put a finger on exactly what home points I've transferred to Singapore. The place is familiar, it's comfortable, I've got some friends here. I don't have a whole heap of friends here but I've got friends here, just walking down the street or going to the local hawker centre and stuff, it's so familiar. I know the faces. All those little things that sort of make a place feel like home. I've sort of put down some small little roots here. It's a nice place and everything, and I sort of feel comfortable. Yeah. So, to that extent, Australia is sort of less like home, because I am comfortable living in Singapore. And, theoretically, I could live here for the rest of my life. It's just that my brain, my logical, conscious decisions, tells me that I wouldn't, because it's just too damn stressful! (Lawyer, Singapore-Australian, one month in Singapore)

However, redefining home is a difficult transition involving surrender, and a problematic area to analyse when taking into account that several expatri-ates interviewed have adopted a strategy whereby a posting is imagined as home. If they did not play this trick on themselves the chances of project failure, particularly in more difficult countries, increased as the expatriate is constantly longing for somewhere else. It would be an area for further research, to examine the moment of choice, the moment of surrender of previous familiarities, practices, values and relationships, and the motivations for making those choices.

Mobile identities

The third response to their professional migration is to develop a sense of comfort with the mobility of identity. This appeared as a strategic device to enable the transnational employee to slot more easily back into life in Australia on return, and to operate more effectively in Asia both in the work-place and socially. An indication of this strategy is the convoluted narratives of participants, such as the young lawyer above and the consultant below who struggled to define 'home'.

I think I'm just in a pattern of calling Sydney my home, you know? That's what it is. Sydney's my home, because that's my pattern of saying, 'Oh, yeah, you know. Where are you from?' People will say, 'Where are you from?' and you're taught to say, 'Sydney'. But really, if I thought about it, where am I from? I'm from Singapore. You know? (*Is that question from Asians or other expatriates?*) Other expats. Even Asians will say, 'Where are you from?', but the funny thing is, when Asians ask me, I say, 'Singapore'. When expats ask me, I say, 'Sydney'. When Asians ask me, I say, 'I'm from Singapore. I've lived here for six years'. And they go, 'Aah, where from originally?' and I say, 'Sydney'. (Consultant, six years in Singapore)

In the scenario narrated above, identity is the answer to a question depending on the context and on who is asking. This participant also feels she 'ocker's things up' when socialising with Australians. Time appears as an important factor in this scenario. The expressions of mobility, the realisation of the potential of elisions of meaning associated with identity referents, and at times associated confusion, was more prevalent among participants who had been in-country for longer periods of time. One of the areas of potential when the established meanings of identity referents began to slip related to the idea of migration as a way to leave behind the past. One interviewee felt that each time she moved to a new country or back to Australia, it was an opportunity to recreate herself. In Singapore she was free from the typecasting associated with the place she grew up in – Camden (an outlying suburb of western Sydney, regarded in the general parlance of other Sydney-siders as an area lacking in sophistication). Only other Sydney-siders would know the stereotypes associated with coming from Camden. In Singapore she need only respond that she is from Australia. Similar feelings are expressed by the consultant below, who is no longer burdened by the memories of other people and their expectations of his behaviour.

> I feel a different person here than in Australia. I feel, in Australia, that I'm constrained by the peers who knew me as a younger guy and what I was doing back then. I'm constrained by my family. My family still see me as a mad six-year old running around! ... I feel like I'm a real person here, ... I feel like I'm somebody here, whereas in Australia I don't. I feel like I don't have as much sense of identity, or personal identity, as I do here. And I like that. (Consultant, seven years in Singapore)

The difficulty with developing such chameleon-like flexibility is the potential for the anxiety that comes with loss of certainties. But rather than extremes, participants tended to adopt more supple responses. They engaged in recreating Australia and reconstituting home to differing degrees at different times and places. They demonstrated different levels of belonging, impacted on by the strength of individual insertion into the norms, practices and networks of relationships that demarcated their definition of the key locational terms of home, Singapore, Australian, and Expat.

Conclusion

The strength of place-making by these transnational professionals would work against the thesis that the mobility of this group is leading to 'denationationalised' identities. While globalisation is related to deterritorialised processes, such as flows of capital and people, it would seem that transnational migration is, in this case at least, as Thomas Faist (2000) suggests, anchored in or spanning two or more states. The relationship between transnational and local spaces consisted of multiple connections between Australia and Singapore at differing levels of engagement, from corporate transactions to personal relationships. A bi-directional process of interaction ensued between TNC employees and Singapore, and within the 'community' of expatriates itself. Personal values and frames of reference were challenged, identity reconstituted, and home recreated in their narratives. The varied and nuanced responses towards the host country, related to the strength and focus of defining home, highlighted the heterogenous reactions by these transnational businesspeople to intercultural exchange.

As these expatriates interacted with Singapore in the process of establishing new routines of everyday practice and relationship networks, they subscribed to or created a place marked by characteristics of familiarity. This included reasserting Australianness and elements of a national imaginary, reconstituting 'home' in the Singaporean context with necessary adaptations, or the realisation of the mobility of identities and the subsequent deliberate adoption of flexibility in different home/host country contexts. The confusion that such identity re-evaluation can engender was seen in convoluted narratives as they struggled to find the words to express a sense of belonging.

Narratives reflected an ability to utilise social and material practices to reconceptualise place, especially apparent in the strategic use of nostalgia, the reformulations of relationship networks, and in the redefining of 'being a local'. The development of competencies to manage movement between Singapore and Australia, between the Singaporean workplace and the expatriate community, required the acquisition of what Floya Anthias refers to as 'translation skills by strangers or travellers from one society to the other' (2001:622). She refers to the utilisation of these skills to manage a condition of marginality, however, these competencies were also used by elites in this research to manage the acculturation process they found themselves in.

There are similarities between these processes of change management and those that mark other less-'wanted' migrant communities as seen in the papers in this edition. However, there are also striking differences in terms of motivations, the push and pull factors, and the level of choice. For these Australians, they have greater choice in whether they leave Australia or not, and more choice in determining how long they stay and when they return. The decision to migrate is not mainly based on economic necessity (although many are financially better off in Singapore) but is more likely to be based on a desire for challenge, newness and cultural curiosity.

The impact of their re-evaluation of place is the development of increasingly complex interconnections which link, in this case study, Australia and Singapore; shifting the idea of place as settled, enclosed and coherent, and reinforcing Massey's point that place can be a meeting point, an intersection of activity, relationships and influences (1995:72). But this place must be given a name, 'home', and there is a tendency towards giving that home geographic qualities, usually one or the other, Australia or Singapore, but at times with a concomitant feeling of not quite being either. Whether it is possible to feel about the world in the same way as home, I would argue there is no evidence in this research that the attachment to being a 'global citizen' (a descriptor used by some participants) overrides the need to feel the ground beneath their feet.

References

American Chamber of Commerce (2003) Personal correspondence, Mr N. De Boursac, Executive Director, 28 November, www.amcham.org.sg

Anthias, F. (2001) 'New Hybridities, Old Concepts: the Limits of 'Culture', *Ethnic and Racial studies*, Vol. 24, No. 4: 619–41.

Appadurai, A. (1977) *Modernity at Large: the Cultural Dimensions of Globalisation* (New Delhi: Oxford University Press).

Bauman, Z. (1998) *Globalisation: The Human Consequences* (London: Polity Press).

Faist, T. (2000) 'Transnationalism in International Migration: Implications for the Study of Citizenship and Culture', *Ethnic and Racial Studies*, Vol. 23, No. 2 (March): 189–222.

Fitzgerald, D. (2004) 'Beyond "Transnationalism": Mexican Hometown Politics at an American Labour Union', in *Ethnic and Racial Studies*, Vol. 27, No. 2 (March): 228–47.

Glick-Schiller N., L. Basch and C. Szanton-Blanc (eds) (1992) *Towards a Transnational Perspective on Migration: Race, Class, Ethnicity and Nationalism Reconsidered* (New York: New York Academy of Sciences).

Government of Australia, Department of Foreign Affairs and Trade (2002) Statistics provided to the Southern Cross Group, http://www.southern-cross-group.org/archives/Statistics/Numbers_of_Australians_Overseas_in_2001_Feb_2002.pdf

Guarnizo, L. and M. Smith (1998) 'The Locations of Transnationalism', in M. Smith and L. Guarnizo (eds) *Transnationalism from Below* (London: Transaction Publishers).

Hannerz, U. (2002) *Flows, Boundaries and Hybrids: Keywords in Transnational Anthropology*, Working Paper, Transnational Communities Project, Oxford University.

Hewison, K. (2003) 'Working in Hong Kong: The Experience of Thai Migrant Workers'. Conference paper presented at *Migrant Labour in South East Asia: Needed, Not Wanted*, Faculty of Economics, Business and Law, University of New England, Armidale, 1–3 December.

Huntington, S. (2004) 'Dead Souls: The Denationalisation of the American Elite', *The National Interest*, No. 75 (Spring): 5–18.

Jameson, F. (1984) 'Postmodernism, or the Cultural Logics of Late Capital', *New Left Review*, Vol. 146: 53–92.

King, R. (1995) 'Migrations, Globalisations and Place', in D. Massey and P. Jess (eds) *A Place in the World? Places, Cultures and Globalisation* (UK: Open University Press) pp. 5–44.

Kivisto, P. (2001) 'Theorising Transnational Immigration: A Critical Review of Current Efforts', *Ethnic and Racial Studies*, Vol. 24, No. 4: 549–77.

Lee, E. F. and Yeo Yen Fang (2003) 'Singapore's Demographic Trends in 2002', *Statistics Singapore Newsletter*, (September) Population Statistics Section, Singapore Department of Statistics. http://www.singstat.gov.sg/ssn/feat/nov2003/pg10–13. pdf, accessed 23 December 2003.

Massey, D. (1995) 'The Conceptualisation of Place', in D. Massey and P. Jess (eds) *A Place in the World? Places, Cultures and Globalisation* (UK: Open University Publishing) pp. 45–85.

Nonini D. and A. Ong (1997) 'Chinese Transnationalism as an Alternative Modernity', in A. Ong and D. Nonini (eds) *Ungrounded Empires: The Cultural Politics of Modern Chinese Transnationalism* (London: Routledge) pp. 3–36.

Portes, A. (1999) 'Conclusion: Towards a New World – the Origins and Effects of Transnational Activities', *Ethnic and Racial Studies*, Vol. 22, No. 2 (March): 463–77.

Portes, A., Luis E. Guarnizo and L. Patricia (1999) 'The Study of Trans-nationalism: Pitfalls and Promise of an Emergent Research Field', *Ethnic and Racial Studies*, Vol. 22, No. 2: 217–37.

Sassen, S. (2002) *Globalisation*, seminar organised by the Migration and Multicultural Research Centre, University of Sydney (21 October).

—— (2000) *Cities in a World Economy* (California: Pine Forge Press).

Singapore Department of Statistics (2002) 'Singapore's Changing Population Trends'. Paper presented at the Conference on Chinese Population and Socio-economic Studies, Hong Kong University of Science and Technology (19–21 June) Hong Kong SAR, http://www.singstat.gov.sg/papers/seminar/poptrends.pdf

Sklair, L. (1998) *Transnational Practices and the Analysis of the Global System*. Paper presented at the Transnational Communities Programme Seminar series, Oxford University, UK.

Velayutham, S. (2003) 'Responding to Globalisation: Nation, Culture and Identity in Singapore', Unpublished PhD thesis, Centre for Cultural Research, University of Western Sydney.

Vertovec, S. (1999) 'Conceiving and Researching Transnationalism', *Ethnic and Racial Studies*, Vol. 22, No. 2: 447–62.

Yeoh, B. (2004) *Migration, International Labour and Multicultural Policies in Singapore*, Asia Research Institute Working Paper Series, No. 19, February 2004, National University of Singapore.

Yeoh, B. and K. Willis (1998) *Singapore Unlimited: Configuring Social Identity in the Regionalisation Process*, Working paper, the Oxford Transnational Community Project, Oxford University, UK.

Zsuzsa, G. and S. O'Riain (2002) 'Global Ethnography', *Annual Review of Sociology*, Vol. 28, No. 1: 271–95.

10

Indian Professional Workers in Singapore

Seema Gaur

Falling fertility in most developed countries, as well as in high-income developing countries like Singapore, has led to population ageing, and is causing serious labour shortages. Consequently, the achievement of growth objectives has become increasingly dependent on foreign labour. Globalisation, the expansion of multinational corporations (MNCs), growing intra-firm linkages, the demands of a knowledge-economy requiring highly skilled workers and the need to maintain international competitiveness, are adding to this process. Under the globalised production regime based on cost minimisation, multinational firms are relocating production and services as well as outsourcing to cheaper locations. Policy makers in these countries are also facing the dual challenge of rising structural unemployment due to economic restructuring on the one hand, and the need to provide knowledge workers on the other. The question then arises: what role can labour migration play in moderating the effects of population ageing and alleviating labour shortages, as well as maintaining the competitiveness of knowledge-based economies?

Singapore is a highly internationalised, affluent economy with a small and ageing population. Services are increasingly driving Singapore's economy, and contribute more than 60 per cent to the country's GDP. Singapore aims to strengthen its position as a regional and global services hub and develop as a knowledge-based economy (KBE). One of the major constraints in achieving this objective is the shortage of skilled, as well as relatively unskilled labour, due to demographic constraints (Sen *et al.*, 2000). Hence, Singapore maintains a policy of being open to foreign talent. India is a rich source of internationally competitive skilled labour that can be absorbed by Singapore as Singapore moves towards KBE. In fact, India has been providing internationally competitive and culturally compatible labour to Singapore at all levels. Recently, Singapore and India signed a Comprehensive Economic Cooperation Agreement (CECA), covering labour migration in addition to trade in goods, services and investments.

This chapter examines the role of Indian labour, particularly skilled labour, in Singapore's globalisation strategy. The paper begins with a discussion of

Singapore's globalisation strategy. Its need for foreign labour, its foreign labour policy, and the size of its foreign workforce are then analysed. The size of the Indian workforce in Singapore and the human resource complementarities between Singapore and India are examined in the next section. Indian labour's contribution to Singapore's competitiveness and globalisation-related goals in several areas are also discussed. The chapter concludes with a discussion of constraints, and suggests steps to facilitate the entry of Indian labour in Singapore.

Singapore's globalisation strategy

Given its diminutive geographical size, Singapore's aim of becoming a developed country relies on globalisation (Khan and Abheysinghe 2002). In fact, globalisation has been part of Singapore's industrial policies since the early 1960s. Within a span of three decades, Singapore transformed itself from a regional entrepôt to a leading global manufacturing and logistics hub. Its success in attracting foreign investments in manufacturing as well as services has contributed to Singapore being one of the most internationalised states in the world (Asher and Sen 1999). Singapore is following its Industry 21 Blueprint (EDB 1998) initiated in January 1999 to develop into a vibrant and robust global hub of knowledge-driven industries with a strong emphasis on technology and innovation. The Economic Review Committee (ERC) (2003) has now endorsed this vision of Singapore as a Knowledge Based Economy (KBE). KBE is a new globalised economic environment which is characterised by

- the importance of talent and education;
- innovation and entrepreneurship as the driving forces for growth;
- re-inventing businesses and industries in the face of global competition;
- upgrading to higher end manufacturing operations and innovative services (ERC 2003).

Manufacturing will continue to be an important growth engine of the new global strategy. The state aims to upgrade key industry clusters of electronics, chemicals, biomedical sciences and engineering, which now form the core of high value-added activities. It also aims to promote the services sector as the second growth engine in order to become a regional services hub and tap major new opportunities in Asia. New, exportable services like healthcare, education and creative industries are intended to be promoted, while also pushing forward in established areas like trading, logistics, info-communications technology (ICT), financial services, and tourism (ERC 2003). In an increasingly competitive environment the main economic challenge for Singapore is to maintain its competitiveness. As the cost of providing the traditional factors of production such as land and labour has risen, knowledge or intellectual capital will provide a competitive advantage to differentiate Singapore from its competitors.

Singapore's labour constraints

Since 1975, Singapore has been experiencing a Total Fertility Rate (TFR) below replacement levels that suggests a rapid ageing of the population and consequent labour shortages (Shantakumar 2002). Augmentation of the human resource base through the importation of foreign workers is therefore necessary for the country to fulfil its economic goals. From a small population base of 1.9 million in 1965, Singapore has successfully leveraged foreign labour in its development strategy. There are shortages of unskilled/semi-skilled labour as well as highly skilled labour in critical sectors like informational and communication technology, the services and biomedical sectors and others. Labour force projections clearly indicate that a continuation of the current inflow of permanent migrants is necessary to sustain reasonable rate of growth for the Singaporean economy in the twenty-first century (Hui 2002).

Restructuring of the economy from labour-intensive to capital-intensive production and services has changed Singapore's occupational structure. The proportion of the workforce in managerial, professional and technical jobs increased from 11 per cent in 1970 to about 40 per cent in 1999. Conversely, production jobs requiring lower educational levels dropped from a peak of 46 per cent in 1980 to 29 per cent in 1999 (Hui 2002). As global competition intensifies and a knowledge-based society takes hold, the nature of jobs to be created in manufacturing and services is expected to change even further. The Singapore Economic Development Board estimates that two out of three jobs resulting from new manufacturing investments will require skilled labour. In comparison, only 15 per cent of the labour force had tertiary qualifications in 2000 (significantly lower than in developed countries), while 38 per cent had pre-secondary educational levels (ERC Subcommittee 2002). Numbers of graduates at more advanced levels is small relative to the projected demand (Mui 2002). Thus foreign talent infusion in Singapore is required to allow Singapore to survive and even thrive in an uncertain global economic environment (as reiterated by ERC Subcommittee on human talent 2002).

Singapore's foreign labour policy

Singapore's foreign labour policy follows a dualistic approach with the objectives of maximising the contribution of foreign workers and minimising social costs. To minimise costs, lower skilled workers are denied the opportunity to establish roots in Singapore by the maintenance of a revolving pool of such workers on fixed employment terms. On the other hand, highly skilled workers are encouraged to seek permanent residency and those with advanced new economy skills are even offered citizenship. The two main flows of foreigners admitted to Singapore include low-skilled contract labour (earning less than S$2,500 a month) on work permits and skilled professional and managerial workers on employment passes. Concerns over the potential negative effects of a large immigrant population have led to the introduction of controls over foreign worker inflow in the form of work permits with differing residency conditions, levies on the employment of unskilled workers, sector specific dependency ratios, restrictions on the sectors allowed to employ foreign labour, and ceilings on the proportion of foreign staff in a firm (Hui 2002). Not only is immigration policy integrally linked to macroeconomic policy to achieve growth targets and to increase market share, but it also complements population policy (Ruppert 1999).

In recent years, rising structural unemployment and retrenchments due to a mismatch between available job skills and the increased need for higher skills are becoming a serious concern. Singaporeans are increasingly questioning the appropriateness of the government's foreign worker policy and the quality of talent recruited (Mui 2002). The government has tried to explain the need to tap and augment the labour pool, especially at the top end, with foreign talent. According to Senior Minister Lee Kuan Yew

> Singapore's foreign talent policy cannot change, as doing so will undercut the nation's capability to grow and expand. There are four million people in Singapore; one million of which are foreigners. You get rid of this one million and many will not find jobs. (*Business Times* 13 November 2003)

It has to be emphasised that foreign labour has helped Singapore's international competitiveness, and the benefits of foreign labour generally exceed costs (Low 2000). For example, a study by the Ministry of Trade and Industry (MTI) Singapore found that 37 per cent of the GDP growth during the 1990s was contributed by employment pass holders (skilled foreigners) and 4 per cent by work permit holders (low/unskilled foreigners) (Tan 2001). A recent MTI study (Chia *et al.*, 2004) has concluded that foreign labour complements (rather than substitutes) local labour, primarily through its role in supporting industrial development. ERC (2003) has reiterated that

> Our openness to global talent will be a key competitive advantage for a Singapore that aspires to become a global city. Foreign worker policies should be flexible enough to allow companies to employ the workers they need, keep their overall costs of production down and make their operations here more viable.

Therefore, Singapore has no option but to continue to recruit foreign talent in spite of rising structural unemployment and concern among its population.

The size of the foreign workforce in Singapore

Official data/statistics on foreign workers in Singapore are patchy. However, the six-fold increase in the proportion of non-residents in the

Singapore population from 3 per cent in 1970 to 18.8 per cent in 2000 (Table 10.1) is a consequence of Singapore's policies to attract and rely on foreign workers.

These figures provide ample indication of the increasing role of foreigners in the Singaporean economy over the last three decades. In fact, in the 2000 census, foreigners formed about 26 per cent of a total population of over 4 million, when permanent residents (which are included in the category of residents) are taken into account. During 1990–2000, citizens registered only a 1.3 per cent population growth, compared to 10 per cent for permanent residents and 9.3 per cent for the non-resident population: thus foreigners account for most of Singapore's population growth rate. This has resulted in the share of permanent residents almost doubling from 3.7 to 7.2 per cent during the 1990s, with the non-resident share increasing from 10.2 to 18.8 per cent, as shown in Table 10.2.

Estimates by some authors indicate that Singapore's foreign workforce has increased from 3.2 per cent of the total work force in 1980 to about 30 per cent in 2000 (Table 10.3).

Hui (2002) has estimated that according to the preliminary 2000 census returns, out of the 1,045,000 foreigners (inclusive of non resident as well as permanent residents), an estimated 600,000 are in the workforce, accounting for 30 per cent of total employment. These include an estimated 110,000 highly skilled and better-educated employment pass holders in the manufacturing, commercial, and business sectors. The remaining 49,000 comprise low skilled work permit holders, including about 130,000 domestic

Table 10.1 Singapore: changes in population categories, 1970–2000

Census/year	Total population[1] — Population (annual rate of growth)	Resident population — Population (annual rate of growth)	% of total	Non-resident population — Numbers (annual rate of growth)	% of total
1970	2,074.5 (2.8)	2,013.6 (n.a.)[2]	97.0	60.9 (5.6)	3.0
1980	2,413.9 (1.5)	2,282.1 (1.3)	94.5	131.8 (1.7)	5.5
1990	3,047.1 (2.3)	2,735.9 (1.7)	89.7	311.3 (2.9)	10.3
2000	4,017.7 (2.8)	3,263.2 (1.8)	81.2	754.5 (9.3)	18.8

Notes
1. The Census divides the population into residents and non-residents. Residents further comprise citizens and permanent residents who are also foreigners. The non-resident population includes individuals holding passes for short-term stays in Singapore (including employment passes, work permits, dependent's passes, long term social visit passes), but excludes tourists and transients.
2. n.a. = not available.

Sources: Department of Statistics (2000), Wong (1997), Yeoh (2004).

Table 10.2   Singapore: total population by residential status, 1990–2000

Residence status	Percentage of total population		Annual growth rate
	1990	2000	1990–2000
Residents	89.8	81.2	1.8
Citizens	86.1	74.0	1.3
Permanent residents	3.7	7.2	10.0
Non residents	10.2	18.8	9.3
Total population	100.0	100.0	–
Total population ('000)	3,016.4	4,017.7	2.8

Source: Shantakumar (2002).

Table 10.3   Singapore: size of foreign labour force, 1970–2000

Year	Total labour force	Foreign workers	Percentage of total labour force
1970	650,892	20,828	3.2
1980	1,077,090	119,483	7.4
1990	1,480,000	200,000	13.5
1995	1,690,000	350,000	20.7
2000	2,000,000	600,000*	30.0

Notes: Figures for 1970 to 1995 have been taken from Wong, 1997 and for 2000 from Hui, 2002.
* The foreign work force is estimated from the population figures by excluding those below 20 and above 60 years of age.

Source: Wong (1997); Hui (2002).

workers, 210,000 construction workers, and about 150,000 employees in the manufacturing, marine and service industries.

The picture that emerges from the above tables is that despite immigration restrictions, the size of the foreign workforce has increased significantly in Singapore. This is because the small size of the domestic population could not have supported the rapid expansion of the economy. Without the contribution of overseas workers, Singapore would not have seen an average quarterly growth of 7.8 per cent during the 1990s (Tan 2001).

Indian labour in Singapore

The origins of Indian labour migration to Malaya/Singapore go back to the colonial period when workers from India were recruited for a myriad of tasks. Indian labourers proved indispensable for the success of many tasks aimed at Singapore's growth and development (Sandhu 1993; Krishnan 1936 cited in Mani 1993). In time, educated Indians were drawn to serve the British administrative machinery. Teachers, policemen, clerks, interpreters, overseers, lawyers, draftsmen and other subordinate posts were filled by Indians. The rapidly expending economy, coupled with a liberal open door policy on immigration drew ever-increasing number of immigrants including Indians. According to Tan and Major (1995),

> There can be little doubt that Indian labor, enterprise and initiative in almost every sphere of society during 19th and 20th century contributed immensely to laying the foundation which essentially enabled an independent Singapore to thrive and prosper.

Despite strict immigration controls after independence in 1965, the 1970s again saw an influx of Indian guest workers who were recruited to ease pressure on the labour market. The period 1980–95 witnessed an influx of better-educated Indians as well as unprecedented labour immigration from the Indian sub-continent into Singapore's construction and infrastructure sectors.

At present, Indian labour is employed in two distinct categories. The first category includes various labour-intensive sectors such as construction and shipping where labour is employed on two-year work permits. These workers are expected to return home after a contractual period, unless they have acquired further training or obtained trade certificates in Singapore's vocational and technical institutes. This enables their re-classification as skilled workers who can then continue to work locally over the longer term (Shantakumar 1999). The second category comprises skilled workers who are found mainly in tertiary institutions and in the engineering, information technology, business, banking and financial sectors. Many are university-educated professionals working as senior executives in local and multinational companies, or doing high-tech research work, or running their own businesses as IT professionals, engineers and accountants (*Straits Times*, 3 August 2003). These professionals are encouraged to become permanent residents (and ultimately citizens), based on the skill requirements of the economy. Both categories of Indian workers have contributed to the growth of Singapore's economy because of their technical proficiency, cost-effectiveness, productivity and their ability to assimilate into Singaporean society (Shantakumar 1999).

Since data on Singapore's workforce has always been shrouded in regional geopolitical sensitivities, it is not possible to provide accurate figures on Indian labour in Singapore. However, the proportion of Indians in the total population increased from 7 per cent to 7.9 per cent during the 1990s, as shown in Table 10.4.

Table 10.4 The Indian[1] population in Singapore, 1821–2000

Year	Population ('000)	Proportion in total population	Growth rate (% p.a.)
1821[2]		2.8	–
1871	11.5	11.8	–
1881	12.1	8.8	0.5
1891	16.0	8.8	2.8
1901	17.7	7.8	1.0
1911	27.8	9.2	4.6
1921	32.3	7.7	1.5
1931	50.8	9.1	4.6
1947	69.0	7.4	1.9
1957	129.6	9.0	6.5
1966	135.8	7.0	0.5
1970	145.1	7.0	1.7
1980	154.6	6.4	0.6
1990	190.9	7.0	2.3
1995	190.0	6.4	−0.1
1997	230.6	7.4	10.2
2000	257.8	7.9	n.a.[3]

Notes

1. The Indian Diaspora currently resident in Singapore refers to the diverse peoples of the sub-continent: Indians, Pakistanis, Bangladeshis, Sri Lankans, Nepalese, Bhutanese, Maldivians and Sikkimise. Censuses from 1970 enumerate these peoples collectively as 'Indians', while distinguishing them by place of origin, country of birth and languages spoken.

From 1980 onwards, the table reflects the resident population only, and not the total Indian labour that may have been working in Singapore on work permits and employment passes. However, it includes those working as permanent residents.

2. The number of Indians in 1821 was 132. There were no female residents at this time.

3. n.a. = not available.

Source: Sandhu (1993), p. 774; Shantakumar (1999); Census, Dept. of Statistics, Singapore (2000).

The rising share of permanent residents and non-residents in the country (Table 10.2) indicates that Indians have made a substantial contribution to the growth of the permanent resident and non-resident populations. Further, since the share of foreigners (inclusive of permanent residents) in the total labour force during this period increased from 20.7 per cent to 30 per cent, this implies that the share of Indian workers in the total labour force must have also gone up during the 1990s. Watson Wyatt, a consulting company, found in its survey of 363 companies in 2001 that almost 50 per cent of the expatriates in Singapore were from India, with China and Malaysia following closely behind. Indian expatriate leaders of informal groups and associations estimate that there are several hundred thousand immigrants, most of whom are permanent residents with the rest holding employment passes (*Straits Times*, 3 August 2003). Incidentally, the officially sanctioned influx of skilled immigrants (of all countries of origin) is about 35,000 in annual terms excluding families. Some 7 to 10 per cent of these could be expected to be Indians (Shantakumar 1999).

Human resource complementarities between Singapore and India

Singapore's transition to a knowledge-based society will be highly dependent on the skills and knowledge of the workforce. The Singaporean vision is to develop a world-class workforce in the twenty-first century, which means having a cost competitive workforce with outstanding capabilities (CSC 1998). With its vast pool of high-quality, technically qualified and English-speaking labour force, India can meet Singapore's needs. India's 250 universities, 1500 research institutions, and more than 10,000 institutes of higher learning churn out more than 500,000 engineers and technical trained graduates and postgraduates every year. Indian labour is culturally and socially compatible, adaptive and internationally competitive, a crucial factor if Singapore is to maintain competitiveness in its transition to a fully developed economy (Shantakumar 1995). Therefore, Singapore looks to India as a significant source in the upgrading of its human resources. On the other hand, Singapore also holds an attraction for Indian professionals due to its proximity to India, a congenial socio-cultural environment, world-class infrastructure in terms of housing and education facilities, and low taxation. Thus complementarities exist in the human resources field between Singapore and India.

The India–Singapore Joint Study Group (JSG) (2003) has taken full cognisance of these opportunities. The JSG's recommendations have been largely incorporated in the CECA, which India and Singapore signed in June 2004, providing an easing of visa restrictions for professionals of both countries.

The role of Indian labour in Singapore's globalisation strategy

Maintaining competitiveness in manufacturing and services

Maintaining international competitiveness has always been a crucial issue for Singapore, given its extreme openness to international trade and the importance of international trade in generating its GDP (Wilson and Abeysinghe 2002). Indian skilled labour can relieve critical labour shortages in key sectors of Singapore's economy, and contribute towards cost reduction and the maintenance of Singapore's competitiveness and its globalisation drive. A few high potential sectors (illustrative, not exhaustive) are discussed below.

Information and communications (infocomm) industry

Singapore aims to develop as the infocomm hub of Asia. Information and communications services have been identified as one of the 12 hub services by Singapore's Committee on Competitiveness (CSC 1998). It is estimated that about 11,000–13,000 people per year will be needed in this field for next few years (IDA 2000). There is evidence that demand far outstrips supply, judging from the high overall turnover rate of 25 per cent in the infocomm industry, and 11 per cent in infocomm end user organisations in 1998 (Hui Weng Tat 2002). Without the inflow of foreign talent, it will be almost impossible to bridge the remaining demand for infocomm labour. Since India is among the world's largest sources of high quality low cost IT labour, a large number are likely to be sourced from India. A study by Watson Hyatt found that the cost of an Indian IT engineer is one-fifth that of a Singaporean engineer (cited Soo *et al.*, 2001).

India also has been the largest source of foreign IT professionals in Singapore during the 1990s (Soo *et al.*, 2001). Singapore's positioning as a test bed for new ICT technology and its strong government emphasis on IT make it an attractive place for Indian IT professionals to develop their careers. The Economic Development Board (EDB) and Contact Singapore have organised missions to India to recruit labour. The Infocomm Development Authority (IDA) has established offices in Chennai and Bangalore for this purpose. Various collaborations between Singapore and Indian organisations are being forged (e.g., IDA-NIIT, NASSCOM-SITF) for cooperation in ICT. Under CECA, both India and Singapore have recognised infocomm professionals in 18 areas of computer related services including systems design and analysis, software engineering and programming, database analysis, information technology, quality assurance and computer engineering. Professional bodies would be encouraged to negotiate Mutual Recognition Agreements. This can be expected to increase the presence of Indian infocomm professionals in Singapore.

Banking and finance

Singapore aims to become the regional and global hub for the management and distribution of financial services. The CSC has recognised that the pool of available skilled personnel required to support the growth of the sector in key areas is limited. Persistent shortages of qualified personnel will result in an overall decline in professionalism and escalate business costs as local professionals become too expensive. India is already contributing to Singapore's needs in this sector through its Indian Institutes of Management (IIMs), and other reputable management institutes. Most of these professionals are generally qualified engineers, thus having a blend of technical and management education, vital in this sector.

Healthcare

Singapore aims at developing into a medical hub for a whole spectrum of healthcare services as well as a global centre for medical research, education and advanced patient care. Further, Singapore's fertility rate is currently below the replacement rate, which coupled with improvement in life expectancy has resulted in a rapidly ageing society. Therefore, demand for skilled healthcare personnel is expected to grow in the next five years, but Singapore faces a severe shortage of health personnel. The most pronounced shortage in the sector is for nurses and healthcare assistants, where there is difficulty in recruiting Singaporeans in spite of the economic downturn (Contact Singapore.com). Currently, only 70 per cent of healthcare assistants and 21 per cent of nurses are Singaporeans.

India has a comparative advantage in the supply of doctors, premedical staff and nurses at competitive prices. However, in spite of these shortages, Singapore has imposed stringent entry barriers. Now, under CECA, a whole range of health sector professionals ranging from general physicians and surgeons to various specialists like cardiologists, dentists, pharmacists, pathologists and others have liberalised access to Singapore. This will provide employment opportunities for Indian medical professionals and will relieve health sector human resource shortages in Singapore. Hospitals are also exploring joint ventures such as the Apollo Gleneagles Hospital, which has been set up in Kolkota, India. Singapore's hospitals can also combine with Indian hospitals in jointly establishing a commercial presence in third countries using Singapore's management and clinical expertise and low cost Indian human resources (Mukherjee *et al.*, 2003).

Education

Singapore aims to develop into a world-class education hub. With over 6000 MNCs, Singapore is also well suited to become a centre for corporate training. With increasing inflows of international students, there is likely to be shortage of teachers, faculty members and other administrative staff. Again, India can meet Singapore's needs for teachers and related staff. Opportunities exist for the two countries to establish partnerships in educational services and training of infocomm personnel. The countries can also leverage Singapore's technical knowledge and India's low cost skilled labour in developing e-learning content and customised e-learning solutions to serve the Asian region. Further, collaboration in IT-enabled services would help increase their share in the world trade in educational services. There are significant entry barriers in Singapore for Indian educational labour (Mukherjee *et al.*, 2003). However, under CECA, university and polytechnic lecturers have been recognised. This implies that after Mutual Recognition Agreements are reached, suitably qualified Indian lecturers will be able to gain employment in Singapore's universities and polytechnic colleges.

Research and development efforts

As part of Singapore's strategy to become globally competitive KBE, national resources devoted to research and development (R&D) have increased from 0.9 per cent of GDP in 1991 to 2.1 per cent in 2001 (Toh *et al.*, 2002). However, there is a considerable gap between the R&D outputs of Singapore and that of more advanced KBEs (Toh and Choo 2002). Singapore does not have enough research scientists and engineers and other knowledge workers with an RSE (Research, Scientists and Engineers) ratio per 10,000 labour force of 66, compared to 98 for Japan, 94 for Finland and 74 for United States (Mui 2002). The Economic Reforms Committee (2003:chap 10, 71) have recognised the constraint: 'A ready and abundant supply of highly trained scientific and technical labour will be an important competitive factor as industry's R&D activities extend upstream beyond product and process development to applied R&D and our industries become more technologically advanced and science based'. Lack of R&D talent is also identified as a critical factor in Singapore's development as a biomedical R&D hub (DBJ 2001).

India has emerged as the R&D hub (*Business Line*, 24 March 2003) for the world with more than 100 MNCs like IBM, General Motors and others setting up R&D centres in India to enhance their competitiveness. Average annual salaries paid for an Indian graduate engineer is US$15,000 to 30,000 for PhD holders – one-fifth of the salary paid to graduates with comparable qualifications in the United States. In its quest to become an R&D hub, Singapore can also carry out some of its R&D functions by setting up subsidiaries in India. According to the Infocomm Development Authority of Singapore (IDA), India is soon likely to become an R&D hub for several Singapore companies like Purple Ace, Xinergy 21, Cleardata Voice and others (*Financial Express*, 15 December 2003).

Cost reductions through outsourcing

Globalisation implies not only capital mobility but also job mobility as the global economy is increasingly based on lowering labour costs. Indian labour could contribute to Singaporean competitiveness not only in physical terms, but also by cost reductions through outsourcing. Bringing cheaper labour to Singapore's doorsteps has costs: search costs, accreditation, accommodation, transport, and compensation (Shantakumar 1995). By outsourcing, some of these costs can be saved. A recent study established that American companies need to move offshore in order to overcome domestic labour shortages (due to slow population growth and an ageing population) and maintain global competitiveness (Evalueserve 2003). It is not difficult to draw a parallel between the United States and Singapore and recognise that the same imperatives apply to Singapore.

Leading global business intelligence and consultancy firms such as Evalueserve, Giga, Forrester Research, McKinsey & Co. and Forbes have shown that India is fast emerging as the global outsourcing hub, drawing MNCs to India to gain competitive edge (www.nascomm.org). With over 1.5 million English speakers graduating each year, India has attracted outsourced customer services, healthcare, fund management, web design, financial services, pharmaceutical testing, and animation services (*Straits Times*, 23 August 2003). Singapore can outsource to India in the area of embedded design, offshore software exports, accounting, insurance, medical transcription services, call centres, back office operations and others. Companies like Singapore Airlines are already outsourcing to India for some of their operations. Singaporean companies can also open subsidiaries in India for outsourcing operations like how many United States companies are doing.

In fact, Singapore can benefit from the Indian outsourcing boom since many global firms prefer to diversify risks by locating certain critical functions like confidential transactions and disaster recovery in more than one location to ensure business continuity in the event of major disruption. The National Association of Software and Service Companies (NASSCOM) and IDA are promoting the idea of Indian business outsourcing (BPO) players establishing a front-end in Singapore and a back-end in India. Scandent, a BPO firm with Indian promoters, has already set up its international headquarters in Singapore with its back-end operations in India. Such businesses require a combination of managerial and technical expertise – skills that are in short supply in Singapore. Indian labour can thus contribute to Singapore's objective of becoming a major player at the high end of the outsourcing market.

A global labour market

The ERC aims to establish a significant presence of Singaporean companies in China, India and the Asian region (ERC). Indian professional labour could prove critical in Singapore's regionalisation drive, especially in China and India. In fact, Indian labour could be a cost-effective workforce for Singapore's knowledge-based business services anywhere in the world. Of 6000 MNCs in Singapore, 3600 have set up regional headquarters and 260 have their international headquarters in Singapore. Further, as more MNCs operating in Singapore also establish themselves in India, opportunities for the international division of labour will increase (Sen 2002). Economic linkages between India and Singapore may well intensify after the signing of CECA, which is likely to substantially increase the Singaporean presence in India. Indian labour is already proving valuable to Singaporean economic expansion into India. For example, infocomm companies like Crimson Logic, First Apex, FTD technology and others have established their presence by leveraging skilled labour available in India.

Unskilled/semi-skilled workers

During the last three decades Singapore has required a pool of unskilled/low skilled workers, not only due to declining birth rates and an ageing population, but also because Singaporeans shun 3-D jobs. Unskilled workers were also required for infrastructure development and to maintain Singapore's competitiveness in the export-oriented manufacturing sectors. Indian labour has traditionally contributed to maintaining Singapore's competitiveness in sectors like construction. However, as Singapore moves up the value chain towards a knowledge-based economy, demand for unskilled/ low skilled workers will decline. To meet the challenge of worsening structural unemployment, the government is trying to modernise traditional sectors to absorb Singaporeans. Construction 21, launched in 1998, aims to transform the sector into a progressive and productive industry that would attract more locals. Construction 21 also aims to reduce foreign labour through a progressive reduction of the Man Year Entitlement (MYE) allocation formula. This formula, introduced in 1998, allocates a certain number of foreign workers based on the nature of the project and its contract value. It ensures that contractors do not employ an excessive number of foreign workers (www.mom.gov.sg). Therefore, the traditional role of Indian labour in construction is likely to decline in the long run. However, it is likely that the demand for professionals such as architects and engineers could grow which, given the shortage of skills in Singapore, may be filled by Indian expertise provided Indian qualifications are recognised. Demand for Indian female labour is likely to grow in the field of domestic work as the number of Indian professionals in Singapore increases. Further, the government has raised the educational criterion for low levy foreign workers (skilled work permit holders) to ensure that a greater proportion have at least completed secondary four or its equivalent, or possess National Training College (NTC) (practical) certificates. This implies that the educational levels of lower-skilled Indian migrants will gradually rise.

Constraints and measures

Administrative, legal and institutional barriers implemented by nation states control the movement of labour. In the GATT context, India and other countries have called for the recognition of labour exports in global liberalisation strategies. Although Singapore generally maintains a friendly regime towards foreign skilled labour, the cross-country movement of professionals is restricted by barriers such as registration requirements, nationality and citizenship requirements and the lack of mutual recognition of qualifications. Several ways of enhancing flows of Indian labour to Singapore are discussed below:

The JSG has recognised that the mobility of people and liberalisation of professional services will significantly enhance economic links between both countries. JSG has therefore recommended that both countries should

- encourage and facilitate negotiations between relevant professional bodies and institutions on the recognition of professional qualifications between both countries, especially in the areas of IT, accountancy, architecture and urban planning, engineering, and health (medical, dental, nursing, physiotherapy and paramedic jobs);

- explore ways to lower barriers to the movement of people between both countries with emphasis on business people, professionals and students.

As noted earlier, CECA, which is based on recommendations of the JSG, has provided mutual liberal market access to 127 categories of professional occupations. The list includes computer-related professionals, medical professionals, scientists, social scientists, accountants, auditors and architects. Under CECA's provisions, recognised professionals would be able to practice/seek employment in the other country after professional bodies in both countries reached Mutual Recognition Agreements. Since Singapore has a scarcity of labour in all sectors, flows are likely to be from India to Singapore.

Foreign students provide a potentially highly qualified labour reserve familiar with the prevailing rules and conditions in host countries. This is why OECD countries increasingly seek to attract foreign students, particularly in the fields of science and technology (Hugo 2002; Martinelli 2002). ERC (2003) recognises that 'As more educational institutions are developed and nurtured, Singapore will continue to attract top talent from all over the world, resulting in a larger inflow of international talent to supplement Singapore labour needs'. Due to its abundance of labour and proximity, India could be targeted at as a source of such students. At present, Indians form one of the largest groups of foreign students studying in Singaporean universities, and numbers are increasing.

To augment the supply of skilled labour, the Singapore government and businesses provide scholarships to foreign students that bind them to work in Singapore for a certain number of years. Although precise data is not available, there has been an increase in scholarships provided by the Singapore Government and Government-linked companies (like Singapore Airlines) to Indian students for pursuing post secondary and tertiary level education in Singapore (Mukherjee *et al.*, 2003). The Singapore Government also provides substantial tuition fee concessions. These concessions/ scholarships bind students to work in Singapore for three to six years after the completion of their studies. Such students not only provide a ready labour pool for companies in Singapore, but are also seen as a strategic resource for Singaporean companies even after their return to India, due to their familiarity with, and knowledge of, Singaporean work practices. Recognising this, JSG has recommended easing barriers on student flows, including a flexible, expeditious and transparent visa application and processing system. Although CECA does not mention easing student flows specifically, Singapore is making efforts to attract Indian students at all levels. A substantial number of these students can be expected to contribute to Singapore's labour requirements over time.

Singapore and India should devise specific education and training programmes with Singapore's needs and India's strengths in mind. Singaporean
companies could invest in technical centres for training software programmers
and engineers, especially for the Southeast Asian and East Asian markets
(Shantakumar 1995). Partnerships between institutes of higher learning in
India like IITs, Indian Institutes of Management (IIMs) and the like
and industry in Singapore should be encouraged, as training ensures that
local infocomm labour is equipped with critical networking skills
(Mukherjee *et al.*, 2003). In fact, collaborative initiatives between acade-
mic/research institutions are already taking shape. For example, the AEC
Group of Singapore has formed a joint venture with the Shriram Group of
Chennai and Ceylico of Sri Lanka. It is expected that these links will be
enlarged and strengthened under CECA.

Concluding remarks

As economic development becomes increasingly knowledge-based, competitiveness will hinge on the ability of countries to complement each other
and share their pool of creativity and knowledge. This chapter has shown
that Singapore's demographic constraints and its need to attract high quality
foreign talent, along with India's comparative advantage in supplying cost
effective knowledge workers, provide strong human resource complementarities between the two countries. Indian labour has a great potential to
complement Singapore's globalisation strategy as it moves towards becoming a knowledge-based economy. The two countries should exploit the full
potential of these possibilities. One major step in this direction is the signing
of CECA, which provides liberalised market access in Singapore to a wide
range of Indian professionals. Temporary labour migration within a regional
perspective is attractive, since it gives importing countries greater control
over labour inflows, while permitting labour exporting countries to derive
benefits on a sustained and fairly predictable basis. India now plans to
use CECA in World Trade Organisation negotiations as a model for seeking
preferential access for its professionals in other countries.

References

Asher, M.G and R. Sen (1999) 'Economic relations between Singapore and the IOR-
    ARC: trends, strategies and prospects', Occasional Paper No. 7, Curtin University of
    Technology, Indian Ocean Centre.
Business Line, 24 March 2003, 'India emerges global R&D base for MNCs'.
Business Times, 13 November 2003, 'Foreign talent policy here to stay: SM'.
Chia, Benedict, S.M. Thangavelu and Heng Toh Mun (2004) 'The Complementary
    Role of Foreign Labour in Singapore', *Economic Survey of Singapore, First Quarter, 2004*
    (Singapore: Ministry of Trade and Industry).

Committee on Singapore's Competitiveness (1998) *Report* (Singapore: Ministry of Trade and Industry).

Contact Singapore, www.contactsingapore.com

Department of Statistics (2000) *Census 2000*, Singapore.

Economic Development Board (1999) *Industry 21*, Singapore.

Economic Review Committee (2002) Sub-Committee on Policies on Enhancing Human Capital (Singapore: Ministry of Trade and Industry).

Economic Review Committee (2003) *New Challenges Fresh Goals: Towards a Dynamic Global City* (Singapore: Ministry of Trade and Industry).

Evaluserve (2003) *The Impact of global sourcing on the US economy, 2003–2010*. Report commissioned by NASSCOM, New Delhi.

Financial Express, 15 December 2003, 'Singapore tech cos eye India as research hub'.

Government of Singapore (2000) *Infocomm Development Authority* (IDA).

Hui, Weng Tat (2002) 'Foreign Labour policy in Singapore', in Koh Ai Tee, Lim Kim Lian, Hui Weng Tat, Bhanoji Rao and Chng Meng Kng (eds) *Singapore Economy in the 21st Century – Issues and Strategies* (Singapore: McGraw Hill) pp. 29–50.

Hugo, G. (2002) 'Migration Policies Designed to Facilitate the Recruitment of Skilled Workers in Australia', *International Mobility of the Highly Skilled* (Paris: OECD) pp. 291–320.

Joint Study Group (2003) 'Report on India-Singapore comprehensive economic cooperation agreement' (CECA) available on the website of the Singapore Ministry of Trade and Industry, www.mti.gov.sg.

Khan, H. and T. Abeysinghe (2002) 'Tourism in Singapore: Past Experience and Future Outlook', in Koh AI Tee, Lim Kim Lian, Hui Weng Tat, B. Rao and Chng Meng Kng (eds) *Singaporean Economy in the 21st Century – Issues and Strategies* (Singapore: McGraw Hill) pp. 466–91.

Low, Linda (2000) 'Labour Migrants in Asia: Bane or Boon'. Research Paper Series (Singapore: Department Of Business Policy).

Mani, A. (1993) 'Indians in Singapore Society', in K.S. Sandhu and A. Mani (eds) *Indian Communities in Southeast Asia* (Singapore: Institute of Southeast Asian Studies, Times Academic Press) pp. 789–810.

Martinelli, D. (2002) 'A Brain Drain among Young Ph.Ds: Mirage or Reality'. *International Mobility of the Highly Skilled* (Paris: OECD) pp. 125–32.

Ministry of Labour (1999) *Labour 21: Vision of a Talent Capital*, Singapore.

Mukherjee, A., A. Modi , N. Taneja and R. Sachdeva (2003) *India-Singapore Trade in Services: Enhancing Co-operation*, Working Paper no. 98 (New Delhi: Indian Council for Research on International Economic Relations).

Ruppert, E. (1999) *Managing Foreign Labour in Singapore and Malaysia: Are There Lessons for GCC Countries*. Policy Research Working Paper Series No. 2053 (Washington DC: World Bank).

Sandhu, K.S. (1993) 'Indian Immigration and Settlement in Singapore', in K.S. Sandhu and A. Mani (eds) *Indian Communities in Southeast Asia* (Singapore: Institute of Southeast Asian Studies, Times Academic Press) pp. 775–88.

Shantakumar G. (2002) 'Population and Labour Force: Changing Dynamics and Policy Implications', in Koh Ai Tee, Lim Kim Lian, Hui Weng Tat, Bhanoji Rao and Chng Meng Kng (eds) *Singapore Economy in the 21st Century – Issues and Strategies* (Singapore: McGraw Hill) pp. 2–28.

—— (1999) 'Singapore Indians at the Millennium: Demographic and Developmental Issues', *Demography India*, Vol. 28, No. 2:179–214.

—— (1995) 'Human Resource Complementarities Between Singapore and India: Formulating Strategy for a Win-Win Situation', in Yong Mun Cheong and

V.V. Bhanoji Rao (eds) *Singapore-India Relations: A Primer* (Singapore: Centre for Advanced Studies, Singapore University Press) pp. 246–69.

Sen, R., A. Mukul and R. Chandru (2000) *India and Singapore: Emerging Trade Opportunities and Challenges*. Research Paper No. 19, Centre for Advanced Studies (Singapore: National University of Singapore).

Sen, R. (2002) 'Singapore – India Economic Relations in the Context of Their Globalisation Strategies'. PhD Thesis, National University of Singapore.

Soo, Cheng Ghee and Lim Teng Kiat (2001) 'Economic Linkages between Singapore and India: The IT Connection', *Economic Survey, Third Quarter, 2001* (Singapore: Ministry of Trade and Industry).

Straits Times, 6 February 2004, 'EDB vision for infocom and media cluster: back office India and front office'.

———, 3 August 2003, 'Asian expats – insight: in Singapore for now or forever'.

———, 23 August 2003, 'Service jobs take flight'.

Tan, Kong Yam (2001) 'Has foreign talent contributed to Singapore economic growth: An Empirical assessment', *Economic Survey of Singapore, Third Quarter 2001* (Singapore: Ministry of Trade and Industry).

Tan, Tai Yong and Andrew J. Major (1995) 'India and Indians in the Making of Singapore', in Yong Mun Cheong and V.V. Bhanoji Rao (eds) *Singapore–India Relations: A Primer* (Singapore: Centre for Advanced Studies, Singapore University Press) pp. 1–20.

Toh, Mu Heng, Tang Hsui Chin and Choo Adrian (2002) 'Mapping Singapore's knowledge based economy', *Economic Survey of Singapore, Third Quarter, 2002* (Singapore: Ministry of Trade and Industry).

Toh, Mun Heng and Choo Adrian (2002) 'Economic contribution of research and development in Singapore', *Economic Survey of Singapore, 2002* (Singapore: Ministry of Trade and Industry).

Wilson, P. and T. Abeysinghe (2002) 'International Competitiveness', in Koh AI Tee, Lim Kim Lian, Hui Weng Tat, B. Rao and Chng Meng Kng (eds) *Singaporean Economy in the 21st Century – Issues and Strategies* (Singapore: McGraw Hill) pp. 272–99.

Wong, D. (1997) 'Transience and Settlement: Singapore's Foreign Labour Policy'. *Asia and Pacific Migration Journal*, Vol. 6, No. 2:135–67.

Yap Mui, Teng (2002) 'Singapore: Migration and the labour market in Asia: recent trends and policies'. Workshop on International Migration and the Labour Market in Asia (Paris: OECD and Japan Institute of Labour) pp. 367–75.

Yeoh, Brenda S.A. (2004) *Migration, International Labour and Multi cultural Policies in Singapore*, Working Paper Series No. 19 (Singapore: Department of Geography, National University of Singapore).

Part III

Managing the Border: Governance of Recruitment, Facilitation of Remittances and Migrant Workers' Rights

11

The Recruitment of Foreign Labour in Malaysia: From Migration System to Guest Worker Regime

Diana Wong

Introduction

In 1997, when the Asian Financial Crisis struck the high-gear economy of Malaysia, it precipitated, among other measures, a major repatriation of the foreign labour force, both legal and illegal, in the country (see Battistella and Asis 1999). Registered foreign workers at that time numbered an estimated 1,471, 645 and the number of undocumented workers was anybody's guess, although a ratio of 1:1 was often cited (*New Straits Times*, 27 June 2001). The measures were effective. By the year 2000, the number of legal workers had declined sharply to an estimated 740,000, with another estimated 400,000 in the country illegally (*Mingguan Malaysia*, 27 January 2002). Since then however, numbers have picked up again. Today, five years after the crisis, and with the economy still struggling to get back on its feet, the foreign share (legal) of the Malaysian labour market has almost fully recovered to pre-crisis levels – at 1.2 million (*New Straits Times*, 14 October 2003).

Nonetheless, it would be a mistake to infer from this figure that there has been no change in policy or practice with regard to foreign labour in the country. In this paper, I trace the evolution of Malaysia's foreign labour policy over the last 30 years, beginning from the early 1970s, when labour scarcity first emerged in the national labour market, until the year 2002, five years after the 1997 financial crisis had put an end to the spectacular economic growth of the preceding decades. The relentless demand for labour generated by the high growth rates of this period was awesome. Between 1987–93 alone, 14 million new jobs were created, at a labour market growth rate of 3.9 per cent. The domestic labour force grew in the same period however, at a mere 3.1 per cent. The gap, as noted by the World Bank, was filled by migrant workers (World Bank 1995:58). The recruitment of foreign labour was thus a fundamental prerequisite of Malaysia's economic policies of growth.

Malaysia's foreign labour policy and its record of foreign labour management however, have been the source of much ambivalence and confusion, and have been characterised as a directionless 'stop-go' process (Pillai 1999), in marked contrast to that of neighbouring Singapore (see Wong 1997). Notwithstanding the complexity of the policy-making process with respect to foreign labour in Malaysia, and the competing interests which help determine, and also reverse, policy outcomes, certain broad continuities (see Kanapathy 2001), as well as shifts, in policy orientation over the last three decades, I argue, can be clearly discerned. Indeed, I shall be arguing in this paper that profound changes to the foreign labour recruitment regime, culminating in changes to the system introduced in the last two years, mark the end of the recruitment regime/migration system which had emerged in the early 1970s.

Two developments here are worthy of note. It would appear that the number of illegal migrant workers has diminished substantially in the last two years, (in tandem with the steep rise in the number of work permits issued), although no official figures are currently available. Whilst still accepting the necessity of a large but transient foreign labour force as fuel for its economy (Kanapathy 2001), the state thus seems to be winning its battle of institutionalising a coherent foreign labour recruitment regime, against the 'chaotic' forces of unauthorised migration. This shift in the composition of the foreign labour force in terms of the ratio of legal to illegal workers (certainly no longer 1:1) has been accompanied by a further significant shift – in terms of the countries of origin from which foreign workers are recruited. Hitherto, Indonesians have constituted the main source of migrants to Malaysia, accounting for circa 80 per cent of both the legal and illegal stock. Indeed, for reasons discussed in greater detail below, Indonesians were the 'migrants of choice'. In 2002 however, an 'Indonesian Last' policy was announced and since then, a concerted policy to widen the range of source countries – to include such 'non-traditional' sources such as Vietnam and Kazakhstan – has been in place.

I review below the history of contemporary labour migration to Malaysia with a focus on Indonesian migrants, who comprise about 80 per cent of the migrant labour flows. I argue that over the course of the last thirty years, foreign labour recruitment has shifted from a regional migration system based on cultural affinity and settlement to a guest worker system based on cultural distance and transience. The term 'migration system' is borrowed from Kritz (1992), but is used in this paper in a more restrictive sense of an informal system of transnational mobility facilitated by 'linkages formed by shared history, culture, geography, and economic ties as well as social networks', as well as constrained by restrictive migration policies (Battistella and Asis 2003:2).

Through the channels established under a migration system, foreign workers are indeed fed into the labour market. Nevertheless, characteristic of a migration system, as intended here, is that it is not exclusively defined by the labour market: petty traders and entrepreneurs, students and political refugees, religious teachers and expatriates, constitute the people on the move as well. Many *remain* as settlers in the country. In an earlier paper, I have characterised the movement of Indonesians to Malaysia as constituting a regional migration system (Wong and Afrizal 2003).

A guest worker regime on the other hand refers to a *state regulated* institutionalisation of the recruitment of foreign contract workers for the local labour market. Its origins in the European system of foreign labour recruitment, no longer in operation since the policy was ended in 1974, are clear. Although there are differences in the actual conditions under which foreign workers are recruited into the labour market, and the rights accorded to them therein, the guest worker regime as used here is defined by two key principles: first, that of labour market exclusivity – only workers are channelled through the system, and second, that of transience – the worker returns at the end of their contract.

Growth of foreign labour in Malaysia

Before the country became an independent nation state in 1957, its demographic composition had been transformed by massive waves of immigration – primarily from China, India and Indonesia – under the aegis of British imperial rule. One of the first pieces of legislation passed by the new nation state was an Immigration Act (1959), which regulated the movement of non-citizens into its territory. Migration came to a halt and thousands of non-citizen workers, some of whom had been resident in the country for their entire lives, were repatriated. One telling exception, however, was made: immigrants from the neighbouring islands of the Archipelago, such as Sumatra and Java, did not fall under the legal category of aliens. In this, the new nation state merely followed the practice of the previous colonial state.

During the colonial period, the 1931 Aliens Ordinance which put an end to the open immigration policy under which thousands of migrant labourers from India, China and the then Netherlands Indies had been brought to British Malaya, was not applied to Indonesians. (Indians, as 'British' subjects, also did not fall under the category of 'aliens'.) Unfettered movement of people, transported along with other goods of the age-old barter trade, continued into the post-colonial regime of national passports and immigration control, including the 1958 Immigration Act mentioned above. Not until the outbreak of military hostilities between the two new nation states in the mid-sixties, and the accompanying ban on the barter trade, did this steady trickle of people movement across the Straits come to a complete halt.

In 1968, at a time when the country was facing serious unemployment, an Employment Restriction Act was passed which required non-citizens to be in possession of a work permit for employment in the national labour market (Mazumdar 1981). The institution of the nation state was thus made legally coterminous with that of a closed labour market; citizenship conferred the right of residence to a nationally defined territory as well as the right of unhindered entry to the labour market.

Within less than a decade of the passing of this legislation to close the national labour market to foreigners however, the labour market in the country had begun to absorb foreign labour in noticeable volume. Dramatic changes in the economic and political landscape of the country were the direct causes. Following racial riots in 1969, a regime change saw the emergence of a highly interventionist, developmentalist state bent on using the state as a vehicle for economic growth and social engineering. In conjunction with changes in the regional division of labour in East and Southeast Asia associated with Japan's rise as a regional economic power, and as a result of the massive rural–urban migration which the state's New Economic Policy promoted, profound changes were effected in the country's labour market.

By the mid-1970s, labour shortages had emerged in the rural sector. The resumption of Indonesian migration to Malaysia in the early seventies coincided with the incipient labour shortage which large-scale development projects, in particular the massive land development schemes undertaken and managed by government agencies, were beginning to generate. Unlike in earlier times, when Indonesian migrants were themselves land pioneers, they now came as contract workers employed by sub-contractors to whom the task of jungle-clearing, as well as various other maintenance jobs, had been commissioned (see Devi 1988). The simultaneous conversion of the plantation labour economy (oil palm and rubber plantations were then major contributors to the GDP) from one based on a settled and permanent labour force to that of casual, contract labour reinforced the demand for migrant labour.

The 1980 census was soon to confirm the significant shift in Malaysia's migration history which had taken place in the decade of the 70s: for the first time in its post-war and post-independence history, a net migrational surplus was recorded, reversing the large net migrational deficits of the preceding decades (Saw 1988:50). Malaysia had become a labour-importing country again. Twenty thousand Indonesians had entered the country in the previous six years, almost half of whom (7219) were enumerated in the rural areas. By 1981, there were an estimated 130,000 Indonesian estate workers in Peninsular Malaysia; this would have then comprised about half the total labour force in that sector (Mehmet 1988).

This initial influx in the decade of the 70s was to grow into a flood. In the 1980s, a construction boom in the urban centres of the country led to a frenetic demand for foreign labour in the construction sector. Similarly, urban double-income households began having to rely on foreign domestic workers to manage the household chores. The migrant workers who came in to fill these new labour market gaps were no longer confined to remote plantation sites. This move to the homes and construction sites of the growing metropolitan centres infused a new quality to the phenomenon. The migrant presence became visible. So did popular hostility to their presence. As the mid-80s crisis struck, this visibility was underscored by their emergence in the informal sector of services and petty trading in the main streets of Kuala Lumpur. And a further discovery was made: that foreign labour had become localised. Recruitment was no longer merely confined to the arduous task of labour importation. By the late-80s, over 12,000 Indonesians were living in 56 squatter settlements in Kuala Lumpur itself (Kassim 1996).

It was only then that the first attempts to regularise the importation of labour were undertaken (see below). Notwithstanding the various bureaucratic interventions however, the size and scope of the foreign labour force continued to expand in the 1990s. The precipitous economic expansion of the early-90s also saw, in 1994, permission granted for the recruitment of foreign labour into the manufacturing and service sectors. Acute shortages of key personnel in the public service sector, in particular of health personnel, has also since led to the deployment of foreign labour in the public sector.

The 1990s also witnessed the recruitment of migrant workers from countries other than Indonesia, including significant numbers of men from Bangladesh. By the end of the decade, the Bangladeshi share of the formal foreign labour market had risen to 17.5 per cent (Kassim 2003). The Indonesian share remained high at 73 per cent, and in fact, these two nationalities had a virtual monopoly of the market, with Filipinos, Thais, Pakistanis and Others constituting miniscule shares. The composition of the informal labour market was a mirror image of the formal one.

This excessive dependence on foreign, and in particular, Indonesian, labour, drawn to a large extent from informal migratory channels, was characteristic of the Malaysian labour market when the bubble burst in 1997. These informal channels were mediated by kin networks as well as professional brokers, who helped with the organisation of the journey and access to the labour market (see Wong and Afrizal 2003 for an account of the modes of entry of Indonesian migrants to Malaysia). The cost of the passage was usually raised by the migrant themselves (or their family) although there was also the possibility of 'selling' oneself to a labour broker who would advance the cost of the passage and recover expenses by 'selling' the migrant to an employer in Malaysia (see Wong and Afrizal 2003).

Evolution of state immigration policy

Four distinct phases of state policy towards foreign labour migration, I suggest, can be distinguished. The first, which lasted from the early-70s till 1989, was manifested in the benign indifference to, if not tacit encouragement of, undocumented or irregular migration on the part of the state. The second, from 1990 to 1996, consisted in the various attempts at legalising the existing stocks of irregular migrant labour in the country. The third involved the parallel existence of an underground irregular migration system and a state-managed foreign contract worker system based on off-shore recruitment. The fourth, which took effect from 2002, marks the attempt to reduce the share of Indonesian labour in the foreign labour market.

As noted earlier, migrants from Indonesia comprise close to 80 per cent of the formal and informal labour markets. Neither the earlier pre-colonial or colonial state however, had considered 'people from across the Straits' to be aliens. The movement of peoples across the Straits of Malacca, and indeed, throughout the Malay Archipelago, goes back several centuries to a pre-colonial past in which a vibrant network of busy trading emporia had constituted a shared cultural world and what was understood to be a common racial stock. The colonial transformation of these maritime societies in the nineteenth and early twentieth centuries led to an intensification and extensification of these movements, as well as changes to their character. The early traders and warriors of these pre-colonial societies were joined by large numbers of agricultural contract workers (from Java) and independent land colonisers (from Sumatra) who eventually settled in the post-colonial state of Malaysia. As noted earlier, neither colonial nor immediate post-Independence immigration legislation had an impact on this flow, as such migrants did not fall under the category of 'aliens'. Not until the outbreak of military hostilities between the two new nation states of Malaysia and Indonesia in the mid-60s did this steady flow of people movement across the Straits come to a complete halt.

The resumption of migration across the Straits of Malacca in the early-70s can thus be taken to mark the commencement of a new chapter in an old migration history. It was treated as such, it would appear, by the Malaysian state authorities. Little effort was made to prevent the inflow of Indonesian migrants who gained access to work immediately upon entry into the country, and in countless instances, also acquired Malaysian permanent residential status within three months of their arrival (see Darul Amin 1990). By the mid-80s, numerous Indonesian settlements had sprung up within the city precincts.

In the 80s, recognition of the market need for foreign labour led to a number of legal measures to establish an official channel of labour recruitment. This included the 1981 Act passed to allow for the establishment of legal recruitment agencies for foreign contract labour, the establishment of a Committee for the Recruitment of Foreign Workers in 1982 and the 1984 Medan Agreement signed with Indonesia for the government-to-government regulated supply of Indonesian labour for the plantation and domestic sectors. With this set of measures, a legal channel, based on a government-to-government mechanism, was finally established, some ten years after the fact, for the legal recruitment of foreign labour (see Kassim 1993, 1996; Pillai 1992, 1995, 1999). This however, did little to stem the tide of what had now become formalised as irregular labour migration. The inefficacy of this first attempt to regulate the demand and supply of foreign contract labour on a government to government basis can be seen from the fact that from 1985 to 1989, only a total of 31,420 work permits were issued, against an estimated 550,000 foreigners employed in the labour market in the country by the end of the 1980s. The market continued to be supplied by a largely 'free' flow of network-based chain migration, issuing in illegality, but with rapid and cheap access to legal settlement status. Children born of parents with permanent resident (PR) status are entitled to citizenship.

The practice of easy acquisition of PR status, which in effect transforms, in legal terms, migrant status to that of settler status, ended in 1989. The severity of the economic recession in 1985–86 however, and the new visibility of Indonesian migrant workers in the informal sector and squatter settlements of Kuala Lumpur, the traditional preserves of the local migrant working class, had led to a profound shift in public sentiment which the state could no longer afford to ignore. The year 1989 saw the first in a series of attempts to regain control of the situation by freezing the further importation of foreign labour while regularising the status of Indonesian migrants already in the country. It marked the beginning of what has been identified in this paper as the second phase of contemporary Indonesian labour migration to Malaysia, characterised by the regularisation of the status of the existing stock of migrant workers in the country. Indeed, it could be maintained that it was only then that a foreign labour policy as such came into being.

The first 1989 legalisation programme was limited to Indonesian workers in the plantation sector and was largely an exercise in futility, due mainly to the cumbersome procedure adopted. A second registration and amnesty exercise launched in 1991, as the start to a five-year policy of containment and regularisation, during which selected economic sectors were to be allowed on-site access to legalised foreign workers, was much more successful. All illegal workers in the country who registered themselves before the deadline would be allowed to remain in the country as legalised workers. Unlike the earlier legalisation exercise however, the amnesty was opened to irregular migrants in the service, plantation and construction sectors, and the procedure was much simplified. The demand was overwhelming. By the time the registration period ended on 30 June 1992, 442,276 workers had registered. Indonesians accounted for 83 per cent of all those who registered.

Supplementing this slew of measures were two enforcement exercises known as *Ops Nyah* I (literally, *Get Rid of Operations* I) and *Ops Nyah* II. Both operations are still ongoing. Ops Nyah I is designed to prevent illegal landings on Malaysia's long coastline and is directed by the Police Field Force. Arrested illegal immigrants are turned over to the Immigration Department which is responsible for their deportation. Ops Nyah II is directed at irregular migrants already in the country and takes the form of raids on work sites and squatter settlements.

Although this second registration and enforcement exercise was more successful than the first, it failed to regularise the status of all the workers already in the country. The legalisation exercise set a precedent however, for the easy on-site procurement of foreign workers for local employers. It also promoted the use of labour contractors and agents to obtain foreign workers.

In 1996, with the end of the interim five-year period, the stage was to have been set for the third phase, the final eradication of the system of local, *on-site* illegal recruitment of labour to be replaced by the implementation of an official migrant labour system of work-permit and contract-based *off-shore* recruitment. This was preceded by a third massive registration exercise for illegal workers from Indonesia, Thailand, the Philippines, Bangladesh and Pakistan. 554,941 illegal workers registered, although it has been claimed that another million refused legalisation. Upon registration and payment of the levy, two-year legal work permits could be obtained. Raids and deportation exercises were stepped up. Nonetheless, the problems persisted, not the least of which was the inability of the bureaucratic infrastructure to manage the legal procedures established. By late 1996, the Foreign Workers Task Force had accumulated tens of thousands of unprocessed applications for workers, and there were allegations that the Task Force itself was into the business of detaining workers from one employer and releasing them into the hands of another (Jones 2000:35).

What emerged in effect was a parallel structure of labour importation – a foreign contract worker system based on off-shore recruitment, co-existing with a large reservoir of foreigners, in particular Indonesians, living and working outside of this formal system. This reservoir of foreigners was marked by a distinction of existential import – those in possession of PR status, and those who were 'illegals'. The two categories of people were often however, intimately linked, as the immediate employers and labour brokers of illegal migrants were often those in possession of settlement status in the country, and were often responsible for initiating their migration (see Wong and Afrizal 2003). 'Illegals' continued to be hounded by police raids and the occasional large-scale enforcement and deportation exercise.

Nevertheless, the resolve underpinning the policy measures of the mid-90s can be seen in the high-level political attention which the whole question of foreign labour, both legal and illegal, began to attract after 1995. As noted by Pillai, it was only after 1995 that the Prime Minister and his deputy began to make public statements on the issue, and although the issue had been touched upon in the 1991 General Assembly, it was only in the 1996 General Assembly of the key ruling party United Malays National Organisation (UMNO) that it was openly discussed and debated (Pillai 1999). Nonetheless, the policy ambiguity and gaps between policy pronouncements and practice persisted, and despite the legalisation exercises and much-publicised law enforcement efforts, foreign workers were estimated to number over 1.7 million in 1997 (Bank Negara Malaysia 1997:63).

It was the economic and financial crisis of 1997–98 which appears to have marked a turning point in policy resolve towards regularising and limiting the foreign labour market (see Pillai 1999). The Prime Minister, Dr Mahathir Mohamed, underlined the determination of the government by noting in a speech on 21 July 1997, 'The country cannot go on depending on foreign workers. We have 20 million people and 1.7 million foreign workers. If we allow this to go on we would risk losing control of our country' (*Bulletin Imigresen* 1997).

1998 saw the policy of containment implemented with far greater rigour and vigour. A final amnesty programme was announced. Unlike the earlier three legalisation exercises however, this amnesty only permitted irregular migrants to register and leave without penalties imposed, with no provision for their status to be regularised. The number of foreign workers who took advantage of this amnesty to leave the country was 187,486. Work permits which expired in August 1998 (apart from exceptions made for some categories), were not renewed and 159,135 foreign workers left the country legally upon expiry of their work permits. Altogether, 409,346 work permits lapsed without any renewal (Department of Immigration Annual Report 1998). In addition, a freeze on fresh labour recruitment meant that out of the employer request for 225,275 work permits in 1998, only 2876 were granted.

The administrative machinery for a comprehensive system of migrant labour recruitment and management was streamlined and improved. A work-permit system based solely on *off-shore recruitment* was put in place. Under this work permit system, foreign workers are recruited abroad and are issued with calling visas for entry into the country; once in the country, the calling visas are converted into work permits, or in the official terminology, visit passes (temporary employment). As is evident in the terminology itself, the system is designed for temporary employment. The passes are employer and location-specific. The worker is not allowed to bring in his /her family. He/she has to leave the country upon cancellation or expiry of the visit pass. In 2001, the duration of the work permit was reduced from six years to three years.

Workers are covered by an insurance scheme for foreign workers, are to be paid on par with local workers, but are subject to a foreign worker levy. The rates of levy for foreign workers vary according to sector and to skill-category, and although officially imposed on the employer, are often passed on to the worker. In 1998, revenue from the levy on foreign workers amounted to RM 415,807,112.95 (Department of Immigration Annual Report 1998). As of January 2002, the number of work permits issued stood at 769,566, of which 566,983 were held by Indonesians (*New Straits Times*, 29 January 2002). Foreign workers are allowed to be recruited for certain designated sectors, such as the construction industry, the plantation sector, services (domestic servants, hotel industry, trainers and instructors) and the manufacturing sector. Foreign workers permitted to work in the above sectors in this country were limited to nationals from ASEAN countries that is, Indonesia, Thailand, Philippines, Cambodia and other countries such as Bangladesh and Pakistan. At the same time, legislative and police action to combat irregular migration was strengthened. Legislative action included the stiffening of penalties for employers as well as for migrants. A maximum fine of RM 10,000 or five years jail can be imposed for illegal entry, as well as for over-staying. Law enforcement measures have been markedly intensified. This is most evident in the deportation figures, which reached 100,000 in the year 2000. In 2001, 158,420 irregular migrants were deported, of whom 120,770 were Indonesians (*Sun*, 11 April 2002). In the early 90s, the numbers deported had hovered around 12,000 a year.

The massive enforcement and deportation exercises came at a cost – to the state, and in particular to the detainees. The detention camps in the country were not able to handle the large number of detainees, and conditions have verged on the intolerable. Deaths have occurred and an NGO activist was sentenced to a jail term of one year for 'maliciously publishing false news' after she released a memorandum at a press conference in August 1995 about alleged torture and deaths in the camps for illegal immigrants (she has so far escaped imprisonment). Well-publicised instances of violence directed at camp authorities have also occurred.

It should be noted here that notwithstanding the above-mentioned actions, the *enforcement* of law and policy with regard to irregular migration still left much to be desired. In a rare official statement on this matter, the Minister of Law, Rais Yatim, observed recently that existing laws like the Immigration Act and the Penal Code were adequate to give powers to authorities to deter the influx of illegal immigrants, but the 'lackadaisical attitude of some authorities' in enforcing the laws was a cause for worry (*Business Times*, 5 February 2002). In the face of what appears to be extensive corruption, between 1999 and 2001, only 21 police officers have been charged with taking bribes (*Star*, 13 March 2002). Furthermore, whereas migrant workers have been targeted, employers have not. As of the end of 2001, only 13 Malaysians had been charged under the Immigration Act for recruiting, 7 for hiring, and 154 for harbouring 'illegal aliens' (*Sun*, 13 March 2002).

This was to change in 2002. The trigger for a renewed policy shift was a highly publicised clash between police and about 450 Indonesian workers at the Hualon Textile factory in Nilai in mid-January (Azizah Kassim 2003:332). Following this, a new round of measures was undertaken, in which two main policy thrusts can be identified: the tightening of the legal noose on illegal migration, and regulatory changes to the formal contract labour recruitment system.

The government passed amendments to the Immigration Act that saw mandatory six-month jail sentences, as well as six strokes of the cane, for illegal migrants. A four-month amnesty period for illegal migrants to leave the country was granted, after which a resolute crackdown began. Again, the rhetoric of the country being held hostage to illegal migrants was aired, and again, the scale of the operation as well as the hardships encountered by those deported, attracted much media attention. Of greater significance perhaps is the fact that employers of illegal migrants were, under the amendments, also to be subject to a fine, imprisonment, and whipping. Thirty five court cases against employers are currently pending at the time of writing (*New Straits Times*, 12 October 2003).

Of particular import however, and representing a major shift in policy, were the simultaneous changes made to the formal contract worker system. About 80 per cent of the contract workers originate from Indonesia, as would be the case for migrants in the informal sector as well. The formal system of labour recruitment, devised and implemented in the 1990s, had restricted labour recruitment to a few countries, with a definite bias for Indonesia. The government announced plans to diversify its source countries of recruitment, in order to reduce the share of Indonesians in this market. The new list was to include, among others, Vietnam, Kazakhstan, Turkmenistan and Uzbekistan. 'National security' was quoted as a justification (Liow 2002), following a number of incidents in which Indonesian migrants were engaged in violent altercations with state authorities. In fact, Indonesians were initially to be restricted only to the plantation sector and domestic work. This regulation was later rescinded, although the 'Indonesia Last' regulation has been retained.

Migration system versus the guest worker regime

In an earlier period of Malaysian migrant labour history, the massive importation of labour from China and India, according to Beeman (1985), had given rise to two parallel systems of labour recruitment. Chinese migration, which occurred through informal channels as well as under the 'credit-ticket' system, was 'spontaneous/speculative' in character, in contrast to the regulated system of Indian migration, organised under the auspices of the colonial state. As Beeman shows, the two contrasting systems had different implications and outcomes for both migrants and employers.

One key question concerned the payment of passage. The rubber industry, then a major employer of migrant labour, provided assisted passage for Indian labour to be directly recruited into the industry. An Indian Immigration Fund, managed by the colonial authorities was established, from which the passage of Indian migrant labourers to the plantation sector was paid. Indian labour recruited in this fashion was confined to the plantation which had paid for the cost of passage and recruitment. The full force of the state was brought to bear on those who 'absconded' from their contract, which in fact did happen with alarming frequency, averaging over a quarter of the total labour force (Beeman 1985:170).

Chinese labour entered a much more diversified and open labour market either as free emigrants who paid their own passage, or as non-paying passengers under the 'credit-ticket' system. Because of the potential for abuse and exploitation in this system, it was widely reviled and viewed with distaste and suspicion. Contrary to the public opinion of the day however, they constituted an insignificant percentage of the Chinese migrant labour. Most of this labour, according to a 1910 report, was locally recruited free labour. The Chinese labour thus recruited was also highly mobile, moving constantly in search of higher wages and better working conditions, whilst Indian labour was confined to the low-wage plantation economy.

The 'Indian' system, Beeman argues, was reliant on the role of the state in enforcing labour circulation, restricting labour mobility and maintaining the powerlessness of the migrant (Beeman 1985:20). The 'Chinese' system, on the other hand, was 'spontaneous and speculative' in character.

It was spontaneous because much of the movement from China to Malaya was by those who paid their own passage and were seeking economic opportunities or avoiding political turmoils. The latter reason helps explain why migration remained quite high even when economic conditions in Malaya were very poor. But Chinese immigration was also speculative, for contractors and lodging-house keepers worked to maximize their profits based on the demand for labour. Thus, a good deal of Chinese immigrants were assisted through this system to provide unskilled labour in Malaya. (Beeman 1985:146)

The parallel here to the Indonesian migration to Malaysia in the final three decades of the twentieth century is, I suggest, unmistakable, as well as the parallel between the 'Indian' system, and the formal system of off-shore labour recruitment which the state has since implemented. Informal Indonesian labour migration into Malaysia since the early 1970s has been essentially 'spontaneous and speculative' in character. Much of the labour is recruited locally by local employers and there is a high rate of job mobility, especially in the construction and agricultural sectors (Wong and Afrizal 2003). Whilst labour brokers continue to play an important role in the transportation and job placement of the new migrants, their role as financiers of 'indentured' labour, comparable to the 'credit-ticket' system of old, is limited.

The official contract worker system on the other hand, or the *guest worker* system as it is often known today in the literature on international migration, appears comparable to the earlier system of Indian labour with assisted passage, the key feature of which is the immobilisation (and hence control) and rotation of migrant labour. Foreign worker passes in Malaysia today are issued for employment with a specified employer and are limited to a specified length of time. Under the present Malaysian regulations on the recruitment of foreign labour, employers are responsible for the payment of the worker's return passage. According to the official regulations, Malaysian employers are also enjoined to withhold and keep the passports of foreign contract workers until their due date of departure. They are to leave the country upon termination of the contract. It should also be noted that foreign contract workers are not allowed to marry – neither locals nor fellow-contract workers – during the duration of their contract.

It is in this regulation that one further key distinction between what I have termed here a migration system as against a guest worker regime can be seen. Recruitment of foreign labour through the informal channels of a migration system is generally based on cultural if not ethnic *affinity*, and is often related to implicit or explicit policies of settlement. Recruitment regulated through a guest worker regime on the other hand tends to prioritise cultural or ethnic *distance*, in order to maintain social distance and transience. The policy *raison d'être* here is the minimisation of the 'social' cost of foreign labour deployment in the economy.

This comes at the price of labour productivity and is generally opposed by employers and indeed, problems have already arisen in the Malaysian context with the recruitment of workers (from Vietnam for example) without a command of English or Malay. For sectors such as construction, agriculture and services, the possibility of immediate on-site recruitment is invaluable. Similarly, there are advantages to the migrant from working within the informal migration system. Transaction costs are lower, implementation of the migration project can be almost immediate, and job mobility is possible. These advantages to both parties in the labour market help account for the continued existence of the informal migration system as a mode of labour recruitment. Although the policy has shifted from the one (relying on an informal migration system) to the other (reliance on a formal guest worker system), the result is the parallel existence of both systems in the current foreign labour market in Malaysia.

Conclusion

Labour, it is a truism, is not a factor of production like any other. As such, at least three issues arise with respect to a foreign worker policy: first, the extent to which market demand should be satisfied, that is, the question of volume, second, the status to be accorded the non-citizen worker – illegality/ transience/settlement, and third, the protection of the rights of the recruited workers.

The third – the question of rights and protection – is still barely visible on the official agenda. On the first issue, that of volume, policy has remained liberal and indeed, expansive, notwithstanding calls from trade union quarters to limit recruitment, most recently in light of increasing retrenchments in the manufacturing sector (*New Straits Times*, 13 October 2003). Here, the overriding priority has been the objective of economic growth, for which a larger and cheaper workforce has been deemed essential (see Kanapathy 2001). There are signs however, that this single-minded pursuit of quantity is being re-considered, especially in light of economic data which suggest that the availability of cheap foreign labour is hindering the restructuring vital for advancement up the technology ladder (see Tham and Liew 2002).

In the past thirty years however, policy attention has been focused on the second concern, namely, the status to be assigned to the foreign worker. Here, there has been a discernible shift from a recruitment system based on illegality and settlement – drawing upon an unregulated informal migration system – to one based on transience and regulated by a state-managed formal contract worker system. This shift could be described in terms of the establishment of a new 'border regime', whereby the above discussion makes clear that the policing of the *territorial* border in itself, although it has received the most media attention, was not necessarily the decisive measure. The policing of the boundaries of the labour market (the 2002–imposed employer sanctions), and the policing of the boundaries of local society (restrictions on marriage, ethnic selection of the labour force etc.) are obviously critical elements of the border regime as well. Thus while foreign workers in Malaysia have been needed, and wanted, over the last thirty years, the terms of entry, and stay, have changed.

References

Bank Negara Malaysia (1997) *Annual Report* (Kuala Lumpur).
Battistella, G. and M.B. Asis (2003) 'Southeast Asia and the Specter of Unauthorized Migration', in G. Battistella and M. Asis (eds) *Unauthorized Migration in Southeast Asia* (Manila: Scalabrini Migration Center) pp. 1–34.
—— (1999) *The Crisis and Migration in Asia* (Quezon City: Scalabrini Migration Center).
Beeman, M.A. (1985) 'The Migrant Labor System: The Case of Malaysian Rubber Workers'. Unpublished PhD thesis, University of Illinois.
Business Times, 5 February 2002.
Darul Amin A.M. (1990) *Pendatang Indonesia dan Implikasinya Terhadap Negara Malaysia (1970–1989): Kajian Kes di Kuala Lumpur*, Latihan Ilmiah, Jabatan Sains Politik, Fakulti Sains Kemasyarakatan dan Kemanusiaan, Universiti Kebangsaan Malaysia.
Department of Immigration (1998) *Annual Report* (Kuala Lumpur).
—— (1997) *Bulletin Imigresen* (Kuala Lumpur).
Devi, P. (1988) 'Features of Labour Utilization: The Contract System' in *Current Issues in Labour Migration in Malaysia*, Seminar Organised by National Union of Plantation Workers and Population Studies Unit, Faculty of Economics and Administration, University of Malaya. Kuala Lumpur, pp. 225–66.
Jones, S. (2000) *Making Money Off Migrants. The Indonesian Exodus to Malaysia* (Wollongong: Centre for Asia-Pacific Transformation Studies).
Kanapathy, V. (2001) 'International Migration and Labor Market Adjustments in Malaysia: The Role of Foreign Labor Management Policies', *Asia and Pacific Migration Journal*, Vol. 10: 429–61.

Kassim, A. (1997) 'Illegal Alien Labour in Malaysia: Its Influx, Utilization and Ramifications', *Indonesia and the Malay World*, Vol. 71:50–82.

—— (1996) 'Alien Workers in Malaysia: Critical Issues, Problems and Constraints' in Carunia Mulya Firdausy (ed.) *Movement of People Within And From The East and Southeast Asian Countries: Trend, Causes and Consequences* (Jakarta: Indonesian Institute of Sciences).

—— (1993) 'The Registered and the Illegals: Indonesian Immigrants in Malaysia'. Paper presented at the seminar on Movement of People in Southeast Asia, organised by PMB-LIPI, Jakarta, 17–19 February.

Kritz, May, Lim Lin Lean and H. Zlotnik (1992) *International Migration Systems: A Global Approach* (Oxford: Clarendon Press).

Liow, Joseph (2002) *Desecuritising the 'Illegal Indonesian Migrant Worker' Problem in Malaysia's Relations with Indonesia* (Singapore: IDSS).

Mehmet, O. (1988) *Development in Malaysia: Poverty, Wealth, and Trusteeship* (Kuala Lumpur: Insan).

Mingguan Malaysia, 27 January 2002.

New Straits Times, 14 October 2003.

——, 13 October 2003.

——, 12 October 2003.

——, 29 January 2002.

——, 27 June 2001.

Pillai, P. (1999) 'The Malaysian State's Response to Migration', *Sojourn*, Vol. 14, No. 1:178–97.

—— (1995) 'Labour Migration in Asia: Malaysia', *ASEAN Economic Bulletin*, Vol. 12, No. 2:221–36.

—— (1992) *People on the Move: An Overview of Recent Immigration and Emigration in Malaysia* (Kuala Lumpur: ISIS).

Saw, Swee-Hock (1988) *The Population of Peninsula Malaysia* (Singapore: Singapore University Press).

Star, 13 March 2002.

Sun, 11 April 2002.

——, 13 March 2002.

Tham, Siew Yean and Liew Chei Siang (2002) 'Foreign Labour in Malaysian Manufacturing: Enhancing Malaysian Competitiveness?'. Unpublished paper presented to the International Conference on *Globalization, Culture, and Inequalities: In Honour of the Work of the Late Professor Dr. Ishak Shari (1948–2001)* UKM, Bangi, 19–21 August.

Wong, D. (1997) 'Transience and Settlement. Singapore's Foreign Labour Policy', *Asian and Pacific Migration Journal*, Vol. 6, No. 2:135–67.

Wong, D. and T. Afrizal, T. Anwar (2003) 'Migran Gelap: Irregular Migrants in Malaysia's Shadow Economy', in Battistella and Asis (eds) *Unauthorized Migration in Southeast Asia* (Manila: Scalabrini Migration Center) pp.169–227.

World Bank (1995) *Malaysia: Meeting Labor Needs, More Workers and Better Skills*, Washington, DC.

12

After Nunukan: The Regulation of Indonesian Migration to Malaysia

Michele Ford

Introduction

Labour migration from Indonesia is a complex phenomenon. Migrants enter Malaysia via a range of formal, semi-formal and informal channels, primarily through Sumatra and Kalimantan. Although Indonesian authorities make little effort to stop semi-formal and informal migration flows, the Malaysian government constantly adjusts its policies towards both documented and undocumented labour migrants according to the condition of its labour market. Periodically these adjustments have involved the mass arrest and deportation of undocumented workers, for example when hundreds of thousands of Indonesian workers were expelled from Eastern Malaysia to the tiny town of Nunukan in East Kalimantan in mid-2002. Both the Indonesian and Malaysian governments have failed to recognise the impact of the Malaysian government's policies on transit zones such as Riau and East Kalimantan, and that more serious efforts at bilateral cooperation must be made in order to lessen the social costs of labour migration in these zones.

On 1 August 2002, the Malaysian government enacted Immigration Act No.1154/2002 and began the mass deportation of undocumented foreign workers. Immigrant settlements were destroyed, and almost 400,000 Indonesians working without appropriate documentation were deported to Belawan, Batam and Dumai in Sumatra, and Pontianak and Nunukan in Kalimantan. It was certainly not the first time the Malaysian government had forcibly repatriated undocumented workers. However, it was the largest single repatriation ever undertaken. The number of workers deported to Indonesia in August and September 2002 far exceeded the capacity of return points in the transit provinces of Sumatra and Kalimantan, particularly Nunukan on Kalimantan's east coast, to accommodate them. The sudden influx of deportees to Nunukan, a small island on Indonesia's border with the Malaysian state of Sabah with a permanent population of just under 40,000 people caused a humanitarian crisis which became a critical point in the management of Indonesia's migration flows to Malaysia.

In the 1980s and 1990s, Suharto's New Order government (1967–98) had adopted a strongly interventionist approach towards the regulation of overseas labour migration though official channels. After the Suharto regime's demise in 1998, the Department of Manpower (now the Department for Manpower and Transmigration) continued to pass regulations determining the process through which potential labour migrants would be recruited, trained, and managed, and to issue licences to private sector companies (or PJTKI, *Perusahaan Jasa Tenaga Kerja Indonesia*) to undertake those processes (Jones 2000:17–21; Tirtosudarmo 2001:10–12). However, during this period, labour migration was dealt with using a model that concentrated primarily on official flows leaving by plane from Jakarta and other major cities in Java directly to receiving countries. Although officially sanctioned labour migration flows occurred through the transit zones of Sumatra and Kalimantan to the Southeast Asian destinations of Malaysia and Singapore, policy-makers paid relatively little attention to them. Meanwhile undocumented migration flows, which occurred primarily through these transit zones (Hugo 2001), were almost totally ignored. As a result of this approach, before the Nunukan crisis in August 2002 the New Order government and its successors made little attempt to acknowledge – let alone mediate – unofficial labour flows to neighbouring Malaysia. They paid even less attention to the social impact of those flows, particularly large-scale forced repatriations of undocumented migrants from Malaysia, on the transit provinces in Kalimantan and Sumatra. The regulation of labour migration remains Jakarta-centric, but events during and after the Nunukan crisis have forced Indonesia's central government to, at the very least, acknowledge the extensive social ramifications of undocumented labour migration flows through the transit provinces in Sumatra and Kalimantan through which labour migrants pass on their way to and from Malaysia and Singapore.

This chapter examines the Malaysian government's management of Indonesian labour migrant flows and the Indonesian government's responses to Malaysia's labour immigration policies, with a particular focus on the changing relationship between the Indonesian central government and the provinces since regional autonomy was implemented. It is divided into four parts. The first provides an overview of Indonesian labour migration, with an emphasis on the significance of Malaysia as a destination for both official and unofficial labour migration flows. The second examines the Malaysian government's policies towards Indonesian labour migrants, culminating in the mass deportation of unregistered workers under the 2002 Immigration Act, which caused the humanitarian crisis at Nunukan. This second section provides context for the final two parts of the chapter, which examine the Indonesian government's policies towards labour migrants before and after Nunukan and their implications for the transit provinces. The chapter draws on data from government sources, NGO reports and interviews with key NGO activists – including humanitarian volunteers present in Nunukan in 2002.

It offers a preliminary analysis of tensions between sending provinces, transit provinces and the central government over Indonesia's labour migration policy, arguing that although the central government has retained control over labour migration, local and provincial governments in the transit zones must play an increasingly important role in the regulation of migrant labour if future crises are to be avoided.

Indonesia's migrant workers: an overview

Although significant numbers of workers migrated from the Indonesian archipelago for work during the colonial period and after Independence, it is only relatively recently that Indonesia became a major supplier of migrant workers to the Middle East, East Asia and to wealthier countries within Southeast Asia. In the five years between 1969 and 1974, just 5624 workers were placed under the government's official labour migration programme. A quarter of a century later, 1,461,236 Indonesians were sent overseas under government-approved labour migration schemes between 1994 and 1999 (Hugo 2001:2).

As shown in Table 12.1 below, overseas migrant workers are an important source of foreign currency income for Indonesia (Table 12.1). Successive Indonesian governments have come to depend quite heavily on these remittances. In 2002 the government set a target of US$ 5 billion for 2004

Table 12.1 Number of documented labour migrants and remittances by region, 2001–03

Region	2001		2002		2003	
	Persons	Remittances ($US)	Persons	Remittances ($US)	Persons	Remittances ($US)
Asia-Pacific	217,555	355,088,125	238,324	1,181,660,673	109,722	n.a.
Middle East and Africa	121,180	180,839,612	241,961	384,693,651	183,770	n.a.
North America	228	1,532,160	40	221,760	171	n.a.
Europe	29	194,880	68	443,520	31	n.a.
Total	338,992	537,654,777	480,393	2,198,019,604	293,694	n.a

Note: Indonesian statistics are problematic, so these and other figures cited in this chapter should be treated as indicative rather than as authoritative. There were some errors in the labelling of these tables on the Depnakertrans website. They were corrected by comparing them with Depnakertrans (2003b; 2002b; 2001b). The remittance data on the website for 2003 was clearly erroneous, and has been omitted.

Source: Depnakertrans (2003a; 2002a; 2001a).

(Jacob Nuwa Wea quoted in *Bisnis Indonesia*, 17 February 2002). Economists later estimated that remittances have the potential to reach as much as US$ 12 billion in future years (*Bisnis Indonesia*, 3 September 2003). However, these figures have proven to be wildly optimistic. After remittances reached over US$2 billion in 2002 (Depnakertrans 2002a), they dropped sharply in 2003 and 2004 (Depnakertrans 2003a; 2004a). The decrease occurred primarily because the number of Indonesians officially employed in Asia-Pacific receiving countries contracted dramatically after 2002, not least because of changes in Malaysia's policy towards Indonesian migrant labour. Official statistics, which do not account for labour migration occurring outside official channels (estimated to outstrip official migration levels), indicate that Saudi Arabia and Malaysia are the largest receiving countries for documented Indonesian labour migrants, as shown in Table 12.2 below.

Although Saudi Arabia received more documented Indonesian labour migrants than Malaysia through the 1980s and most of the 1990s (ILO 1998), and has since reasserted its dominance, Malaysia is a particularly important destination for Indonesian migrant labour because of its geographical proximity and the shared cultural and linguistic heritage of the two countries. Indonesian migration to Malaysia has a long history (Kaur 2004). In 1950, almost 200,000 residents were noted as having been born in Java – a 111 per cent increase from 1930. A further 62,200 were born in South Kalimantan, while 26,300 were born in Sumatra (Mantra 2000:144). Indonesian migration levels grew again as a result of changes in immigration priorities after Independence was granted to Peninsular Malaysia in 1957 and Sarawak and Sabah in 1963.

In the colonial period, labour recruitment policies were designed to meet the labour requirements of export industries such as rubber and tin, but after 1957 efficient production of export commodities was no longer the government's primary concern. Instead, attention was focused on the implications of racially targeted labour migration for the Malayan population. Ethnic Malays (including Indonesians) accounted for fewer than 50 per cent of the

Table 12.2 Historical distribution of documented labour outflows from Indonesia to Saudi Arabia and Malaysia

Destination	1983	1987	1991	1995	1999	2003
Saudi Arabia	17,116	48,741	64,785	49,517	131,157	169,038
Malaysia	2,967	5,763	40,715	47,380	169,177	89,439
Malaysia as % of of all legal outflows	10.2%	9.7%	32.3%	26.5%	39.6%	30.4%

Source: Adapted from ILO (1998), p. 3; Depnakertrans (2000; 2003b); Soeprobo (2003).

population of Peninsular Malaysia, whilst some 37 per cent of the population was Chinese and a further 11 per cent was Indian (Dorrall 1989:290). As a direct result of concerns about the growing imbalance between the migrant Chinese and Indian communities and the Malays, the government banned unskilled labour migration from China and India soon after Independence. This policy was taken one step further after the race riots of 1969, when the government repatriated a number of Indian plantation workers and moved to encourage the in-migration of large numbers of Muslims from Indonesia and the Philippines, particularly to the East Malaysian state of Sabah.

Since the 1970s, there have been three broad trends in labour migration to Malaysia (Kanapathy 2004). First, as manufacturing grew, Malaysia experienced a high level of internal migration from rural areas to the towns, which gave rise to labour shortages in the agricultural sector in general and in the new oil palm industry in particular. Overseas migrant workers were used to overcome the shortages first in agriculture and then in construction in the late 1970s and early 1980s. The second wave occurred as Malaysia's export-oriented industrialisation policies succeeded, and demand for foreign workers grew in manufacturing from the late 1980s. A third wave occurred after the 1997–98 Asian economic and financial crisis, when flows of overseas migrant labour stabilised in response to the Malaysian government's stricter enforcement of its immigration policy. An important characteristic of contemporary officially sanctioned Indonesian labour migration to Malaysia is its gender balance, which is different to that of other large receiving countries of Indonesian migrant workers, particularly Saudi Arabia, as shown in Figure 12.1. Whereas most Indonesians working abroad are females employed in informal sector, particularly in domestic work (ILO 1998; Hugo 2001), most Indonesian labour migrants leaving through official channels to Malaysia are males seeking work in the plantation, construction, transportation and manufacturing sectors. Moreover, a much larger proportion of female Indonesian labour migrants in Malaysia are employed in the formal sector than in other major receiving countries, where the majority of women are employed as domestic workers. In 2001, almost one-third of women officially placed in Malaysia were employed in formal sector occupations (Depnakertrans 2001c; 2001d). By 2003, the proportion of women placed in the formal sector had risen to over two-thirds, as a result of the Malaysian government's 'employ Indonesians last' policy (Depnakertrans 2003c; 2003d).

The fact that many more workers leave for Malaysia through semi-formal or informal channels than through official programmes (Hugo 2001) has important implications for the areas of Indonesia close to the border with Malaysia. Access to Peninsular Malaysia from Riau and North Sumatra is relatively easy by sea, while Sabah and Sarawak in East Malaysia share a long land border with the provinces of East and West Kalimantan. It is important

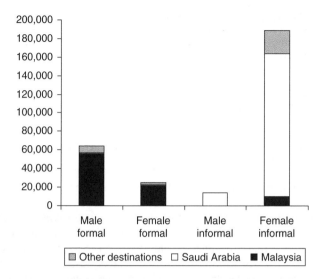

Figure 12.1 Sectoral distribution of all overseas migrant workers officially placed in 2003 by gender and destination

Source: Raw data taken from Depnakertrans (2003c; 2003d).

to note, in the context of the transit provinces' role in migration between Indonesia and East and Peninsular Malaysia, that not all workers leaving through these unofficial channels are undocumented. This is reflected in the fact that the transit provinces of East Kalimantan, West Kalimantan, Riau and North Sumatra record relatively high numbers of labour migrants officially leaving for Malaysia (and, from the Sumatran provinces, to a lesser extent for Singapore), despite their relatively small populations (Hugo 2001). Although local people from the transit provinces undoubtedly do become labour migrants, these figures are swelled by large numbers of Javanese and people from West Nusa Tenggara who are issued local papers. Many registered and unregistered agents recruit intending workers at village level or elsewhere in the sending provinces then take them to a transit province, where they arrange a local identity card from which a passport can be issued. Local immigration officers are paid 'special fees' to issue local identity cards and then passports (see, e.g., Ford 2001). In Nunukan, for example, illegal agents simply have to telephone the immigration department, and they can produce hundreds of passports within days (personal communication with Riwanto Tirtosudarmo, 14 July 2003). While having been obtained illegally, these passports are authentic, official documents. Such documents are commonly described as being *aspal* (*asli tapi palsu*, original but fake). The large numbers of 'semi-formal' migrants who enter using *aspal* documents are reflected in the differences between the overall arrivals and departures figures for

Table 12.3 All arrivals and departures of Indonesian citizens to Malaysia, 2000–03

Year	Arrivals	Departures	Difference between arrivals and departures	Difference as % of all Indonesian arrivals
2000	790,769	416,387	374,382	47.34
2001	1,046,376	526,862	519,514	49.65
2002	1,247,003	696,958	550,045	44.11
2003	1,557,240	856,610	700,630	44.99

Source: Data from Department of Immigration Malaysia (2000; 2001; 2002; 2003).

Indonesians issued by the Malaysian Department of Immigration, as shown in Table 12.3.

The enormous numbers of Indonesians leaving for Malaysia officially, semi-officially and unofficially each year through the transit provinces in Sumatra and Kalimantan suggest that those provinces should long have been a major focus for Indonesian policy-makers. Instead, while semi-legal and illegal entry to Malaysia was – and continues to be – aided and abetted by local immigration officials in the transit provinces, the Department of Manpower (the department responsible for handling overseas labour migration) paid almost no attention to the transit provinces until after the crisis at Nunukan. As is suggested below, Indonesia's failure to address migration flows through these provinces has periodically caused significant difficulties in relations between Indonesia and Malaysia. Perhaps more importantly, however, those flows had serious social and economic implications for Indonesians living in those provinces and the migrants passing through them.

Regulating the flow of Indonesian labour migrants

In contrast to Indonesia's failure to properly acknowledge and accommodate the flows of migrants through the transit provinces of Sumatra and Kalimantan – let alone address the problems associated with those flows – Indonesian immigration has long been a focus for Malaysian policy-makers, not least because of public reactions to the influx of Indonesian migrants. Although Indonesians were initially welcomed in Malaysia because they shared the racial and religious background of the Malays – many of whom are descended from earlier waves of migration from the Indonesian archipelago – over time, the enormous influx of migrants brought considerable criticism within Malaysia. During cyclical economic downturns, Indonesians and other migrant workers were seen to represent a threat to Malaysian citizen's economic security. Malaysians have also long been uneasy about the motives, morality and behaviour of Indonesian migrant workers. In the 1980s, for example, concerns were expressed that although the majority of Indonesian were Muslim, some Indonesians were spreading

Christianity amongst the ethnic Malay community (Dorall 1989:305). Reports in the late 1980s also highlighted drug-trafficking, burglary involving the use of black magic and kidnappings involving Indonesians. For many Malaysians, the large numbers of Indonesians living in squatter settlements continued to represent a moral and social risk two decades later. Crinis's (2004) survey of English-language Malaysian newspapers, including the government-sanctioned *New Straits Times*, shows that media coverage continues to focus on the social problems associated with migrant labour, particularly drugs, violence, murder, disease, rape and prostitution. Indonesians are also perceived as competing unfairly for jobs and for living space in the cities, as Hing has demonstrated using data from interviews with middle-class and working-class Malaysians (2000:231).

In response to pressure from the public and foreign policy and economic imperatives, the Malaysian government has varied the intensity with which it enforces border control as means of enhancing its social and labour market regulation. The Malaysian government formally began trying to regulate inflow of foreigners unilaterally in the early 1980s. Bilateral attempts to regulate the flow of spontaneous labour migration were subsequently formalised in 1984 when the government initiated the Supply of Workers Agreement, known as the Medan Agreement, with Indonesia (Tirtosudarmo 2001). Similar agreements were later signed by the Malaysian government and the governments of the Philippines, Thailand and Bangladesh. The government increasingly sought to limit migration during the 1985–87 recession, but as the economy recovered, demand for foreign workers grew once more, and the government again encouraged labour migration. As a result, the number of documented migrant workers allowed into Malaysia in the period between 1986 and 1990 was one and a half times higher that of the previous five years (Lim 1996:322).

In conjunction with its attempts to regulate new arrivals, the Malaysian government moved to control undocumented foreigners already working in Malaysia. In 1989, the government undertook its first major initiative, namely to establish the Foreign Worker Regularisation Programme, which was designed to minimise the employment of illegal Indonesian plantation workers. Under the scheme, foreign workers employed on plantations were offered three-year contracts in return for registration, and the employment of new workers from Indonesia was frozen from 1 January 1990. The programme was only moderately successful: it is estimated that only one-third of foreign plantation workers registered at the centres (Kanapathy 2004). In the 1990s, the government ran another series of campaigns in a renewed attempt to regularise undocumented foreign workers already employed in Malaysia and to minimise undocumented border flows to Peninsular Malaysia (Kassim 2000:102–3). In October 1991, the government implemented the Comprehensive Policy on the Recruitment of Foreign Workers. This policy streamlined recruitment processes for employers in the plantation, construction, manufacturing and services industries, and mandated a number of social security measures for foreign workers (Kanapathy 2004). Additional policies were subsequently implemented to discourage over-reliance on foreign labour, including an annual levy on foreign labour in 1992, and bans on various categories of low-skilled foreign workers between 1993 and 1995.

Two major amnesties and registration and deportation campaigns were also run in the early-mid 1990s under the names *Ops Nyah* I and *Ops Nyah* II. Of those arrested between 1992 and 1995, some 78 per cent, or almost 147,000 people, were Indonesian (UNESCO-MOST n.d.). During that same period 402,508 other Indonesians found to be working illegally in Malaysia were allowed to register as legal foreign workers (UNESCO-MOST n.d.), while in 1996–97 over 300,000 more undocumented Indonesian workers were regularised (Hugo 2001). A total of 413,832 unregistered foreign nationals were registered between March and August 1997 in Sabah alone, of whom 294,704 were Indonesians (Kurus 1998:282). After amendments were made to the Immigration Act in January 1997 heavier fines were imposed on illegal foreign workers, employers and agents in an attempt to reduce unauthorised entry and employment of foreigners. In August the same year, a total ban was imposed on new recruitment of foreign workers. The ban was lifted shortly after protests by businesses and employers of domestic workers, but was re-imposed in January 1998 for workers in the manufacturing, construction and service sectors (Kanapathy 2004).

During the Asian economic and financial crisis of 1997–98, the Malaysian government again strengthened its dual strategy of migration control. In an attempt to deal with increasing unemployment once again it simultaneously sought to limit the number of Indonesians entering Malaysia through official channels and to expel Indonesians already working illegally in Malaysia. In late 1997, the government announced that 200,000 foreign workers would lose their jobs in 1998, and that work permits for 700,000 foreign workers (excluding domestic workers) would not be renewed on expiry (Pillai 1998:268). In early 1998, levies on foreign labour were raised, and conditions under which foreign domestic workers could be employed were tightened (Pillai 1998:269). Stricter border checks were imposed, unregistered migration agents were arrested, and a number of Immigration officers were arrested on the suspicion that they were issuing forged documents (Pillai 1998:271). As a result, in 1997–98, the overall number of official placements of overseas labour migrants dropped 55 per cent, primarily because of the changes in the Malaysian government's labour migration policies aimed at softening the effect of the crisis on local Malaysians (Feridhanusetyawan and Gaduh 2000:14).

However, when bans were again lifted in mid-1998, as Figure 12.2 suggests, numbers quickly rebounded. By 1999, they had reached two-thirds of the 1996–97 levels (Depnakertrans, 2003a) – levels that were artificially high

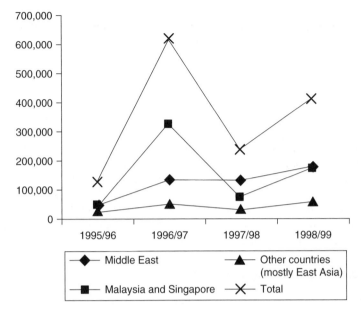

Figure 12.2 Effects of the 1997–98 crisis on placement of overseas migrant workers in major destinations, 1995–1999

Sources: Depnakertrans (2001, 2002).

because a large number of undocumented workers in the service sector were legalised in that year (Hugo 2001). While the number of migrant workers arriving in Malaysia through official channels again rose after the crisis, the Malaysian government continued its anti-Indonesian policy, particularly with regard to undocumented workers. It deported 30,000 undocumented workers in August 2000 as part of a plan to halve the number of Indonesians working in Malaysia from 900,000 to 450,000 (*Surabaya Post*, 27 January 2002). In December 2000, the government announced that it had commenced deporting another 66,000 undocumented Indonesians, and in January 2001 declared that around 120,000 more would be deported in the near future (AMC 2002:62–3). In November 2001, Zainal Abidin Zin, Malaysia's Deputy Minister for Internal Affairs announced the government would deport 10,000 undocumented Indonesian immigrants per month (*Detik.com*, 28 November 2001). Some 2500 Indonesians were immediately repatriated on two navy ships (*Suara Merdeka*, 21 November 2001).

In January 2002, the Malaysian government responded to riots by Indonesian workers in an industrial zone in Negeri Sembilan and in Cyberjaya on 20 and 27 January respectively by threatening to end Indonesian labour migration to Malaysia (*Kompas*, 27 January 2002). On 21 January 2002, after the first riot, Deputy Prime Minister Abdullah Ahmad Badawi announced that Indonesian labour would be banned altogether (*Kompas*, 23 January 2002), whilst Prime Minister Mahathir announced a 'hire Indonesians last' policy. These announcements were again met by protests from Malaysian business organisations, which argued that their members required access to Indonesian labour to effectively run their business concerns (see, e.g., *Suara Merdeka*, 31 January 2002). Another amnesty for undocumented workers was announced two months later. Between 22 March and 11 July, 145,578 Indonesians left Malaysia voluntarily under the amnesty, which was then extended to July 31 (*Nakertransnet*, n.d.). In mid-2002, the Malaysian government deported 3200 Indonesians working illegally in Malaysia in the lead-up to the implementation of the Immigration Act on 1 August (*Satunet*, 22 July 2002), after which at least 140,000 Indonesians were forcibly repatriated. As tensions rose, the Indonesian Foreign Minister, Syed Hamid Albar, and Malaysian Prime Minister, Mahathir, advised Malaysians to temporarily suspend visits to Indonesia (*Pikiran Rakyat*, 29 August 2002).

Responses to the crisis at Nunukan

At the time the mass deportation began in August 2002, Nunukan was already experiencing a population explosion caused by the steady flow of migrants returning under the amnesty in the months leading up to the implementation of the Immigration Act. In July and August 2002 alone, the Indonesian Consulates in the East Malaysian cities of Kota Kinabalu and Tawau registered almost 140,000 undocumented workers returning to Indonesia via Nunukan (Palupi and Yasser 2002:9; Purwanto and Kuncoro 2002:2). In the first half of August, between 5000 and 9000 people passed through Nunukan's Immigration Office every day (Palupi and Yasser 2002:8). According to human rights activists present in Nunukan at the time, most of the deportees were robbed of their assets before returning to Indonesia (Palupi and Yasser 2002:20; Interview with Sri Palupi, June 2003).

The majority of those deported to Nunukan were moved to other areas of Indonesia on Navy and regular ships (Purwanto and Kuncoro 2002:2). However, approximately 25,000 returnees remained in twenty-one camps run by registered labour-sending companies. According to local officials, at least half this number again also remained on the island without being registered (Palupi and Yasser 2002:10). Purwanto and Kuncoro divide those who remained in to three categories: those waiting for their passports to be processed so they could return to Malaysia; those who wished to return to their home provinces, but did not have the means to do so; and those whose family members were still either detained or fugitives in Malaysia (2002:2). In Nunukan, some deportees were housed in tents or buildings owned by labour-sending companies. Others constructed makeshift shelters, or slept in the markets, sheds or on building sites (Palupi and Yasser 2002:13). Sanitation and lack of clean water was a major problem both in the camps and outside them. Deportees experienced major illnesses, including breathing problems, fever, dysentery, malaria, stomach problems, skin diseases, dehydration, and anaemia (Palupi and Yasser 2002:15–16; Purwanto and Kuncoro 2002:15). According to NGO investigations, between 67 and 70 deportees died (Palupi and Yasser 2002:17–18; Purwanto and Kuncoro 2002 Appendix). The effects on the population of Nunukan itself were also severe. Although local residents in some ways profited by providing services and facilities for the influx of people, they were subjected to price rises of up to 100 per cent for basic food commodities, and many took in deportees, sometimes for months. The town's infrastructure did not cope with the sudden quadrupling of its population, and locals as well as returnees suffered from a lack of basic facilities. As could be expected, there was a rise in social problems and crime, as well as significant environmental pollution (Palupi and Yasser 2002:20).

In response to the worsening conditions, local authorities established a crisis response team on 27 July 2002, which became the channel for outside help. The crisis team ran programmes to help the local community prepare for the influx; established security posts in dangerous areas and increased both sea and land patrols; established nine basic health clinics to deal with the returnees' health problems; increased the capacity of the immigration office; prepared emergency accommodation for returnees and arranged with the central government for warships to be sent to Nunukan to transport returnees to their provinces of origin (Palupi and Yasser 2002:10). These measures helped alleviate some of the worst of the suffering, but were insufficient to effectively address even the immediate needs of the deportees. The labour-sending companies that had provided inadequate documentation for the workers they placed in Malaysia were not penalised in any way (Purwanto and Kuncoro 2002:12).

At first, the Nunukan crisis received no response whatsoever from government officials in Jakarta. It was only after considerable critical media coverage of events in Nunukan and a series of NGO campaigns that a number of central government officials and members of parliament visited Nunukan (Palupi and Yasser 2002:22). However, the seriousness of the situation continued to be underestimated. Indonesian President Megawati Sukarnoputri accused the media of overstating the problems experienced in Nunukan, whilst shifting responsibility for handling the issue to Vice President Hamzah Haz, who in turn delegated authority to the Coordinating Minister for Health and Welfare to deal with the problem. After these visits, the central government continued to make little serious effort to deal with either the humanitarian crisis in Nunukan or the underlying causes of that crisis (Purwanto and Kuncoro 2002:11).

NGOs dealing with migrant labour played an important role both in bringing the Nunukan crisis to the central government's attention and in eventually forcing the government to take steps to begin to address the situation in Nunukan and other transit locations. In a letter dated 24 July 2002 to the Coordinating Ministers for Politics and Security, Health and Welfare and Economics and Industry, as well as the parliament and the National Human Rights Committee, these NGOs urged the central government to address the impending mass deportation. They recommended that the central government give priority to finding a diplomatic solution to stop the Malaysian government's arbitrary treatment of Indonesians; prepare for future large-scale deportations by establishing dedicated taskforces in the locations to which undocumented migrant workers are generally returned; instruct the local governments of sending areas to become involved and provide protection for workers from those areas and undertaking necessary steps required to return Indonesian migrant workers to their families if deported; and undertake a complete revision of the process under which workers are placed overseas and the protection of those workers whilst overseas (*Konsorsium Pembela Buruh Migran Indonesia* [KOPBUMI]; Interview with Wahyu Susilo June 2003).

When these recommendations were initially ignored, a number of these NGOs filed a citizen's lawsuit against nine government officials, including President Megawati Soekarnoputri, in September 2002 (KOPBUMI), in which they argued that the President had failed to fulfil her duty under the human rights and anti-corruption laws of 1999. The text of the lawsuit incorporated a chronological account of the humanitarian crisis at Nunukan in the evidence section, which included references to the President's claims that journalists were overstating the severity of the situation, poor coordination between Ministers, failure to react in a timely manner to Malaysia's announcement of its plans to deport large numbers of overseas migrant workers and failure to sign a Memorandum of Understanding in Bali at a Meeting of Senior Officials in August 2002.

In response to NGO activity, a number of government departments set up new initiatives to address the overseas migrant worker question, in addition to providing some emergency aid directly to Nunukan (Palupi and Yasser 2002). The Department of Manpower's Decision No. 312A/D.P2TKLN/2002 attempted to mandate the protection of overseas migrant labour through bilateral agreements, placement and work contracts, insurance, the regulation of placement costs and the provision of legal aid for overseas migrant workers (KOPBUMI). The decision included provision for the setting up of a protection unit to deal with complaints and establish protocols for handling migrant worker cases; to verify information concerning the accuracy of migrant workers' documents and information about placement, the health and safety of migrant workers awaiting placement and the suitability of placement; and to organise the return of all fees to migrant workers who are not successfully placed. More importantly, in the context of this discussion, the unit was to liaise with the police, the courts, local and provincial governments. This requirement was one of the first concrete measures in which the central government recognised the role of local institutions in managing migrant worker flows.

The year 2002 also saw the introduction of a bill into parliament on the Protection of Indonesian Migrant Workers and their Families. A year later, three competing drafts were being discussed by the parliament, one of which was drafted by KOPBUMI (Solidaritas Perempuan/Komnas Perempuan 2003). The tabling of the drafts and ensuing discussions were followed by a public announcement on 17 November 2003 that the government would set up a migrant advocacy team to provide legal protection for migrant workers in Indonesia and abroad. The agreement, which was signed by a number of relevant Ministers, covered transportation, passports, and the establishment of a special team to deal with returnees (*Kompas*, 14 November 2003; *Jakarta Post*, 18 November 2003). Meanwhile, the Ministry for Women's Empowerment, in conjunction with a number of women's groups, began a pilot project aimed at improving the regulatory environment for overseas domestic work; the Ministry for Social Affairs established a new division focusing on migrant workers and victims of violence, which conducted a series of workshops and established a number of crisis centres for migrant workers; and the Ministry of Foreign Affairs supported a collaborative programme to improve the provision of consular services for overseas migrant domestic workers. A number of other ministries also responded directly to the Nunukan Affair (Solidaritas Perempuan/Komnas Perempuan 2003).

New bilateral and multilateral negotiations were also undertaken after the Nunukan crisis. As noted earlier, negotiations between President Megawati and Malaysian Prime Minister Mahathir Mohamed failed in Bali in August 2002, but Malaysian officials announced in March 2003 that the Memorandum of Understanding, which would include a quota for Indonesian workers to be sent to Malaysia, was to be signed within two months (*Jakarta Post*, 13 March 2003). In May 2004 – almost two years after the Nunukan tragedy – the governments of Indonesia and Malaysia finally signed the long-awaited agreement. The Memorandum of Understanding covered issues including recruitment, medical checkups and transportation, but did not prescribe sanctions for employers who do not meet mandated conditions or deal with issues concerning the deportation of undocumented workers (Forum Kerja untuk PRT Migran). In the same month, officials announced that a new Memorandum of Understanding that dealt specifically with the question of Indonesian domestic workers in Malaysia would be negotiated (Human Rights Watch, 2004). Meanwhile, on 28 August 2003, Malaysian Human Resources Minister Fong Chan Onn announced that Malaysia would accede to the Indonesian government's request not to recruit workers outside the official system of labour-sending agents (*Star*, 30 August 2003). The protection of migrant workers was again discussed at the ASEAN Inter-Parliamentary Organisation (AIPO) meeting in Jakarta in September 2003, at which it was decided that legal instruments were required to provide protection for migrant workers (*Jakarta Post*, 10 September 2003). NGO activists later urged ASEAN to take up the AIPO initiative, arguing that ASEAN's policy of non-interference prevented the satisfactory resolution of issues surrounding migrant labour (*Jakarta Post*, 9 October 2003).

Implications for the transit provinces

So what of the transit provinces? The mass deportation of Indonesian workers from Malaysia under the 2002 Immigration Act was not the first time the transit provinces have had to deal with the negative effects of labour migration. However, under the centralised system established by the New Order, there was little local and provincial governments could do to mitigate those effects. Changes in the political climate after the fall of President Suharto – particularly those associated with the passing of the national laws on fiscal decentralisation and regional autonomy in 1999 – meant that it became possible for regional governments to become actively involved in the regulation of migrant labour. Since then, some sending provinces including East and Central Java and West Nusatenggara have issued regulations and policies concerning overseas migrant workers (Tirtosudarmo 2001, 2004). In addition, demands have were made by local and provincial governments in the transit provinces that the local and provincial governments in sending regions (primarily in Java and Eastern Indonesia) take responsibility for people from those regions who are forced to return to the transit provinces. For example, in late July 2002, representatives of the governments of West Kalimantan and North Sumatra were reported as complaining about the failure of the central government and the governments of sending provinces to take responsibility for dealing with the crisis caused by the large numbers of migrant workers deported to Kalimantan and Sumatra (*Sinar Harapan*, 29 July 2002).

Such complaints do not negate the fact that the local government of Nunukan did receive some assistance from the central and provincial levels, and from neighbouring local government regions during the Nunukan crisis, although this assistance was nowhere near enough to meet the needs of the deportees (Palupi and Yasser 2002:11). Most commonly sending provinces contributed to the transportation of migrant workers returning to their provinces of origin. For example, by the end of August 2003 the provincial government of East Java had outlaid Rp 2.3 million for the return of 208 deported workers (*Bisnis Indonesia*, 29 August 2003). However, overall the transit provinces of North Sumatra, Riau and West and East Kalimantan received little help from either the sending provinces or the central government with regard to deported migrant workers, and most of the burden of housing, feeding and repatriating deported workers fell on the governments of those transit provinces themselves. Central government initiatives to lessen the flow of deportees through the transit provinces were also only partially successful. Although the Department of Manpower later requested that the Malaysian government repatriate Indonesians to the large Javanese ports of Tanjung Priok in Jakarta and Tanjung Perak in Surabaya rather than just paying repatriation costs to the nearest Indonesian port (*Media Indonesia*, 14 November 2003), no effective formal mechanism was established to achieve this, let alone create structures for handling normal flows of migrant labour through those transit zones. More recent attempts to establish a series of 'one-roof' processing centres for deportees have also been relatively unsuccessful (interview with Lisa Humaidah, Komnas Perempuan, July 2005).

Perhaps most importantly, despite the Malaysian government's best efforts to regulate the flows of migrant workers from Indonesia, Malaysia's borders with Indonesia remain extremely porous, and workers continue both to enter Malaysia illegally and be deported. In 2003, the Malaysian government announced that another 48,000 Indonesians working illegally in Malaysia would be repatriated (*Media Indonesia*, 14 November 2003). Between January and September 2003, the Malaysian government deported an additional 5552 undocumented workers to Medan's Belawan Port alone (*Kompas*, 10 September 2003). In July 2004, plans were announced to deport a further 1.2 million illegal workers, in the lead-up to the introduction of micro-chipped identity cards for foreign workers (*Malaysiakini*, 12 July 2004; *Jakarta Post*, 20 July 2004). Although at that time the Indonesian government asked that Indonesians working illegally in Malaysia be regularised, the government of Malaysia refused (*Suara Pembaruan*, 20 July 2004).

In July 2004, NGOs and the Minister for Manpower warned that the new round of deportations could result in a 'second Nunukan' (Migrant Care 2004; *Kompas*, 19 July 2004). Only a few months later, the local government in Nunukan announced it was 'ready to receive the influx of tens of thousands of illegal Indonesian migrant workers to be deported ... in the next few months', having prepared barracks for the deportees and budgeted for their travel expenses back to their provinces of origin (*Jakarta Post*, 27 September 2004). Although the local government may be more prepared for this 'second Nunukan', repeated influxes of deportees would still most certainly put unbearable strain on local resources.

Conclusion

Although the repatriation of illegal immigrants is set to continue, the Nunukan Affair of 2002 was a critical point both in bilateral relations between Indonesia and Malaysia. It also put significant pressure on the relationship between Indonesia's central government and the provinces through which migrant workers pass on their way to Malaysia, and to which Indonesian migrant workers no longer welcome in Malaysia are deported. Local governments' new-found political power (and financial responsibility) following the implementation of regional autonomy laws in 1999 has greatly increased their willingness to speak out about problems associated with migrant labour flows through the transit provinces and demand support from both the sending provinces and the central government. Yet although the Nunukan Affair has forced Indonesia's central government to attempt to respond more systematically to deportations of workers from Malaysia, central government departments have overwhelmingly continued to seek centralised solutions to the detriment of the interests of the transit provinces. This is clearly demonstrated in Law No. 39/2004 on The Placement and Protection of Indonesian Workers Overseas, which was finally signed on 18 October 2004 (Depnakertrans 2004b). Instead of dealing comprehensively with issues concerning mass deportations and their effects on the transit provinces, the only article that referred to deportation simply stated that in the case of deportation, workers were to be returned to their region of origin (Law No.39/2004, Article 73).

The pressures associated with the repeated mass deportation of Indonesian migrant workers from Malaysia mean that the regulation of labour migration flows through the transit provinces, and their effects on the communities through which they pass, can no longer be ignored. However, the central government's continued marginalisation of the transit provinces suggests that while regional autonomy has highlighted the problems associated with migrant flows, it is yet to provide a framework in which those problems can be addressed. Until such a framework is created and the transit zones are properly resourced to deal with the contingencies associated with migration flows to and from Malaysia, future humanitarian disasters in the transit provinces cannot be avoided.

References

Asian Migrant Centre and Migrant Forum in Asia (2002) *Asian Migrant Yearbook 2001: Migration Facts, Analysis and Issues in 2000* (Hong Kong: Asian Migrant Centre/Migrant Forum in Asia).

Bisnis Indonesia, 3 September 2003.

——, 29 August 2003.

——, 17 February 2002.

Crinis, V. (2004) 'The Silence and Fantasy of Women and Work'. Unpublished PhD Thesis, University of Wollongong.

Detik.com, 28 November 2001.

Depnakertrans (2004a) 'Penerimaan Devisa dari TKI Menurut Kawasan Tahun 2004', http://nakertrans.go.id/pusdinnaker/tki/Devisa%202004.htm (accessed 24 July 2004).

—— (2004b) 'Undang-Undang Republik Indonesia Nomor 39 Tahun 2004 tentang Penempatan Dan Perlindungan Tenaga Kerja Indonesia Di Luar Negeri', http://www.nakertrans.go.id/perundangan/undang-undang/uu_39_2004.php (accessed 25 July 2005).

—— (2003a) 'Penerimaan Devisa dari TKI Menurut Kawasan Tahun 2003', http://nakertrans.go.id/pusdinnaker/tki/Devisa%202003.htm (accessed 24 July 2005).

—— (2003b) 'Penempatan TKI Formal dan Informal ke Luar Negeri Tahun 2003', http://nakertrans.go.id/pusdatinnaker/tki/TKI%202003.htm (accessed 10 August 2004).

—— (2003c) 'Penempatan TKI Formal ke Luar Negeri Tahun 2003', http://nakertrans.go.id/pusdatinnaker/tki/TKI_Formal%202003.htm (accessed 10 August 2004).

—— (2003d) 'Penempatan TKI Informal ke Luar Negeri Tahun 2003', http://nakertrans.go.id/pusdatinnaker/tki/TKI_Informal%202003.htm (accessed 10 August 2004).

—— (2002a) 'Penerimaan Devisa dar TKI Menurut Kawasan Tahun 2002', http://nakertrans.go.id/pusdatinnaker/tki/Devisa%202002.htm (accessed 10 August 2004).

—— (2002b) 'Penempatan TKI Formal dan Informal ke Luar Negeri Tahun 2002', http://nakertrans.go.id/pusdinnaker/tki/TKI%202002.htm (accessed 24 July 2005).

—— (2001a) 'Penerimaan Devisa dar TKI Menurut Kawasan Tahun 2001', http://nakertrans.go.id/pusdinnaker/tki/Devisa%202001.htm (accessed 10 August 2004).

—— (2001b) 'Penempatan TKI Formal dan Informal ke Luar Negeri Tahun 2002', http://naker trans.go.id/pusdinnaker/tki/TKI%202002.htm (accessed 24 July 2005).

—— (2001c) 'Penempatan TKI Formal ke Luar Negeri Tahun 2001', http://nakertrans.go.id/pusdinnaker/tki/TKI_Formal%202001.htm (accessed 10 August 2004).

—— (2001d) 'Penempatan TKI Formal dan Informal ke Luar Negeri Tahun 2001', http://nakertrans.go.id/pusdatinnaker/tki/TKI_Informal%202001.htm (accessed 10 August 2004).

—— (2000), 'Tabel 11.1: Jumlah Tenaga Kerja Indonesia (TKI) yang Ditempatkan di Luar Negeri Menurut Negara Tujuan, 1999–2000', http://www.nakertrans.go.id/PINAKER/Statistik/table_111.htm (accessed 3 August 2003).

Dorrall, R. (1989) 'Issues and Implications of Recent Undocumented Economic Migration from the Malay World', in Noleen Heyzer and G.Lycklama (eds) *The Trade in Domestic Helpers: Causes, Mechanisms and Consequences Helpers: Causes, Mechanisms and Consequences* (Kuala Lumpur: APD Centre).

Feridhanusetyawan, T. and Gaduh, A. (2000) 'Indonesia's Labor Market During the Crisis: Empirical Evidence from the *Sakernas*, 1997–1999', *Indonesian Quarterly*, Vol. 28, No. 3: 294–315.

Ford, M. (2001) 'Indonesian Women as Export Commodity: Notes from Tanjung Pinang', *Labour and Management in Development*, Vol. 2, No. 5: 1–9.

Hing Ai Yun (2000) 'Migration and the Reconfiguration of Malaysia', *Journal of Contemporary Asia*, Vol. 30, No. 2: 221–45.

Hugo, G. (2001) 'Women's International Labour Migration'. Paper presented at the 2001 Indonesia Update, Australian National University, Canberra, 22 September.

Human Rights Watch (2004) 'Help Wanted: Abuses Against Female Migrant Domestic Workers in Indonesia and Malaysia' *Human Rights Watch*, Vol. 16, No. 9(B): 1–91 (Plus Appendix).

International Labour Organisation (ILO) (1998) 'Emigration Pressures and Structural Change: Case Study of Indonesia', http://www.ilo.org/public/english/protection/migrant/chapters/emindo ch3.htm. (accessed 19 April 2001).

Jakarta Post, 27 September 2004.

——, 20 July 2004.

——, 18 November 2003.

——, 9 October 2003.

——, 10 September 2003.

Jakarta Post,13 March 2003.

Jones, S. (2000) *Making Money off Migrants: The Indonesian Exodus to Malaysia* (Hong Kong and Wollongong: Asia 2000/CAPSTRANS).

Kanapathy, V. (2004) 'International Migration and Labour Market Developments in Asia: Economic Recovery, the Labour Market and Migrant Workers in Malaysia'. Paper presented at the 2004 Workshop on International Migration and Labour Markets in Asia, 5–February.

Kassim, A. (2000) 'Indonesian Immigrant Settlements in Peninsular Malaysia', *Sojourn*, Vol. 15: 100–22.

Kaur, A. (2004) 'Mobility, Labour Mobilisation and Border Controls: Indonesian Labour Migration to Malaysia since 1900'. Paper presented at the 15th Biennial Conference of the Asian Studies Association in Australia, Canberra 29 June–2 July.

Komnas Perempuan (2005) 'Draft Temuan Studi Pendahuluan Kehidupan Buruh Migran Perempuan Tak Berdokumen Indonesia di Malaysia: Studi Kasus Bone-Sulawesi Selatan, Sambas-Kalimantan Barat, Lombok Tengah-Nusa Tenggara Barat, Lumajang-Jawa Timur, dan Jakarta'. Unpublished Draft Report, Komnas Perempuan, Jakarta.

Kompas, 19 July 2004.

——, 14 November 2003.

——, 10 September 2003.

——, 23 January 2002.

——, 27 January 2002.

Kurus, B. (1998) 'Migrant Labor: The Sabah Experience, *Asian and Pacific Migration Journal*, Vol. 7, No. 2–3: 281–95.

Lim, L. (1996) 'The Migration Transition in Malaysia', *Asian and Pacific Migration Journal*, Vol. 5, No. 2–3: 319–37.

Malaysiakini, 12 July 2004.

Mantra, I. (2000) 'Indonesian Labour Mobility to Malaysia (A Case Study: East Flores, West Lombok and the Island of Bawean)' in Sukamdi, A. Haris and P. Brownlee (eds) *Labour Migration in Indonesia: Policies and Practice* (Yogyakarta: Population Studies Center Gadjah Mada University) pp. 143–84.

Media Indonesia, 14 November 2003.

——, 29 August 2003.

Migrant Care (2004) 'Pernyataan Sikap Migrant Care: Nunukan Jilid 2 Akan Segera Terbit', Statement by Migrant Care issued on 16 July.

Nakertransnet, n.d.

Palupi, S. and Yasser, N. (2002) 'Laporan Investigasi Buruh Migran Indonesia (TKI) di Nunukan: Korban Praktek Perbudakan Terselubung Indonesia – Malaysia', unpublished report produced by the Jaringan Relawan Kemanusaiaan untuk Nunukan.

Pikiran Rakyat, 29 August 2002.

Pillai, P. (1998) 'The Impact of the Economic Crisis on Migrant Labor in Malaysia: Policy Implications', *Asian and Pacific Migration Journal*, Vol. 7, No. 2–3: 255–80.

Purwanto, E. and Kuncoro, W. (2002) 'Laporan Perjalanan dari Nunukan Tanggal 21–29 Agustus 2002: "Menjadi Kuli Kontrak di Malaysia, Semakin Tertindas di Negeri Sendiri" '. Unpublished report produced by KOPBUMI and Jarnas BMI.

Satunet, 22 July 2002.

Sinar Harapan, 29 July 2002.

Star, 30 August 2003.

Soeprobo, T. (2003) 'Country Report: Indonesia', available at http://www.jil.go.jp/foreign/event_r/event/documents/2004sopemi/2004sopemi_e_countryreport4.pdf (accessed 16 August 2004).

Solidaritas Perempuan and Komnas Perempuan (2003) 'Indonesian Migrant Domestic Workers: Notes on its [sic] Vulnerability and New Initiatives for the Protection of their Rights'. Unpublished draft Indonesian country report to the UN Special Rapporteur on the Human Rights of Migrants.

Suara Merdeka, 31 January 2002.

———, 20 July 2004.

———, 21 November 2001.

Surabaya Post, 27 January 2002.

Tirtosudarmo, R. (2004) 'Cross-border Migration in Indonesia and the Nunukan Tragedy' in A. Ananta and E. Arifin (eds) *International Migration in Southeast Asia* (Singapore: ISEAS) pp. 310–30.

——— (2001) 'The Politics of Regulating Overseas Migrant Labor in Indonesia'. Paper presented at the Workshop on Labor Migration and Socio-Economic Change in Southeast and East Asia, Lund University, Sweden, 14–16 May 2001.

UNESCO-MOST (n.d.) 'Issues Chapter from Malaysia', http://www.unesco.org/most.apmrnwp9.htm (accessed 19 April 2001).

13
The State and Labour Migration Policies in Thailand

Patcharawalai Wongboonsin

Introduction

Thailand's rapid economic growth has resulted in an increased demand for highly educated and skilled workers than the country can currently supply. In order to overcome this skilled manpower shortage, the Thai government has approved the recruitment of foreign PTK (professional, technical and kindred) workers. This policy, which does not take into account the movement of unskilled workers into Thailand, has resulted in an increase in undocumented labour migration into the country. Thailand is also experiencing changes in the composition of labour migrants. In the past, the assumption was that Thailand would become a net labour exporter. But it has now become both a labour-sending and a labour-receiving country.

Labour emigration from Thailand can be traced to the mid-1970s when there was temporary and circular migration to the Middle East associated with the demand for construction workers. This represented a shift from the permanent settlement of skilled Thais in the West in the previous decades. The late 1980s saw another major shift in terms of migration destination, from the Middle East to East and Southeast Asia (Phuaphongsakorn 1982; Pongsapich 1986, 1994; Thosanguan and Chalamwong 1991). The number of emigrants increased from 105,988 migrant workers in 1987 to 183,671 in 1997 (Ministry of Labour and Social Welfare 1989 and 2001).

Figure 13.1, based on official records, suggests a continuation of such a trend after the 1997–98 economic and financial crisis, with an increase from 191,735 migrants in 1998 to 202,416 in 1999. The start of the twenty-first century constitutes another shift, from a sloping I-curve to a sloping E-curve pattern of labour emigration. This reflects an almost 30 per cent decline in labour emigration – to 147,769 migrants in 2003, with a decreasing proportion to ASEAN and other Asian destinations.

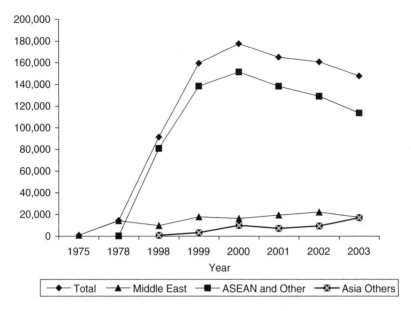

Figure 13.1   Thai migrant labour flows by destination, 1975–2003
Source: Ministry of Labour, Thailand: 1975–2003.

Migration streams have also changed. The proportion of low-end unskilled emigrants (equipment operators and service workers) showed a decline in 2000. This decline was accompanied by an increase in irregular or undocumented emigration from Thailand. One explanation for this trend was the more stringent regulation of migrant flows by the major destination countries as Singapore and Japan, as well as a reduction in job opportunities in other countries such as Korea (Lee 1998; Park 1998; Watanabe 1998; Atipas 1999; Ito 1999; Chalamwong 2001). A second explanation may be traced to a new policy by the Thai state to proactively promote labour emigration via bilateral agreements with countries that were relatively less affected by the Asian economic and financial crisis, in order to mitigate the impact of unemployment in Thailand (Wongboonsin 2000:54). The Thai government's crackdown on crime syndicates involved in labour recruitment was an additional factor.

Labour migration into Thailand

Labour migration into Thailand rose during the period 1990–2003. This increase, from under 10,000 in 1990 to more than 80,000 in 2003, is shown in Table 13.1 below. These migrants, who went mainly to Bangkok, comprised mainly business and high-end skilled workers.

Table 13.1　Regular migrant labour in Thailand in 1990 and 2003

Province	Total		Promoted Establishment		Non Promoted		Aliens under Section 12	
	1990	2003	1990	2003	1990	2003	1990	2003
Bangkok Metropolis	6,856	44,014	2,271	9,156	4,560	30,511	25	1,508
Provinces around								
BKK	1,236	6,798	958	2,264	277	4,103	1	431
Central and East	518	13,298	344	5,412	143	4,566	31	3,320
North	213	12,846	55	546	138	2,616	20	9,684
Northeast	384	1,444	23	349	65	798	296	297
South	382	9,628	183	585	194	8,501	5	542
Total	9,589	86,205	3,834	19,328	5,377	52,095	378	15,782

Note: Data excludes 14,423 migrants working in Thailand before 13 December 1972 and granted permanent work permits 2003 data are those as of 25 December 2003.

Source: Calculated by author, based on data from Ministry of Labour (2003).

These skilled workers were predominantly from East Asia and the Western countries, as shown in Table 13.2 below.

They and less-skilled workers were recruited under the state's policy of prioritising establishments that were allowed to hire foreign labour. There were three main categories. In the first category, the promoted establishments included enterprises that are promoted by the Board of Investment under investment promotion and other related legislation. These enterprises are seen by the government as a vehicle to attract foreign investment into Thailand. East Asians providing mostly managerial and technical services dominated this category in 2003 (Table 13 A1).

The second category, although referred to as the 'non-promoted' category, is nevertheless involved in 'important' economic activities in Thailand. Workers recruited for enterprises in this category include a small proportion who hold permanent resident status that carries lifetime work permits. In 2003 migrant workers from East Asia and Western countries providing managerial and professional services dominated in this category (Table 13 A2).

In the third category are included workers who entered the country without documentation. They are allowed to work on a temporary basis, but are subject to deportation under section 12 of the Alien Employment Act. This category includes those whose deportation status is still pending and foreign nationals who entered Thailand illegally and who were in the process of being deported from the country. This category also includes persons born in Thailand but who have been denied Thai nationality under the state's National Executive Council Announcement No. 337 dated 13 December 1972 or similar legislation. In 2003, 'migrants' who came under this category included skilled and semi-skilled workers, employed in retail, the agricultural

Table 13.2 Documented migrants in Thailand: by nationality and occupation as on 25 December 2003

Occupations	TOTAL	Japanese	British	Indian	Chinese	American	Taiwanese	Filipino	Australian	German	Others
Executive, managerial	42,438	11,134	3,041	4,363	3,168	1,941	3,039	579	1,256	1,387	12,530
Professionals	14,221	1,881	2,279	627	705	2,214	170	1,673	747	299	3,626
Technical	5,292	1,448	317	284	845	216	293	278	101	136	1,374
Clerical	839	226	23	33	53	28	29	35	25	23	364
Service and sales	3,403	208	34	106	259	28	62	18	25	44	2,619
Skilled in agricultural and fishery sector	1,834	1	1	1	14	4	6	1	2		1,804
Skilled, other sectors	2,160	270	47	85	245	21	85	34	22	19	1,332
Plant/Machine operators and assemblers	875	119	45	18	123	40	30	38	24	13	425
Trainees	153	26	5	1	27	1	1	5	1	15	71
Others	14,990	1,425	424	399	569	334	530	158	196	169	10,786
TOTAL	86,205	16,738	6,216	5,917	6,008	4,827	4,245	2,819	2,399	2,105	34,931

Note: Excludes 14,423 aliens working in Thailand before 13 December 1972 and granted with a permanent work permit; 2003 data are those as of 25 December 2003.

Source: Ministry of Labour (2004c).

and fishery sector, and elsewhere. They comprise mainly ethnic minorities from the country's western and northern margins (Table 13 A3).

Temporary migrant workers under work permit rules

The official data cited above does not include those working legally under work-permit regulations. There are three categories under these regulations. The first is the Alien Employment Act exemptions, including members of diplomatic corps; members of consular missions; representatives of member countries and officials of the United Nations Organisations and its specialised agencies. It also includes personal servants (domestic workers) from abroad who are employed to work exclusively by the persons listed above. The second includes those who fall under the Royal Decrees B.E. 2522 and B.E. 2528. These workers are allowed to work without a permit on a very limited and highly discretionary basis. This category includes those performing duties under an agreement between the Thai government and an international organisation or foreign government; those carrying out duties associated with education, culture, arts, sports, or other activities prescribed by Royal Decree; and those working on a temporary basis at a local convention or exhibition for a period of less than 30 days. This category also includes workers performing work of 'an urgent and essential nature' for a maximum period of 15 days.

Irregular/undocumented migration

As noted earlier, the Thai state's immigration policy towards unskilled migrants has resulted in an increase in the inflow of irregular migrant labour over the past decade. The magnitude of irregular migrant labour is difficult to quantify. Estimates vary from source to source and year to year, and range from 200,000 to more than two million migrants. A widely cited estimate in 2002 was 1,222,143 irregular migrants. This compares with an estimate of 200,000 irregular migrants in 1993, an Immigration Bureau estimate of 525,480 irregular migrants in 1994, and a Ministry of Labour survey of 943,745 irregular migrants in 1997 (Table 13.3). Who are these irregular migrants?

Migrants from Myanmar dominate the irregular or illegal flows, and estimates of other illegal migrants vary according to the sources cited. According to official Immigration Bureau statistics (1994), an estimated 300,000 irregular migrants were from Myanmar in 1994. Additionally, there were about 100,000 irregular migrants from China, 10,000 from Indochina, and 80,000 from South Asia. This compares with an estimated 8300 highly skilled migrants working illegally in Thailand in 1990 (Sussangkarn 1995). Skilled migrants typically enter the country on a three-month tourist visa and continually renew their visas on expiry at Thai embassies or consulates in other parts of Southeast Asia. Some of these migrants include people born in Thailand who reside abroad, or children of Thai parents born and raised abroad, particularly in the United States (Havanon 1998, Stern 1998).

Low-end/unskilled irregular labour migration into Thailand falls into three categories, and precise information is unavailable on this migration

Table 13.3 Irregular migrants in Thailand, 1992–2004

Year	Source	Size
1992	Estimated total number	Not available
	Registered (Ministry of Labour)	706
1993	Estimated total number (National Security Council, based on news intelligence)	211,492
1994	Immigration Bureau, Ministry of Interior	525,480
1995	Not available	Not available
1996	Estimated total number (Ministry of Labour)	741,999
	Registered (Ministry of Labour)	282,511
1997	Survey (Ministry of Labour)	943,745
	Estimated total number (Institute of Population and Social Research, Mahidol University)	970,903
	Targeted repatriation for local replacement (Ministry of Interior)	300,000
	Repatriated irregular migrants (Ministry of Interior)	249,817
1998	Estimated total number (Ministry of Labour)	709,418
	Registered (Ministry of Labour)	90,911
	Quota for registration	158,253
	Demand claimed by the private sector	230,617
1999	Estimated total number (Ministry of Foreign Affairs)	600,000
	Registered (Ministry of Labour)	99,974
	Quota for registration	106,000
	Demand claimed by the private sector	Not available
2000	Estimated total number	Not available
	Registered (Ministry of Labour)	99,656
	Quota for registration	106,000
	Demand claimed by the private sector	Not available
2001	Estimated total number	Not avilable
	Targeted registration	2,000,000
	Registered (Ministry of Labour)	568,249
2002	Widely-cited estimates	1,222,143
	Response to registration and work permit renewals (Ministry of Labour)	430,074
2003	Estimated total number	Not available
2004	Estimated total number	Not available
	Expected registration	800,000
	Registered as of July 18	540,000

Source: Compiled by the author from various official sources and media reports.

stream. Migrants include daily commuters; seasonal, and annual migrants. A large number of them reside along the country's margins and borders, while others commute from other parts of the territory. Women and children who are trafficked from neighbouring countries and South Asia fall under this

Table 13.4   Location of irregular migrants in Thailand, 1997

Location	Number	Percentage of total irregular migrants
Border areas	256,146	27.1
Coastal areas	313,896	33.3
Bangkok region	223,288	23.7
Non-Bangkok region	150,415	15.9
Total	943,745	100.0

Source: Ministry of Labour and Social Welfare (1997).

Table 13.5   Population of Thai provinces bordering Myanmar, 2002

Province	Official population	Registered migrant labour	Registered migrant labour from Myanmar	Estimated Non-registered migrants	Registered camp populations
Chiang Rai	1,266,815	10,804	10,495	20,000 to 50,000	0
Chiang Mai	1,587,466	28,926	28,874	30,000 to 100,000	0
Mae Hong Son	232,697	3,431	3,431	20,000 to 50,000	41,972
Tak	481,875	47,489	47,486	75,000 to 150,000	55,284
Kanchanaburi	776,812	11,491	11,220	>50,000	3,706
Ratchaburi	818,564	11,710	11,296	~20,000	8,700
Phetchaburi	456,367	3,280	2,720	~5,000	0
Prachuap Khiri Khan	475,246	6,913	6,206	~15,000	0
Chumphon	456,218	14,216	13,732	~25,000	0
Ranong	156,681	25,281	25,281	20,000 to 80,000	0
Total	6,708,741	163,225	160,741	280,000 + 465,000	109,662

Sources: Ministry of Public Health (1999); Ministry of Labor and Social Welfare (2001); Ministry of Labor and Social Welfare (2001); Estimates given to WHO Border Health Officer by Health Authorities and International Health Workers in border provinces; UNHCR Thailand, as of 31 January 2002.

migration stream. According to a survey by the Ministry of Labour, irregular migrants (as of October 1997) were predominantly located in the coastal areas of Thailand and in Bangkok (Table 13.4). Nevertheless, the proportion of irregular migrants residing in the Thai-Myanmar border regions was substantial (around 6.6–9.4 per cent), compared to the local population in 2002 (as shown in Table 13.5). Estimates of 465,000 non-registered migrants suggests that the majority of them remained undetected. The state's registration programme was an attempt to discover the actual extent of irregular labour migration from Myanmar, Lao PDR and Cambodia. This was done with the objective of regularising migrant labour (Kasem 2004).

Employment categories

Undocumented workers were mainly hired in the following sectors: agriculture, construction and domestic work, as shown in Table 13.6.

Table 13.6 Registration of irregular migrant labour by sector and nationality according to cabinet resolution of 28 August 2001

Sector allowed	Myanmar	Lao PDR	Cambodia	Total
Farm, orchard work	90,223	5,701	7,414	103,338
Mining	1,305	48	34	1,387
Pottery	3,329	180	39	3,548
Construction	39,856	2,133	5,331	47,320
Rice milling	5,880	129	186	6,195
Husbandry	22,348	3,517	3,748	29,613
Fishery	80,029	2,102	21,244	103,375
Warehouse	9,743	899	3,448	14,090
Domestic service	61,381	16,828	4,180	82,389
Special activities				
With employer	117,350	23,614	9,318	150,282
Without employer	19,891	4,207	2,614	26,712
Total	451,335	59,358	57,556	568,249

Source: Ministry of Labour (2002a).

Table 13.7 Irregular migrant labour with work permit extension between 24 February and 25 March 2002

Sector allowed	Myanmar	Lao PDR	Cambodia	Total
Farm, orchard work	70,054	3,993	4,506	78,553
Mining	1,137	16	9	1,162
Pottery	2,777	160	34	2,971
Construction	31,010	1,389	3,255	35,654
Rice milling	4,572	100	115	4,787
Husbandry	15,915	2,293	2,105	20,313
Fishery	59,592	1,307	15,045	75,944
Warehouse	7,022	655	2,508	10,185
Domestic service	47,536	12,681	3,100	63,317
Special activities	109,649	19,602	7,937	137,188
With employer	99,738	17,551	6,452	123,741
Without employer	9,911	2,051	1,485	13,447
Total	349,264	42,196	38,614	430,074

Source: Ministry of Labour (2002b).

The provision/extension of work permits (whereby illegal migrant workers are allowed to change their status from illegal to legal workers) shows that this category of workers were mainly from Myanmar. The breakdown of migrants with approved extensions by country of origin shows that most of them were from Myanmar (85.81 per cent), followed by Lao PDR (7.38 per cent), and Cambodia (6.81 per cent), as shown in Table 13.7 (Ministry of Labour 2004a).

Clearly, migrant workers form Myanmar dominate this stream and this may be a consequence of geography and political conditions in Myanmar.

Causes and consequences of labour migration into Thailand

Disparities in economic and employment opportunities, income inequality and demographic differences between the source and destination countries are key factors in low-end irregular labour migration to and from Thailand (Phuaphongsakorn 1982; Pongsapich 1986;Thosanguan and Chalamwong 1991; Pongsapich 1994; TDRI 1994; Ratanakomut 2000; Kittisuksathit and Punpuing 2002). Research also indicates that unskilled labour migration into Thailand co-occurs with unskilled Thai labour emigration. Moreover, the conditions facilitating such out-migration have also made Thailand attractive for in-migration of low-end labour. Part of the explanation lies in the emergence of a dual labour market during the 1980s and 1990s, resulting from the Thai state development strategies to transform Thailand from a largely agricultural economy to an industrial economy.

Additionally, income and employment disparities and unemployment in rural areas led to a rural–urban drift. Rural workers either moved into the manufacturing sector or emigrated to work overseas. The latter shift was associated with the oil crisis of the 1970s, the construction boom in the Middle East and the role of private employment agencies in the recruitment of large numbers of temporary contract labour destined for the Middle East. Moreover, this was in keeping with Thailand's fifth National Development Plan (1982–86), whereby labour emigration was seen as a strategy to reduce unemployment; as a source of foreign exchange; and as a factor in reducing the country's trade deficit. Despite rapid economic development in the late 1980s and the 1990s, remittances of migrant workers were still considered a source of household and national income.

Rural unemployment

According to a labour force survey conducted in the early 1990s (National Statistical Office n.d.), employment in the agricultural sector dropped from 79.2 per cent in 1971 to 60.32 per cent in 1991. This contrasted with an increase from 4.1 per cent to 11.1 per cent in the manufacturing sector and a decrease from 14.3 per cent to 12.1 per cent in services during the same period. Moreover, as shown in Table 13.8, employment rates increased at a faster rate than the growth in labour supply.

Concurrently, there was an expansion in labour-intensive industries in the country. The resulting demand for manual, low-wage labour, which would not exercise pressures on the wage structure, provided an impetus to the persistent flows of irregular migrant labour as a substitute for local labour (Thosanguan and Chalamwong 1991; TDRI 1994; Kittisuksathit and Punpuing 2002).

Table 13.8 Thailand: labour force and employment growth rates, 1975–91 (%)

Period	Labour force	Employment
1975–80	4.48	4.38
1980–85	3.59	2.79
1985–90	3.21	3.59
1990–91	1.58	2.08

Source: Labour force survey, National Statistical Office cited in Pongsapich 1994, p. 17.

The majority of the migrant workers were male adults and comprised largely Thai rural migrants and migrants from Myanmar (see Table 13.9). Moreover, younger and slightly better educated Myanmar migrants met the demand for workers in labour-intensive industries. These findings are based on a survey conducted in 1998–99 of Thai rural migrants in Udon Tani and Chayapum and those from Myanmar in Ranong, a province along the Thai–Myanmar border with a high number of migrants engaging in a variety of jobs (Wongboonsin 2001). It was also apparent from the survey that while most rural Thais saw migration as an opportunity to develop new skills, most of the migrants from Myanmar gained other experiences apart from skill development. In Thailand they also had more political and employment security compared to life in Myanmar (Wongboonsin 2001).

Turning to Thai workers, the major reasons for movement to the urban areas or overseas was largely due to the draw of higher incomes, opportunities to improve their skills, and their unskilled status in Thailand. The survey findings also revealed that the migration decisions of migrants from Myanmar were influenced by political and economic pressures in Myanmar, the promise of higher incomes, and the structural demand for low-wage services in the Thai labour market. Kinship and family ties played a role in migration both into and out of Thailand (Wongboonsin 2001).

A study by Chantavanich *et al.* (2000b) on Cambodian migrants in Thailand indicates that higher incomes appear to be the major reason for illegal Cambodian migration into Thailand. Improvement in economic and political development in these countries may lead to a reduction in labour migration from Lao PDR, Cambodia, and Myanmar to Thailand.

Additionally, intermediaries and migration networks played an important role in the outflow of Thai migrants. Migrants from Myanmar and Cambodia, on the other hand, were less reliant on brokers or agents. The latter mostly either migrated with their family or followed the first member of the family who had migrated (Wongboonsin 2001; Chantavanich *et al.*, 2000b). Given the policy shortcomings discussed below, one may expect the role of brokers and agents to increase rather than decrease in the migration process.

Table 13.9   Socio-economic background of migrant labour

Socio-economic background		Thai migrant labour	Myanmar migrant labour in Thailand
Sex	Male	91.7%	87.0%
	Female	8.3%	13.0%
	Total	100.0% (528 migrants)	100.0% (301 migrants)
Age	19 and below	–	12.7%
	20–29	25.9%	50.9%
	30–39	41.5%	27.8%
	40–49	27.6%	22.1%
	50 and above	4.9%	2.7%
	Total	100.0% (528 migrants)	100.0% (299 migrants)
Marital status	Married	87.9%	40.0%
	Separated, Divorced, Widowed	2.8%	5.7%
	Single	9.3%	54.3%
	Total	100.0% (528 migrants)	100.0% (300 migrants)
Education	0–4 Years	52.7%	30.1%
	5–7 Years	30.5%	48.5%
	8–12 Years	16.9%	20.4%
	Higher Education	–	1.0%
	Total	100.0% (528 migrants)	100.0% (299 migrants)
Number of family members	1–4	55.9%	54.9%
	5–9	43.8%	30.2%
	10 and above	0.4%	14.9%
	Total	100% (528 workers)	100% (301 workers)

Source: Wongboonsin (2001).

Management of migrant labour inflows

The management and regulation of labour migration has become a key issue in Thailand. The government's opinion is that immigration levels were too high and emigration levels too low in 2000 compared to the satisfactory levels of 1990, despite the migration stock reaching only 0.6 per cent of the population in Thailand (see Table 13.10).

While Thailand adopted a labour-export policy, and has recently attempted to deal with labour emigration on a proactive basis, the situation is different for labour immigration. Without the implementation of proper policies regulating immigrant labour, the Thai state has to confront issues such as immigration and the employment of migrant labour on an ad hoc basis. Relevant institutional intervention in Thailand may be characterised as follows: incoherent, selective, and impractical measures pertaining to the

Table 13.10   Thai migration indicators, 1990 and 2000

Indicator		1990	2000
Population			
Number (*thousands*)		54,736	62,806
Rate of natural increase per 1,000 population[1]		14.2	13.5
Rate of growth per 1,000 population[1]		14.1	13.4
Migration stock[2]			
Number (*thousands*)		386	353
Per cent of population		0.7	0.6
Refugees[3]			
Number (*thousands*)		99.8	105.0
Per cent of migrant stock		25.8	29.7
Net migration[1]			
Number (*thousands*)		−5	−5
Rate per 1,000 population		−0.1	−0.1
Government positions concerning migration			
Immigration levels	View	Satisfactory	Too high
	Policy	Lower	Lower
Emigration levels	View	Satisfactory	Too low
	Policy	No intervention	Raise

Notes
1. Estimates represent annual averages for 1990–1995 and 1995–2000.
2. Estimated mid-year number of non-citizens with the addition of refugees.
3. Data compiled by UNHCR and refers to the end of the year.

Source: United Nations (2002).

supply-side of labour migration; and a lack of policy relating to irregular migration.

The Immigration Act BE 2522 (1979) does not prohibit employment of migrants, except for those engaged in manual labour. Policy regimes governing the employment of migrants may be viewed under two categories: first, the recruitment of documented migrants at the skilled level and above. These workers are encouraged, but variable standards are applied to regulation. And second, unskilled migrants who are formally prohibited, but tolerated in practice.

These variable standards are applied to laws governing the employment of regular migrants in Thailand. Migration under laws relating to investment promotion, petroleum and industrial settlement are facilitated and awarded with privileges. For others, employment in Thailand is allowed on an 'as and when necessary' basis. According to the Alien Employment Act BE 2521 (1978) and subsequent revisions/additions, rather than relying on labour market demand, or skills criteria, educational background or income, migrant workers are subject to assessment in terms of the contribution to the economy on a discretionary basis. They are also subject to quotas with strict control on the types of professions and jobs or occupations (Laws and Development Research Center 2000). Royal Decrees on Prohibited Professions and Occupations for Aliens BE 2522 (1979), BE 2536 (1993), and BE 2543 (2000) prohibited migrants workers from 39 types of employment ranging from unskilled jobs to professional occupations in all areas of the country. This is shown in Table 13.11.

Table 13.11   Types of employment prohibited from alien engagement in Thailand

Labouring work[1]	Work in agriculture, animal breeding, forestry, fishery (excluding work with specialized skill, specialized work, or farm supervision)[2]	Masonry, carpentry or other construction work	Driving of motor vehicles or non-motorized carriers (except piloting international airplanes)
Hair dressing, beautician work	Thai musical instrument fabrication	Mat weaving or fabrication of wares from reed, rattan, kenaf, straw, or bamboo pulp	Manual fibrous paper making
Shop attendant and window salespersons	Pottery and ceramics making	Goldsmith, silversmith, or other precious metalwork	Bronzeware fabrication
Gem cutting or polishing	Wood carving	Hand weaving	Nielloware fabrication
Lacquerware making	Alms bowl fabrication	Thai character typesetting	Hawking business
Thai doll making	Mattress or padded blanket fabrication	Manual silk reeling and weaving	Manual silk product fabrication
Buddha image making	Knife making	Paper or cloth umbrella fabrication	Shoemaking
Hat making	Cigarette rolling	Dressmaking	Tourist guide or tour agent
Auctioning	Clerical or secretarial work	Legal or litigation services[3]	Architectural work
Brokerage or agent (except international business)	Accounting and auditing (except occasional internal auditing)	Civil engineering (except work requiring specialised skills)	

Notes
1. Changed by Royal Decree on Jobs and Occupations Prohibited from Alien Engagement (2) BE 2536 (1993) to 'Labouring work, except labouring work on fishery carriers'.
2. Changed by Royal Decree on Jobs and Occupations Prohibited from Alien Engagement (2) BE 2536 (1993) to 'Work in agriculture, animal breeding, forestry, fishery, excluding work with specialized skills, specialized work, farm supervision, or labouring work on maritime fishery carriers'.
3. Except for arbitrator, and such services in arbitration under non-Thai laws. The exception is provided by Royal Decree on Jobs and Occupations Prohibited from Alien Engagement (3) BE 2543 (2000).

Source: Unofficial translation by author, based on Royal Decree on Jobs and Occupations Prohibited from Alien Engagement BE 2522 (1978), and Royal Decree on Jobs and Occupations Prohibited from Alien Engagement (2) BE 2536 (1993).

An analysis of the list of jobs denied to migrant workers shows that this prohibition is mainly based on the notion of job security for the local workforce and the preservation of Thai heritage according to the prevailing nationalistic political culture. The regimes governing employment of foreigners do not align with the current employment needs within Thailand. Complicated procedures for work permit renewals result in a number of skilled migrants sidestepping regulatory procedures to work without authorisation in Thailand (Havanon 1997; and Prachusanond *et al.*, 2000). Despite the labour ministry's recognition of the problem, major improvements in regulation need to be made (Prachusanond *et al.*, 2000).

For unskilled and irregular migrants, while state policy prohibits the recruitment of unskilled manual workers, weak enforcement measures explain the persistence of irregular migrant labour flows from neighbouring countries and beyond. The government relies on five ad-hoc measures to deal with temporary migrant labour flows, namely border controls; a series of short-term registration-amnesty measures; information campaigns; anti-trafficking laws; and the repatriation of irregular migrant labour. Registration is the most important among all these measures.

The twelve cabinet resolutions that permitted irregular migrant workers to be employed with a work permit in specified sectors and provinces for a limited period of time between 1992–2002 are listed in Table 13.12.

The measures introduced in 1992 deal with illegal migrants from Myanmar in nine border provinces, as recorded in the Cabinet Order BE 2535 (1992) on The Problem of Undocumented Migrant Labor from Myanmar. The second cabinet resolution (1993) expanded the scope of coverage to include migrant labour from Myanmar, Lao PDR, and Cambodia in 22 coastal provinces and fisheries. The 1996 cabinet resolution allowed the employment of irregular migrant labour from the three sources listed above in 8 industries in 43 provinces. In 1997 and January 1998, massive crackdowns were implemented aimed at removing up to 600,000 irregular migrants. Meanwhile, entrepreneurs along the borders were encouraged to employ locals instead of irregular migrant workers. This was in response to rising unemployment among Thais as a consequence of the 1997 economic crisis. The April 1998 resolution was based on the pre-crisis approach, and incorporated border commuters into the regularisation process, expanding the spatial coverage to 54 provinces. There was a retreat from this policy in 1999 when only 18 sectors in 37 provinces were regularised and the 2001 cabinet resolution encouraged irregular migrant labour in all provinces to register with an unlimited number of work permits in ten sectors. The latter also included 'special activities' deemed relevant, which reflected an even wider job coverage than previously. The 2002 cabinet resolution referred to in Table 13.12 maintained most of the earlier regulations while extending periods for registration and work permit renewal.

Table 13.12 Thai cabinet resolutions on irregular migrant labour, 1992–2002

Date of resolution	Migrants covered	Decisions	Requirements	Remarks
17 March 1992	From Myanmar	10 border provinces allowed	Bt 5,000 bond; Bt 1,000 fee	706 migrants registered but 101,845 purple cards issued
22 June 1993	From Laos Cambodia and Myanmar	22 coastal provinces and fisheries allowed		Not implemented in fisheries until 1979 law amended
25 June 1996	From Laos Cambodia and Myanmar	39 (later 43)provinces and 7(later 11) industries allowed	Bt 1,000 bond; Bt 1,000 fee; Bt 500 health fee	2-year work permits for those register from 1 Sept–29 Nov. 1996; 372,000 registered and 303,988 permits granted
29 July 1997	From Laos Cambodia and Myanmar	Improve border and interior enforcement; Remove 300,000 migrants in 1997	provincial committees to deal with migrants; factories in Thai border areas encouraged to hire locals	
19 Jan. 1998	From Laos Cambodia and Myanmar	Improve border and interior enforcement; Remove another 300,000 in 1998		
28 April 1998 8 May 1998	From Laos Cambodia and Myanmar	54 provinces and 47 jobs allowed; border commuters allowed; extension of work permits from Aug. 1998 to Aug. 1999	Bt 1,000 bond; Bt 700 medical exam. Fee; Bt 500–1,200 provincial health fee	Maximum 158,000 but 90,911 registered
3 Aug. 1999 2 Nov. 1999	From Laos Cambodia and Myanmar	37 provinces and 18 sectors in 5 industries allowed	Bt 1,000 bond; Bt 700 medical exam. Fee; Bt 1,000 health card	Max 106,000 one year work permits to expire 31 Aug. 2000; 99,974 registered

29 Aug. 1999	From Laos Cambodia and Myanmar	37 provinces and 18 sectors allowed		Allowed 106,684 migrants to in 18 sectors and 37 provinces to work until 31 Aug. 2001
28 Aug. 2001	From Laos Cambodia and Myanmar	Wider business types entitled for registration. The migrant workers who registered and got certificates entitled to medical treatments under the health insurance scheme of the Thai government. The Ministry of Labor is the sole body responsible for registration.	Registration: Bt 3,250 Fee per worker (including Bt 1,000 bond; Bt 1,200 health insurance premium; Bt 900 fee; Bt 150 ID card). Medical exam. 6 months after registration with Bt 300 fee for check up and Bt 900 fee per worker	568,249 registered (80% Myanmar; 10% Laotian; 10% Cambodian) Bangkok ranked highest (109,099 migrant workers registered). Patalung in the South ranked the lowest (52 migrant workers registered).
27 Aug., 25 Sept. and 1 Oct. 2002	From Laos Cambodia and Myanmar	Extended periods for registration and work permit renewal; re-categorising sectors; changing employers allowed; illegal crews in fishery sector registered; upgrade of role of MOPH in medical exam. And birth control	Maintaining the 2001 Resolution	Work permit renewal after six months: 430,074 worker; after one year: 353,274 workers; Mostly in fishery (77,577 workers) followed by general labour (70,005 workers)

Source: Compiled by author, based on various Ministerial Orders, 1992–2002.

In 2003 the Department of Employment Regulation on Criteria and Conditions for Alien Employment Authorisation BE 2545 was issued. Article 6 (10) allows foreign workers (without the imposition of quotas) to carry out jobs performed by local labour in cases of local labour shortages. Nevertheless, such an authorisation is only on an 'as and when necessary' basis.

In 2004 a new labour migrant management regulation was implemented with a registration process scheduled for a one-month period beginning on 1 July. This allowed migrant workers from three source countries (Myanmar, Cambodia and Laos) to register for a one-year work pass, which allowed the pass-holder to work or to seek employment for a year. Those who qualified for temporary work passes had their details sent to the relevant embassy in Bangkok for review before receiving an official work permit during the period 22 August–15 November 2004. The official work permit is for a two-year term and may be renewed once. A total fee of Thai Baht 3800 was required to complete the process. Regularised migrant workers are also allowed to change employers, while registered employers are entitled to replacement labour all year round. Deportation rules apply if the migrant workers could not find employment within a year (Ministry of Labour 2004b). Thailand expected around 800,000 migrants to register in 2004. As of July 18, roughly 560,000 migrants had registered for work permits (Chann 2004a, 2004b).

Two general observations can be drawn from the above. First, the registration-amnesty measures applied only to a limited number of target groups   those from Myanmar, Lao PDR, and Cambodia. Second, there is an expanding range of jobs and spatial coverage encompassed by the regularisation process. In official terms, the registration and amnesty measures included these four aspects of migration management: to discern the size of irregular labour migration; to control its magnitude and whereabouts; to register workers in demand so as to obtain temporary work permits for those otherwise awaiting repatriation in provinces where there was a labour shortage; and to repatriate superfluous irregular migrant labour.

None of these aims have been achieved in full. The real magnitude of irregular labour migration is still unknown. All registration drives achieved low responses. As shown in Tables 13.4 and 13.12, only 706 migrants joined the registration drive for Myanmar migrants in 1992. In 1996, of an estimated 741,999 migrants from Myanmar, Lao PDR and Cambodia, there were 282,511 registered workers. In 2002, of the targeted two million migrants, there were 568,249 registered migrant workers from those three sources.

Rather than controlling the magnitude and ascertaining the whereabouts of irregular migrant labour, the registration-amnesty schemes unintentionally spread irregular migrant labour flows from the border areas to the rest of the country. This has been the case since the first two resolutions were initiated. Moreover, the registration schemes unintentionally became a magnet to new flows of irregular low-end migrant labour before effective enforcement was introduced (Chann 2004a, 2004b; Charoensuthiphan 2004; Charoensuthiphan and Phanayanggoor 2004).

Labour regulation and its shortcomings

The poor responses to the registration drives were reportedly due to complicated procedures and high fees set in order to placate government agencies which were opposed to the registration drive (ARCM 2000, 2001; Chann 2004a, 2004b; Charoensutthipan 2004; Charoensutthipan and Phanayanggoor 2004). As suggested in Table 13.12, registration costs were reduced from a TB 5000 bond in 1992 to a registration fee of TB 4450 for a one-year permit covering annual health insurance, work permits, and repatriation guarantees in 2001, and then to a total of TB 3800 in 2004.

Couettee and Pack (2002) nevertheless maintain that employers prefer to continue hiring irregular migrant labour by bribing local officials. This is confirmed in a study based on interviews with migrants employed in a textile and garment workers in the Mae Sot district in northern Thailand. Employers in these industries who did not want to register their migrant labour asked them to leave during the registration period, and return after the registration period was completed (Kittisuksathit and Punpuing 2002).

Complicated procedures and high fees were also said to encourage job brokers and other intermediaries from extorting money from irregular migrant workers (Chann 2004a, 2004b). These reportedly included: TB 2000 for the broker to falsely represent themselves to be an employer; TB 1000–3000 to transport workers for registration with local authorities; and a payment to owners of rented houses and flats of TB 1200 in order to make accommodation arrangements appear 'legal' (Charoensuthiphan 2004; Charoensuthiphan and Phanayanggoor 2004). The Thai Farmers Research Center (2001) maintains that there were a large number of persons and businesses reaping profits from irregular migrant labour both directly and indirectly. The registration-amnesty scheme appeased some segments of the business community. It was also described as a series of employer-initiated measures to defer the planned removal of migrants (Broadmoor 2001).

It is my contention that flaws in the policy were due to ad hoc measures. This problem was particularly pronounced during the early 1990s and during the 1997–98 economic crisis. Relevant policies and border regimes introduced during the said periods were more in response to socio-political security concerns, misgivings about the real demand for migrant labour and threats of nationwide strikes (NESDB 1997; UN 1998; P. Wongboonsin 2000;

Ministry of Public Health 2003). The latter concern was particularly expressed by the Thai Labour Congress, whose members feared that the employment of migrant labour would result in hundreds of thousands of Thai workers losing their jobs, and would also lead to social problems (UN 1998). At other times, the Labour Congress was more responsive to calls from the private sector for business survival and Thailand maintaining its international comparative advantage.

The dilemma was also due to the convoluted regulation system and insufficient knowledge of factors impacting on migrant labour flows, particularly in terms of the real demand and supply of migrant workers; the role of employers, brokers, and other migration infrastructures; the real cost and benefits of labour migration; and the strengths and weaknesses of existing mechanisms. This also helps explain the reasons for irregular migration flows.

In Thailand the perception of a culture in policy making exists wherein decisions are based upon visions of high-ranking officials rather than on detailed research on labour supply. Despite the fact that such a culture is under transformation, there is a lack of systematic links between research and policy-making units (Kanchai and Yee 2002). This is particularly the case for non-commissioned research. Despite the fact that databases are compiled by relevant agencies, these are difficult to access and review. As a result, they are not appropriately utilised for management and policy purposes (Archavanitkul 1998).

Moreover, Thailand has problems with striking a balance between three perceptions: national social and political security based on nationalistic fervour; economic 'security' based on a neo-liberal attitude towards international comparative advantage and competitiveness; and human rights and labour protection based on humanitarianism. Thailand also maintains complicated legislative and regulatory regimes governing the entry and stay of foreign nationals. This position partly reflects the more than 20 Acts, Royal Decrees, Ministerial Orders, and Regulations governing the entry and stay of migrant workers in Thailand.

Towards a demand-side and successful development-based approach

At the turn of the twenty-first century, control-based management strategies of the supply-side approach of labour migration were shown to be self-defeating. Both migrant labour and the Thai economy have been 'damaged'. Thailand has failed to control irregular labour migration and the economy is in danger of losing its competitive advantage internationally. The negative effects are expected to linger for some years to come. Moreover, recent research findings have shown that irregular migrant workers did not take jobs away from the local workforce (IAS, TDRI 2003). The prevalence of unskilled and semi-skilled labour irregular migrant labour has resulted in the private sector's hesitation to invest in more skilled and productive human resources. As a result, exploitation of migrant labour continues whilst the development of their skills is relegated to the background.

The shortcomings of existing institutional intervention limit the opportunity for Thailand to capitalise on its demographic advantage to move towards a value-added and competitive industry based on managerial expertise and higher technical skills. According to K. Wongboonsin (2003) Thailand has an opportunity to benefit from a 'demographic dividend' of better economic performance and a higher standard of living. A demographic transition has taken place in Thailand with an increasing proportion of the population in the labour force age bracket (15–59), from 55.64 per cent in 1980 to 61.68 per cent and 65.92 per cent in 1990 and 2000, respectively. One may expect this demographic dividend to provide a sustained period of economic well-being and a higher standard of living in Thailand. However, this projection is based on demographic assumptions without taking other key factors into consideration. Chief among these factors is the productivity of the labour force.

The demographic dividend in Thailand may even fade in the near future. Labour force participation is predicted to increase to a maximum of 67.08 per cent in 2009, then decline to 62.05 per cent in 2025. Thereafter, Thailand will be facing an increasing old-age dependency ratio (K. Wongboonsin and P. Wongboonsin 2004a).

Given such a significant change in demographic structure and the current restructuring of the Thai economy to compete effectively in the knowledge-based economy, the demand for labour needs to be geared towards skills-based competitiveness. Migration management in Thailand needs to shift from the supply side to the demand side in a development-based approach that would lead migrants, returnees and other local labour, as well as the Thai economy into sustained growth (K. Wongboonsin and K. Wongboonsin 2004b).

This can partly be facilitated by new developments during 2003–04 to integrate returnees into better skilled job segments within Thailand, and to add a bilateral approach to unilateral migration management for an orderly flow of labour migration from neighbouring countries. A recent Memorandum of Understanding on cooperation in labour employment between the Ministry of Labour and Lao PDR, Cambodia, and Myanmar strengthens a new initiative to encourage economic cooperation amongst the three neighbouring countries. The opportunities are endless for the Thai state and its neighbours.

Appendix

Table 13.A1 Documented migrants in promoted establishment category by nationality and occupation as on 25 December 2003

Occupations	Total	Japanese	British	Indian	Chinese	American	Taiwanese	Filipino	Australian	Malaysian	Others
Executive, managerial	10,893	5,422	410	545	651	468	1,031	145	241	243	1,437
Professionals	1,834	874	87	115	165	124	61	96	37	45	1,437
Technical	2,464	1,083	70	162	489	60	169	52	32	53	236
Clerical	364	114	6	10	22	11	19	15	15	12	124
Service and sales	90	23	6	2	5	4	1	–	9	2	38
Skilled in agricultural and fishery sector	4	–	–	–	–	1	2	–	–	–	1
Skilled, other sectors	697	235	30	68	139	16	57	21	9	12	92
Plant/Machine operators and assemblers	359	80	36	8	70	35	70	31	23	5	9
Trainees	8	5	–	–	1	–	–	–	1	–	1
Others	2,615	818	157	264	214	131	403	57	69	41	419
Total	19,328	8,654	802	1,174	1,756	850	1,759	417	436	413	2,596

Note: Excludes 14,423 aliens working in Thailand before 13 December 1972 and granted with a permanent work permit; 2003 data are those as of 25 December 2003.

Source: Ministry of Labour (2004d).

Table 13.A2 Documented migrants in non-promoted category by nationality and occupation as on 25 December 2003

Occupations	Total	Japanese	British	Indian	Chinese	American	Taiwanese	Filipino	Australian	German	Korean	Others
Executive, managerial	42,438	11,134	3,041	4,363	3,168	1,941	3,039	579	1,256	1,387	1,097	12,530
Professionals	14,221	1,881	2,279	627	705	2,214	170	1,673	747	299	367	3,626
Technical	5,292	1,448	317	284	845	216	293	278	101	136	40	1,374
Clerical	839	226	23	33	53	28	29	35	25	23	16	364
Service and sales	3,403	208	34	106	259	28	62	18	25	44	54	2,619
Skilled in agricultural and fishery sector	1,834	1	1	1	14	4	6	1	2			1,804
Skilled, other sectors	2,160	270	47	85	245	21	85	34	22	19	9	1,332
Plant/Machine operators and assemblers	875	119	45	18	123	40	30	38	24	13	3	425
Trainees	153	26	5	1	27	1	1	5	1	15		71
Others	14,990	1,425	424	399	569	334	530	158	196	169	24	10,786
Total	86,205	16,738	6,216	5,917	6,008	4,827	4,245	2,819	2,399	2,105	1,611	34,931

Note: Excludes 14,423 aliens working in Thailand before 13 December 1972 and granted with a permanent work permit; 2003 data are those as of 25 December 2003.

Source: Ministry of Labour (2004e).

Table 13.A3 Regular migrants under section 12 of the Alien Employment Act by Nationalities and Occupations as on 25 December 2003

Occupations	Total	Tai Yai tribe	Tai Loe tribe	Karen tribe	Mon tribe	Myanmar	Illegal Myanmar migrants (permanent)	Chinese	Independent Chinese ho (from Yunnan)	Eko tribe	Vietnam	Others
Executive, managerial	158	31	17	1	1	18	1	6	13	–	55	15
Technical	17	1	–	2	–	2	–	2	–	–	–	10
Clerical	284	3	–	104	43	92	–	2	2	–	–	38
Service and sales	24	2	–	1	–	–	–	7	7	1	–	6
Skilled in agricultural and fishery sector	2,192	454	112	32	16	571	22	119	242	55	100	469
Skilled, other sectors	1,804	622	72	96	95	702	10	10	12	31	7	146
Plant/Machine operators and assemblers	1,103	238	56	59	179	303	11	20	31	22	28	156
Trainees	336	18	6	110	47	303	–	5	6	9	12	42
Others	–	–	–	–	–	–	–	–	–	–	–	–
Total	9,864	3,411	607	573	351	2,298	373	205	340	238	55	1,401

Note: Excludes 14,423 aliens working in Thailand before 13 December 1972 and granted with a permanent work permit; 2003 data are those as of 25 December 2003.

Source: Ministry of Labour (2004f).

References

Archavanitkul, K. (1998) 'International Population and Policy Options for Importation of Foreign Labour into Thailand'. Paper presented at the Regional Workshop on Transnational Migration and Development in ASEAN Countries organised by Institute for Population and Social Research (IPSR), Mahidol University, May 25–27, Thailand.

Asian Research Center for Migration (ARCM) (2001) 'Alien Labour Policy and Solutions in the Short (2001) and Long Terms'. Unpublished Research Report submitted to Ministry of Labour and Social Welfare, Bangkok, June.

—— (2000) 'Labour Shortages in Thailand: 2000'. Unpublished Research Report submitted to Ministry of Labour and Social Welfare, Bangkok, July.

Atipas, P. (1999) 'Thai Workers in Singapore'. Paper presented at the International Workshop on Thai Migrant Workers in South-east and East Asia, organised by Asian Research Center for Migration, Institute of Asian Studies, Chulalongkorn University, Bangkok, 18–20 November.

Broadmoor, T. (2001) 'Labour Pains', *Irrawaddy*, Vol. 9, No. 7, Aug–Sep., p. 1.

Chalamwong, Y. (2001) 'Recent Trends in Migration Flows and Policies in Thailand', in paper presented at OECD Conference on *International Migration in Asia: Trends and Policies* (Paris: OECD).

Chann, N. (2004a) 'Migrants Sidestep Crackdown to Register to Work', *Irrawaddy*, 17 June.

—— (2004b) 'Restrictions Eased for Migrant Workers in Thailand', *Irrawaddy*, 21 July.

Chantavanich, S., A. Germershausen and A. Beesey (eds) (2000a) *Thai Migrant Workers in East and Southeast Asia 1996–1997*, Asian Research Center for Migration (ARCM), Institute of Asian Studies (Chulalongkorn University, Bangkok: Chulalongkorn University Printing House).

Chantavanich, S., Bessey, Amaraphibal, P., Suwanachat, P., and Wangsiripaisal, P. Shakti (2000b) *Cross-border Migration and HIV/AIDS Vulnerability at the Thai-Cambodia Border, Aranyaprathet and Khlong Yai*, Report submitted to WHO Thailand by Asian Research Center for Migration, Institute of Asian Studies (Chulalongkorn University, Bangkok: Seven Press and Promotion, Co. Ltd).

Charoensuthiphan, P. (2004) 'Illegal Labour Registration: Door Opens Again for Extortion Racket', *Bangkok Post*, 7 July.

Charoensuthiphan, P. and P. Phanayanggoor (2004) 'Registration of Alien Workers Starts Today', *Bangkok Post*, 1 July.

Couettee, T. M. and M. E. Pack (2002) 'Pushing Past the Definitions: Migration from Burma to Thailand', www.soros.org/publications/burma/thai.html.

Havanon, N. (1997) *Illegal Practice of Side Stepping Regulations on Employment of Skilled Foreign Workers* (Nakhonpathom, Institute for Population and Social Research, Mahidol University [in Thai]).

Immigration Bureau (1994) *Annual Report 1993*, Ministry of Interior (in Thai).

Institute of Asian Studies (IAS), Chulalongkorn University, Thailand Development Research Institute, and the Institute for Population and Social Research, Mahidol University (2003) 'A Study on the Demand for Hiring Foreign Labor in Thailand during 2003–2005'. A draft research report for submission to the National Security Council, September (in Thai).

Ito, C. (1999) 'Interviews with key informants on Thai migrant workers in Japan'. Paper presented at the International Workshop on Thai Migrant Workers in South-east and East Asia, organised by Asian Research Center for Migration, Institute of Asian Studies, Chulalongkorn University, Bangkok, 18–20 November.

Kanchai, S. and Yee May Kaung (2002) *Migration Research and Migration Policy Making: A Case Study of Thailand*. Asian Research Center for Migration, Institute of Asian Studies (Chulalongkorn University, Bangkok: Chulalongkorn University Printing House).

Kasem, S. (2004) 'Illegal Labour Up to 2 Million Aliens Targeted', *Bangkok Post*, 9 July.

Kittsuksathit, S. and S. Punpuing (2002) 'Improving Migration Policy Management With Special Focus on Irregular Migration: A Case Study of Textile and Garment', Institute for Population and Social Research, Mahidol University (Unpublished paper).

Lee, J. S. (1998) 'The Impact of the Asian Financial Crisis on Foreign Workers in Taiwan', *Asian and Pacific Migration Journal*, Vol. 7, Nos. 2–3: 145–70.

Ministry of Public Health (2003) *Alien Labour and the Public Health in FY2002* (Bangkok: Samcharoenpanich [Bangkok] Co. Ltd. [in Thai]).

—— (1999) *Annual Epidemiological Surveillance Report* (Division of Epidemiology, Office of the Permanent Secretary [in Thai]).

Ministry of Labour (2004a) "Discussions in 'News Talk', Broadcast via UBC19 on 26 April 2004," Department of Foreign Workers Administration (in Thai).

—— (2004b) 'Alien Labour Management 2004', Department of Foreign Workers Administration RNG0307 June (in Thai).

—— (2004c) 'Foreign Workers in Thailand', Office of Foreign Workers Administration in www.doe.go.th/workpermit/data/remain_oin46/remainterm_m12/htm.

—— (2004d) 'Foreign Workers in Promoted Establishment Category in Thailand', Office of Foreign Workers Administration in www.doe.go.th/workpermit/data/remain_oin46/remainpro_m12/htm (in Thai).

—— (2004e) 'Foreign Workers in Non-Promoted Category in Thailand', Office of Foreign Workers Administration in www.doe.go.th/workpermit/data/remain_oin46/remaintem_m12/htm (in Thai).

—— (2004f) 'Alien Workers Under Section 12 in Thailand', Office of Foreign Workers Administration in www.doe.go.th/workpermit/data/remain_oin46/remainmt12_m12/htm (in Thai).

—— (2003) 'Number of Migrant Workers', in www.doe.go.th/Workpermit/data/remain/kddec2546.htm (in Thai).

—— (2002a) 'Registration of Irregular Migrant Labour by Sector and Nationality According to Cabinet Resolution on August 28, 2001', Alien Registration, Office of Administration Commission on Irregular Immigrant Workers, 24 December (in Thai).

—— (2002b) 'Irregular Immigrant Workers with Work Permit Extension', Alien Registration, Office of Administration Commission on Irregular Immigrant Workers, 24 December (in Thai).

Ministry of Labour and Social Welfare (2001) 'Registered Immigrant Workers', Office of Administration Commission on Irregular Immigrant Workers (unpublished, in Thai).

—— (1989) 'Registered Immigrant Workers', Office of Administration Commission on Irregular Immigrant Workers (unpublished in Thai).

—— (1997) 'Survey of Irregular Migrants in Thailand'. Department of Employment. In www.thaieconwatch.com/articles/m98_2/m98_2_t7.htm (in Thai).

NESDB (1997) 'Problems of Labour Migration in Thailand', *Thai Society 1996*, National Economic and Social Development Board, Bangkok (in Thai).

National Statistical Office (n.d.), *Labour Force Survey (Various Years)* (Bangkok: National Statistical Office, Office of the Prime Minister [in Thai]).

Park, Y. B. (1998) 'The Financial Crisis and Foreign Workers in Korea', *Asian and Pacific Migration Journal*, Vol. 7, Nos. 2–3: 219–34.

Pongsapich, A. (1994) 'International Migrant Workers in Asia: The Case of Thailand'. Paper presented at the International Conference on Transnational Migration in the Asia-Pacific Region: Problems and Prospects, 1–2 December, Bangkok.

Phuaphongsakorn, N. (1982) 'Thai Migrant Workers in Foreign Countries: Causes, Impacts, Problems and Politics', Document for the 11th Workshop of NIEO held on 27 April, Bangkok, Thammasat University.

—— (1986) *Migrant Workers to the Arab World – Thailand*, A report submitted to the United Nations University (Bangkok: Chulalongkorn University Social Research Institute).

Pongsapich, A. (1994) 'International Migrant Workers in Asia: The Case of Thailand'. Paper presented at the International Conference on Transnational Migration in the Asia-Pacific Region: Problems and Prospects, 1–2 December, Bangkok.

Prachusanond, C., S. Tanitkul, and P. Wongboonsin (2000) *Comparative Study of Laws Governing Alien Employment in Thailand and Other Countries for Future Development.* A report submitted to Department of Employment, Ministry of Labour and Social Welfare (Bangkok: Laws and Development Research Center, Faculty of Laws, Chulalongkorn University [in Thai]).

Ratanakomut, S. (2000) 'Issues of International Migration in Thailand', in S. Chantavanich, A. Germershausen and A. Beesey (eds) *Thai Migrant Workers in East and Southeast Asia 1996–1997* (Bangkok: Chulalongkorn University Printing House).

Stern, A. (1998) *Thailand's Migration Situation and its Relations with APEC Members and Other Countries in Southeast Asia*, Asian Research Center for Migration (ARCM), Institute of Asian Studies, No. 11 (Jan.).

Sussangkarn, C. (1995) 'Labour Market Adjustments and Migration in Thailand', *ASEAN Economic Bulletin*, Vol. 12, No. 2.

Thailand Development Research Institute (TDR) (1994) 'The Thai Economy: First Step in a New Direction', Macroeconomic Policy Program (Mimeo).

Thai Farmers Research Center (2001) 'Executive Summary: 2001's Alien Labor Registration Generates More than Bt3 Billion', www.trfc.co.th.

Thosanguan, V. and Y. Chalamwong (1991) 'International Migration and Its Transformation in the Industrialization Process of Thailand'. Paper presented at the Second Japan-ASEAN Forum on International Labour Migration in East Asia organised by the United Nations University, Tokyo, 26–27 September.

United Nations (1998) *International Migration Policies*, Department of Economic and Social Affairs, Population Division ST/ESA/SER.A/161 (New York: United Nations). www.un.org/esa/population/publications/ittmig2002/locations/764.htm

Watanabe, S. (1998) 'The Economic Crisis and Migrant Workers in Japan', *Asian and Pacific Migration Journal*, Vol. 7, Nos. 2–3: 235–54.

Wongboonsin, K. and P. Wongboonsin (2004a) 'Modern Population Trends and the Family.' Paper presented at the Asia Pacific Family Dialogue, 11–13 October, Kuala Lumpur.

—— (2004b) 'To Enhance International Competitiveness via Labour Repositioning from the Middle and Low Levels', *Journal of Demography*, Vol. 20, No. 1: 15–38 (in Thai).

Wongboonsin, K. (2003) *Demographic Dividend Rendered by Demographic Transition in Thailand* (Monograph Series 295, College of Population Studies, Chulalongkorn University, Bangkok, Chulalongkorn University Printing House).

Wongboonsin, P. (2001) 'Transnational Migration', in P. Wongboonsin, V. Prachuabmoh, N. Chongwatana, S. Vibulset and M. Nokyungtong, *Research Report on the Impact of Migration on Transnational Labor Migrants: The Case of Thailand*, College of Population Studies in cooperation with Institute of Asian Studies, Chulalongkorn University, Bangkok, Chulalongkorn University Printing House (in Thai).

—— (2000) 'Impact of Economic Crisis on ASEAN Labour Migration', *Journal of Demography*, Vol. 16, No. 1: 25–58 (in Thai).

14
The State and Facilitation of Financial Flows (Remittances) by Temporary Workers: The Case of Bangladesh

Kenneth Jackson

This chapter focuses on the impact of remittances on development and examines the experience of Bangladesh as a case study. Bangladesh is one of the few significant Asian recipients of remittance flows reflecting a long history of Bangladeshis looking to overseas for employment opportunities. Remittances represent an important source of funds for development in this case and in the eyes of recipients it is considered to be the 'best form of aid' possible, in that it is spent in the ways they determine to be in their own best interests. From a market driven perspective it can be hypothesised that such a decision-making process is likely to be more allocatively efficient than either official or Non-governmental Organisation (NGO)-sourced Aid finance, since the decisions and expenditure are all undertaken locally by the consumers directly.

Introduction

A survey of some of the vast literature on the topic of migration and remittances shows that a large number of studies have increasingly become focused on the impact of short-term international migration and the counter flow of remittances generated which in turn may be viewed as equivalent to a payments stream derived from the export of labour services. Such income streams are critical for the balance of payments of many developing countries, with the movement of labour seen as a key opportunity for many people in a globalised world, where direct foreign investment has often meant little in the way of expanded employment opportunities. Many developing economies have also found they face continuing obstacles to the full realisation of their anticipated returns from improved market access and tariff reductions for their goods and services expected to result from trade liberalisation. Opposition to labour movement in the receiving countries is a fundamental problem for those seeking employment opportunities. Migrant labour is often needed for work nationals will not perform, because of its danger, dirty nature or other reasons. Temporary permits and other expedient devices are common ways to ensure a supply of services, but with no long-term settlement rights being granted. Migrants are clearly needed in this respect, but equally clearly are not wanted as permanent migrants.

The literature

There is a an old established tradition of a literature related to development through macro-economic variables in general and export growth specifically, not least in the staple approach of Canada as exemplified in the work of Harold Innis (1995) and others, some of whom included labour as representing a major staple for many developing countries. The aim was to demonstrate the importance of labour as an abundant factor, in contrast to the scarcity of capital. As a derivative of the 'vent for surplus' approach to development through export growth, the approach looked at abundant labour surplus as a resource. There are still features of the 'vent for surplus' approach in the studies of migrant labour in the present era. Migration did not feature in the staple approach, however, a fact that prompted Noel Butlin (1964:138–58) to effectively dismiss it as a really effective tool in analysing development. Others, besides the users of the staple approach, look at labour demand and explanations for fluctuations in it and its impact upon development. Thirlwall provides a concise description of some of the how and why of labour input fluctuations, balance of payments constraints and export-led growth (Thirlwall 2003:648–9).

The use of labour surplus as a staple in analysing development resulted in much research and publishing in the 1960s and 1970s and initially was concentrated on the so-called regions of recent settlement. General problems with the staple approach, its static rather than dynamic nature included, left it in something of a blind alley of description rather than analysis, despite the best efforts of many such as Caves (1965), to instil some theoretical rigour to the case. Despite trenchant criticism, adherents of this form of analysis continue to develop it today. Morris Altman's recent article gives not only a background to the theory, but develops it further for analytical purposes (Altman 2003). Bangladesh is heavily reliant upon remittance income, which may be viewed as receipts for the export of labour as a staple product.

Regardless of the explanatory power or lack of it, in the staple approach many countries, not just Bangladesh, have in their past and still now been reliant upon the attractions of cheap labour to bring in a considerable inflow of overseas direct investment and look to this to produce a boost to employment and the importation of new and innovative technology. This has not, however, always been either welcomed or successful, especially in generating employment. There is a tendency for new low-cost areas to always be sought out by investors driving all down to the least cost. This is reflected in current interest in Eastern Europe as a cheap labour source, since it is one that is blessed with high levels of human capital, meaning low labour unit costs. This distinguishes it from the usual concentration on just low-wage rates per se. Most usually it is these raw wage costs that attract the attention of the opponents of shifts of production to low-cost areas. Similarly the raw wage levels are often looked at when examining conditions in the migration source countries such as Bangladesh. Opposition to movement from such countries means the emigrant labour is also not wanted in the destination countries.

Growth in opposition to international migration has occurred simultaneously with the growth in numbers of 'economic' migrants globally. The list of freely welcoming receiving countries is now probably somewhat smaller than in the past. Australia, the United States and New Zealand are generally listed as part of a small group that will accept migrants with some and varying degrees of welcome. There is some economic justification for this stand of the developed North, along the lines of the arguments developed by Wood (1994, 1995) amongst others. Movement of jobs to developing countries or migration of labour from there tends to boost global welfare, but may well represent a net loss to the developed world's labour force. For this reason opposition to migration does not always result in development assistance to provide employment in the source countries.

The inflow of migrants represents an increase in the labour supply in the receiving country and imposes downward pressure on wage levels, reinforcing feelings of their not being wanted amongst the national labour force. Equity and other issues run counter to this, by suggesting that from the developing country perspective there is a net gain, both to the individuals themselves and to the society they come from. The distinction has been made in the literature that migration of labour represents a movement of both the factor and the income stream, whereas with capital the factor moves country, but the income stream remains as before (Foreman Peck 1983:50). With remittances this distinction is at least blurred if not rendered invalid. The factor moves, but only some of the income stream does, some of it is returned to the country of origin, through both official and unofficial channels. It is the length of time over which such remittance flows are maintained and the level of those flows that then become important in terms of their impact on development.

Much as the analysis of Wood has met criticism, including that the biggest impacts come not from the developing on the developed, but within the developed group itself, the reality is that perceptions of such damage from Least Developed Countries' (LDC) labour, however small, result in political movements and actions that are deleterious to the developing world. The developing country migrants are shown as the scapegoats in this exercise regardless of how great an impact they may have in reality. The accuracy and the exactness of Wood's findings are less important than the power of the rhetoric the process has prompted. The more general critique is that the focus on imports from cheaper countries and immigrants from lower wage countries has switched attention away from the positives of openness when looked at from an export position. One Australian study has found positive labour market outcomes for workers in the national economy from export growth, with exporting firms paying their workers some 60 per cent higher wages than non-exporters, allowing for size and sector variations (Harcourt 2000).

If openness is good for the North then it should be equally good for the South and there should be no restriction on goods and services trade or migration. If Wood is correct and there are particular groups in the North who lose out, then the concentration should be on the issues of equity and fairness and how to compensate losers rather than restriction, protection and continuing impoverishment for all.

Equity and fairness also come into the picture with respect to internal versus external migration. Adams's study of Pakistan started from the general finding of several investigations that internal migration led to a reduction in income inequality whilst the opposite was true of overseas migration (Adams 1996:149–50). External migration was held to have a positive effect, however, on rural development since it was richer groups who were believed to migrate externally. Richer rural households invest their extra income, including that from remittances, into assets including land and livestock holdings. Internal migration and remittance flows were thought to accrue predominantly to the lower income groups (Adams 1996:165–6). Thus the idea that external migration is simply an extension of rural to urban internal migration and will result in similar outcomes is considered somewhat fallacious. Internal migration, however, may well meet less opposition than international migration, although underneath it is no more welcomed in receiving areas, by those whose jobs may be under threat.

Some of the drivers underlying both internal and international movement may be expected to exhibit similarities, even though there may be differences in outcomes between them. Models of a Harris-Todaro (1970) type, which focused on differentials in expected earnings, have some validity in terms of the underlying motivation for movement, but in cases such as Bangladesh it may be the chance of any employment, rather than the disguised unemployment of the family farm, that drives the movement. In Pakistan, and elsewhere in South Asia, it can be suggested that the contribution of remittance flows has been marked in terms of encouraging economic growth. Impacts on the sending countries' unskilled labour markets have sometimes been quite small, if not negligible, whilst having major impacts on the markets for the skilled and on occasion have been successful in opening up opportunities for women to enter the labour force (Knerr 1996:203). All of these aspects can impact on financial flows and have significant social implications, whether desirable or not.

The reverse flow mechanism of urban–rural migration is less in the case of international migration. This paper looks at some of the impacts in a more positive way than is taken in some of the Migration, Remittances and Bureaucracy (MIRAB) model approaches, derived from such work as that of Bertram and Watters on Pacific Island States (1985), which suggested dependence on overseas remittances and foreign aid was only fine as long as the rents kept coming. Other interpretations suggest this is no way to develop. Here remittances are seen, as acceptable and in a positive light, they reflect a return for the export of labour services and are a reflection of an open and dynamic economy rather than a dependent one. In effect the underlying concept of the staple approach is there, although more is suggested for analysis than just the staple approach. In keeping with a macro-level approach, the micro foundations of the underlying reasons for migration are largely omitted.

Bangladesh: the state, migration strategies and migrant labour flows

Bangladesh has been said to be in danger of too great a dependence on foreign assistance in the form of foreign aid and the unreliability, or unsustainability, of that source of funding, reflecting some of the fears of the MIRAB studies approach. Fluctuations in the overall level of funding as the result of political or other changes are always present. Similar concerns are evident with respect to remittance flows. The overall suggestion is that this is a valuable, but risky, route to take in seeking funds. Barriers to migration can change and consequently impair the flow of funds. The events of 11 September 2001 have resulted in some considerable tightening of restrictions on travel and financial flows generally and upon Muslims in particular. Events such as this seriously impact upon the level of receipts. More generally, however, some comfort is afforded by the fact that there has not been as great a problem with volatility of receipts in the past as might have been feared, as may be judged by the figures provided in Table 14.2, which are graphed below (Figure 14.1), showing little volatility at least since the early 1990s.

Bangladesh is not alone in this respect; its experience is similar to that of other areas. The Southern European and Middle Eastern countries, which were traditionally reliant on a supply of guest workers to Europe, also have not suffered. The Mediterranean experience over a forty-year period has been revealed to show a fairly long-term secure position for its migrants (Glytsos 2002:7–13).

The literature has concentrated on the financial aspects, rather than the more qualitative aspects such as cultural or social impacts of this facet of globalisation. This chapter too scopes the financial effect in respect of Bangladesh, but attention is also paid to the other aspects of the situation.

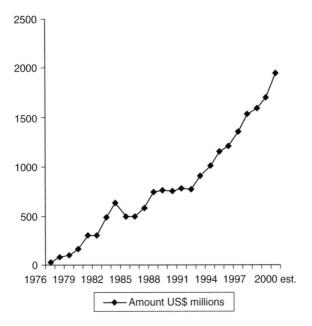

Figure 14.1 Bangladesh: remittance receipts, 1976–2000
Source: Table 14.2.

Similarities exist in the types of analysis used in rural–urban drift studies and the international ones especially when considering short-term migration. Such migration is a relatively recent phenomenon for *large-scale* international migration. The numbers of migrant workers and the remittances they generate have both grown markedly in the recent past. There are cases where remittance income is relatively more important than it is for Bangladesh, but these are generally smaller in size in comparison to the Pacific Islands or Kosovo for example, with 25 per cent or more of their population engaged in overseas employment. A survey undertaken in Kosovo in 1999 showed over 40 per cent of families had migrant workers abroad (RIINVEST 2001:175). The impact and significance of both the migration flows and the remittance flows is large and of itself raises questions as to their desirability. To what extent are they need or want driven?

Bangladesh has relatively fewer such migrants and consequently is less reliant upon remittance income, but it has a considerable absolute number of people engaged in overseas work, both long and short term, with a resultant relatively large amount of remittance income flowing back to the home country, even as judged by the underestimates of the officially reported statistics. Table 14.1 summarises the general findings of such statistics.

Table 14.1   Bangladesh: migrant outflows, 1977–99

Year	Knerr migrant outflow	Siddiqui and Abrar estimates
1977–99	62,669	63,029
1980–82	143,935	148,622
1983–85	192,677	193,628
1986–88	210,797	210,796
1989–91 (S&A)		352,669
1992–94		618,958
1995–97		780,334
1998–99		534,859

Sources: Knerr (1996) p. 215 and Siddiqui and Abrar (2003) p. 16.

The figures are not totally identical for the two sources, but the general trends are consistent. The later study is rather better in terms of a breakdown by skilled, unskilled and semi-skilled, although that is not reported here, as well as for the length of the time period it covers. It also demonstrates that the 1997 spike was almost entirely due to a rise in semi-skilled migrants from 34,689 in 1996 to 193,558 in 1997 (Siddiqui and Abrar 2003:16). This spike was followed by the Asian economic and financial crisis and a reduction in demand for migrant labour.

The fluctuations in figures in recent times are at least as much due to particular events as to any general theoretical proposition. Catastrophic floods in the late 1990s adversely affected the current account, but were offset by an estimated 9 per cent growth in remittance income. The economic need was growing at this time. The more recent global economic slowdown of the early years of the new millennium has seen a fall in global demand for Bangladeshi labour, as well as that from other migrant sending countries. The source countries are numerous and the absolute number of potential migrants is also large. The level of competition on the supply side is high, that on the demand side less so. Labour is needed and even wanted, by the demanders, but they may be indifferent as between Bangladeshi and other nationals. On the supply side both push and pull factors are at work in determining the number of potential migrants in the pool, whilst political, social and institutional factors also play their part in determining the actual number who will make the move. For many migrants the work is needed and desired, for some the need is paramount.

Prior to 1990, remittance income was limited until around the late 1970s and the start of migration to the Middle East. From the late 1970s it rose steadily to the level given in Table 14.2 below with minor downturns in 1982 and 1985 (Knerr 1996:215–17).

Beyond 1998, remittances have continued at a high level, growth slowing around the turn of the millennium as a result of the downturn in the global

Table 14.2 Remittance income flows
to Bangladesh, 1976–2000

Year	Amount US$ millions
1976–78	213.4
1979–81	778.27
1982–84	1,618.21
1985–87	1,823.8
1988–90	2,302.28
1991–93	2,680.36
1994–96	3,710.45
1997–99	4,840.01
2000 est.	1,949.32

Note: 1984 and 1985 were estimates of
doubtful accuracy given a value of 500 million each. Since all official remittance flows
are serious underestimates this is not sufficient a problem as to require their removal
from the analysis.

Source: Siddiqui and Abrar (2003) p. 16
based on Bangladesh Bank data.

economy and a falling off in the demand for migrant labour. The 2000 figure
is disputed and gives rise to different estimates from different sources. More
recently still the level of remittances have picked up again and managed to
totally offset the merchandise balance of trade deficit. The expansion in the
amount of receipts showed a 22 per cent annual increase from the 2002 to
the 2003 financial year as well as exhibiting the usual seasonal fluctuations.
It is argued generally that the official estimates for remittance income may
be as much as 50 per cent below their real level, since they reflect only transfers through official sources and miss many informal transfers. For Bangladesh
a possible 46 per cent of remittances by volume passing through official
sources has recently been estimated from survey results (Siddiqui and Abrar
2003:4). Exchange rate and interest rate differentials have been considered as
possible explanatory variables for changes in the percentage of remittances
going through official channels. A recent study for Egypt found a significant
relationship for these variables, although others have not found such a link
(El Sakka and McNabb 1999).

Latest figures indicate that whilst the growth rate of remittances is still
positive, it is far less than the rate of increase in new migrants going overseas
(0.8 per cent as compared to 12.1 per cent for the second quarter 2003, ADB
2003:6). This is partly explained by problems with a Saudi Exchange house
interrupting some payments for a while. However, it is also likely that less-
skilled migrants have formed much of the increase in migration, with lower

rates of pay, so as average remittances per migrant have fallen, the increase in their overall numbers has compensated to keep up the overall total. It is conceivable that the need is again on the rise for people to migrate for economic reasons. If the Bangladesh experience is like that elsewhere, the general finding that a 10 per cent increase in remittances brings a 1.6 per cent reduction in the proportion of people living in poverty (Adams and Page 2003:21) should be viewed positively. Falling per capita remittance flows, however, will not assist in achieving rapid growth in the amounts remitted.

The Bangladeshi Government wishes to promote an increased remittance flow, but there are issues concerning the recruitment of migrants and the treatment they receive from the private sector employment agents. The Bangladeshi state has shown limited interest in governing the recruitment process of workers heading overseas, this is largely unrestricted and operated by private contractors and corporations. There are cases of exploitation and poor treatment on the part of some operators and some overseas employers. As De Bruyn and Kuddus state 'the efforts taken to promote labour migration are not matched by the efforts to protect the rights of migrants in the destination country or in the migration process' (De Bruyn and Kuddus 2005:46).

More interest has been shown by the Government in wishing to control the remittances rather than the conditions of the workers. Three aims have become apparent in this respect, namely

1. Attempting to foster the greater use of formal channels for remittance transfers;
2. Trying to influence the way in which remittances are used, including providing Investment facilitation as an outlet for remittance use; and
3. Seeing remittances as an important source of income therefore encouraging labour migration so as to increase the level of remittance flows as well reduce unemployment.

The introduction on the website of the Bangladesh Overseas Employment and Services Limited (BOESL) (www.bdcom-online.com/boesl) talks of the pressing need for foreign exchange and that encouraging both skilled and unskilled worker migration is a major source of such income. Established in 1984 this government-owned company competes with over 600 private formal recruitment organisations. How many informal operators exist is difficult to estimate, but their number is likely to be significant as with the informal transfers of remittances. Certainly large numbers of short-term migrants are seen as having gone to the Middle East through 'informal' channels (IOM 2005:273). More than 50 per cent of overseas employment obtained by Bangladeshis is estimated to be informal (IOM 2005:100). This significantly reduces the effectiveness of the apparently stringent regulations relating to emigrants from Bangladesh that are enshrined in statute and regulation. It is also worth noting that the supposed purpose of BOESL is to look after the interests of the overseas employers first and foremost rather than the workers themselves. Whilst the 2001 formation of the Ministry for Expatriate Welfare and Overseas Employment should have improved conditions for expatriate workers, there are still many areas in which worker's rights are not acknowledged. As with BOESL and the Bureau of Manpower and Training (BMET), it is increasing the numbers going overseas and enhancing the remittance flows back in that is the key objective. The same is likely to be true of any bilateral agreements on labour movement that eventuate in future. To date there is only a bilateral agreement with Kuwait on the books.

Recruitment is governed in lacklustre fashion, in part because of the desire to encourage migration and thus generate overseas exchange, remittances officially equate to some 20 per cent of foreign exchange earnings (De Bruyn and Kuddus 2005:40). Tax benefits, relaxing of exchange regulations and bond issues to attract remittance income into channels under more official control are policies designed more to encourage the repatriation of migrant earnings and influence the use of remittance flows, rather than to directly encourage migration itself, but they do have a positive impact on the willingness of people to migrate. Facilitating remittances seems to mean that the Government is keen to see more coming through official channels and that more is used in particular ways, essentially state-directed investment.

Impacts on the exchange rate appear to have resulted in a real appreciation with an increase in demand for non-tradable with employment and output in that sector growing (Hossain 1997). If the supply of labour overseas is taken to represent a staple export product it is having some supply-side shock effects on the economy of Bangladesh. Remittances represent additional 'export' receipts and increased demand for domestic tradable and non-tradable goods as well as for imports, whilst a reduced labour supply will tend to push up wages, which the non-tradable sector can better cope with than can the tradable sector. Thus the immediate positive effect of the remittances on the external balance may be offset in the longer term by a less competitive tradable sector and an appreciating currency making imports more attractive. Currently, however, the effect of remittance income is to more than offset the balance of trade deficit, effectively assisting in closing the foreign exchange gap. The long-term desirability of such effects from a macro-economic perspective, depend upon the eventual outcome.

Official remittances now equate to some 4.5 per cent of total income (Table 14.A1), significant enough although not in the international top 15 (Table 14.A2). These appendices demonstrate that Bangladesh is a big world player in terms of absolute numbers of migrants and remittances, but not a major player in a relative sense. If the 4.5 figure is doubled to approximate estimated total remittances, both through official and unofficial channels, then at 9 per cent of GDP the figure is highly significant. From a world view, Bangladesh figures prominently in only one aspect, that of total remittances (Appendix Table 14.A1) where it is ranked thirteenth, appearing with only two other Asian countries, India and the Philippines, which rank third and fourth respectively. At the family level the impact of remittances is significant. Parents constitute over half of remittance recipients in recent village surveys done for the International Labour Office (ILO) (Siddiqui and Abrar 2003:24–5). An absence of social security programmes for old age render such payments very much in the needed and wanted categories from the parents' perspective. Seasonal fluctuations are in part associated with non-economic factors, including a boost in the level of remittances in the period (November for 2004) leading up to the celebration of the Eid-ul-Fitr festival. Some of the non-financial effects, along with some of the additional components and determinants of such factors, are briefly considered in the next section of the paper.

Qualitative aspects of the Bangladesh case

Much of the existing literature concentrates on the financial aspects of the migration and remittance flows, with less attention paid to the more qualitative aspects such as cultural or social impacts of this facet of globalisation. Remittances certainly do play a major part in financial analysis, as they represent a financial flow. They also, however, impact on many other aspects of community development, not least by their often requiring migrants to be absent from the family home, and therefore play a very different (limited) role in everyday social relationships.

Among the social changes of expanded remittance levels, it is suggested women have become more mobile and economically active. It is also suggested that poverty has been alleviated (Afsar 2003:82). Short-term poverty alleviation through increased consumption is valuable in itself, but at some point it may be achieved only temporarily, at the expense of long-term alleviation through foregoing the alternative of asset accumulation.

The sheer numbers of people making international movements suggest that all effects, both financial and non-financial, are likely to be significant. For Asia as a whole by the late 1980s there were well in excess of 2,000,000 people migrating overseas every year. Twenty years earlier the estimated level was a negligible figure. It is frequently suggested that, as with remittances, these official figures are an underestimate and that there are far higher numbers of people who, although they do not meet the official classification criteria, are moving internationally nonetheless (Skeldon 1992:4). Older estimates of Asian migration are even less clear, but leave the impression of major movements in the past and with far higher rates of return migration, especially under the indentured labour systems, than was the case for European migrants of the time. The estimate of Asian movements to the less densely populated areas of the tropics in the nineteenth century are very imprecise, but there were certainly many millions of people involved, including some from South Asia to Malaysia, one of the significant destinations for Bangladeshi migrant workers of the present day. Only Indonesia was sending a higher number of migrants than Bangladesh to Malaysia in the 1990s.

Lewis has reckoned the historical gross total of Chinese and Indian migration to the tropics, as exceeding that of European migrants to the temperate zone countries (1978:185–6). By 1930 Indian residents were found to be living in a range of overseas countries, although their net migration level was estimated to be only about 25 per cent of the total number of people moving. Most returned to the country of origin. With short-term contracts facilitated through overseers (Kangani), common in what was then called Ceylon and Malaya as well as elsewhere, as early as 1900 (Latham 1978:106), a long run pattern of short-term international migration with remittance flows can be seen to have been historically established, well before the 1980s. Migration patterns from India and Pakistan are given in Latham (1978:105–8) with his table 23 summarising these. This table is based on earlier work by Kingsley Davis (1951:115–16).

In Bangladesh the impact of such migration is not so long-lived. Work on British ships in the 1940s is talked of as the origins of this. Internal migration has a longer history than external migration and will still outweigh international migration in terms of the numbers of migrants. The vast majority of people still do not travel outside their own national boundaries, even temporarily. Something like 2 per cent may travel internationally for work. Their social impact is greater than the internal one, however. The loss of day-to-day contact and social interaction is offset by a substantial inflow of income. Receiving families on average had their incomes lifted by over 100 per cent with a family member overseas, according to the ILO survey (Siddiqui and Abrar 2003). The absence is, however, long term with the average migrant spending five years or so overseas (Siddiqui and Abrar 2003:31). There may be problems too with returning migrants since they, especially the unskilled, may experience lengthy periods of unemployment upon return. All of this creates social dislocation and social costs not apparent in the in the financial flows alone. For the present the immediate need to find employment outweighs any consideration of future possible loss, the future is discounted highly.

Social and family contacts are maintained in the modern context by the use of air travel and the possibility of short-term holiday returns, which were not possible in the historical case, mitigating adverse social impacts, although not entirely removing them. During such visits remittances in kind are often given, with electronic goods, jewellery and other expensive items appearing as well as cash. The use of money couriers as a means of transfer is also significant from the survey data (Siddiqui and Abrar 2003:34–5). A high frequency of return migration and the high frequency of support of aged parents in this case, suggest that the rate of sustainability of the remittance flows is likely to be high. Generally, studies have suggested that the rate of decay of the remittance inflow can be rapid unless there is a likelihood of return. In such cases the society will typically look to a rapid replacement of the remittance flow, by the simple expedient of sending more people overseas. Bangladesh does not fall into this category and in consequence the remittance flows is expected to be sustainable.

With respect to the characteristics of those who migrate, of the millions that have engaged in international migration from Bangladesh in the last thirty years or so, almost half have been unskilled, with current figures from BMET suggesting that the unskilled along with the semi-skilled continue to dominate the overall number (IOM 2005:96–7). Given the large number of undocumented migrants and, that these are likely to be both unskilled and female, the official numbers almost certainly understate the dominance of the unskilled and overstates that of males in the process.

Saying what constitutes a typical migrant worker is difficult due to paucity of reliable data. According to official data, less than 18,000 women migrated between 1991–2003, or less than 1 per cent of the total. This contrasts with the unofficial estimate of 45,000 women going to the Persian Gulf alone, between 1998 and early 2002 (De Bruyn and Kuddus 2005:18–19).

United Kingdom (UK) figures suggest that the gender split for immigrants from Bangladesh was more even than the official BMET statistics suggest, with some 100 females for each 109 males from Bangladesh counted as entering in 2003 (De Bruyn and Kuddus 2005:19). At an estimate of 500,000 people (De Bruyn and Kuddus 2005:18) the United Kingdom was equal with the United States as the dominant host nation of Bangladeshi migrants amongst the industrialised countries. Families being brought back together after the initial movement of male workers alone, could account for some of this, but the likelihood remains that unofficial movement of female workers is likely to have occurred. The 2:1 ratio of illegal to legal migrant workers from Bangladesh found for Malaysia (IOM 2005:96 table 2.1) is unlikely to have been repeated in the UK case, but the small number of official female migrants is most unlikely to be correct.

Most of the temporary migrants are heading for the Middle East or Southeast Asia. Saudi Arabia alone absorbed 42 per cent of Bangladesh's total labour migrants between 1976 and 1999, and in 2003 it accounted for two-thirds of the total followed by Malaysia, the United Arab Emirates, Kuwait, Qatar, Oman and Bahrain in more recent times (IOM 2005:274). This flow to Asia is dominated by short-term migrant flows in contrast to the flows to Europe which are typically longer term, although shorter term, illegal movement is not unknown there too. As at 2003 the unskilled formed over half the total of migrants (IOM 2005:275) and a large, if unquantifiable number, were from rural areas, between their late teens and early thirties, of low educational achievement and essentially heading overseas in response to the push factors of low wages and unemployment, either explicit or disguised. Only those found in the United States are uniformly likely to have high educational levels, largely since they migrated essentially for higher education opportunities.

Reflections and conclusions

The initial survey of some of the vast literature available on this topic at a macro-level, from both economics and development studies disciplines, revealed an increasing focus on the impact of short-term migration of an international character. When problems either temporary or permanent have arisen then these reverses have been found to result in significant negative impacts on the balance of payments of the immigrant source countries and on private economic development activity in those societies. Remittance income has also been *said by recipients to be the most productive form of financial assistance*, rather than aid or foreign loans, meaning this is found to be an important aspect of the development process for Bangladesh. A similar viewpoint is to be found in ILO reporting (ILO 2004:127–8). At 9 per cent of GDP remittances are important in a macro-economic sense and as they are favoured by recipients, they are effective and important at an individual level as well.

There is both internal and international migration with remittances in the case of Bangladesh. The general literature would suggest this is likely to see a move towards a more equal income distribution as a result of rural urban migration, offset by a move in the opposite direction through international migration. As Bangladeshi international migrants are, however, largely unskilled, this move to less equality, as is normal, from international movement should be less pronounced or even reversed, since the general findings rest on the assumption that the unskilled move internally and the skilled internationally. A full test of such an hypothesis may be worth undertaking in future research. It may well encounter some difficulties of good data availability, but there is at least a case to be made to suggest that here is an example which runs counter to the conventional wisdom. The positive impact on rural economic and social development that is normally associated with international migration may also need to be re-considered carefully in this case.

The role of remittance income in the macro-economic field, at least in a short-run, static sense, is to increasingly cover the foreign exchange gap arising from a chronic balance of trade deficit and to generate additional sources of income, in return for a virtual export of labour services. It has also generated some restructuring within the Bangladesh economy, by boosting demand for non-tradable and by raising the demand for currency, resulting in a real appreciation of the exchange rate. In the longer term there are some possible adverse affects on growth rates and particularly on export-led growth, through a supply-side shock, favouring the non-tradable sector and raising wage costs in the export sector. The recent move to a floating exchange rate will not have had time to impact on the situation as yet, but should reveal such effects and trends more plainly than was possible in the past under controlled and fixed rates.

How effective remittances are in generating growth relative to foreign aid inflows and direct investment is open to question, but theoretically they could be anticipated to respond to market forces relatively well and to meet the requirements of economic allocative efficiency. Further analysis would be needed to estimate the overall outcome. A supply-side shocks approach might provide some negative results, but perhaps less so than a MIRAB one. Either way the case of Bangladesh suggests that the staple resource of surplus labour is clearly evident in the modern era and is playing a significant role in the way in which the society is affected by this aspect of globalisation.

It can also be surmised that the movement out of rural areas in Bangladesh to overseas will have positive effects. Some of the remittance flows appears likely to be put into investment in land development with long-term benefits, unlike the normal associations of international migration as impacting negatively on the rural sector. The ratio of skilled to unskilled workers in the Bangladesh emigrant mix could in part explain any such outcome. Specific institutional and cultural characteristics, such as the ethnic mix of migrants, also give particular characteristics to the Bangladesh case. The study suggests that remittances can be seen as a positive economic influence at both the macro-economic and the individual household level, rather than as solely the pessimistic residual outcome implied by the early MIRAB modelling.

Appendix

Table 14.A1   Top 15 countries with the highest total remittances received, 2001

Country	Total remittances (in US\$ millions)[1]	Total remittances as percentage of GDP	Total remittances per capita US\$
Mexico	9,920	1.6	97.37
France	9,220	0.7	154.55
India	9,160	2.0	9.14
Philippines	6,366	8.9	78.24
Spain	4,692	0.8	117.05
Germany	3,800	0.2	46.18
Portugal	3,573	3.3	354.95
Belgium	3,493	1.5	340.49
Egypt	2,911	3.0	40.49
Turkey	2,786	1.9	41.90
United States	2,380	*	8.35
Italy	2,266	0.2	39.17
Bangladesh	2,105	4.5	15.83
Greece	2,014	1.7	189.57
Jordan	2,011	22.8	390.23

Note

1. The remittance data presented in the above table are from IMF (2003). 'Total remittances' refers to the sum of: 1 workers' remittances, 2 compensation to employees, and 3 migrant transfers reported by each country.

The remittance data presented for all countries are for 2001 except the data for India, which are for 2000.

For additional information on how remittances are defined and measured, see chapter 7 in Bilsborrow *et al.* (1997).

* Figure is not significant, that is, it rounds to 0.0.

Table 14.A2 Top 15 countries with the highest total remittances received as a percentage of the GDP, 2001

Country	Total remittances (in US$ millions)[1]	Total remittances as percentage of GDP	Total remittances per capita US$
Lesotho	209	26.2	112.80
Vanuatu	53.3	25.0	276.14
Jordan	2,011	22.8	390.23
Bosnia and Herzegovina	860.1	18.0	219.29
Albania	699	17.0	199.12
Nicaragua	335.7	16.2	68.25
Yemen	1,436.9	15.7	82.21
Moldova (Republic of)	223.1	15.1	50.34
El Salvador	1,925.2	14.0	308.64
Jamaica	1,058.7	13.6	397.17
Dominican Republic	1,982	9.3	233.85
Philippines	6,366	8.9	78.24
Uganda	483	8.5	19.98
Honduras	541	8.5	85.09
Ecuador	1,420	7.9	107.71

Source: As per note 1 of Table 14.A1.

Acknowledgement

This is a revised version of a paper presented at The University of New England Asia Centre & School of Economics, International Conference, 'Migrant Labour in Southeast Asia: Needed, Not Wanted', Armidale, NSW, Australia, 1–3 December 2003. My thanks are due to the helpful comments of participants at the conference and for a helpful discussion with Chris Butler, Director ASIA 2000.

References

Adams, R. H. Jr (1996) 'Remittances, Inequality and Asset Accumulation: The Case of Rural Pakistan', in David O'Connor and Leila Farsakh (eds) *Development Strategy, Employment and Migration: Country Experiences* (Paris: OECD) pp. 149–70.

Adams, R. H. Jr. and J. Page (2003) *International Migration, Remittances and Migration in Developing Countries*. World Bank Policy Research Working Papers, 3179, Washington.

ADB (2003) *Asian Development Bank Quarterly Economic Update Bangladesh*, September, Dhaka, Publication stock number 010401.

Afsar, R. (2003) 'Gender, Labour Market and Demographic Change: A Case Study of Women's Entry into the Formal Manufacturing Sector in Bangladesh', in Garcia, Brigida, Richard Anker and Antonella Pinelli (eds) *Women in the Labour Market in Changing Economies: Demographic Issues* (Oxford: OUP) pp. 59–86.

Altman, M. (2003) 'Staple Theory and Export-Led Growth: Constructing Differential Growth', *Australian Economic History Review*, Vol. 43, No. 3: 230–55.

Bertram, G. and R. Watters (1985) 'The MIRAB Economy in the South Pacific Microstates', *Pacific Viewpoint*, Vol. 26, No. 3: 497–520.

Bilsborrow, R. E., Huge G., Oberai A. S. and H. Zlotnik (1997) *International Migration Statistics: Guidelines for Improving Data Collection Systems* (Geneva: International Labour Office).

Butlin, N. G. (1964) 'Growth in a Trading World, Heavily Disguised', *Business Archives and History*, Vol. 4, No. 2: 138–58.

Caves, R. E. (1965) 'Vent for Surplus Models of Trade and Growth', in R. E. Baldwin (ed.) *Trade Growth and the Balance of Payment* (Chicago: Rand McNally) pp. 95–115.

Davis, K. (1951) *The Population of India and Pakistan* (Princeton: Princeton University Press).

De Bruyn, T. and U. Kuddus (2005) *The Dynamics of Remittance Utilisation in Bangladesh*, IOM Migration Research Series No. 18, Geneva.

El Sakka, M.I.T. and R. McNabb (1999) 'The Macroeconomic Determinants of Emigrant Remittances', *World Development*, Vol. 27, No. 8: 1493–502.

Foreman-Peck, J. (1983) *A History of the World Economy: International Economic Relations since 1850* (Brighton: Harvester-Wheatsheaf Press).

Glytsos, N. P. (2002) 'The Role of Migrant Remittances in Development: Evidence from Mediterranean Countries', *International Migration*, Vol. 40, No.1: 5–25.

Harcourt, T. (2000) *Why Australia Needs Exports: The Economic Case for Exporting* (Canberra: Australian Trade Commission).

Harris, J. R. and M. P. Todaro (1970) 'Migration Unemployment and Development: a Two-Sector Analysis', *American Economic Review*, Vol. 60, No.1: 126–42.

Hossain, A. (1997) 'The Real Exchange Rate, Production Structure and Trade Balance: The Case of Bangladesh', *Indian Economic Review*, Vol. 32, No. 2: 155–77.

ILO (2004) *Towards a Fair Deal for Migrant Workers in the Global Economy*. Report VI of: *International Labour Conference, 92nd Session*, International Labour Office, Geneva.

IMF (2003) *Balance of Payments Statistics Yearbook 2002* (Washington: IMF Publications Services).

Innis, H. (1995) 'The Importance of Staple Products in Canadian Development', in D. Drache (ed.) *Staples, Markets, and Cultural Change: Selected Essays of Harold Innis* (Montreal: McGill-Queen's University Press).

IOM (2005) *Labour Migration in Asia* (Geneva: International Organisation for Migration) [IOM].

Knerr, B. (1996) 'Labour Migration from South Asia: Patterns and Economic Implications', in David O'Connor and Leila Farsakh (eds) *Development Strategy, Employment and Migration: Country Experience* (Paris: OECD) pp. 203–28.

Latham, A. J. H. (1978) *The International Economy and the Undeveloped World* (London: Croom Helm).

Lewis, W. A. (1978) *Growth and Fluctuations, 1870–1913* (London: G. Allen & Unwin).

RIINVEST (2001) *Post-war Reconstruction of Kosova: Strategies and Policies*. Prishtina, RIINVEST.

Siddiqui, T. and A. R. Chowdhury (2003) *Migrant Worker Remittances and Micro-Finance in Bangladesh*, Social Finance Programme, Working Paper 38, Geneva, ILO.

Skeldon, R. (1992) 'International Migration and the ESCAP Region: A Policy Oriented Approach', *Asia Pacific Population Journal*, Vol. 7, No. 2: 3–22.

Thirlwall, A. P. (2003) *Growth and Development: With Special Reference to Developing Economies* (Basingstoke: Palgrave Macmillan).

Wood, A. (1994) *North-South Trade, Employment and Inequality: Changing Fortunes in a Skill-Driven World* (Oxford: Clarendon Press).
—— (1995) 'How Trade Hurt Unskilled Workers', *Journal of Economic Perspectives*, Vol. 9, No. 3(Summer): 15–32.

15
Regional Perspectives on the 1990 UN Convention on the Rights of All Migrant Workers

Nicola Piper

With the ratification by El Salvador and Guatemala on 14 March and Mali on 5 June 2003, the *International Convention on the Protection of the Rights of All Migrant Workers and Members of Their Families* (hereafter ICRM), adopted by General Assembly resolution 45/158 of 18 December 1990, has finally entered into force on 1 July 2003. To date, from among the 34 countries that have ratified, or acceded to, the ICRM, there are only three situated in the Asian region: the Philippines, Sri Lanka and East Timot (with Bangladesh and Indonesia having signed only). The Asian region, however, has emerged as a particularly important source for the export and import of labour, and there is substantial evidence of the violation of the human rights of migrant workers as stipulated by international standards (Piper and Iredale 2003; Piper 2004). These violations are not necessarily specific to the Asian region. In the light of migrants constituting a highly vulnerable group of people, the ICRM – being a migrant worker specific human rights document – could offer an important source for protection if widely ratified and implemented. Furthermore, the potential and real relevance of the ICRM is reflected in the vigorous NGO activism that has been taken place, particularly in the Philippines and by Filipinos abroad who have been at the forefront of migrant rights' activism, campaigning among other issues also for the ratification and implementation of this Convention.

Introduction: intra-regional migration patterns and rights issues

Migratory flows

Historically, cross-border migration in Asia (as much as in other regions) is not at all a new phenomenon. The multi-ethnic composition of many states in Asia is an indication of a long history of human mobility beyond geographic boundaries. However, in regard to contemporary labour flows, patterns and conditions of international migration have undergone considerable changes, whereby the changes within the economic as well as legal sphere are attributed by many scholars to broader globalisation processes or more specifically to the global trend towards neo-liberalism (Gills and Piper 2002; Bell and Piper 2005). This has resulted in reducing the benefits of migration for the individuals involved by increasing the burden being placed upon them. This is so for various reasons.

One of these reasons revolves around the feminisation of migration – a phenomenon which has become a recognised fact among migration scholars, but not yet sufficiently by policy makers (cf. Lim and Oishi 1996). Women have been drawn onto the international labour market in increasing numbers on account of rising male unemployment, the reduction in demand for male labour due to economic slowdowns, and the shift in economic emphasis to the service industries (Gills and Piper 2002). Most women migrants generate income through jobs which are considered unskilled, are poorly paid and often performed in the domestic/private domain (where such jobs are typically not recognised as 'proper' work) or related to the expansion of the service industry. These low- or un-skilled types of jobs are often not a reflection of these women's actual educational or skill levels, but purely a reflection of the kind of jobs available to them. The majority of female migrants in East and Southeast Asia still work in a narrow range of unskilled, reproductive and productive labor. Domestic work on contract has been the most common occupation among migrant women throughout the region (Constable 1997; Chin 1998; Yeoh *et al.*, 1999). Specifically female forms of migration are also the 'maid trade', 'wife trade' and foreign women in the sex and entertainment industries. In all these forms, women are often regarded as more vulnerable than men.

The other source of social hardships which seems to be a specific feature of intra-Asian cross-border migration is the high occurrence of transnationally split families whereby either one spouse works abroad while leaving the other behind charged with the upbringing of children and so on or whereby both spouses work abroad, albeit in different destinations. This has to do with the tendency of labour migration to take place in the context of short-term contracts and without family reunification possibilities. There are only a few 'pockets' on today's global migration scene where family migration for those classified as unskilled is still possible (e.g., Pacific Island migration to New Zealand, legal migration to Europe and North America to some extent, albeit more limited than in the past). Except through international marriage, very little settlement migration is taking place these days, resulting in phenomena such as return and/or circular migration and transnationally split households becoming the norm. Transnationally split households have become a social phenomenon with serious implications for parenthood and children (Scalabrini Migration Center *et al.*, 2004).

Another feature of contemporary migration flows contributing to high levels of vulnerability and abuse is the ever-increasing proportion of undocumented or irregular migration which is linked to the ever-decreasing legal avenues of entry, limited availability of work permits, and a dominating anti-immigration stance reinforced since the September 11 tragedy and the ongoing counter-terrorism rhetoric. Being an undocumented or an overseas contract worker also often results in repeat or circular migration, whereby the individual foreign worker is repeatedly subjected to 'state exactions' (to use the preferred phrase by Migrante, a global NGO active on behalf of Filipino migrants) by the country of origin forcing individual migrants to pay recruitment or travel fees several times.

Over the last few decades, intensified migration pressures have resulted in the supply-side of migrant labour out-balancing the demand, resulting in increased competition, with the effect that the benefits for migrants have been reduced, as wages have been pushed down and recruitment fees pushed up. Furthermore, these market pressures allow for less protection, meaning migrants are subjected to higher levels of exploitation. On the labour-exporting front, new source countries such as Nepal, Cambodia, Vietnam, and Mongolia have emerged. This has resulted in increased competition and lower standards of labour migration policies at the receiving end, where economic downturns and rising unemployment among the local workforce have lowered existing protective mechanisms and reduced the prospects of implementing rights-based regulations for non-citizens. Certain abuses have become more common, such as the non-payment of wages. This reflects the current state of the economy in many receiving countries where unskilled migrants are usually employed in small- and medium-sized firms, which typically take the brunt of increased global competition. Hence, the costs of migration have come to be disproportionately borne by the migrants themselves.

In this context, it is very difficult for sending countries to initiate negotiations with receiving countries that could result in Memoranda of Understanding (MOU), Bilateral Agreements (BLA) or Free Trade Agreements (FTA). MoUs are more common, but they hardly ever contain protection clauses based on receiving countries' politico-economic power position.

To sum up, policies commonly practiced by sending countries aimed at limiting the duration of migration and the integration of foreign workers all impact upon migrants' rights as stipulated by international standards since they classify migrants as workers or labourers to be deposed off when convenient. Such policies also reduce the economic benefits for individual migrants who are often forced into repeat or circular migration. Also, there is a tacit approval of irregular migration in much of the region (as elsewhere).

Rights' issues

Many countries in the Asia-Pacific have adopted a permanent residence/population policy directed at retaining highly skilled or professional migrants and a temporary worker labour policy for the unskilled, whereby the latter are required to leave on expiry of their contracts (for Singapore, see Wong 1997). These policies impinge upon migrants' social and economic rights as they reduce the migrants to the status of 'manpower' by ignoring the human side of migration.

Migrants are subject to an array of abusive practices which go against the principles/standards set out by the ICRM at all stages of the migration process in the pre-departure phase, while working abroad and upon return. In the pre-departure process, would-be migrants typically become victims of deceitful and incomplete information about the whole migration process and quite often also victims due to falsification of travel documents.

In both sending and receiving states, a major issue is the modus operandi of recruitment agencies, many of which are either illegal from the outset, or even if legally registered, often engage in some kind of illegal practices. Preferential treatment to certain categories of migrants, based on their ethnicity (e.g., Nikkeijin in Japan) or skill-level, practiced by all receiving countries, is another source of human rights violations.

While working abroad, the following human rights' violations are commonly reported:

- Deprivation of freedom of movement (most contract workers, including trainees and entertainers in Korea and Japan, as well as domestic workers in Malaysia, Hong Kong, Singapore, are deprived of any choice with regard to employers);
- The non-existence of standard contracts for migrants leading to discrimination between workers (e.g., Filipino and Indonesian migrant workers);
- Non-payment or under-payment of wages;
- Unfair dismissal;
- Work-related accidents (no compensation);
- Withholding of passports;
- Insufficient staff and lack of support by embassies;
- Abuse by state authorities (detention centres, police and immigration officers' raids);
- Deprivation of the right to organise (especially for domestic workers);
- Absentee voting rights legislation not in place.

Upon return, migrants are supposed to be provided with reintegration assistance which is usually lacking.

The politics of migrants' rights – search for an analytical framework

In this section, my aim is to develop an analytical framework which would help us understand the complexities involved in migrants' human rights issues in the country of origin and employment as reflected in the ICRM's ratification, or obstacles thereto. In other words, how can we explain why a major sending country like Indonesia – whose migrating citizens encounter serious abuses at their receiving destinations – has not yet ratified the ICRM, but the Philippines has? And has ratification made the Philippines government more active in responding to migrant rights violations abroad and at home?

To answer these questions, an integrated approach is required which looks at inter-state and intra-state relations. Such a framework necessarily draws on studies from multiple fields. When investigating external factors, inter-national relations literature and its sub-discipline international political economy provide crucial contributions. In other words, to replicate the legal and political issues at stake here in a transnational setting within which international labour migration takes place, we have to look at inter- and intra-state relations. But in addition to the traditional state-centred nature of international relations, we also have to bring non-state actors into the discussion whose role in promoting UN conventions and achieving ratifications has been crucial ever since the UN system opened itself up toward NGO involvement. As the 'history' of other UN Conventions has shown (such as the Convention on the Elimination of All Forms of Discrimination against Women [CEDAW] and the Convention on the Rights of the Child [CRC]), the involvement of non-state actors, particularly NGOs, has been crucial in the lobbying process (pre-ratification) and the monitoring of implementation (post-ratification); but to do so, there has to be 'democratic' space for NGO activism.

An analysis of such issues involves internal and external aspects at the level of the state and also non-state actors. A holistic approach is needed in addressing the Human Rights of migrant workers and the obstacles to the ratification and implementation of the ICRM. With international migration involving at least two different states, we have to look at these issues from many angles, and from the viewpoint of both sending and receiving countries:

1. Political structure of the state – transition from dictatorship or authoritar-ianism; space for civil society activism; approach to human rights (Uhlin 1997; Bauer and Bell 1999; Christie and Roy 2001);
2. International relations and international political economy. Here there are two strands:
   State-centred traditional approach: this is important to explain the different power position of sending and receiving countries (for example, in the case of country X which was close to ratifying but was threatened by receiving country Y that the latter would not accept its workers upon rat-ification of the ICRM; there are also problems with negotiating Bilateral Agreements and Memoranda of Understanding); it is also worth exploring why a certain sending country does not confront a receiving country

which might engage in the violation of the sending countries' citizens (Muslim Indonesia does not want to offend another Muslim country for example those in the Middle East).

Non-state-centred approach: inclusion of NGO/civil society activism. As the history of the ratification and implementation of UN conventions shows, the most successful ones such as CEDAW and CRC involved lobbying and engagement by NGOs at all stages, nationally and internationally; even human rights used to be seen as a matter of violations on the part of states; but this understanding has changed to include the possibility of human rights violations by non-state actors.

3. The concept of transnational politics challenges conventional under-standings of civil society and social movements as well as international relations that have traditionally been approached from a (nation) state-centred perspective.

The emerging research area of transnational activism has generated impor-tant studies within several different scholarly disciplines, including interna-tional relations. First, international relations scholars, opposing the state-centred paradigm of an anarchical international political system, have analysed non-state actors in international politics. Risse-Kappen (1995), drawing on Keohane and Nye's writings in the 1970s, has helped to reintro-duce this perspective. Other scholars following this tradition have made use of social movement theory and focused explicitly on trans-national activism. Keck and Sikkink (1998) provided a path-breaking study in this respect, which was followed by others (e.g., Risse *et al.*, 1999; Scholte 1999; O'Brien *et al.*, 2000; Khagram *et al.*, 2002). Second, studies of transnational activism from an International Political Economy perspective have stressed issues of power and authority in the international system (Higgott *et al.*, 2000) and tend to treat transnational activism mainly as resistance to neo-liberal globalisation (Mittelman 1999; Gills 2000).

In the transnational sphere in which international labour migrant takes place, the politicisation of migrant workers' vulnerable position has to be addressed in an equally transnational manner bringing at state as well as sub-state level, that is, a synergetic framework of intra- and inter-state dynamics with non-state actors/activism is needed.

The 1990 UN convention on migrants' rights

Introduction

Until fairly recently, neither relevant institutions within the UN system nor governments which had played an influential role in the drafting process had made efforts to promote this Convention. The marginalisation of the ICRM might also be related to the fact that it did not officially come into effect until July 2003. Unlike the six UN core conventions, the ICRM is a smaller convention that has never been given much priority and has not even been supported by European governments, which are usually at the forefront of ratifying international human rights instruments. Until 1996 even obtaining its text was difficult, and until the beginning of 2001 no single person anywhere in the world was engaged on a full-time basis in promoting this Convention. On the contrary, there is evidence that a number of governments strongly discouraged attempts to do so. The limited success of the ICRM and the fact that it has so far only been ratified only by labour-sending countries is related to the power position of states (or blocs of states).

The late 1990s, however, witnessed intensified civil society activism, notably in Asia which has the most advanced migrant worker NGOs and regional networks; the launching of a Global Campaign in 1998; the appointment of an UN Special Rapporteur on Human Rights of Migrants in 1999; and the official launching of International Migrants Day on 18 December 2000 by the UN (Taran 2003). In April 2000, the United Nations Commission on Human Rights in Geneva passed a resolution calling upon 'all member states to consider the possibility of signing and ratifying or acceding to the Convention as a matter of priority'.

UN conventions in historical perspective

In recognising that the increasing presence of non-national workers has resulted in a growing need for concepts, institutions, and legal instruments to protect the rights of migrant workers, it is pertinent to note that international concern for the rights of migrant workers began with the establishment of the International Labour Organisation (ILO) in 1919 (it became a UN specialised agency in 1946). There are a number of ILO Conventions specifically relevant to migrant labour commencing with the 1975 *UN Convention on Basic Human Rights of Migrant Workers* whose text provided a primary model (along with ILO Convention 97 of 1949) for the drafting of the ICRM. The latter broke new ground by clarifying the full application of the human rights law to migrant workers, defining what constitutes a migrant worker and covering the entire migration process. Thus far, it has gained only limited support from states generally and no support at all from labour-receiving countries. This stands in stark contrast to other UN conventions (such as the CEDAW and CRC) covering other vulnerable groups such as women and children.

The CEDAW and CRC

The ICRM specifically addresses the fundamental human rights of migrant workers and members of their families based on their vulnerability as non-nationals in states of remunerative employment and states of transit. The types of migrants covered range from unskilled to skilled, including itinerant, project-tied, those in specified employment, self-employed migrant workers and seasonal workers. Explicitly excluded are seafarers, business people (traders, investors), trainees and asylum seekers. Given the impact of global migration for employment, the Preamble of the Convention emphasises the need to 'harmonize the attitudes of States through the acceptance of basic principles concerning the treatment of migrant workers and their families'.

With international migrants moving between states, an additional problem is that the ICRM – in order to provide full and comprehensive protection – needs to be ratified by both sending and receiving countries, but there are no supra-national agencies which can enforce that. The Convention thus underscores the age old conflict between the international norms of human rights and state sovereignty. Ultimately, the 'rights of states' clearly prevail over the 'rights of migrants' with states retaining the right to set the conditions under which foreigners may enter and reside in their territory. Many of the problems migrants face, however, are directly connected to their visa status or type of work permit. Migrants who hold valid work permits/visas tend to be in a better position than irregular migrant workers but they are typically subject to state restrictions and their working conditions are usually poor. The situation is usually much worse for irregular migrant workers who are given little or no legal protection and face the constant threat of deportation. Despite its flaws, the ICRM is nevertheless considered as 'the first universal codification of the rights of the migrant workers and their family members in a single instrument' and although 'some of the provisions can be found in other international instruments, the fact that they are brought together in one Convention gives them validity' (Loennroth 1991:735).

So, why is it then that there have been so few ratifications, with even a labour-exporting country such as Indonesia not among the state parties to this Convention? And what are the implications of ratifying the ICRM in the Philippines for improving migrants' welfare?

Obstacles: the state

All receiving countries discriminate against migrants in one way or another – according to visa status, perceived and/or real skill level, and/or ethnicity. There are many legal loopholes between sending and receiving countries and this hampers the use of protective mechanisms that exist at national levels. But governments are generally not prepared to consider the rights of migrant workers and rights-based emigration/immigration policies because of the existence of high levels of corruption/collusion between government and the intermediaries in the 'migration industry', particularly in the context of recruitment of migrants at both ends of the migration process. This is related to the prevailing view that migrants do not share the same entitlements to the full protection of human rights law as citizens do (de Varennes 2002). In this context, an international convention extending rights to migrants throughout the entire migration process (pre-departure, working abroad, return) gains enormous importance and could potentially close these loopholes if widely ratified and implemented.

In the sending and receiving countries discussed here, the ICRM is known about in government circles, largely due to the promotion by very active NGOs. This does not, however, mean that the document is fully understood in all its details. On the technical legal level, apart from Japan (which is the only Asian country that joined the Working Group deliberations at least during the final phase of the drafting process), none of the other countries discussed here have gone so far as to investigate clause by clause the exact legal implications of ratifying this Convention. This is also the reason why it was only Japan where the issue of 'duplication' (of ICRM with other human rights instruments already ratified) was mentioned.

Overall, a better understanding of the Convention and the implications of ratification are needed in both sending and receiving countries. The overwhelming perception of the ICRM among receiving countries is to see it as an instrument for liberal immigration policies. There is little understanding that this Convention actually encourages the control of clandestine migratory movements and does not infringe upon the rights of States' to establish criteria governing admission of migrant workers and their families (with some minimum standards, though). Sending countries, on the other hand, fear that they would have to grant migrant workers within their own midst (mainly highly skilled professionals from developed countries) rights which are superior to local workers' rights. This would be beyond their means. Hence, there is much confusion as to what the gains and losses are in the case of ratification, and it is assumed in both sending and receiving countries that the losses are bigger than the gains. A change of mindset is needed as well as the need to address unnecessary fears about 'being first' to ratify this document.

Another issue is the novelty of the concept of the 'rights of migrants'. Once governments ratify a UN Convention, they need to address their obligations. With regard to foreign migrant workers, they are typically not prepared to do so either at the labour-sending or receiving end and this position is largely supported by public opinion. In the receiving countries, migrant workers are seen as well protected in their capacity as workers (although their visa status often poses an obstacle to claiming labour rights in practice), but addressing their social, economic and cultural rights as stipulated in the ICRM is a different matter. In countries with social welfare policies, this has to do with the current restructuring and reduction of welfare provisions. In countries having a multi-ethnic population, this has to some extent to do with ethnic politics and existing minority groups whose rights often have not been protected according to international standards.

In receiving countries, the granting of rights to migrants is dependent upon the control of migratory flows and only a small minority of highly skilled migrants are given an array of rights. Regarding the majority of the less skilled migrants, the objective is to treat them as temporary workers. The perception is that migrants coming from less developed countries are given the chance to earn much higher wages, hence there is no need to give them rights or offer treatment not available to them in their country of origin. Any demands for their rights are seen as not legitimate. Also, many receiving countries want to keep their immigration policies flexible so that policy changes can occur frequently, often on an ad hoc basis, in response to economic fluctuations and public opinion. There is no willingness to provide scope for protection or a rights-based approach to labour importation.

In labour-sending countries, extending rights to migrants is seen as a problem with regard to the numerically small group of professionals who – coming from developed countries – are used to services of high standard. Countries such as Indonesia do not have the capacity to meet such standards.

Priority is another issue hampering closer examination of the ICRM by governments. Since 11 September 2001, it is reported that counter-terrorism conventions take precedence and there are certain deadlines to be met which keep relevant ministries occupied with little time left to consider other conventions. The current priority given to 'national security' issues is reinforced by the multi-ethnic composition of many countries in this region and the existence of extremist groups. This means that other conventions, including the ICRM, are further down the line of priorities. In this context, anti-trafficking issues are considered more important than conventions dealing with broader migrant worker rights.

Obstacles: non-state actors

A combination of interests which act against the granting of rights to foreign workers – including recruitment agencies, employers, governmental officials – constitute a huge force that is not easily counter-acted by NGOs and sympathetic individuals within the governmental structure. At the NGO level, a major problem is the lack of resources available to campaign for the ICRM. As a result, NGOs often decide to concentrate on the improvement of national legislation first instead of promoting the ICRM. The Convention is seen as too far removed with little hope of success, especially in the receiving countries, so that making an effort and spending resources is seen as a waste of time. NGOs feel that the pressure to compel labour-receiving countries to ratify the Convention has to come more from the outside. But unless it comes from the UN, this external pressure will not come about easily because no Western labour-receiving country has ratified the ICRM.

Given the general disinterest in the protection of migrant workers' rights at state level, the NGOs' role in preparing the ground and pushing policy makers is essential. Although NGOs in both sending and receiving countries are currently lobbying for national laws or bills to be implemented or amended rather than concentrating on promoting the UN Convention alone, NGOs in the sending countries engage more strongly in lobbying their governments to ratify the ICRM. In contrast, NGOs in the receiving countries feel that if they focus on the promotion of the ICRM it would result in a backlash, with even smaller-scale improvements slipping away. NGOs in receiving countries take the view that the political timing (owing to the economic downturn and the need to protect undocumented workers) is not right to push for the ICRM's ratification. They prefer to concentrate on lobbying for changes within the national legislation that are less comprehensive than the ICRM. This does not mean that NGOs based in the receiving countries do not support the principles of this Convention. In fact, they engage in transnational networking and give full support to NGOs in the sending countries. But their strategy is to get national legislation amended first and then plan to follow up with campaigns for the ratification of the ICRM at a later stage.

On the whole, the NGOs' advocacy efforts are just one of the many activities they engage in and rarely is advocacy the specific focus of any NGO concerned with migrant workers. In addition, many NGOs engaged in migrant worker issues are often general human rights organisations, women's or labour watch groups. Hence, forceful campaigning on behalf of migrant workers is not happening. Alliance building is also scattered and relatively weak at the national as well as at the transnational level.

Visibility of this Convention has also not been extended into the wider public sphere, which is an essential ingredient in generating wider acceptance of the notion of migrants' rights. Knowledge of human rights in general is reasonably good, particularly in the receiving countries where standards of education are on average higher, but the concept of the human rights of migrants is neither given much attention nor sympathy. The media are partially to be blamed. In addition, human rights divisions at the ministerial level in most countries tend to be under-staffed and under-funded and this shows a general lack of priority given by governments. The shortage of experts in the areas of international law and human rights is also a common problem.

Sending countries: Indonesia as a case study

The ratification and implementation processes of any UN convention are expensive undertakings and the government budget and staff assigned to such matters are limited. Another huge problem is the allegedly high level of collusion between government officials and those involved in the labour export business (recruitment agencies). The creation of an environment of 'good governance', which would involve broad level reforms to render ratification of this Convention meaningful, is needed.

The biggest obligation for Indonesia would be in the area of pre-departure information campaigns and training sessions, monitoring of workers abroad and the imposition of sanctions on brokers and recruiters operating illegally.

Under the current infrastructure arrangements, this is a difficult task. Recruitment has been increasingly privatised as governments have sought to take this function out of the public sphere. Alternate types of recruitment agencies, for example, trade unions and local councils, need to be found to minimise exploitation by private recruiting firms (see Iredale *et al.*, 2003). NGOs in Indonesia are campaigning on behalf of the ICRM and also for national legislation. A consortium of concerned NGOs in Indonesia has drafted a national Migrant Worker Bill modelled after this Convention. The Philippines' Migrant Workers Act of 1995 (RA 8042) was also used as a frame of reference and this resulted in the inclusion of a gender perspective into the Indonesian bill – an element missing from the ICRM. This Bill is still with the Parliament. A consortium of NGOs has also lodged a class action court case (Indonesian citizens verus the government) in connection with the Nunukan tragedy. The High Court has accepted this case, but has postponed its decision indefinitely.

On the whole, major problems include the lack of resources at the governmental and NGO levels, by lack of awareness or ignorance on the part of the migrants themselves, and the vested interests involved in the 'migration business'.

Receiving countries

The receiving countries under investigation here can be clustered together in the following categories with regard to their immigration policies on the one hand, and political systems and attitudes towards human rights on the other. They include one, Malaysia and Singapore; two, Japan and Korea; and three, Hong Kong.

In countries where human rights are generally restricted as in Malaysia and Singapore, rights advocacy work by NGOs targeting governments is next to impossible. In addition, migration policies and procedures are treated in a highly non-transparent and uncoordinated manner between the many ministries. Outside of government circles, nobody knows which ministry is in charge of what migrant worker-related aspect. In this environment, it is hard for NGOs to find allies within the governmental structure, and trade unions tend to be too closely linked with the ruling elite.

In Japan and South Korea, the political system allows for political activism on the part of civil society and there are migrant-supporting networks run by concerned local citizens in both countries. A major obstacle to ratification of the ICRM here is that both countries consider themselves as strictly mono-ethnic/mono-cultural and non-immigration promoting countries. Governments feel that if they ratified the ICRM, this would result in a large scale influx of and settlement by foreign workers. In addition, protecting undocumented migrants is considered unacceptable.

In Hong Kong there is very little illegal migration and a lot of space for political organising not only by concerned local citizens, but even more so by fellow citizens of migrant workers. The administrative and legal systems inherited from colonial times have put in place labour laws and channels of redress that are available to migrant workers as well. The main obstacles to ratification of the ICRM here stem from the comprehensive nature of this Convention: it is seen as too detailed and extensive, thus rendering this document even more complicated than the CRC. The cost of administering it would be prohibitive and the reporting obligations alone a nightmare.

In all the receiving countries under investigation, there are links between immigration policies and discriminatory practices based on visa status or ethnicity. The preference for certain ethnic groups of migrants is related to the importance given to maintain the (often false) mono-ethnic/mono-cultural nature of society or to maintain a balance with existing ethnic groups. Although the Convention allows individual countries to determine and design immigration policies suitable to their national situation and national interests, the problem is that the visa status and rights as provided by national legislations (labour laws) are tightly linked with migrants not being able to use existing rights in practice. This is also related to the complex issue of 'irregular' or undocumented migrants. No government is prepared to extend rights to irregular migrants and there is very little critical assessment of how migrants become 'illegal'.

Problems with recruitment agencies exist in all countries. States typically protect employers more than foreign workers and this is typically approved of by the public at large. Although most receiving countries claim that they have sufficient legislation in place, by excluding trainees and domestic workers from coverage under their employment or labour laws, a substantial part of the foreign migrant worker population is without protection.

Ratification by the Philippines

The quantitatively most significant labour exporter in the region is still the Philippines, which also has the longest history of state-driven labour-exporting policies. Not surprisingly, Filipinos constitute the globally most widespread workforce, with an almost equal proportion of men and women taking up employment abroad. During the Marcos era, there were also substantial numbers of political migrants, often highly educated Filipinos, many of whom engaged in NGO activism while abroad.

Although the Philippine government did not take part in the ICRM's deliberation and drafting period, it has emerged from among all labour-sending countries as the one country with the most comprehensive laws for the protection of its migrants on paper. How did this happen? One of the major impetuses, which triggered the passing of various migrant worker-related bills, is related to comparatively strong migrants' rights activism at home and abroad. As one interviewee expressed: 'The key to successful campaigning abroad is a strong movement "at home" '. Migrant worker activism needs to be seen in the general context of the Philippines' comparatively long tradition of a vibrant civil society and its political engagement. Migrant worker NGOs all grew out of the national democratic movement, which was anti-dictatorship and multi-sectoral. With the Philippine government having been an active promoter of labour export for a long time, NGOs have been highly involved in this process for quite some time also. Hence, with Filipinos being the most globalised workforce, it is not surprising to find supportive NGOs organised by themselves all over the world. Unlike in Indonesia, Filipino NGOs have been able to work within a more open political system and even have access to elite allies within the government structure although there are a lot of frictions and conflicts in government – NGO relations concerning labour migration (Villalba 1997). The Catholic Church has also played an instrumental role in supporting migrant workers (Asis 2002). The church's role in a more political type of advocacy might be questionable but even so, it has provided an important physical space for migrants to come together, to obtain and exchange information. On the whole, since Aquino, NGOs have grown more independent from existing political organisations. There is a widely shared understanding that the state has an important role to play in the distribution of resources.

The actual ratification of the ICRM was achieved in 1995, as a response to the Flor Contemplacion case – a domestic worker who was executed in Singapore for killing her employer – which created a massive outcry in the Philippines and among Filipinos abroad, resulting in daily demonstrations etc. (Hilsdon 2000). One of my informants, a government official, said that the then President Ramos was apparently very surprised at the scale of public outcry in reaction to one single domestic worker (whose plight of course symbolised in many ways the plight of female migrant workers at large). In order to calm public opinion, the ICRM was ratified and the Migrant Workers and Overseas Filipino Act, or RA 8042, hastily passed. The Philippines is in fact the first country to pass a local law like the RA 8042.

It is important to acknowledge that ratification of the ICRM did not happen in a vacuum and was in fact proceeded by other small 'success stories' lobbied for by migrant worker NGOs, mainly operating from Hong Kong: the alliance UNIFIL and their campaign to have the government order forcing migrant workers to send remittances home abolished (Law 2002; Lindio-McGovern 2003). In this sense, before ratifying comprehensive legal instruments like the ICRM and passing the RA8042, the Philippine government or policy makers were already to some extent aware of migrant worker issues due to NGO activism at home and abroad.

The latest legal accomplishments are the passing of the Absentee Voting Rights' Bill (RA 9189) and the Anti-trafficking in Persons Act (RA9208), both in 2003. The latter was achieved because there was already a high level of awareness and a core of committed people in place, due to eight years of lobbying by migrant and women groups. The former was achieved through engagement of overseas Filipinos and local NGOs forming a campaign described by one NGO activist as 'a global thunder' as it involved the broadest possible participation (nationally and transnationally) at highest level possible (i.e., allies among congressmen). Both of these bills have been described as even more progressive than the ICRM or anti-trafficking laws that exist in Thailand and the United States.

The combined quantity and quality of all of these protective bills, however, does not mean that there are no issues left for further activism. Legal bills are typically a political compromise and from the viewpoint of NGOs often 'watered down' end products. Lobbying for amendments is still going on. But the most crucial issue left is actual implementation. According to the Commission for Human Rights, the RA8042 for instance was not backed up with a budget ensuring its proper implementation (interview). Thus, despite comprehensive legislation existing on paper, many rights violations are left unaddressed by the government.

Another question worth raising is the extent to which the Philippine government can challenge receiving countries regarding the treatment of Filipino migrants on the basis of having ratified the ICRM, but none of them have done so. The Philippine government made some 'noise' in Hong Kong when domestic workers were faced with a wage cut. The government has generally improved the staffing of its embassies, with labour attaches stationed in crucial receiving destinations. But the numbers of migrants are so large that embassies still are overwhelmed in their ability to provide services. Embassies, however, rarely engage in confronting receiving countries for diplomatic reasons. In addition, the widespread existence of undocumented migrants also makes it difficult to demand protection from receiving countries which typically criminalise such workers as 'illegals'. Politically, there is very little that a ratifying country such as the Philippines can demand of receiving countries that have not already done so.

Concluding remarks

It appears that the obstacles to the ratification and implementation of the ICRM can be summarised as related to three major issues: intra- and inter-state politics; mis-information about the implications of ratifying; and public opinion (in the receiving countries, largely anti-immigrant). All of these more or less involve the state and non-state actors, nationally as well as transnationally. Ratification and implementation depends on political factors as well as material resources (although the latter is to some extent also a political factor related to budgetary priorities).

In the interim, if not the UN Convention, what other alternatives are there? ILO conventions, other conventions (CEDAW, CRC) and national laws modelled after international standards. Migrant women could claim their rights under the heading of 'women's rights' rather than 'migrants' rights' (right to marry, reproductive and health rights) and CRC (their kids from locals etc.). This explains why this chapter has been silent on gender issues so far: these issues are more complex because female workers are often discriminated against locally so that the 'equal treatment' for female migrant workers does not result in rights protection.

In view of their low ratification record, however, issues of protection are left to national employment or labour laws and employment contracts. Even where national employment or labour laws exist, the biggest problem is enforcement and monitoring. As stated by one NGO supporting migrant workers in the region: 'There are all those laws out there, but then when it comes to reality, there is nothing'. Legal regulation in any context is meaningless without proper enforcement mechanism and channels through which to file complaints. What makes the situation of foreign workers particularly precarious is their doubly insecure position as unskilled workers in the 'three D' or informal sectors of the economy, compounded by their status as temporary contract workers. In addition, migrant workers often tread a thin line between their status as documented and undocumented worker, sometimes sliding into an 'illegal' status beyond their control or with no avenues open to them to reinstate their originally legal status. Also, to become a legal contract worker, migrants are required to sign contracts that often explicitly stipulate that they are not allowed to join trade unions or organise in any other way and require them to accept wages below the going rate for local workers, and various other unfair conditions. Particularly damaging are employment contracts for domestic workers. Owing to the nature of their work, domestic workers are explicitly excluded from coverage by national employment laws everywhere in Asia. Even when in theory covered by protective provisions set out in national labour laws or employment contracts, in practice foreign migrant workers often cannot file court cases because their legal visa status is tied to their employment status. Without work, they are either legally not allowed to remain in the country (and subsequently deported) or they cannot afford to do so and depend on their embassies' (financial and housing) assistance or on NGOs whose resources are also limited.

As mentioned above, related to the non-enforcement of existing laws on the national level in the receiving countries, and the unwillingness or inability to design protective laws in the sending countries, is the issue of colluding interests between government and business circles. Highly corrupt 'security forces' (police, immigration officials) and a weak 'rule of law' works to the disadvantage of many migrant workers. In the end, as expressed by one NGO representative – 'the state protects the employers'. This is reinforced by the prevailing attitudes among bureaucrats in many receiving countries in Asia – as in the words of this NGO representative:

> Officials or bureaucrats either do not know about the law or they are not active in using it. There is a kind of psychological campaign to not use it. Also, some officials are very prejudiced people through the media.

To address the challenges posed by these combined forces is not an easy task. But increasingly, NGOs are taking up these issues engaging in campaigns to support foreign migrant workers, in both the sending and receiving countries. The political and material problems involved in implementing protective or rights-based legislation also point to the limitations of legislation in addressing the root problems of migration that are leading to the violation of human and labour rights. This is captured very well by Patrick Taran, an experienced migrant rights' activist, who wrote that '(w)hile States appear focused on devising *national security*-based responses to migration that contradict their own future needs and defy labour and economic market laws, elaboration of alternative, rights-based approaches to governance of migration is desperately lacking' (2003:10). This led him to conclude that unless 'options and political support for alternative approaches can be generated from civil society and international organizations, it seems unlikely that addressing international migration in the context of international standards will advance'. This switch in focus is the result of the global changes in the last ten years or so and Taran (2003:10) now places little faith in governments providing 'moral, political and practical leadership in assuring a rights-based approach to international migration'. One way of achieving improvements in legal protection is through empowerment programmes developed by NGOs. Empowerment of women migrants is seen by NGOs as an important method by which to raise consciousness about rights and to involve migrant workers in political activism. Another way, ideally happening simultaneously, is the mounting of a global campaign involving NGOs, sympathetic individuals within national and international policy making positions.

Acknowledgement

The author would like to acknowledge the support of the Australia Research Council (grant no. DP0343303) in supporting this research; UNESCO; and SEARC at City University of Hong Kong. She would also like to thank Dr Delia Monares for helpful comments.

References

Asis, M. M. B. (2002) 'Being church for migrants: The Catholic Church and the Care of Migrants in Asia', Paper presented at the Conference 'Gender, Migration and Governance in Asia', Australian National University, Canberra, December 5–6.

Bauer, J. R. and D. A. Bell (eds) (1999) *The East Asian Challenge for Human Rights* (New York: Cambridge University Press).

Bell, D. A. and N. Piper (2005) 'Justice for Migrant Workers? The Case of Foreign Domestic Workers in East Asia', in Will Kymlicka and Baogang He (eds) *Multiculturalism in Asia* (Oxford: Oxford University Press, 2005) pp. 196–222.

Chin, C. B. N. (1998) *In Service and Servitude: Foreign Domestic Workers and the Malaysian Modernity Project* (New York: Columbia University Press).

Christie, K. and D. Roy (eds) (2001) *The Politics of Human Rights in East Asia* (London: Pluto Press).

Constable, N. (1997) *Maid to Order in Hong Kong: Stories of Filipina Workers* (Berkeley: University of California Press).

De Varennes, F. (2002) 'Strangers in Foreign Lands – Diversity, Vulnerability and the Rights of Migrants', *UNESCO-MOST Strategy Paper*, 9 September.

Gills, B. K. (ed.) (2000) *Globalization and the Politics of Resistance* (Basingstoke: Macmillan).

Gills, D. S. and N. Piper (eds) (2002) *Women and Work in Globalizing Asia* (London: Routledge).

Hilsdon, A. (2000) 'The Contemplacion Fiasco: The Hanging of a Filipino Domestic Workers in Singapore', in A. Hilsdon, M. Macintyre, V. Mackie and M. Stivens (eds) *Human Rights and Gender Politics* (London: Routledge).

Iredale, R., N. Doloswala, T. Siddique, and R. Tirtosudarmo (2003) 'International Labour Migration in Asia: Trends, Characteristics, Policy and Interstate Cooperation', *Paper delivered at Labour Ministers' Meeting* organised by IOM, Colombo, Sri Lanka, 1–2 April.

Keck, M. and K. Sikkink (1998) *Activities Beyond Borders: Advocacy Networks in International Politics* (Ithaca: Cornell University).

Khagram, S., J. V. Riker and K. Sikkink (eds) (2000) *Restructuring World Politics: Transnational Social Movements, Networks, and Norms* (Minneapolis: University of Minnesota Press).

Law, L. (2002) 'Sites of transnational activism: Filipino Non-Government Organisations in Hong Kong', in S. A. Brenda Yeoh, Peggy Teo and Shirlena Huang (eds) *Gender Politics in the Asia-Pacific Region* (London: Routledge).

Lim, L. L. and N. Oishi (1996) 'International Labour Migration of Asian Women: Distinctive Characteristics and Policy Concerns', *Asian and Pacific Migration Journal*, Vol. 5, No. 1: 85–116.

Lindio-McGovern, L. (2003) 'Labour Export in the Context of Globalisation: The Experience of Filipino Domestic Workers in Rome', *International Sociology*, Vol. 18, No. 3: 513–34.

Loennroth, J. (1991) 'The International Convention on the Rights of all Migrants in the Context of International Migration Policies: An Analysis of Ten Years of Negotiations', *International Migration Review*, Vol. 25, No. 4: 710–36.

Mittelman, J. H. (1999) 'Resisting Globalisation: Environmental Politics in Eastern Asia', in K. Olds *et al.* (eds) *Globalization and the Asia-Pacific* (London: Routledge).

O'Brien, R., M. Williams, A. M. Goetz, and J. A. Scholte (2000) *Contesting Global Governance – Multilateral Economic Institutions and Global Social Movements* (Cambridge: Cambridge University Press).

Piper, N. (2004) 'Rights of Foreign Workers and The Politics of Migration in Southeast and East Asia', *International Migration*, Vol. 42, No. 5: 71–97.

—— (2003) 'Bridging Gender, Migration and Governance: Theoretical Possibilities in the Asian Context', *Asian and Pacific Migration Journal*, Vol. 12, Nos 1–2: 21–48.

Piper, N. and R. Iredale (2003) *Identification of the Obstacles to the Signing and Ratification of the UN Convention on the Protection of the Rights of All Migrant Workers: The Asia Pacific Perspective*, Asia Pacific Migration Research Network (APMRN) Working Paper 14 (Wollongong: University of Wollongong).

Piper, N. and A. Uhlin (eds) (2004) *Transnational Activism in Asia: Problems of Power and Democracy* (London: Routledge).

Risse-Kappen, T. (1995) *Bringing Transnational Relations Back in Non-State Actors, Domestic Structures and International Institutions* (Cambridge: Cambridge University Press).

310 *Nicola Piper*

Risse, T., S. C. Ropp, and K. Sikkink (eds) (1999) *The Power of Human Rights International Norms and Domestic Change* (Cambridge: Cambridge University Press).

Scalabrini Migration Center *et al.* (2004) *Hearts Apart – Migration in the Eyes of Filipino Children* (Manila: SMC).

Scholte, J. A. (1999) 'Global Civil Society: Changing the World?', University of Warwick, Coventry: Centre for the Study of Globalization and Regionalisation, *Working Paper* no. 31/99.

Siddiqui, T. (2001) *Transcending Boundaries – Labour Migration of Women from Bangladesh* (Dhaka: The University Press Limited).

Taran, P. (2003) 'To Be or Not to Be Ruled by Law: Migration in the 21st Century and the 1990 International Convention'. Paper presented at workshop Eighth International Metropolis Conference, Vienna, 15–18 September.

Uhlin, A. (1997) *Indonesia and the 'Third Wave' of Democratization: The Indonesian Pro-Democracy Movement in a Changing World* (Richmond, Surrey: Curzon Press and New York: St. Martin Press).

Villalba, M. (1997) 'Protecting Migrant Workers Rights: Government-NGO Conflict and Cooperation', in Marlon A. Wui and Ma. Glenda S. Lopez (eds) *Philippine Democracy Agenda, Vol. 2: State-Civil Society Relations in Policy-Making* (Quezon City: Third World Studies Centre).

Wong, D. (1997) 'Transience and settlement: Singapore's Foreign Labour Policy', *Asian and Pacific Migration Journal*, Vol. 6, No. 2: 135–67.

Yeoh, B., S. Huang and J. Gonzalez (1999) 'Migrant Female Domestic Workers in the Economic, Social and Political Impacts in Singapore', *International Migration Review*, Vol. 33, No. 1: 114–36.

Index

acculturation, 172, 190
Aceh: workers to Malaysia, 39, 46
administrative constraints, 67
agency fees, 35
agency, issue of, 6
agrarian/agriculture sector: decline, 28,
    141, 143, 145, 256; modernisation, 33,
    43; overpopulation and migration, 25;
    workers, 42–43
Alger Hiss case (1950), 16
Algeria, war of independence, 14
Annan, Kofi, 134
Asia Pacific Economic Co-operation
    (APEC) forum, 27
Asia Pacific system, 31
Asian Regional Initiative Against and
    Trafficking of Women and Children,
    Manila, Philippines, 123
aspal documents, 233
Association of South East Asian Nations
    (ASEAN), 27, 31, 32, 43, 59, 66, 69, 98,
    222, 248; Economic Community, 52,
    63; ASEAN Framework Agreement on
    Services (AFAS), 52, 61; commitments,
    64, 66–67;—migration policy, 63–64,
    68; ASEAN Free Trade Agreement
    (AFTA), 102; intra-ASEAN investment
    flows, 56; ASEAN Inter-Parliamentary
    Organisation (AIPO), 242; policy of
    non-interference, 242
asylum seekers, 8, 20; and migrants, 9
Australasia: Filipino nurses, 91
Australia, Australian, 38; Australian
    Chamber of Commerce (AustCham),
    186; Department of Immigration,
    Multiculturalism and Indigenous
    Affairs (DIMIA), 174; Immigration
    Restriction Act (1901), 11–12;
    migration/migrants, 9, 20, 277;
    European, 17;—inflow encouraged by
    state, 14;—from Malaysia, 43, 100;—in
    refugee-humanitarian category, 15,
    80;—professional workers in
    Singapore, 172–91;—skilled, 35;

—student migrants, 77; mail order
    bride system, 79, 93; and Singapore,
    bilateral trade agreements, 173; racism,
    12; refused asylum to Kurds, 8; sex
    ratio, 97, 100; women migrants, 78–79,
    81;—Burmese, 96;—Filipino, 88, 91;
    —Malaysians, 100;—Thai sex workers,
    93, 95;—from Vietnam, 80, 92
Australia New Zealand Association
    (ANZA), 186
authoritarianism, 296

Badawi, Abdullah Ahmad, 238
Bagong Bayani (New Heroes), 33, 34
Bahrain, Indonesia labour migrants, 153
balance of payment (BOP), 274, 275
Bangkok: *Declaration on Irregular
    Migration*, 134; migrants, Burmese,
    96;—Thais, 249, 254
Bangladesh, 45, 47, 292; Ain O Shalish
    Kendra (ASK), 160; Bangladesh
    Association of International Recruiting
    Agencies (BAIRA), 160–61; Bangladesh
    Legal Aid and Services Trust (BLAST),
    160; Bangladesh Overseas
    Employment and (BOESL), 160, 169,
    282–83; Bangladesh Society for
    Enforcement of Human Rights
    (BSEHR), 160; Bangladeshi Women
    Migrants Association (BWMA), 161;
    Christian Commission for
    Development in Bangladesh (CCDB),
    160; Bangladesh Migrant Centre
    (BMC), 161; Bureau of Manpower,
    Employment and Training (BMET),
    159, 163, 165, 167, 283, 286;
    economy, 281, 283, 287; Emigration
    Ordinance (1982), 159; labour
    export/migration/migrants, 43, 157;
    —to Malaysia, 217, 220, 222, 285–86;
    —gender split, 286;—qualitative aspect,
    284–86;—and remittances, 274–75,
    279, 281–85, 287; Migration,
    Remittances and Bureaucracy

Bangladesh – *continued*
(MIRAB), 278, 288; recruitment
process, 282–83; SHISUK, 160; state
and migration policy, 158–62, 278–84;
Welfare Association of the Bangladeshi
Returnee Employees (WARBE), 160;
women migrations, contributing
factors, 165–67;— a gendered
perspective, 162–65;—regulation,
161–62;—trafficking, 156;
Berlin wall, fall of, 9
bilateral agreements and national
policies, impact on migration, 61–63,
173, 294, 296; to protect the rights of
migrants, 133–34, 241;—women, 106
Bolshevik Revolution, 1917, 13
bonded labour, 123
border control regimes, 6, 10–11, 13, 14,
15, 23, 27; in Australia, 13; in Japan,
17–18; and immigration policies in
Singapore and Malaysia, 43–49,
61–64, 66–67, 68, 213–14, 217–23,
226; in the post-cold war world,
18–20
Boyce, Ralph, 123
brain drain effects, 55, 77, 96, 102,
119, 126
Brunei: migration/migrants/labour
import, 5, 31, 117; male, 98;
Indonesian, 144, 153; from Malaysia,
100; policies, 66; unskilled, 35, 59;
skilled, 81; women, 79, 98;
—Indonesian domestic
workers, 88, 98
Brunei-Indonesia-Malaysia-Philippines
East ASEAN growth area
(BIMP-EAGA), 32
bureaucracy, 5, 13, 18, 23, 307
Burma, *see* Myanmar
business, skilled and professional
migrant workers, 60–61

Cambodia: migration/migrants/ labour
export, 5, 31, 294;—feminisation,
164;—policies, 66;—restrictions and
limitations on migrants, 66–67; and
Thailand, bilateral agreements on
migration, 63; temporary labour
migration (TLM), 64; trading relations,
27; women migrants, 97–98;—illegal,
96;—refugee, 81, 95

Canada, 38; migrants, 257, 310;—Filipino
domestic workers, 88;—Malaysian,
43;—refugees, 15, 92;—Thai, 95;
—Vietnamese, 92; staple approach, 275
capital: deterritorialisation, 174;
internationalization, 3
caregivers, 91
Caribbean Community and Common
Market (CARICOM), 54
Catholic Church, role in supporting
migrant workers, 305
chain migration, 30, 219
China, Chinese, 182; disruptions due to
rebellions, 25; gender ratio, 26; and
Japan, passport-free travel, 14;
migrants/labour migration from, 26,
57, 285;—illegal, 96;—male, 26;
—contract labour in Malaysia, 26, 215,
223–24, 232;—in Singapore, 200;
Vietnamese, 80, 93; women
migrants, 26, 80
citizenship, 3, 13, 31
civic and social rights of refugees and
migrants, 15
civil society activism, 4, 5, 296–97, 303,
305, 308; *see also* non-governmental
organizations (NGOs)
Cold War, 9, 14–15, 17; border controls
in the post period, 18–20; and the
control of subversives, 15–16
Collaer, Nicholas, 17
colonial rule in Southeast Asia,
colonialism, 3, 23–24, 26;
immigration policy, 44
Common Economic Relations, 54
Commonwealth Passport Act (1920), 13
communism, communists, 13, 27;
capitalists, confrontation, 19
community development, 284
competition, competitiveness, 3, 56, 62,
117, 193–96, 201–04, 206, 266, 294
conservatives, 16
constitution, 10
contract labour system, 24–26, 74,
115, 116, 126, 144, 195, 295; in
Malaysia, 26, 29, 218–20, 225–26;
women, 106, 119
Convention on the Elimination of All
Forms of Discrimination Against
Women (CEDAW), 296, 297,
298–304, 306

Convention on the Rights of Child (CRC), 296, 297, 298–304, 306
convergence, 4
co-operation, 27
Coordination of Action Research on AIDS and Mobility (CARAM), 160
corporate capitalism, 11
corruption, 299
cosmopolitanism, 186
cost reductions through outsourcing, 204–205
counter-terrorism conventions, 301
cross-border movements, 26, 56–59, 63, 68, 292–93
cross-cultural challenges, 180
culture, cultural, 174, 178, 214, 266; adaptation, 172; change, 172; clash, 93; codes, shifting, 182–89; cues, 185; distance and transience, 214, 225; diversity, 4, 6; isolation, 168; and language maintenance, 108; mobilisation, 13
Czech Republic, Vietnamese migrants, 93

daily commuting workers, 32
debt-bondage, 100–101
decolonisation, 3, 15, 27
democracy, 9–10, 20–21
democracy-free zone, 9
demographic patterns, 28, 32, 146
deprivation of freedom, 295
despatialisation, 19
destination countries, conditions of employment, 167–68
development and economic integration in Southeast Asia, 29, 55–56
discrimination, 128, 158, 166, 295
displaced persons, displacement, 14, 97, 155
domestic workers, 34, 35–36, 60, 76, 83, 119, 143, 157, 168, 293
Downer, Alexander, 8
dulang workers, 26

East Timor: women migrants, 80
Eastern Bloc, 27
economic: crisis, 52, 57, 59, 60, 134, 139, 140–42, 152, 213;—in Indonesia, 29;—and international labour migration (ILM), 29–30; in Malaysia, 29, 48, 213, 221, 236;—in Thailand, 29, 248, 261, 265; impact of migration, 148–49, 168–69; integration in Southeast Asia, 55–56; restructuring, 4; and social issues, 13, 53, 139, 172; stagnation, 27; transformation, 31, 248
economy, 3, 140–41, 146; international/global, 3, 23, 27; of Malaysia, 27, 31; of Singapore, 193, 195, 197–99, 201, 208; of Thailand, 31, 248, 266–67
education, 28, 29; India and Singapore cooperation, 203
emigration policy and gender implications, 107
emotional deprivation, 149
empires and labour migration in Southeast Asia (1870–1940), 23–27
entertainment and sex industry/prostitution and women migrants, 76, 157–58; Burmese, 96; Filipino, 76, 89, 90, 91, 95, 118–19, 121–23; Indonesian, 76, 86; Malaysian, 100; Thai, 76, 93–95
Entikong-Tebedu Border post, 32
ethnicity, ethnic relations, 4, 15, 30, 178, 225, 295, 300
Europe: female migrant domestic workers, 75; Filipino, 88;—nurses, 91; political turmoil, 14; skilled migration flows, 35; system of foreign labour recruitment, 215
European Union (EU), 20
Evian Accord (1962), 14
expatriate workforce, 37, 177–78, 179–89, 190
exploitation of migrants, 76, 83, 92, 103–106, 108, 156–58, 163, 166, 294

family migration, 75, 78, 91, 92, 293
family relations and the migration, 34, 130
female international migration, *see* women
feminisation of labour migration, 5, 19, 26, 33, 73, 75, 130, 156, 164, 293
Filipino, *see* Philippines
Flor Contemplacion case, 305

Flores, East, 86
forced labour, 35, 156
foreign direct investment (FDI) flows, migration and, 60–60–62, 115
France: Algerian migrants, 14; refugees from Cambodia, 97

gender dimension/gendered nature of migration, 6, 33–34, 36, 39, 42, 73, 107–108, 119–23, 145–46, 156, 158, 166, 183
General Agreement on Trade in Services (GATS), 54, 64, 68, 173
Geneva Conventions, *see* United Nations Conventions
Germany: genocidal policies of Nazi government, 14; trafficking of Thai women, 95; undocumented Vietnamese, 93; West, *Gastarbeiter* system, 14
global capitalism, 175
Global Commission on International Migration (GCIM), 134–35, 136
global governance norms, 4–5
global health and epidemiological surveillance, 48
global labour market, 172–73, 205; and labour transformation in Southeast Asia since 1970s, 27–30
global war on terror, 10, 13, 15, 20
globalisation, 3–4, 6, 20, 27, 30, 53, 126, 135, 139, 152, 172, 175, 189, 193, 194–95, 208, 284, 288
gross domestic product (GDP), 55–56
growth triangles, 27, 31
guest worker system, 14–15; in Malaysia, 214, 223–26
Gulf states, infrastructure development, 118

Hamzah Haz, 239
health industry: India and Singapore cooperation, 203; migrant women, 77
Hong Kong, 178, 182; labour import/migration/migrants, 5, 117, 303–304;—Filipino, 33, 89, 91, 121, 127;—Indonesia, 88, 142, 143, 153; —illegal, 143, 303;—Malaysians, 101;—skilled, 35; newly industrialised country, 27; women migrants, 88–89, 91, 121, 127;— Thai sex workers, 95

host countries, *see* labour importing/receiving countries
housekeeping, 33
Howard, John, 20
human rights, 4, 5, 6, 16, 20, 121, 135–36, 240, 266, 296, 298–99, 302; abuse/violations through labour export, 19, 134, 158, 295; *see also* United Nations
humanitarianism, 266
hybridization, 172, 186

identity re-evaluation, 172, 184–85, 190
illegal/undocumented migrant workers, 15, 29, 34, 36, 39, 42, 43, 47, 96, 121, 134, 143, 148, 155, 156–57, 294; in Malaysia, 36, 38, 42, 46, 47, 48, 49, 98, 128, 213, 214, 217–20, 222–23, 226, 228, 234, 236–37, 243; in Thailand, 248, 250, 252–54, 257, 261–63, 266; women, 75, 88, 95, 103, 139
income and wage differentials, 31
India, Indian, 45, 182; Emigration Act (1922), 26; labour migration from, 26, 57, 285; National Association of Software and Service Companies (NASSCOM), 205; and Singapore, Comprehensive Economic Cooperation Agreement (CECA), 193, 201–203, 205, 207–208;—economic linkage, 205;—human resource complementarities, 201;—Joint Study Group (JSG), 201, 206–207;—Mutual Recognition Agreements, 202–203, 207; professional workers in Singapore, 193, 198–208;—constraints and measures, 206–208; women migrants to Malaya, 26
individual and the state, relationship, 10
Indo-China: women migrants from, 80
Indo-Chinese war, 97
Indonesia, 45, 46, 64; creation of, 24; development plans, 40; economic development/foreign currency income through remittances by labour export, 32, 230–31, 302–303; formal sector, 140–41, 145; has not ratified the Geneva Convention, 296, 302–303; government's response to Malaysia's labour immigration policies, 229, 234, 239; labour migration, migrant

Indonesia – *continued*
flows, 5, 31–32, 39–42, 57–58,
230–34;—documented, 231;—illegal/
undocumented, 139, 143, 148;—in
Malaysia, 29, 31, 34, 46, 47, 60, 82–83,
86–87, 142, 143, 144, 146, 151, 153,
214–20, 222, 223, 228–29, 231–32,
235–38;—official programme, 230;
—Saudi Arabia, 231;—size and
composition, 142–48;—skilled and
professional, 60, 64;—unskilled, 59; and
Malaysia, bilateral relations, 243–44;
National and Regional Manpower
Planning Policy, 139; New Order
Regime, 140, 229, 242; open economy,
27; Placement and Protection of
Indonesian Workers Overseas, 244;
population, 28, 140; poverty, 140;
recruitment procedures and practices,
146–48; regional autonomy, 242, 244;
women migrants, 81, 83–88;—domestic
workers, 76, 83, 86, 87, 88;
—entertainment and sex industry, 76,
86;—policy issues, 103–106
Industrial Revolution, 3
industrialisation, 23, 45, 146; export-led,
3, 43, 46
inequality, 30
information and communication
(Infocomm) industry, 202, 205
intermediaries and private labour
brokers, 25, 26, 31, 33, 36, 92, 151,
233, 257, 265, 299
international community, 134
international contract labour migration
(ICLM), 129; women, 106
international cooperation, 21
international institutional structures, 4
international labour market, 162
international labour migration (ILM),
46, 53, 60, 115, 116, 148, 159; Asian
economic crisis and, 29–30; and
domestic labour markets, 125–28;
institutionalisation, 33;
non-permanent, 93; and
the state, 30–34
International Labour Organisation (ILO),
35, 152, 284, 287, 298, 306
international law, 5, 6, 20
International Monetary Fund (IMF), 4
International political economy, 296–97

International relations, 296–97
International Symposium on Migration
Towards Regional Cooperation on
Irregular/Undocumented
Migration, 134
international treaty commitments, 9
Intra-regional migration pattern and
rights issues, 292–97
intra-regional trade and investment, 59
Irian Jaya: women migrants to
Papua-New Guinea, 80
Italy: Filipino domestic workers, 121

Japan, 14; economic boom after World
War II, 18; entertainment and sex
industry, 93–95, 121; Immigration
Ordinance (1899), 12; migration/
labour migrants, 5;—illegal, 17–18;
—Indonesia, 144, 146;—lower class,
12;—Malaysian, 43, 100;—overstayers,
100;—skilled, 35;—Thai, 93–95, 249;
—transition, 38;—temporary, 122;
—undocumented, 128; Migration
Control Ordinance (1951)/Law (1952),
17; political activism, 303; women
migrants;—Burmese, 96;—family
migration, 91;—Filipino, 33, 88, 121;
—illegal, 89;—Malaysian prostitutes,
100;—Thai, 93–95;—victims of slavery,
94;—from Vietnam, 80, 93
Japanese Yakuza, 122
Java, Javanese, 229, 233, 242; contract
labour in Malaya, 26, 39
job classification system, 26
Jolo, Filipino migrants, 42

Kalimantan, the transit zone of deported
Indonesian migrants, 32, 56, 86, 228,
229, 232, 234, 242
kangani system, 26
kinship, role in migration, 6, 30, 31
knowledge-economy, 193, 194
Konsorsium Pembela Buruh Migran
Indonesia (KOPBUMI), 240–41
Korean War, 16
Kota Kinabalu crisis, 238
Kurds, 8
Kuwait: Bangladeshi female workers,
165, 283, 286; Filipino domestic
workers, 121; Indonesia labour
migrants, 153

labour deployment policies, 32
labour export, 294; impact on economy,
    32, 274–75
labour exporting/sending countries, 33,
    53, 157, 292, 299–303; and importing
    nations, inter-state relations, 116
labour force: deployment, 59; impact of
    female migrants, 157–58
labour import policies and bilateral
    agreements, 61–63
labour importing/receiving countries,
    33, 63, 121, 127, 134, 275, 292,
    300–302, 303–304; migration policies,
    61–68
labour, international division, 3, 33
labour laws, 35
labour management regulations,
    36–39
labour market, 23, 24, 28–29, 31–33, 35,
    52, 54, 55, 129, 134, 139, 152, 159;
    impact of migration on domestic,
    125–28; and the illegal/undocumented
    migrants, 36; in Malaysia, 28, 29, 33,
    46, 213–17, 226, 228; segmentation,
    34; in Singapore, 28, 29, 33, 45–46;
    urban, 33
labour migration, economic and social
    effects on economy, 148–49;
    international context, 53–54; living
    conditions, 152; social impacts,
    129–31; in Southeast Asia
    (1870–1940), 23–27
Labour receiving countries, *see* labour
    importing/receiving countries
Labour sending countries, *see* labour
    exporting/sending countries
labour shortage, 29, 115, 157, 193; in
    Japan, 18; in Malaysia, 29, 38, 45, 146,
    232; role of migration, 193; in
    Republic of Korea (ROK), 146; in
    Singapore, 37, 193, 201, 206; in
    Thailand, 29, 146, 264
labour surplus, 29, 288; in Indonesia, 24;
    staple approach, 275
Laos PDR, Laos; migration/migrants/
    foreign workers, 5, 31, 97;—policies,
    66;— restrictions and limitations on
    migrants, 66–67; and Thailand,
    bilateral agreements on migration, 63;
    trading relations, 27; women

migrants, 79, 96–97;—illegal, 96;
    —into entertainment and sex
    industry, 76;—refugees, 95;—seasonal,
    96;—to Thailand, 96;—from Vietnam,
    93, 97
Lee Kuan Yew, 196
less developed countries (LDCs), 53–54
Libya, Vietnamese migrants, 93
Lombok, workers to Malaysia, 39

Mahathir Mohammed, 221, 238, 241
mail order bride schemes, 79, 93
Malays, 38, 43, 232
Malaysia (Malaya), 30, 44, 103; Aliens
    Ordinance (1931), 215; British colonial
    administration, 24; capital outflow, 29;
    Committee for the Recruitment of
    Foreign Workers, 47, 218; construction
    industry, 46, 47, 216, 219; creation of,
    24; demographic transition, 28;
    Employment Restriction Act (1968),
    215; Foreign Workers' Medical
    Examination and Monitoring Agency
    (FOMEMA), 49; Foreign Workers
    Regularisation Programme, 235;
    Foreign Workers' Task Force, 220; guest
    worker system, 214, 223–26;
    Immigration Act (1958–59), 215,
    222;—(1997), 236;—(2002), 228, 238,
    242; labour import/receiving region,
    38, 217, 303; labour outflow, 38, 43;
    Malaysian Agricultural Producers
    Association, 40; Malaysian Federal
    Land Development Authority Scheme,
    39; Malaysian Trade Union Congress
    (MTUC), 40; Medan Agreement (1984),
    218; migration/migrants/foreign
    workers, 5, 31, 43, 213–14, 285;
    Bangladeshis, 217, 220, 222, 285–86;
    —Cambodian, 222;—Chinese, 26, 215,
    223–24, 232;—Filipinos, 33, 42, 46, 47,
    60, 62, 121, 127, 217, 220, 222, 232;
    —illegal/undocumented migrant
    workers, 36, 38, 42, 46, 47, 48, 49, 86,
    98, 128, 213, 214, 217–20, 222–23,
    226, 228, 234, 236–37, 243;
    —immigration policy and border
    controls/policy issues, 43, 46–49,
    61–64, 66–67, 68, 213–14, 217–23,
    226;—Indian, 26, 215, 223–24, 232;

Malaysia – *continued*
—Indonesian, 29, 34, 46, 47, 60, 82–83, 86–87, 142, 143, 144, 146, 151, 153, 214–20, 222, 223, 228–29, 231–32, 235–38;—legal, 99;—management/ regularisation, 38–39, 40, 46–47, 219–20, 234–38;—Pakistani, 217, 220;—recruitment system, 46–48, 213–26, 231, 235–36;—registration and enforcement exercise, 219–20, 222, 232, 235–36;—skilled, 35, 60–61, 62, 64;—Thai, 42–43, 95, 217, 220, 223; —unskilled, 35, 59, 224, 232; —Vietnamese, 93, 214;—women migrants, 26, 28, 49, 60, 88, 98–101, 232;—domestic workers, 60, 62, 87, 89, 121, 127, 217;—from Indonesia, 29, 34, 60, 82–83, 86–87;—into entertainment and sex industry, 76, 86, 95;—Thai, 95; *Ops Nyah* I & II, 219, 236; origin and destination, both, 98; population, 28, 232; public health policy, 48–49; punishment for overstay, 36; reactive approach, 36; repatriated undocumented Indonesian migrants, 39–41, 228–30, 235–38, 242–44; New Economic Policy (NEP), 38, 43, 216; refugees, 46; slavery ended contract labour, 26; temporary labour migration (TLM), 56; United Malays National Organisation (UMNO), 220
Malaysia-Thailand border, 32
male dominance in migration, male migrants, 26, 75, 80, 86, 88, 93, 98, 148
manufacturing sector, 42, 157; in Thailand, 256
marriage migration, 78–79, 91, 92–93, 293; and labour migration, distinction, 78
mass media, role in migration, 31
McCarran, Pat, 16, 17
Mekong sub-regional system, 31, 56, 59
Memoranda of Understanding (MoUs), 294, 296
Mexico, 115
Middle East: construction sector, 119, 248; labour importing region, 116–17, 157; migration/migrant labour; —Bangladeshi female workers, 166,

278, 280, 282, 286;—Filipino, 57–58, 77, 118, 119, 121, 128;—Indonesian, 57–58, 77, 139, 144, 148, 230;—Thai, 248; women migrants, 75, 86; —skilled, 77
Migrant Care and Federasi Organisasi Buruh Migran Indonesia (FOBMI), 49
migrant fee charges, 151
migrant workers, problems and constraints, 149–52
migration goals temporary worker schemes and regional pattern in Southeast Asia, 34–43
migration industry, 299
migration policies, *see* policy issues in migration
migration process/system, 5, 75, 214–15, 295; permanent and non-permanent, 74, 88
migration zone, 20
Mindanao: Filipino migrants, 42; Muslim separatist movement, 46
mindset change, 300
mining labour force, 26
mobile identities, 188–89
mobility, international labour migration (ILM) and the state, 30–34
Mongolia, labour export, 294
morality, 14
motivations, 181
multinational corporations (MNCs), 193, 199, 204, 205
Myanmar (Burma/Burmese), 64; British colonial administration, 24; creation of, 24; economic isolation, 27; labour-out migration/emigrants, 5, 31, 58, 96;—illegal, 96;—unskilled, to Thailand, 29, 59, 60; per capita income, 56; and Thailand, bilateral agreements on migration, 63; women migrants, 79, 80;—into entertainment and sex industry, 76;—policy issues, 103; —refugees, 81, 95;—undocumented, 95

nation state, 9
national education systems, 11
national mobilisation, 13
national security aspect, security concerns and the migration, 19, 21, 49, 308

nationalism, 174
nationality, 8, 80
neo-liberalism, 293
Nepal, labour export, 294
New Zealand, 179; Malaysian migrants, 43; women migrants, 78–79;—Thai, 95
newly industrialised countries (NICs), 27, 43, 157
non-governmental organizations (NGOs) activism and the issue of migration/rights of migrants, 21, 292, 294, 296–97, 298, 300–302, 307–308; in Bangladesh, 167, 169, 170, 274; in Indonesia, 86, 104–105, 151, 229, 302–303; role in Nunukan crisis, 239–42; in Philippines, 127, 305
non-state actors, 301–2
North America: Filipino nurses, 77, 91; migrants from Singapore, 101; refugees from Cambodia, 97;—from Laos, 97
North American Free Trade Agreement (NAFTA), 54
nostalgia, 186
Nunukan, humanitarian crisis, 228–30, 239;—response to, 238–43; illegal agents, 233; the transit point of deported Indonesian migrants, 228–30

occupational segmentation, 75
OPEC, oil crisis, 115, 116, 118, 131
open economy, 27
outsourcing, 204–205
overseas contract workers (OCWs), 73–74, 83, 129, 294; Filipino, 117, 121, 123, 126–28; Indonesian, 81, 83–85, 87, 95, 117, 121; management system, 32; social impact, 129; Thai, 95
overseas workers, rights, 132–33

Pakistan; labour export/migration, 157, 285;—from Bangladesh, 276; —internal and external, 277;—to Malaysia, 217, 220; remittances, 277
Papua New Guinea: women migrants from Irian Jaya, 80
parenthood and children, implications of migration, 293
passports, subversion and mobilisation – the World War I and after, 13–14

per capita income, 55–56, 59; in Brunei, 55, 56; in Indonesia, 56, 140; in Philippines, 56; in Singapore, 55; in Thailand, 55, 56; in Vietnam, 56
permits and quotas, *see* work permit system
Perusahean Jasa Tenaga Kerja Indonesia (PJTKI), 146, 229
Philippines, Filipinos, 178; Absentee Voting Rights Bill, 305; Anti-trafficking in Persons Act, 305; Aquino administration, 124; Commission on Filipinos overseas, 116; creation of, 24; domestic workers, 158; Department of Labour and Employment (DOLE), 128, 131, 132; ratification of the Geneva Convention, 292, 296, 299, 304–306; economic development by labour export, 32–33, 34, 116, 123–25, 127, 131, 135; family unit, 130; foreign direct investment (FDI), 124; labour export/migrants/ domestic workers, 5, 31, 42, 52, 57–58, 157;—impact on domestic labour market, 125–28; —gendered, 119–23;—illegal, to Japan, 18;—to Malaysia, 33, 35, 42, 46, 47, 60, 62, 121, 127, 217, 220, 222, 232; —policy, history and critique, 102, 103, 131–35;—sex ratio, 79;—to Singapore, 35, 60;— skilled and professional, 60, 63, 77, 118–19, 129;—unskilled, 59; labour trade, 116–18; and Malaysia dispute over Sabah, 46, 228; Marcos regime, 129; Migrant Workers and Overseas Filipinos Act (1995), 132, 305; Overseas Employment Development Bureau, 131; Overseas Worker Welfare Agency (OWWA), 128; national dependency on hard currency earnings, 123–25; Philippine Nurse Association, 91; Philippine Overseas Employment Administration (POEA), 32, 116–19, 126, 127, 131, 132, 134; population, 28; regulations to protect domestic workers, 35, 131–32; women migrants, 75, 80, 81, 88–91, 118, 129–30;—domestic workers, 75–76, 88–91, 95;—into entertainment and sex industry, 76, 89, 90, 91, 95; —marriage, 78, 91;—nurses, 90, 91; —policy issues, 102, 103

Phnom Penh, 98
plantation and mining sectors, unskilled
    migrants, 35, 39, 42, 57, 60; in
    Malaysia, 47, 216, 219, 223
Pol Pot, 98
policy issues in migration, 27, 52, 63–64,
    68, 73–74, 139, 294, 299; Bangladesh,
    158–62; in host countries, 61–68;
    Indonesia, 103–106, 139; Japan, 17–18;
    Malaysia, 43, 46–49, 61–64, 66–67, 68,
    213–14, 217–23, 226; Philippines, 102,
    103, 131–35; women, 34, 73–74,
    102–108; *see also* border control
political will, 104
politics, 10, 296–97
polling booth and the border post, 9–11
population growth, 24
population regulation, 5
poverty and migration, relation, 31, 32,
    38, 140, 148, 156
preconceptions and prejudices, 10, 15
production, reorganisation, 3, 6
professionalism, 202
prostitution, *see* entertainment and sex
    industry/prostitution
psychological distress, 130
PT Sukma Karja Sejati Jakarta, 146, 147
public health dimension of geographic
    mobility, 48
push and pull factors, 181, 280

Qatar, Indonesia labour migrants, 153

race, racism, 8, 11, 15, 16, 36, 80, 128;
    identification with economic
    function, 38; the migrant labour at the
    start of the twentieth century,
    11–12, 39
recruitment process, 299; in Bangladesh,
    282–83; in Indonesia, 146–48
redefining home, 187–88
refugee issue, refugees, 8, 19–20, 80–81,
    155; and economic migrants, 19; and
    guest workers from World War II to
    cold war, 14–15
regional economy, 27, 31
regulation of migration, 31–33
relationships networks, 185, 190
religion, religious diversity, 4, 8, 80
Republic of Korea (ROK), Indonesia
    labour migrants, 143, 144, 146, 153

restrictions and limitations on migrants,
    66–67, 103
returned migrants, role in migration, 31
Riau, transit zone, 228, 232–33
rights issues, rights of migrants, 106,
    292–97, 299, 301, 308; politics,
    295–97; *see also* non-governmental
    societies
Rohingya Muslim migrants in
    Malaysia, 46
rule of law, 307
rural poverty, 28
rural to urban migration, 25, 33

Sabah, 46, 231, 232, 236; migrant
    workers, 39; women migrants,
    —Indonesian, 86, 228;—Philippines,
    42, 46, 80
sans papiers, 14
Sarawak, 32, 231, 232
SARS outbreak, 117
Saudi Arabia: women migrants;—from
    Bangladesh, 162, 286;—Filipino
    domestic workers, 91, 103, 118, 121,
    127;—from Indonesia, 87, 104–105;
    —exploitation, 83, 103–105
service industry, 54, 119, 121, 293
sex workers, 157
sexual harassment of migrants, 86, 121,
    139, 149–51, 153, 156, 158
Singapore, 30, 214; Australian
    professional workers, 172–91;
    Chinatown and Little India, 177;
    Committee on Competitiveness, 202;
    construction industry, 177, 206;
    Contact Singapore, 202; demographic
    transition, 28; destination of migrants,
    5, 31; Economic Development Board
    (EDB), 176, 195, 202; economic
    development strategy, 31, 172;
    Economic Reforms Committee (ERC),
    204–205, 207; Employment of Foreign
    Workers Act, 1990, 45–46;
    employment regulatory regime, 176;
    expatriate workforce, 37, 177–78,
    179–89, 190; globalisation strategy,
    193, 194–95, 208;—role of Indian
    labour, 201–208; gross domestic
    product (GDP), 196, 201, 204;
    gross national product (GNP), 36;
    Immigration Ordinance (IO), 44, 45;

Singapore – *continued*
Infocomm Development Authority
(IDA), 202, 204–205; Knowledge Based
Economy (KBE), 194, 201, 204, 206,
208; migration/migrants/ foreign
labour, 117, 303;—Filipinos, 33, 60,
89, 91, 101, 121, 158, 177;—illegal
migrants, 101;—Indian labour,
201–208;—Indian professional workers,
193, 198–208;—Indonesian, 101, 142,
143, 144, 153, 177;—immigration
policy and border controls, 43–44,
61–64, 66–67, 68, 194, 195–98, 199;
—after 1965, 44–46, 199;—Malaysian
migrants, 43, 44, 100, 101, 177, 200;
—management, 36–38, 45–46, 62;
—skilled, 36, 60, 62, 63, 64, 172,
177–78, 193, 199;—Thai, 249;—unskilled
migrants, 59, 177, 193, 196, 205–206;
national development strategy, 63;
newly industrialised country, 27, 44;
part of Malaya during colonial period,
44; out-migration to MDCs, 101;
population, 28, 177, 178, 197–98, 200;
punishment for overstay, 36; quotas,
46, 176; Regulation of Employment
Act 1965, 44, 45;—Amendment, 1975,
44; temporary labour migration
(TLM), 56; Total Fertility Rate (TFR),
195; women labour/domestic workers,
28, 34, 60, 88, 89, 91, 101, 121, 158,
177;—from Sri Lanka, 101, 177;—from
Sumatra, 86;—into entertainment and
sex industry, 76, 95; Vietnamese
migrants, 93;—workforce, size, 196–98
Singapore-Johor border, 32
skilled migration flows, 29, 34–36, 55,
60–61, 62, 118–19, 165; women, 77
slavery, 25
social and institutional factors in
migration, 280
social class, 30
social impact of migration, 129–31,
284–85
social indicators, 28
social mobilisation, 13, 297
social networks, relationships, 174–75,
187, 214, 284
social welfare policies, 11
socialist regimes, 27

societal borders, 47
socio-economic and political reasons of
migration, 27
socio-economic development, 170
socio-political security concerns and
migrants, 265–66
South Korea; migration/migrants/labour
import, 5, 33, 117; Filipino, 121;
—transition, 38; illegal out-migration
to Japan, 17–18; newly industrialised
country, 27; political activism, 303;
women migrants from Indonesia, 86
South–North movements, 53, 78
sovereignty, 4, 20, 48, 49
Soviet Union, collapse, 18, 19
sponsorship system, 35
Sri Lanka, 45, 292; Bangladeshi female
workers, 166, 285; labour export, 157;
women migrants domestic workers,
76, 158
state: and individual, relationship, 10;
role in international labour migration
(ILM), 30–34, 296; power, 10, 20; and
society, integration, 14; territorial
role, 6
stereotypes, 182, 186
Sto. Tomas, Patricia, 135
student migrants, 77
subversive immigrants, 17; cold war and,
15–16
Suharto, 83, 140, 229, 242
Sukarnoputri, Megawati, 239–41
Sulawesi, workers to Malaysia, 39, 56
Sumatra, 231; transit province for
Indonesian migrants, 228, 229, 234,
242; migration to Malaysia, 39, 80;
—to Singapore, 86
Sydney, Australia: Thai women in sex
industry, 93

Taiwan: labour import/migrant workers,
5, 33, 116–17;—Filipino domestic
workers, 89, 121, 127;—illegal, 101;
—Indonesian, 88, 143, 146, 153;
—Malaysia, 43;—transition, 38; newly
industrialised country, 27; women
migrants, 88–89;—Burmese, 96;
—marriage migration, 78, 92–93;
—Thai sex workers, 95;—Vietnamese,
80, 92–93

Tawau, 238
temporary labour migration (TLM), 52, 53, 54–55, 67–68, 115, 208; business, skilled and professional workers, 60–61; migration policies, 63–64; unskilled, 59–60; women, 74, 88
temporary permits, 275
temporary worker schemes and regional migration pattern in Southeast Asia, 34–43
Tenagita, Malaysia, 49
territorial sovereignty, notion of, 20
terrorism, 46
Thailand, 30, 45, 46, 47, 98, 178; Alien Employment Act (1978), 250, 252, 259–60; creation of, 24; crime syndicate, 249; demographic transition, 28, 267; employment categories, 254–56, 259; government banned the export of women for domestic work, 95; Immigration Act (1979), 259; labour export, 248, 258; migration/migrant labour emigration/inflow/foreign workers, 5, 31, 60; Bangladeshi female, 166; Burmese migrants, 60, 62; —prostitutes, 96;—Cambodians, 254, 255, 264; cause and consequences, 256–58; Chinese, 252, 257;—decline, 248–49;—documented by nationality and occupation, 251;—Indonesian, 146, 249–56;—Lao, 254, 255, 257, 264;—management, 258–61, 264–65, 267;—from Myanmar, 29, 252, 254–57, 264;—policies, 61–64, 66, 68, 248, 252, 259;—professional, technical and kindred (PTK)/skilled, 60–61, 64, 248;—refugees, 95, 97; registration/amnesty and repatriation, 29, 63, 264–65;—regulation and shortcomings, 265–67;—rural to urban, 257;—temporary, under work permit system, 252–56, 261, 264; —undocumented/illegal, 248, 250, 252–54, 257, 261–63, 266;—unskilled, 35, 63, 248, 249, 250–51, 252–53, 261, 267; migration/migrants, outflow, to Bangkok, 249, 254;—to Japan, 249; —to Malaysia, 42–43, 95, 217, 220, 223;—to Singapore, 249; National

Executive Council, 250; open economy, 27; origin and destination, both, 93, 248; population, 28; women migrants, 28, 93–96;—from Cambodia, 97;—domestic workers, 34;—from Laos, 96, 97;—marriage migration, 78, 79;—from Myanmar, 80;—into entertainment and sex industry, 76, 93–94, 97, 98;—policy issues, 95, 103;—from Vietnam, 98
Thai-Myanmar border region, 254, 257
third world, 95
3D (dangerous, dirty, and degrading/difficult) jobs, 38, 75, 143, 157, 307
total war system, 13
totalitarian regimes, 9
trade and investment, 53, 56, 59
trade liberalisation policies, 3, 27, 33, 46, 48, 53
trafficking of women, 156; Filipino, 122–23; from Myanmar, 96; from Thailand, 94–95
training to migrant women, 103–104, 159
transit provinces, role in migration, 233, 242–43; marginalisation, 244
transnational corporations (TNCs), 173, 176, 179, 190
transnational professionals, circulation, 173–74, 175
transnationalism, transnational relationships, 172, 173, 175, 297
transparency, 4
Truman, Harry S., 16

umroh visa, 86
undocumented migration, *see* illegal/undocumented migration
unemployment, 4, 28, 32, 159, 293; unaffected by Asian economic crisis, 29; Bangladesh, 43; in Indonesia, 28, 139, 140, 142, 147, 148, 152; in Philippines, 28, 116; in Singapore, 28, 37, 196, 206; in Thailand, 28, 29, 215, 249
UNIFIL, 305
United Arab Emirates (UAE): migrants from Bangladesh, 286; Filipino domestic workers, 121

United Kingdom; Aliens Restriction Act
(1914), 13; Filipino nurses, 91
United Nations, 9, 20, 98, 134–35, 155,
252, 296, 301; Convention on Rights
of Migrant Workers and the Members
of their Families, Geneva (ICRM,
1990), 5, 8, 19, 170, 292, 295–98;
Convention on the Protection of the
Rights of All Migrant Workers and the
Members of their Families, 102, 163;
Convention on Status of Refugees
(1951), 14; Development Project
(UNDP), 166; humanitarian schemes,
15; protocol on refugees, 80
United States of America, 27; Central
Intelligence Agency (CIA), 9; House
Committee on un-American Activities,
16; Immigration and Naturalization
Law (1952), 16; immigration policies,
15–16; and Iraq war, 117; Internal
Security Law (MacCarren law), 16, 17;
migrants, Malaysian, 43;—skilled, 35,
43; quota system, 16; refugees, 15;
post-war border control policy, 17;
women migrants, 78–79;—Filipino
domestic workers, 88;—Thai workers,
95;—Vietnamese refugees, 92; attack
on World Trade Centre (WTC), 46
Universal Declaration of Human
Rights, 5
unskilled/semi-skilled migration flows,
34, 35, 55, 57, 59–60, 62, 143, 144,
146, 158, 165; women, 76, 119

values and frames of reference, 190
Versailles Treaty, 13
Vietnam, Vietnamese, 98;
migration/migrants/ labour export, 5,
31, 52, 294;—to Cambodia, 98;—to
Malaysia, 93, 214;—restrictions and
limitations, 66–67; Orderly Departure
Program, 92; trading relations, 27;
women migrants, 92–93;—marriage,
80, 92–93;—prostitutes, 98;—refugees,
81, 92, 95; war, 58

village sponsors, role in labour
recruitment, 146–47

wage differentials/discrimination, 31, 61
Walter, Francis E., 16
welfare systems, 11
West Nusa Tenggara, workers to
Malaysia, 39, 233, 242
Western Bubble, 186–87
wild zone, 21
women, women migrants/ migration,
28, 33–34, 49, 60, 88, 98–101, 148–49,
155–58, 293; contract labour and
irregular, 119; domestic workers, 34,
60, 62, 87, 89, 121, 127, 217;
employment, 33, 163; empowerment,
156, 308; illegal, 86; from Indonesia,
29, 34, 60, 82–83, 86–87;—into
entertainment, prostitution and sex
industry, 76, 86, 95, 118–19, 121–23,
156, 157, 158, 293; service sector, 119,
121, 293; socio-economic conditions,
166; in Southeast Asia, 74–81; status,
73, 76, 158; Thai, 95; Vietnamese, 93,
214; vulnerability and abuse, 118–19,
121–22, 131–32, 136, 156, 157, 294,
295; *see also* women in individual
country names
work permit system, 36, 299; in
Malaysia, 215, 220, 221; in Singapore,
45, 176–77, 196, 199; in Thailand,
252–56, 261, 264
working conditions of migrants, 32, 35,
156, 158, 299
World Bank, 4, 140, 213
World Trade organization (WTO), 4, 63,
64, 68, 173, 208
World War I, 11; passports, subversion
and mobilisation after, 13–14
World War II, 12, 17, 18, 23, 44; post
period, 3; refugees and guest workers,
14–15
Wyatt, Watson, 200

Yemen: Vietnamese migrants, 93